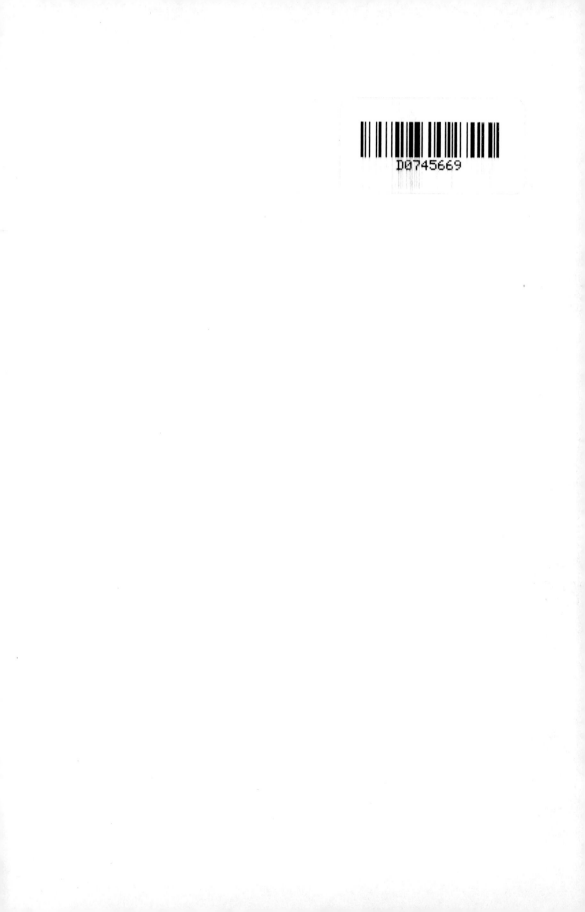

Voices Off

Other titles in the Cassell Education series:

Voices Off

Texts, Contexts and Readers

Edited by
Morag Styles, Eve Bearne and
Victor Watson

CASSELL

Cassell
Wellington House
125 Strand
London WC2R 0BB

215 Park Avenue South
New York
NY 10003

An earlier version of Chapter 4 appeared in *Signal 74*, May 1994, and is reprinted with permission of the publishers, Thimble Press, Lockwood, Station Road, Woodchester, Stroud, Glos GL5 5EQ.

British Library Cataloguing-in-Publication Data
A catalogue record for this book is available from the British Library.

ISBN 0-304-33578-9 (hardback)
0-304-33579-7 (paperback)

Typeset by BookEns Ltd, Royston, Herts.
Printed and bound in Great Britain by Redwood Books, Trowbridge, Wiltshire

Contents

List of Contributors

Kate Agnew has been manager of Heffers Children's Bookshop in Cambridge since 1991. She began bookselling at the Children's Bookshop in Muswell Hill, where she worked first as a student in the holidays, and then full-time after she graduated. She is a reader for the French publisher Gallimard, and she reviews books for the *Guardian*, *TES* and *TLS*.

Holly Anderson is a senior lecturer in Professional Studies and Language at Homerton College, Cambridge. An infant and nursery teacher for 18 years, she became an advisory teacher for language before working in higher education. Her research is primarily in the area of language development in early years education. She was UK project leader for a collaborative research project with Norway which looked at writing development in primary schools in both countries and has published a number of articles within this field.

Eve Bearne has taught English and Drama in schools and colleges for 25 years. She was a project officer for the National Writing Project and co-editor of a number of their publications. As well as being one of the editors of the companion volumes to this book (*After Alice; The Prose and the Passion*) she is co-author of *A Writing Policy in Action* and has edited two collections, *Greater Expectations: Children Reading Writing* and *Differentiation and Diversity in the Primary School*. She is a senior lecturer at Homerton College and is currently involved in research into children's literacy.

Janet Bottoms has taught in a variety of schools and further education colleges and in university and adult education, and her interest in the use and abuse of Shakespeare in education was widened through the international dimension discovered by teaching students from different non-English-speaking countries and cultures and in the USA. She has published a critical survey of school editions of Shakespeare, and is currently working on a study of prose versions written for children. She is also interested in tackling Shakespeare with younger pupils and helping students to use their own knowledge and enjoyment of the plays to good effect in the primary classroom.

Gabrielle Cliff Hodges taught English in Cambridgeshire for many years, and is now a senior lecturer in English at Homerton College, Cambridge. She specializes in the Victorian period and in teaching English in the secondary school. She has a particular interest in reading development within the secondary age range. Recent publications include a chapter on GCSE English Literature in *The Politics of Reading*. An active member of the National Association for the Teaching of English since the 1980s, she is currently the Vice Chair of NATE.

Jenny Daniels has taught in a variety of contexts, including schools, nurseries, further education, special needs, adult literacy and prison education. She is now head of English at Homerton College where she specializes in the Augustan/Romantic period for English Literature and Language in the primary school. Her current area of research is gender and reading practices, particularly as they relate to popular culture. She is also continuing to work on historical analysis of women, representation and literature.

Geoff Fox is well known and highly respected in the world of children's literature. He has been an editor of *Children's Literature in Education* since its inception and is co-author of distinguished texts such as *Teaching Literature 9–14*, and *Writers, Critics, and Children*. A senior lecturer in English and Drama at the School of Education, University of Exeter, he was partly responsible for a series of children's literature conferences in the early 1970s which are still remembered today for their groundbreaking impact. Geoff is much in demand as a speaker and has lectured at conferences in Canada, the USA and Australia, as well as in Britain. He is editor of Collins Cascades Series and reviews extensively for the *TES* and other journals. *Celebrating Children's Literature in Education* was published by Hodder and Stoughton in 1995, marking the 25th anniversary of the journal.

Elizabeth Hammill is currently the Children's Department Manager for Literature at Waterstone's bookshop in Newcastle. She has been a children's bookseller for 16 years and has worked to connect children and books to 'make readers'. To bring this about, she has developed a range of nationally recognized community initiatives and programmes, some in partnership with Newcastle LEA. She is managing director of *In Brief*, a book magazine written for teenagers, by teenagers. She contributes regularly to *Signal*, in particular Fiction 6 to 9. She has co-edited and contributed to two Northern Children's Book Festival Guides, and she regularly writes articles and gives lectures on children's books.

Lesley Hendy, a former first school headteacher, is now senior lecturer in Drama and Creative Arts at Homerton College, Cambridge. She has had much experience teaching drama at primary and secondary level, as well as specializing in drama in the early years. She is co-author of *The Drama Box* (with P. Baldwin, published by HarperCollins) and *Science through Stories* (with Rachel Linfield, published by Pearson Publications).

Mary Hilton has worked in primary schools in Cambridgeshire and is now a senior lecturer at Homerton College. She has been researching community literacy, history and popular culture and is now working towards a PhD in the oral history of teaching. She has contributed to publications such as *Collaboration and Writing* and *The Prose and the Passion*, and is currently editing a book for Routledge entitled *Children, Literacy and Popular Culture*.

Satoshi Kitamura read comics when he was a child, and this had a great influence on his style. He did not train as an artist and began to do commercial work, especially greetings cards, when he moved to Britain. In 1982, Kitamura's artwork was exhibited at the Neal Street Gallery in Covent Garden. Klaus Flugge came to the exhibition and showed him Hiawyn Oram's text of *Angry Arthur*. This was an instant success when it was published in 1982, receiving the Mother Goose Award and the Japanese Picturebook Award. In the years following, Kitamura has become one of the best-known picture book authors in the world. His many works are immediately recognizable by virtue of their individualistic, challenging and often comic style and he is much loved by young readers.

Jan Mark is a distinguished and distinctive writer of fiction for children. Some of her best-known novels are *Thunder and Lightnings*, *Trouble Halfway*, *The Ennead* and *Divide and Rule*; she is also well known for books of short stories such as *Nothing to Be Afraid Of* and *Hairs in the Palm of the Hand*. She is the editor of the excellent *Oxford Book of Children's Stories* and is much in demand as a speaker at conferences and festivals and as a reviewer of children's books.

Helen Nicholson is a senior lecturer in Drama and English at Homerton College; she was head of an Arts Faculty at a Bristol comprehensive school until 1992. She is currently working on a PhD on the values of arts education. She specializes in modern literature and has a particular interest in contemporary theatre. Recent publications include articles on drama education and gender, and drama in an arts curriculum.

Jill Paton Walsh is a popular and highly regarded writer for children. She also writes for adults and her novel, *Knowledge of Angels*, was shortlisted for the Booker Prize in 1994. Among her acclaimed novels for young people are *Gaffer Samson's Luck*, *Grace*, *Unleaving* and *A Parcel of Patterns*. She has received many honours, including the Whitbread Award and the Universe Literary Prize for *A Parcel of Patterns*, and she was the Grand Prix winner of the Smarties Award for *Gaffer Samson's Luck*. Jill Paton Walsh lectures on literature in many parts of the world and works regularly in the USA.

John Rowe Townsend was a journalist, before becoming a highly regarded author of fiction for children. He is a critic of books for children and was the Children's Book Editor for the *Guardian* until 1978. *Written for Children*, of which there have been several editions, is now considered a key text on the history of children's literature. His first book, *Gumble's Yard*, was groundbreaking in its treatment of working-class characters and social realism. He has now published more than twenty books for young people in Britain and the USA. He spends some time in the USA each year where he is, among other things, an adjunct board member of Children's Literature New England. John Rowe Townsend lectures on children's literature in Britain, the USA, Canada, Australia and Japan.

Anne Rowe has been headteacher of two Berkshire primary schools and is now working on a freelance basis on activities related to the learning of literacy and literature; she still manages to spend a lot of time in classrooms. She is 'loosely associated' with the well-known Reading Centre based at Reading University. She is currently taking an Art History course at Oxford which is developing further her passion for picture books.

Brigid Smith taught for many years in schools, was head of Special Needs in a Harlow comprehensive and is now Director of Overseas Education at Homerton College. Her recent publications include *Spelling in Context* (with Margaret Peters), *Teaching Spelling* (UKRA) and *Through Writing to Reading*, which is a book about effective approaches to literacy, based on her research into children's dictated stories. She travels all over the world in her role as Language Consultant for ODA and the World Bank and is involved in literacy projects in India and Pakistan.

Morag Styles is Language Co-ordinator at Homerton College, where she teaches literacy and children's literature. She runs writing workshops with children and teachers, compiles anthologies of poetry, reviews poetry for children and writes on aspects of children's literature. Some recent publications include the *Cambridge Poetry Box*, *Mother Gave a Shout* (poems by women, with Suzannah Steele) and *The Politics of Reading* (with Mary Jane Drummond). She is finishing a book for Cassell on the history of poetry written for children entitled *From the Garden to the Street*, and has completed an edited volume (with Victor Watson) for Hodder, *Talking Pictures*. She is currently researching women writing poetry for children before the twentieth century.

Victor Watson is a principal lecturer in English at Homerton College, Cambridge. He has a special interest in the history and nature of children's books and their relationship both with adult literature and with changing assumptions about childhood. He has made a close study of books for children in the eighteenth and nineteenth centuries, and he has a particular interest in William Blake, Lewis Carroll and Arthur Ransome. He has worked closely with reception children learning to read with picture books and has written for *Signal*, *TES*, the *Cambridge Journal of Education*, the *UKRA Journal* and *Books for Keeps*. He is currently beginning work as the editor of the forthcoming *Cambridge Guide to Children's Books*.

David Whitley is a senior lecturer in English at Homerton College, Cambridge, where his main areas of teaching are in early modern literature and media education. He has written on Chaucer, children and television, and on various aspects of the tradition of the Aesop fable.

Robert Louis Stevenson wrote a brief fable in which a frog rebukes a tadpole thus: 'When I was your age I never had a tail.' 'Just as I thought,' says the tadpole. '*You* were never a tadpole.' It strikes me from time to time that a number of frogs who pronounce upon children's fiction have conveniently forgotten they were ever tadpoles.

Jan Mark

INTRODUCTION

Innocent Children and Unstable Literature

Victor Watson

Journalists, politicians, social commentators and philosophers have many things to say about children's books — about why children should read, what they should read, and how their reading can be seen as an indicator of the cultural state of the nation. This is a relatively new phenomenon; thirty years ago children's literature was a comparatively isolated corner in the wider cultural landscape, of interest mainly to teachers, librarians and a few book-collectors. The children who actually read the books were presumably not interested in their cultural significance.

In considering some of these 'voices off', I am going to begin on a sombre note, the relevance of which may at first seem doubtful. The killing of James Bulger was so terrible that the whole nation seems to have been gripped and frightened by it. My most vivid memory is of two mothers interviewed on television — outside a supermarket, with their children in pushchairs — recommending the death penalty for the murderers. This memory haunts me because of the willingness of these two worried young women to overlook what seemed to me the central problematic fact — that the killers were children too.

We have as part of our cultural thinking assumptions about children as innocent victims. This is well documented. But we also have fears about child demons, or child monsters, or child criminals — and usually the latter are kept safely remote from everyday life in horror films like *Rosemary's Baby*. The innocent child victim and the demon child monster are two powerful cultural icons of our thought. The killing of one child by two others brought into direct and articulate conflict our compassion for the innocent child victim and our fear of the child monster. While there continues to be a national anxiety about juvenile crime (exploited by politicians and journalists when it suits them), we will continue to be haunted by variations of this particular child demon.

In 1994, Marina Warner delivered the Reith Lectures, calling the series *Six Myths of Our Time*.[1] She is the next of the 'voices off' I want to attend to. Warner was clear about what she meant by a myth, explaining:

[that] myths are not always delusions ... that they can represent ways of making sense of universal matters, like sexual identity and family relations, and that they enjoy a more vigorous life than we perhaps acknowledge, and exert more of an inspiration and influence than we think.[2]

One of her talks was on the myth of childhood innocence.

I recommend the published version to anyone interested in the contemporary meaning of childhood. In referring to the James Bulger murderers, she made two points which are particularly interesting to those of us concerned with children's books. First, she suggested that a culture which sets up what she called 'the nostalgic worship of childhood innocence'[3] is likely to be *vengeful and punitive* in its disappointed anger when children fail to live up to the ideal: 'The consecration of childhood raises the real-life examples of children to an ideal which they must fail, modestly by simply being ordinary kids, or horrendously by becoming victims or criminals.'[4] The second point was her suggestion that the myth of the innocent child is associated in particular with children's literature. Of course, she didn't *blame* children's literature, for this is not a simple and direct causal relationship. But she is clearly of the view that the existence of an impossible and damaging ideal of childhood and the growth of children's literature are inextricably enmeshed with one another. The connection began, as Warner pointed out, at the time of the Romantics, and for two centuries inspired 'an unsurpassed imaginative literature for children'.[5] If Warner is right, children's literature may not be responsible, but it is implicated.

This is not a minor academic matter for us, and Warner's 'voice off' is one we should listen to. She reminds us that the ways in which we think about children at present have become seriously problematic, and that children's books have a direct and urgent bearing on that problem.

This is an important question: how far is it true that children's literature has been involved in *the consecration of childhood innocence?*

My search for an answer to this question led me back to *Little Lord Fauntleroy.*[6] And, of course, I found that the hero is a child with absolutely no faults! He is concerned for others before himself; he sees only the good in others, thus shaming them into wanting to be as good as he imagines them to be; he is never angry or resentful; he is never selfish. He is even perfect physically — his body is frequently described as beautiful, sturdy and graceful. The adjective most frequently used of him is, precisely, 'innocent'. Take this account, for example:

His greatest charm was this cheerful, fearless, quaint little way of making friends with people. I think it arose from his having a very confiding nature, and a kind little heart that sympathised with everyone, and wished to make everyone as comfortable as he liked to be himself. It made him very quick to understand the feelings of those about him. Perhaps this had grown on him, too, because he had lived so much with his father and mother, who were always loving and considerate and tender and well-bred. He had never heard an unkind or uncourteous word spoken at home; he had always been loved and caressed and treated tenderly, and so his childish soul was full of kindness and innocent warm feeling. He had always heard his mamma called by pretty, loving names, and so he used them himself when he spoke to her; he had always seen that his papa watched over her and took great care of her, and so he learned, too, to be careful of her.

So when he knew his papa would come back no more and saw how very sad his mamma was, there gradually came into his kind little heart the thought that he must do what he could to make her happy. He was not much more than a baby, but that thought was in his mind whenever he climbed upon her knee and kissed her, and put his curly head on her neck, and when he brought his toys and picture books to show her, and when he curled up quietly by her side as she used to lie on the sofa.[7]

The notion that a loved child is likely to become a loving child is not one we should ridicule. Furthermore, it was a clever idea to contrast not only the innocent little boy with the bitter and selfish old man but also American egalitarian assumptions with British feudal habits. And I cannot help admiring the way in which Frances Hodgson Burnett demonstrated that a children's book could be socially aware of the issues of poverty, alcohol and crime.

But, in spite of those considerations, the quotation above is conclusive evidence that *Little Lord Fauntleroy* is guilty of idealizing childhood, and of consecrating an impossible ideal of incorruptible innocence whose purpose is to redeem others. But why did the author do it? Why did she make for herself what must amount to a tricky technical problem? — for character development is out of the question if your chief protagonist is perfect at the outset.

I suspect that she could not help herself. For three decades Victorian adult novelists had concentrated the minds of their readers on the nature of childhood, and had already established in the minds of the great reading public the image of the innocent child. *Oliver Twist*[8] was the first. A development from the idealized child was the redemptive child, able to restore goodness and joy in the most hardened and embittered adult. Tiny Tim in *The Christmas Carol*[9] is one of the first to do this. Later there were Florence Dombey in *Dombey and Son*[10] and Eppie in *Silas Marner*.[11] Redemptive children were often associated with early death; there were Smike in *Nicholas Nickleby*,[12] Dick in *Oliver Twist*, Paul Dombey, and Little Nell in *The Old Curiosity Shop*.[13] It is significant that Dickens' close friend and biographer, John Forster, claimed that he had urged

Dickens to kill off Little Nell 'so that the gentle pure little figure and form should never change to the fancy'.[14] It would be interesting to know if anyone saw the sinister implications of this danger signal. An ideal of childhood which *requires the child to die* in order to preserve it in the 'fancy' of the adult is not a benign ideal.

However, in *Jane Eyre*[15] Charlotte Brontë resisted the appeal of the redemptive child and its association with early death. In spite of the novel's concern with the early death of Helen Burns, Charlotte Brontë is clearly more interested in the continuity of the growth from Jane's childhood to adulthood. No British writer had shown that continuity before. After *Jane Eyre*, the treatment of childhood became more intelligently searching and there was a developing interest in how child characters survived into adult life. This phenomenon has been treated by many scholars and I do not intend to dwell on it. My purpose here is to suggest that in such a cultural climate it is no wonder that Frances Hodgson Burnett, writing a novel for her own son, should sentimentalize the young hero of her first children's novel.[16]

However, if we look at the three other children's novels she wrote, we see that an interesting development took place in her treatment of child characters. In *A Little Princess*,[17] Sara Crewe is an intelligent, brave and forthright girl. She is still in some ways an idealized child, but the difference is that she is aware of good and evil — and she knows that good has to be worked for. The young Lord Fauntleroy, on the other hand, had acted innocently and was unaware of the effect he produced on people. Sara Crewe's character shows that the author was developing the child figure from one with a simple unconscious innocence into one who *consciously works to do good* in an imperfect world.[18]

There was a further development in *The Secret Garden*,[19] in which both the main characters are realistically presented as thoroughly disagreeable from the start — though she makes it clear that it is neglect that has brought about this condition. Elements of the redemptive child remain: the adults (Ben Weatherstaff and Colin's father) are, as it were, *softened* by the example and influence of the children, but learning is not a simple one-way process. Another difference is that in this novel Burnett takes care to report the inner thoughts and feelings of Mary so that the disapproving reader can at the same time understand her confusion and loneliness.

Frances Hodgson Burnett in her three major children's novels[20] moved steadily away from the idealized innocent child. From Little Lord Fauntleroy to Mary Lennox was a big step. I have concentrated upon her to this extent because I believe that her progress roughly exemplifies what children's literature has tried to do in its presentation of childhood. The Victorian adult novelists had taken childhood into a narrative cul-de-sac, exemplified perhaps by the deaths of Tom and Maggie Tulliver in *The*

Mill on the Floss[21] or the suicide of the children in *Jude the Obscure*.[22] Then, while adult literature lost interest, children's writers *rejected* the innocent, doomed and redemptive children of adult fiction and worked out a different ideal.[23] Children's writers explored alternative versions of childhood — there were comic children and disruptive children,[24] but most of all there were *thoughtful* children trying to work out their place within a community largely composed of adults.

Take Alice.[25] She is certainly innocent, a good child. But it is clear that Lewis Carroll's main purpose was to pay tribute to Alice's *intelligence*, her sense of fun, her awareness of the ridiculous. He was not wishing to consecrate her as a model of redemptive innocence. And if we look at most of the influential works written for children subsequently — for example, the stories of E. Nesbit — we find that writers for children were as far as possible representing real children negotiating their lives in a world of adults. Of course, their success was as varied as their methods. But whether they employed play, humour or fantasy, I believe that children's writers have assumed that their role was to *resist* sentimentalized portrayals of childhood. If we think of our own time, we find, I believe, that many recent and contemporary writers have continued realistically to present thoughtful children trying to work their way through childhood. Today's young readers would not tolerate a consecration of innocent childhood anyway — they know better. In fact, there have been recent complaints that children's books are too grimly authentic.

Child characters in most children's books are, I believe, treated by writers with a mixture of reverence and realism. There is a realistic recognition that children can be selfish, devious, and manipulative — and can rarely rise above the standards of the adults around them. But there is also a reverence for the potential and actual goodness of children, an understanding of their different ways of seeing, and a sympathy for their needs and their vulnerability. Perhaps the best example of what I mean by reverence and realism is to be found in the work of Rumer Godden. Her novels reveal a unique ability to combine authorial sympathy with a truthful and unrelenting severity in her accounts of her characters. This combination is to be found in all her works — *An Episode of Sparrows, The Battle of the Villa Fiorita* and, most powerfully of all, *The Greengage Summer*.[26]

There are numerous examples of child characters being presented in this sympathetic and yet uncompromising way. There is Lucy in the Narnia series, Nicola Marlow in Antonia Forest's brilliant series,[27] Billy Caspar in *Kes*, Jane Gardam's intelligent and difficult young heroines, Geraldine Kaye's Comfort, the complex characters of Margaret Mahy, Kate Tranter in *The Way to Sattin Shore*, the heroine of Anne Fine's *Goggle Eyes*, Amy in Jan Mark's *Trouble Half-Way*, and the grave young people in Anita Desai's *A Village by the Sea*.[28] Even Dahl's characters, though they are often straightforwardly sentimentalized victims, are rarely straightforwardly innocent. There are numerous other examples.

The creators of these fictional children have not been interested in innocence; they have been concerned with *coping*. Yet most adult commentators seem not to have noticed this. It seems to me that we have to consider the intriguing and paradoxical possibility that children's literature is repeatedly and consistently *misread*.

I believe it is possible to understand why this happens. For example, if we read the following extract, we could be forgiven for regarding it as shamelessly sentimental. It is about a boy who is at last given the puppy he has longed for — only to find that he is so disappointed by its timidity that he drives the unhappy dog away from him in an angry and bitter moment of rejection.

> He shut his eyes tight, but he could see no invisible dog nowadays. He opened his eyes, and for a moment he could see no visible dog either. So the brown dog had gone at last. Then, as Ben's eyes accustomed themselves to the failing light, he could pick him out after all, by his movement: the dog had got up; he was moving away; he was slipping out of sight.
>
> Then, suddenly, when Ben could hardly see, he saw clearly. He saw clearly that you couldn't have impossible things, however much you wanted them. He saw that if you didn't have the possible things, then you had nothing. At the same time Ben remembered other things about the brown dog besides its unChiquitito-like size and colour and timidity. He remembered the warmth of the dog's body against his own, as he had carried him; and the movement of his body as he breathed; and the tickle of his curly hair; and the way the dog had pressed up to him for protection and had followed him even in hopelessness.
>
> The brown dog had gone farther off now, losing himself in dusk. Ben could not see him any longer. He stood up; he peered over the Heath. No ...
>
> Suddenly knowing what he had lost — *whom* he had lost, Ben shouted, 'Brown!'
>
> He heard the dog's answering barks, even before he could see him. The dog was galloping towards him out of the dusk, but Ben went on calling: 'BrownBrownBrownBrown!'
>
> Brown dashed up to him, barking so shrilly that Ben had to crouch down and, with the dog's tongue slapping all over his face, put his arms round him and said steadyingly, 'It's all right, Brown! Quiet, quiet! I'm here!'
>
> Then Ben stood up again, and Brown remained by his side, leaning against his leg, panting, loving him; and lovingly Ben said, 'It's late, Brown. Let's go home.'

That is the ending of Philippa Pearce's *A Dog So Small*.[29] Read carelessly or out of context, it can seem to be a tear-jerking and syrupy 'happy ending'. But in the context of the whole novel, it is a profoundly serious ending, about a thoughtful and introspective child who is possessed by a longing to such an extent that the real world is not good enough; but he learns the sad lesson that the real world is all there is — and the comforting lesson that it amounts to quite a lot. Furthermore the careful reader might notice with pleasure the meticulous working out of words of *seeing*, and appreciate the way in which they pick up the theme of sight, which has been dramatically and at one point almost catastrophically central to the action of the novel.

It seems to me that such a misreading of *A Dog So Small* is in miniature what happens to children's literature as a whole: it is read carelessly, or out of context. Or perhaps most adults no longer know how to read a children's book.

My thesis is that children's literature has in general been misread, and that it has had little part in what Marina Warner calls 'the consecration of childhood'[30] — and has in fact sought to work against it.

My next point is that there are influences that lead us into other kinds of misreading. I can demonstrate what I mean by referring to a famous novel in which the heroine is an orphan, not particularly attractive, and at times rather disagreeable. This heroine moves to a big Victorian house where the owner is a remote, austere and rather intimidating man. Here she has an ambiguous relationship with the servants and becomes curious when she hears strange noises at night, perhaps human screams, coming from some distant room.

You will have immediately recognized that I am referring to *Jane Eyre*. But those clues might just as appropriately have led you to think of *The Secret Garden*.

It is not my purpose here to work out the significance of the striking parallels that seem to exist between those two novels, but rather to use them to question our habit of thinking of literature as established and fixed. We are inclined to think of texts as stable. But they are manifestly unstable: they have a capacity to generate new versions, new readings, remakes and ironic intertexts. The diagram on page 8 indicates the complexity in this case: *Jane Eyre* in ways that we do not yet understand seems to have led to *The Secret Garden*, which itself has been remade in various film and television versions. Jean Rhys's *Wide Sargasso Sea*[31] also has an obvious intertextual connection here. Frances Hodgson Burnett's book is also related to Philippa Pearce's *Tom's Midnight Garden*[32] — another novel about a secret garden, and which is in part concerned with an orphaned girl living in an unfriendly family. This too has been filmed for television. There is a further point of interest: Charlotte Brontë wrote

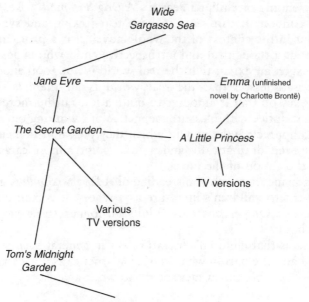

an unfinished novel called *Emma*[33] about a child left by her rich father at a fee-paying school which finds itself responsible for her when the father disappears. There is probably a conscious or unconscious imaginative link of some kind between that and *A Little Princess*[17] — which has itself been made into at least one serialized television version.

It is not my purpose to examine the *meaning* of these connections, but simply to draw attention to their existence. These are texts which seem to speak to one another, or about one another. It is not only 'classic' texts which are capable of this kind of thematic transformation or proliferation. While many new novels are published, read and forgotten, there is in others a seminal principle which ensures that they are repeatedly invoked, copied, adapted and quoted. We have only to think of *Goggle Eyes*.[34] It began as a novel by Anne Fine. When Margaret Meek wrote about it in *After Alice*,[35] the attention of such a respected commentator slightly altered its status. Then it was serialized on television — and no doubt it will eventually be marketed as a video. All this has occurred within a period of about five years. *Goggle Eyes* may not become a classic text, but it has already demonstrated some capacity to become what Peter Hollindale refers to as 'a protean, unstable and evolving one'.

I would like at this point to acknowledge my indebtedness to Peter Hollindale, who wrote an article, called 'Peter Pan, Captain Hook and the Book of the Video',[36] in which he argues that there are some texts which are 'richly generative for other, lesser works of derivation which nonetheless have interest of their own'.[37] His article is a model of the kind of illuminating criticism which can occur when such related texts are attentively read so that their 'intertextuality accentuates rather than overrides their originality'.[37] His concern in that article is the Hook group of texts — surely the most complex intertextual phenomenon in the history of children's books, and of especial significance since *Peter Pan* is the text that is usually cited when people are discussing childhood innocence.

But which text? The story started as an idea in an adult novel — *The Little White Bird*[38] — some parts of which were reissued as *Peter Pan in Kensington Gardens*.[39] *Peter Pan* was first performed as a play in 1904, and later appeared as a story by Barrie. Then there were retellings for younger readers, an authorized school edition, and numerous reissues illustrated by different artists.[40] It also has clear imaginative connections with *Treasure Island*,[41] and perhaps *Swiss Family Robinson*,[42] and Barrie took explicit care that adult readers should understand his indebtedness to William Wordsworth's famous 'Intimations' ode.[43]

In our own time the story's 'elasticity and adaptability'[44] has led to Disney's film version and Steven Spielberg's *Hook*.[45] The latter is not primarily about childhood at all, but the current American cultural anxiety about parenting, especially as it concerns fathers. Spielberg imported into Neverland a number of alien phenomena, including American baseball and sentimental sex — a very safe sex in which Tinkerbell grows to full human size long enough to kiss the adult Peter before shrinking again and becoming sexually inaccessible. The power of such 'generative' texts extends even beyond the boundaries of intertextuality: rather eerily, Barrie's story has links with Michael Jackson, one of the pop idols of the young, who was a boy star with 'exactly that adorable cuddly cuteness that makes grown-ups purr and coo'[46] — and who lives in his own private getaway, a remote ranch to which children were invited and which he calls Neverland. One of the children in Hook says incredulously, 'Peter Pan's *got kids?*' His disbelief is appropriate, for Barrie's Peter Pan *cannot* grow up — and in a weird piece of cross-cultural echoing, Michael Jackson's marriage to the daughter of Elvis Presley recently provoked a similar astonished disbelief and was assumed by some commentators to be a hoax, or a publicity stunt. They were saying, though not in so many words, 'Michael Jackson's *married?*'

It is perhaps worth pointing out that Barrie's *Peter Pan* is another text that has been widely misread. It does not set up an ideal of innocence; it sets up an ideal of play and pretending. Barrie had no illusions about 'innocent' children. Though he saw them as irresistibly attractive, he most frequently described them as crafty, cocky, cunning, disloyal, greedy, faithless and — in particular — heartless. His children possess a unique egocentric capacity *for themselves*; in Spielberg's film, they possess a unique capacity *for their parents*. The message in *Hook* is crude but urgent: the appeal of childhood is so shortlived that a father who spends too long at the office is likely to miss it. But neither Barrie nor Spielberg is concerned with innocence.

I believe that today's young readers are not specially interested in their own innocence — but are perfectly at home with this textual instability and do not find it remarkable or formidable. They live with it, and in it, quite comfortably — though they may not, unfortunately, have equal access to it. And that leads me to some other very powerful 'voices off' — the voices of authority. The present government has shown itself unable to understand textual instability. It prefers a *stable* heritage model of literature — or perhaps we should say 'model literature'. The original proposals for English, despite their apparent innocuousness, were obsessed with Standard English. 'An appreciation of Standard English' was listed as the first characteristic at Key Stage 1. I believe there is a matching, but undeclared, belief in what might (if the writers dared to make it explicit) be called 'standard literature'. This commitment lay behind those prescriptive lists which, with all their inevitable arbitrariness, continued to undervalue media and drama, and ignored popular literature altogether. Government thinking would prefer to exile the canon from vital popular culture. The *New Order*[47] still implies a divided and élitist culture, in which popular and media texts are 'consumed' outside school and 'literature of high quality' is taught inside school. Teachers always do their best, of course, but there is the danger that 'literature lessons' will become a dutiful gesture, devoid of real significance for most pupils. The government's failure to take into account the cultural lives of today's children within the contemporary video culture is breathtaking, and we need always to bear in mind that if teachers are required to teach a literature which *excludes what children actually experience as pleasurable reading*, the consequence is likely to be that prejudice, alienation and cultural fragmentation will be reinforced.

There is today a generation of children whose lives are increasingly likely to be filled with television, film, computer games, virtual reality and CD-ROMS, not to mention the enormous range of comics, newsprint, magazines and popular fiction. Within a few years it will be possible for young viewers to bring Wonderland into their bedrooms via the super-highway. It is already technologically possible not only to watch the story of *Alice* on a video but to go interactively through the looking glass with her — or even to remove Alice altogether and make alternative narrative adventures with yourself as the protagonist. However, in a world in which the children's novel has long lost its 200-year-old cultural dominance, the classroom can still be the place where popular literature and classic literature meet.

Popular literature is unstable; all literature is potentially unstable — children know this and take it for granted. They are born into a world of unstable proliferating texts, and the assumed distinction between 'children's literature' and popular fiction will not withstand scrutiny. An *illusion* of stability — and therefore an illusion of separateness — has been possible through several centuries of print; but now instability, which has probably always been the true condition of the popular arts, is about to demonstrate its powerful and careless creativity.

So we find ourselves in an extraordinary situation: children's writers have for a hundred years resisted damaging ideals of childhood, but the culture at large still perceives children's literature as dealing with sentimentalities. How is it possible that such a serious misreading can persist? Meanwhile we have a government which would have preferred to regard all literature as divorced from the real world of children. Why is it that social critics, commentators, philosophers, journalists and politicians generally misunderstand children's books and their place in the lives of actual children?

One possible explanation, of course, is that most adult commentators have not read any children's books for twenty or thirty years. There is a lot to be said for re-reading.

There may, however, be more deeply rooted cultural reasons. Children's writers generally prefer hopeful endings; and their narrative voices are generally sympathetic to their fictional characters, and — by extension — seem to be concerned for their young readers. But this age is not in sympathy with such qualities and perhaps contemporary adult culture cannot respond to them. Good authorial intentions are fair game for deconstruction. In a postmodernist world, such ideals are regarded cynically and alienation is more in vogue. Even stand-up comedians in the 1990s get their laughs by *insulting* their audiences! Perhaps a literature which is written through affection is bound to be at odds with such a culture. Is it symptomatic of the age that the children's books which have *not* been misread are those with the protective colouring of irony or comedy — Billy Bunter, William Brown and Adrian Mole?

This may not be a new phenomenon; in the middle of the eighteenth century the adult and public culture of the fashionable world was one of savage satire, sneering wit, and the ruthless competitions of capital and politics. But research is cautiously beginning to reveal that in the nurseries there was a quite different educational culture — a private and domestic culture — based on affection for children. Eighteenth-century nursery culture was able to keep its head down in an unsympathetic age, but the children's literature of today is less fortunate; it is publicly exposed and in everyone's gunsights.

In 1994 I read of a local authority which wanted to teach its Year 3 children about AIDS. A Tory MP opposed this, complaining that it would

'destroy young children's innocence'. There is that word again, appearing
— as it so frequently does — in contexts where its meaning has to do with
ignorance, and in particular with sexual ignorance. That kind of comment
gives the game away: our culture seems to want to set aside children as a
safely isolated group, in a cultural reservation called Innocence. But there
is an uncomfortable irony here: although we would prefer them to spend
their time safely reading traditional children's literature, we remain quite
happy that they should be exposed to the sinister 'voices off' of a
multimillion-pound toy industry, with its aggressive marketing and its
images and stereotypes of violence and cruelty.

If a culture herds its children into a corral called Innocence, it is a likely
consequence that it will put children's literature in there too, to separate it
off from the rest of popular culture, and from adult literature.
Fragmentation begets fragmentation. A country where there is such a
genuine difficulty in seeing children as simply *people* is likely to find it
hard to regard children's books as simply belonging to a wider *popular*
culture. Children's books are part of the wider literature in the same way
that children are part of the whole population. So long as we insist on
making unrealistic demands of both the literature and the children, we
will continue both to expect the literature to serve the false goddess
Innocence and to overreact with horror when children become criminals.

The National Curriculum is unlikely to recommend the study of Disney's
recent film version of *Aladdin*,[48] with the voice of Robin Williams as the
Genie. Yet anyone who has seen it will know that almost any extract —
and in particular the first appearance of the self-advertising Genie —
would repay close analysis and should finally refute any lingering belief
that reading a film text is easy or passive. There are more cultural
allusions per 60 seconds in that children's film than in any other film I can
think of. We can dismiss it as exemplifying the worst features of popular
culture: it is brash, vulgar perhaps, and committed to a frenetic show-biz
slapstick which we might dismiss as peculiarly American. But, if we have
children between, say, 7 and 12, which would we rather they watched? —
that? — or a few episodes of *EastEnders*? Which is the more 'innocent'?
Which will show our children more wickedness, bitterness and hope-
lessness? We know the graduation that occurs with soaps: very young
children begin with *Home and Away* and *Neighbours*, they often by-pass
Coronation Street, and then they progress to *EastEnders*. Almost all
human wickedness and unhappiness are there: cruelty, violence, betrayal,
arson, murder, cynicism, adultery, abortion, AIDS — except how to
murder a father and dispose of the body; for that you have to go to
Brookside. I make this point, not to attack the dramatic character of these
compelling soaps, but to draw attention to the inconsistencies in our
assumptions about what is suitable viewing for children.

The old Disney films usually began with a book. First came the credits, and then a leather-bound or gold-covered storybook would appear on the screen, saying *Cinderella* or *Sleeping Beauty*.[49] A voice would read the words on the page, the camera would move in on one of the stills, it would become animated — and the film was launched. The unspoken assumption was that the film was pretending it was a book — or implying that its validity derived from a book. But, significantly, there is no book at the beginning of *Aladdin*. It begins with a storyteller talking directly to the camera. It openly declares its filmic credentials and makes no reference to books. And most of its cultural allusions are to cinema and showbusiness. Meanwhile, information books are showing signs of attempting to disguise themselves as videos and interactive CD-ROMS. It will be interesting to see whether any publisher has the courage to counter the video culture by specifically designing books to emphasize their uniquely 'bookish' qualities.

These are significant developments. If even the conservative Disney can admit that its films have finally moved into a video culture, we probably have to accept that children's poetry and children's novels exist in a different relationship now with the wider popular culture at large. Any serious consideration of children's literature, I believe, must take account of the enormous and perhaps overwhelming changes that are taking place.

I also believe that we will not understand children's literature unless we begin to understand that massive cultural mish-mash which we call childhood, whose appalling contradictions became briefly and tragically obvious at the time of the killing of James Bulger.

Notes

1 Marina Warner, *Managing Monsters — Six Myths of Our Time* (the 1994 Reith Lectures), Vintage, London, 1994.
2 *Ibid.*, p. xiii.
3 *Ibid.*, p. 34.
4 *Ibid.*, p. 46.
5 *Ibid.*, p. 35.
6 Frances Hodgson Burnett, *Little Lord Fauntleroy*, first published 1886.
7 *Ibid.*, pp. 7–8.
8 Charles Dickens, *Oliver Twist*, first published 1837–39.
9 Charles Dickens, *The Christmas Carol*, first published 1843.
10 Charles Dickens, *Dombey and Son*, first published 1846–48.
11 George Eliot, *Silas Marner*, first published 1861.
12 Charles Dickens, *Nicholas Nickleby*, first published 1838–39.
13 Charles Dickens, *The Old Curiosity Shop*, first published 1840–41.
14 David Grylls, *Guardians and Angels: Parents and Children in Nineteenth Century Fiction*, Faber, London, 1978, p. 136.

15 Charlotte Brontë, *Jane Eyre*, first published 1847.
16 Frances Hodgson Burnett had already published a good deal of adult fiction.
17 Frances Hodgson Burnett, *A Little Princess*, first published 1905. There had been an earlier version, *Sara Crewe or What Happened at Miss Minchin's*, first published in 1887.
18 Lesley Shuttleworth, 'Frances Hodgson Burnett and the Evolution of the Child Figure in Nineteenth Century Literature', unpublished dissertation, Cambridge University, 1994.
19 Frances Hodgson Burnett, *The Secret Garden*, first published 1911.
20 F. H. Burnett wrote one more novel for children — *The Lost Prince*, published in 1915. The story is unconvincing and rather badly told, but her move towards a more convincing characterization continued in this work.
21 George Eliot, *The Mill on the Floss*, first published 1860.
22 Thomas Hardy, *Jude the Obscure*, first published 1894–95.
23 American children's literature parted company at about this time and was already developing its own tradition.
24 For example, Billy Bunter, William Brown and Jennings.
25 Lewis Carroll, *Alice's Adventures in Wonderland*, first published 1865; *Through the Looking-Glass*, first published 1871–72.
26 Rumer Godden, *An Episode of Sparrows*, Macmillan, London, 1956; *The Battle of the Villa Fiorita*, Macmillan, London, 1963; *The Greengage Summer*, Macmillan, London, 1958.
27 There are ten novels in Antonia Forest's Marlow series, originally published by Faber. They are the best series of family/school stories ever written but are now mostly out of print and unobtainable. Puffin published four of them as a separate — and therefore misleading — series of school stories.
28 Barry Hines, *Kes*, Michael Joseph, London, 1978; Philippa Pearce, *The Way to Sattin Shore*, Kestrel, London, 1983; Anne Fine, *Goggle Eyes*, Hamish Hamilton, London, 1989; Jan Mark, *Trouble Half-Way*, Viking Kestrel, London, 1985; Anita Desai, *A Village by the Sea*, Heinemann, London, 1982.
29 Philippa Pearce, *A Dog So Small*, Puffin, London, 1964, pp. 155–6.
30 Marina Warner, *op. cit.*, p. 46.
31 Jean Rhys, *Wide Sargasso Sea*, Andre Deutsch, London, 1966.
32 Philippa Pearce, *Tom's Midnight Garden*, OUP, Oxford, 1958.
33 See Charlotte Brontë, *The Professor*, and *Emma, a Fragment*, Dent, London, 1969.
34 Fine, *op. cit.*
35 Margaret Meek, 'Children reading — now', in Morag Styles, Eve Bearne and Victor Watson (eds), *After Alice*, Cassell, London, 1992.
36 Peter Hollindale, 'Peter Pan, Captain Hook and the Book of the Video', *Signal, 72*, Thimble Press, Stroud, 1993.
37 *Ibid.*, p. 172.
38 J. M. Barrie, *The Little White Bird*, first published 1902.
39 J. M. Barrie, *Peter Pan in Kensington Gardens*, first published 1906.
40 Even the title was unstable; versions are variously known as *Peter Pan, Peter and Wendy*, or *Peter Pan and Wendy*.

41 R. L. Stevenson, *Treasure Island*, first published 1881–82.
42 Johann David Wyss, *The Swiss Family Robinson*, first published in various textual forms 1812–18.
43 William Wordsworth, 'Ode: Intimations of Immortality from Recollections of Early Childhood', first published 1807.
44 Peter Hollindale, *op. cit.*, p. 155.
45 Steven Spielberg (director), *Hook*, Tristar Pictures Inc.
46 Marina Warner, *op. cit.*, p. 43.
47 *English in the National Curriculum*, HMSO, London, 1995.
48 Walt Disney, *Aladdin*, video, The Walt Disney Company.
49 Walt Disney, *Cinderella*, video, The Walt Disney Company; Walt Disney, *Sleeping Beauty*, video, The Walt Disney Company.

PART I

The Voices of Children

If popular literature is trash, what are its readers? And if those readers are young, what is their status? How can children begin to appreciate the pleasures of great literature if the books which first give them a sense of literary enjoyment are exiled and branded as rubbish? If great literature is studied in school, and popular literature is enjoyed out of school, what kinds of cultural integration are possible for young readers? If Enid Blyton is such a pernicious influence on young readers, how is it that so many experienced and discriminating adults admit to having loved her books when they were young? These are some of the questions that lie behind the chapters in this Part.

Reading is a double-edged tool. When children's books first began to appear at the end of the seventeenth century, many Puritans believed that the salvation of their children depended on their being able to read the Word of God. They were dismayed to find that their children seemed just as keen to read the word of the Devil in its many forms — inflammatory, bawdy, subversive, even revolutionary. Several generations later, penny dreadfuls and comics caused similar alarm. Today, we find it hard to feel comfortable with the fact that so many developing readers find their reading pleasure outside the classroom, within what we rather enviously (but precisely) refer to as 'popular' literature.

A perceived division between approved literature and exiled literature is not new. Nor is it easy to deal with. Although there seems to be little evidence to suggest that reading popular fiction does children any actual harm, we cannot feel equally confident that it will lead them unaided to an appreciation of more satisfying reading. There are practical and pedagogical difficulties here for teachers; but there is also a more fundamental dilemma which has to do with how *we* relate to texts; we cannot *stop* being adults and reading as adults, and we may feel with some justice that we should not be asked to pretend that we can see no difference between Philippa Pearce and Enid Blyton. We may feel that there are some compromises we should not be asked to make, some convictions we should not be obliged to surrender. Or is this just literary snobbery? We need to find ways of being true to our own sense of literary excellence while at the same time being able to welcome other voices telling us what it is like to be a young reader in today's popular culture.

This dilemma might be easier for us if we could bring ourselves to see children's literature as existing on a continuum with popular literature instead of divided from it. In some ways it is becoming easier to believe in that continuity in a multi-media age in which traditional barriers of form and genre are collapsing and new popular versions of classic texts proliferate — thereby providing teachers with an invaluable resource for comparison and debate.

But in order to engage in a debate, you have to have a variety of speakers representing every point of view. There cannot be meaningful discussion if some perspectives are assumed to be invalid even before they are formulated; if one side of the debate is silenced. In this section Elizabeth Hammill and Kate Agnew are concerned with the many ways in which the voices of children are resolutely and stubbornly disregarded by parents, publishers and reviewers. This is not a trivial matter: it has consequences for young readers and for the quality of the books we produce for them. Jenny Daniels and Charles Sarland show that, when children are genuinely and sympathetically consulted, we can learn important lessons about them as readers, and they may be led into making articulate all manner of subtle readerly distinctions and judgements — engaging in literary discussion, in fact.

If in their early years young readers have shared the best of today's picture books, they will already have learned that reading is interactive and expressive, voluble and volatile. Are all those invaluable hours of early-years book-talk to be wasted? Every effort has been put into encouraging these 4-, 5- and 6-year-old readers to formulate their views, their enthusiasms, their delights, their bafflements — to develop confident voices and find words for their own ways of engaging critically with texts. Is all this energy to be allowed to run into the ground when they move on from picture books? Are these same readers to grow up into a generation of silenced consumers, no longer valuing either what they read or their own opinions?

The themes of this Part are the educational waste and cultural divisions that ensue when the voices of children are silenced, overridden or disregarded; and the potential for increased cultural cohesiveness that might be realized when critical literacy in developing young readers begins to become articulate and is attended to.

CHAPTER 1

'Real' Stories or 'Pretty' Stories
A Question of Criteria

Elizabeth Hammill

Elizabeth Hammill's chapter is concerned with young readers aged between 6 and 9. These are readers who have become familiar with the textual and intertextual challenges of contemporary picture books. What is there, she asks, for such readers to progress to? The answer is depressing. Her chapter provides an account of the ways in which publishers' series have to a large extent replaced one-off publications, and of how this has led to a considerable degree of impoverished uniformity in the stories available to young newly independent readers. She singles out one honourable exception — one series of books which provides a rich, varied and sophisticated range of literacy challenges for readers who are passing through this important transitional stage. She examines this situation in the light of current publishing practices, and she also has some sharp things to say about the amount and the quality of children's book reviewing. Elizabeth Hammill frames her argument within an absorbing analysis of a short story by Mary Norton — a story which is itself a challenge to adult assumptions about young readers and what we think they want. They do not want 'pretty' stories — or indeed pretty series.

It seems appropriate in a chapter concerned with exploring how we develop criteria for selecting books to share with 6- to 9-year-olds that I begin by selecting and sharing a story with you, the reader. It's a little-known short story by Mary Norton, called 'Paul's Tale', and is chosen, I'll admit, with intent.

It begins with 'comfortable' Aunt Isobel attempting to entertain her feverish Godson with a fairy-tale that *she* clearly enjoys. It could be a tale from her childhood, as the dated language suggests:

> 'Ho! Ho!' said the King, slapping his fat thighs. 'Methinks this youth shows promise.' But at that moment the Court Magician stepped forward ... 'What is the matter, Paul? Don't you like this story?'[1]

Paul, far more interested in exploring what it feels like to be a hot-water bottle beneath the bedclothes, admits that he likes 'told stories better than read stories'. What sort? He gives us his criteria.

'I'd like a real story ... You know,' he said, 'quite real. So you know it must have happened.'
    'Shall I tell you about Grace Darling?'
    'No, tell me about a little man.'
    'What sort of little man?'
    'A little man just as high –' Paul's eyes searched the room, '– as that candlestick on the mantelshelf, but without the candle.'
    'But that's a very small candlestick: it's only about six inches.'
    'Well, that big.'[1]

Aunt Isobel, 'disappointed about the fairy story', begins a new 'real' tale about a 'little tiny man' who initially closely resembles the characters in the tale she has just been telling. But not for long.

'He was the sweetest little man you ever saw, and he wore a little red jerkin and a dear little cap made out of a foxglove. His boots –'
    'He didn't have any,' said Paul.
    Aunt Isobel looked startled, 'Yes!' she exclaimed. 'He had boots — little pointed ...'
    'He didn't have any clothes,' contradicted Paul. 'He was quite bare.'
    Aunt Isobel looked perturbed. 'But he would have been cold,' she pointed out.
    'He had thick skin,' explained Paul, 'like a twig.'
    'Like a twig?'
    'Yes. You know that sort of wrinkly, nubbly skin on a twig.'
    Aunt Isobel knitted in silence for a second or two. She didn't like the little naked man nearly as much as the little clothed man: she was trying to get used to him. After a while she went on.[1]

But Paul interrupts and soon Aunt Isobel, in spite of herself, gets caught up in Paul's altogether more earthy and imaginative tale until, believing that Paul is actually keeping the little man in a cake tin in the bedroom, she decides to free him. In the ensuing tension, she drops the tin.

Paul broke the silence with a croupy cough. 'Did you see him?' he asked, hoarse but interested.
    'No,' stammered Aunt Isobel, almost with a sob. 'I didn't. I didn't see him.'
    'But you nearly did.'
    Aunt Isobel sat down limply in the upholstered chair. Her hand wavered vaguely round her brow, and her cheeks looked white and pendulous as if deflated. 'Yes,' she muttered, shivering slightly, 'Heaven help me, I nearly did.'

Paul gazed at her a moment longer. 'That's what I mean,' he said.

'What?' asked Aunt Isobel weakly, but as if she did not really care.

Paul lay down again. Gently, sleepily, he pressed his face into the pillow ...

'About stories. Being real .... .'[1]

This is one of those stories that, in Kafka's words 'bite and sting'. It begins in familiar, comfortable territory — a bedroom, a fire, an aunt, a sick boy, a fairy-tale. We think we know where we are. But it quickly changes to jolt us and Aunt Isobel with the shock of the new. While 'Paul's Tale' has much to teach us as readers — about the variety of ways in which stories can be told, about narrative time, about the reality of stories, about the fact that in the act of storytelling, the listener/reader is just as important as the teller/writer — let us focus, for the moment, on what it can *do* for us in the context of this chapter.

What does it tell us about the relationship between the assumptions we make about young readers and the stories we select to share with them? Aunt Isobel has clearly made assumptions about Paul and the sort of story he, or perhaps a sick child of about 9, might like. Her fairy-tale, of which we only hear fragments, is a possibly childless aunt's notion of a good children's story. It is certainly a story that *she* feels comfortable reading aloud but it is one that neither holds Paul's attention (he is diverted by an eiderdown feather and a hot-water bottle) nor challenges his mind or ear with its flaccid, stilted language. Aunt Isobel has not taken account of Paul himself (we do not know how well she knows him); only perhaps of an idealized Paul/boy. 'How beautiful he looked, she thought, lying there in the firelight, with one curled hand placed lightly on the counterpane.'[1] The Paul we encounter, feverish cold notwithstanding, is an alert, imaginative, curious, physical boy who wants a 'real story ... so you know it must have happened'.[1]

When Aunt Isobel begins her second 'told' story, however, we are once again back in the stock fairy-tale world she first invited Paul to enter. When she introduces a fairy in a tree into the proceedings, Paul asks 'incredulously'. ... 'Do you know that for certain?'[1] This is not a story where he can slip between the words to enter its world and allow himself to believe in it completely. It is a closed story that underestimates Paul's restless intelligence — a 'pretty' story Aunt Isobel thinks, but not right for Paul. When Paul takes over the increasingly collaborative telling, his tale swallows us and Aunt Isobel up with its reality — invented or not. Paul is altogether tougher, wiser and more acute than Aunt Isobel ever imagined. There is nothing condescending or shallow about his story. He knows how to play a flexible text against the listener, in spite of it not being his aunt's kind of story, to make his point about stories being 'real'. When Margaret Meek tells us that reading and storying continually need redefining, that is what Paul's tale is doing for Aunt Isobel and for us.

Knowledge of the reader, then, not assumptions about the reader, is crucial in book selection. What do we know about readers between 6 and 9? We know that children raised on reading schemes or on real picture books will have developed some sense of what counts as reading, what counts as a book, what counts as a story; some expectations of what literature is and what it is good for — expectations not yet solely based on 'literary experience, but (instead) on a prospective reading adventure with the possibility of surprise'.[2] Children who have read and still enjoy the fluid dual texts of picture book makers like Satoshi Kitamura, Anthony Browne, the Ahlbergs, John Burningham, and Jon Scieska and Lane Smith will expect the unexpected in subject, telling and style. Yet most of these same readers, for whom nothing about reading is yet set in stone, will not only become independent readers in these years but will also move from reading pictures with words, to words with some pictures and then to words alone. From the continuing challenge of picture books, they will 'progress' to the early stages of dense text and to an awareness that it is ultimately not the image but the word that we value and that pictures with words can be replaced with pictures in the mind. We know that different readers will make this transition in different ways and that we need a wealth of different books to enable this to happen: books that will hook them as readers, confirm them as readers and extend them as readers. We know too that at 7 or so, children are beginning to judge for themselves what kind of readers they are going to become. They do this in part by viewing their ability to learn and master the workings of text in relation to peers, and in part by assessing what the texts we give them to read tell them about themselves and about our view of them as readers.

What happens to children developmentally between 6 and 9? While home and family are still important, children are now firmly a part of the wider social world of school and neighbourhood, of peers and non-familial adults, and are subject to the rules of both. The common cultures of childhood — the jokes, games, comics, and television programmes shared in the playground, on the street corner, at home or in the classroom — demonstrate an appetite for knock-about humour, for farce and the ridiculous, for wit and wordplay. Play — 'let's pretend' and 'what if' — is still a serious activity through which the young investigate possibilities and 'extend the limitations of their smallness and weakness in the face of adult authority'.[3] Their ability 'to switch in and out of metaphor, ... to live in several worlds at once' enables them through play to 'explore the world they inhabit, hypothesize and experiment as they work out the patterns that govern everyday life'.[4] Reading, then, for the apprentice learner and player on the world's stage, now becomes a 'tool of discovery that can be adapted (not only) to the service of the need to learn and organise new information' about how the wide world works but also to confirm the young's ability to succeed and be competent in it.[5] Reading not only

> images the world; in story form, it also images the reader's role in the world. ... So it is not surprising that the young child's view of reading (say in the years 6 to 9) mirrors both of these preoccupations — learning and mastering.[6]

That this happens we know from observation. How it happens, however, remains a puzzle. The National Curriculum affords us the opportunity to learn by attending to what the young must now share with us about the insides of their reading. Even Aunt Isobel is open to this. The paradox remains, however, that as adults, selecting on behalf of young readers, when we read a book where the implied reader is an apprentice or newly independent one, we are unlikely to read in the way in which it asks to be read. Our natural instincts are to read with adult sensibilities and standards; then, on behalf of the child reader; and then, perhaps, 'to surrender to the book on its own terms', remembering how we *might* have responded as a child.[7] It is here that knowledge of the reader and assumptions about the reader may become blurred. If Aunt Isobel misjudges her choice of story because she assumes that Paul is akin to the reader she remembers she once was, how often do we too do this? If we yearn only for the kinds of texts we enjoyed as children, we miss the point that childhood is changing, books are changing, ways of telling are changing, and what counts as literacy is changing; and we need to carry on growing as readers ourselves if we and the young entrusted to us are not to be left behind. 'Pretty' will not do when 'real' is required.

If we stop for a moment to consider what provision publishers make for readers of 6 to 9 — what we are to select from — a disconcerting picture emerges: one to which all of us who create, select from and share books with the young may unwittingly have contributed; in which 'pretty' is primarily what we are offered. While a review of recent publishing history is not possible here, it is important to note that publishing houses are now multinational enterprises in which money is no longer made in order to publish good books, but books, over 7000 new children's titles annually, are published to make money. Caught in a 'pincer grip' between the demands of schools which 'often display a very limited view of the rewards of reading for pleasure' and ask 'for general children's lists to reflect the boring banality and ... "accessibility" of the reading scheme', and competition from television, many children's publishers have 'lost their nerve under pressures from the money men ... and lowered their standards so that they can increase their output of titles in short print runs that bring quick profit'.[8] Michael Rosen describes the situation thus: 'It is the inexorable anarchy of capitalism that is insisting: more titles, more authors, quick quick, write, write, no time to edit, no time to rewrite, get it out, sell it, drop it, pulp it.'[9] Mammon, not excellence, dictates product, not literature — and nowhere are product and endemic overproduction more evident than in publishing for 6- to 9-year-olds.

In 1986 when I was choosing books as one of the selectors for the *Signal Bookguide Fiction 6 to 9*, we were aware that many stories written for this age group came in series: Gazelles, Blackbirds, Kites, etc. Five years later, in preparing an update for the Bookguide, I found that *most* books published for newly independent readers now appeared in series. Indeed, in 1991, over 50 per cent of *all* fiction published for young people by our 20 major publishers was in series for this age group. While this imbalance has marginally improved, it is clear that an entire sector of children's publishing has been subsumed by what might be called a 'series mentality'. In consequence, it now provides us with an excess of choice, as series, for economic reasons, are published in sets of four or six. Looking back over the past 25 years as reflected in the annual *Children's Books of the Year* selection, we see how series publishing for 6- to 9-year-olds (in the 1970s, it was for 5- to 8-year-olds) has supplanted the book published on its own merit alone. It's a revealing exercise. In 1971, 6 out of 21 titles selected were from series; in 1975, 7 out of 21; in 1979, 10 out of 29; in 1982, 7 out of 25; then after the launch in 1984 of the highly successful Banana Books, in 1985, 18 out of 36; in 1989, 16 out of 20; and in 1993, 20 out of 23. The figures speak for themselves about the shift from one-off publishing to series publishing.

What is the problem with series? They have always provided a useful umbrella for 'bridge' stories of all types for newly independent readers to 'practise on'. Many are competently written and well-intentioned. Despite the limitations on length, shape, and size dictated by the standardization of format, authors can rise to these challenges with tales that are masterpieces of economy, invention, and even poetry. From Arnold Lobel's Frog and Toad tales to James Marshall's stories about the rapscallion Fox to Kevin Crossley-Holland's *Storm*, Jan Mark's *The Twig Thing* and *Taking the Cat's Way Home*, and Bob Wilson's *Ging Gang Goolie, It's an Alien*, there is a long list of fine stories that have appeared in series. Until recently, however, these books were part of a wider pattern of in-between fiction publishing. Now series — a glut of them — are almost all that is being produced for 6- to 9-year-olds. The sheer number of titles and the apparent bandwagon response of some publishers to the educational, commercial and literary success of Banana Books and Jets have had a deleterious effect not only on the overall quality of publishing for this age group but also on our ability to select wisely and well from it; indeed, to think critically about it at all. But think critically we must.

When Peter Hunt laments the fact that children's books now present us with a 'dull featureless plateau of homogenised competence — of knowing where all the buttons are and which ones to push when',[10] he could be talking about much that is published in series for 6- to 9-year-olds. There is a palpable sense in many of these books, in which format (and possibly formula) is emphasized at the expense of individual content and voice, that publisher and author know 'exactly what kind of story will "fit", what the market will bear, what kind of cute little twist (almost obligatory now) is needed to end the story'.[11] When Michael Rosen wonders if Catherine Storr's *Clever Polly and the Stupid Wolf*, a classic of young fiction, would have seen the light of day 'if she had started out writing with publishers standing over her saying: could you shorten that for our new series Whizzers we're launching in the autumn. And could you change biscuits to cookies, we're off to the Bologna Book Fair next week and we're hoping to interest Gulf Oil Children's Books in it', he is questioning whether current publishing practice is compatible with the making of literature.[12] When Julia Eccleshare, in 1993, her final year as selector of *Children's Books of the Year*, deplores a style of writing in series that 'reads as if it is a series of shots being fired from a gun. Short sentences are easy to read. Once hooked, you might go on. Especially if the kids have short, silly names and do short silly things', she is raising other important questions.[13]

Why are we offering this age group a reductive literature — impoverished in form, language and content? Why, when we know that children engage with the complexities in picture books, do we then offer them trivialized experience and expect them to regard it as 'progress'? Is children's intelligence being underestimated and text devalued because there is a fear that reading has become too difficult an occupation because it doesn't work like television or computer games? Is there a consequent assumption that *all* young readers need simplified and accessible texts — 'dumbing down', as they call it in the USA?

If the shortage of good fiction for 6- to 9-year-olds is not a new problem (it is noted in the Bullock and Plowden Reports), if, as early as 1983, we shocked ourselves by discovering that the kind of book we sought for this readership was 'a product of a certain size, length, and shape', selected 'just as the uncommitted wine buyer works by price',[14] and if, as selectors and buyers, we have fallen back on the series product because we have difficulty identifying suitable books — a problem exacerbated by a lack of critical attention to books for in-betweens — then are we not all in some way responsible for the present state of affairs? Add to this the uncertainties of a teaching profession demoralized by government policy and the politics of literacy and reading; a library service divested of children's specialists and funds; the demise of effective national review coverage of children's books; and an increase in specialist reviewing that because there is a target reader — a librarian, a teacher — becomes consumer-led, not book-led, and we see that it is small wonder that publishers get away with producing 'pretty' series books.

Why, when young readers have just learned to master print independently, do we almost unthinkingly abandon them to series? Series may be 'stepping stones' between picture books or reading schemes (from which they naturally follow on) and novels — a transitional literature — but, as such, they need us to attend to them. We use our skills as thoughtful and discriminating selectors earlier in children's reading lives. We need to continue using them at this stage too. While it may be easier to succumb to the marketing ploy of publishers who sell each new set in a series into schools as packages only, led by a flagship author, if we are genuinely concerned about what we give children between 6 and 9 — an in-between stage just as crucial as that other literary transition point in adolescence — then we must start to make the sorts of distinctions between books that the sheer volume of series publishing actively discourages and that we may have hitherto avoided.

This brings us back to the selector, the individual book, and the young reader; to Aunt Isobel, Paul and their tales, and to the question which seems to me to lie at the heart of all selection: what might this book *do for its reader*? 'Paul's Tale' makes it abundantly clear that no text is neutral matter. Whatever its qualities, literary or otherwise, text acts on the reader; indeed, invites the reader to interact with it. Margaret Meek has indisputably shown us this in *How Texts Teach What Readers Learn*.[15] It is because text is active in this way that it places on those of us who create, comment on and select from it for young readers an active responsibility to consider critically just how it will affect those readers.

This 'how', if we look, for example, at what passes for reviewing these days, seems to be narrowly defined in terms of pleasure at its most basic level, accessibility, and suitability: typically, 'I read this to my six and eight year olds and we laughed and laughed'[16] or 'A rattling little story . . . aimed at the newly independent reader who is looking for a short and amusing story told at a good pace'[17] or 'Shades of Gradgrind and Dickens here. . . . I loved it. A read-aloud that appeals to us teachers, with plenty of in-jokes, is long overdue. Oh, yes, the children loved it too'.[18] Do any of these 'critical' comments begin to address what each book might do for its readers? If a story made a family 'laugh and laugh' or was 'amusing', I'd like to know how the writer makes this happen; how the story works; how the shape of the text both controls and frees the reader's response. I'd like to know, for instance, what kind of humour is at play. Is it the 'nudge-nudge' comedy current in much fiction for 6- to 9-year-olds or does it work in subtler, more circumspect, ways? Does it arise from a straightforward joke or from a comic reversal or parody of a traditional character or genre (known perhaps to young readers from television and film)? Is the humour farcical, relying on slapstick or exaggeration for effect? What is it teaching its readers about how a funny book is to be read? Here, for example, is a review of Andrew Matthews' *Dr Monsoon Taggert's Amazing Finishing Academy*, which attempts to do just this and, in so doing, to consider, not just whether children will enjoy this story, but why it is worth their time and attention.

> Let me suggest that boys like most the comedy of the grotesque, the excessive. I fear their preferences are antifeminist. Look at Tony Ross's illustrations for *Dr Monsoon Taggert's Amazing Finishing Academy* by Andrew Matthews. What a ghastly sight is Arabella Armitage, whose parents 'fed her until she swelled up all round like a pink balloon'. The fat-person joke seems to run and run; it is allowable only when the implicit message is 'this is play'. So on her way to the Finishing Academy Arabella becomes thinner as she meets a series of play characters, a talking dog, a talking chair, a highwayman dressed in (removable) polka dots called Spotted Dick, an ogre and an even fatter Lady Carmen. She finds hunger preferable to fright, and learns the lesson that, as far as I know, never comes from a diet sheet. 'When you have nearly been eaten, it makes you see things from the food's point of view.'
>
> The humour in this story is slapstick parable, junior Monty Python action. The reader learns the moral rules of this game: greed is never good. As with Molière you laugh because you know it's really serious and are relieved (the effect of laughter) when Arabella speaks up for herself at last. 'I'm not bossy. I'm determined.' There's family mileage in that phrase I guess. All good read-aloud stuff, with lip-licking wordage in the cream-cake episode. No one would believe a word of it, but as a story it comes well up to scratch with its what-if possibilities.[19]

Underlying this review is first-hand knowledge of children's delight in this particular book and the attendant assumption that others will enjoy it too. Suitability (not a word I often use) is implicit, but not a reductive suitability based on the assumption that the less experience the reader/ listener has of life and literature the more predictable the reaction and the simpler the story has to be, but rather one that assumes that readers of 8 or 9, once secure with story patterns and how an extended text works, will, just as they do with picture books, enjoy stories which 'upturn and subvert the usual order of words on a page' in 'topsy-turveys' whose texts teach that 'a lot goes on under the surface features of the language, making interpretations a significant kind of *deep* play'.[20] Of course, texts for 6- to 9-year-olds need to enable them to make the transition from picture books to ever denser texts — a transition in which the nature of reading subtly changes as text takes over from pictures and the role of illustration changes. But who says this can't be done adventurously?

From the surfeit of series 'products' currently available, one series alone has directly addressed both this change and the changing young reader. Acknowledging and building on the complex lessons about visual narratives learned by the young from television, cinema, computer games and picture books, Jets,[21] though light in feel, take young readers and their new literacies seriously. While the form of the comic, the common literary currency of most 6- to 9-year-olds, and the interactive multi-dimensional narrative experiences it provides (the need to interpret, for instance, several kinds of text at once from straightforward narrative to dialogue in speech bubbles and thoughts in bubbles to pictures) underpin Jets, what distinguishes the series is the judicious, often inventive, blend of texts whose conventions are drawn from a range of contemporary literacies. Comic strip, television-type narratives and dialogue, newspaper and magazine articles, letters, lists and maps are interwoven with line drawings, handwritten and printed text and an emphasis on humour in the form of verbal and pictorial jokes, wordplay and puns by author and illustrator, working out page by page how the mixed media will achieve the desired effect. Shirley Hughes in *Chips and Jessie* and Roger McGough and Tony Blundell in *The Great Smile Robbery* individually showed us the possibilities of this form in the early 1980s. Here it is given a series format — one that is sufficiently flexible to allow a variety of voices to be heard and literary genres encountered. While the kinds of literary experience Jets offer move across a range of difficulty and challenge, children drawn in and along by familiar conventions and forms here experience reading and interpretation as an intriguing game, as known literacies from other media are used in unexpected ways and readers are invited to become insiders in a new kind of intertextual network.

Bob Wilson's *Ging Gang Goolie, It's an Alien* exemplifies what Jets' bookmaking, at its best, might do for its readers. I tried to do justice to its complexity when I reviewed it in 1992. I described it as

> a SciFi romp that interlaces picture and text(s) in an organic way. A deadpan text recounts how the unexpected meeting of an alien Grobblewockian spaceman and the 3rd Balsawood Scout Troop changes the whole course of interplanetary conquest. It is the games Wilson plays around the straightforward narrative that are original and extending. Wilson offers readers several points of view on the action, for instance, by setting a variety of contemporary literacies against it: three completely different lists of 'essential kit' for Garry to take to Scout camp — the Scout leader's, Garry's mother's, and Garry's own; a basic guide to Grobblewockian history and culture; a diagram of the correct way to erect a tent: and handwritten notes from the author to the reader either commenting on the action or on our expectations of the action. He builds up several running jokes — on Scout Derek Twig's brain power, for instance — begun in words and finished in pictures. He offers us two

cultures and two languages — ours and the aliens' (both a kind of pidgin English) — and makes great play on the humorous similarities between them. The Boy Scout motto is 'Be prepared' and the Grobblewockians' is 'Bee Pree! Pear Head'. Each of these literacies acts as more than just a device to tell the story and, at an age when the look of a book matters, they allow for a changing layout of text and picture and size and spacing of types of print and handwriting that continually engage the reader's attention. They enable the reader to experience language and form as playthings with which to explore through story the make-believe question 'What if?' that lies at the heart of so much children's imaginative play between six and nine.[22]

While Jets use familiar literacies to draw young readers into stories where the word is assuming ever greater importance, the illustrations, as in picture books, still need to be read if the whole tale is to be understood. Increasingly, however, in other books for this age, illustrations are no longer an integral part of the text. They break up text so that the reader is not swamped by words but they no longer move the story along or suggest other resonances and layers of meaning. Eventually text will take over completely and the reader will be required to replace pictures on the page with pictures in the mind. To think in images, to visualize, children need to learn to *listen to* the text, to its voice(s), to the unspoken story between and around the words. Images come to us in language: in phrases, in verbal constructs, in poetry. What language itself does for the reader is of vital importance. As we saw in 'Paul's Tale', Aunt Isobel's stock story may conjure up positive images for her but for Paul and us those images don't necessarily work. Indeed, when Paul says he prefers 'told' stories to 'read' stories, it may be that he is giving up on the printed word because it appears to offer him no images to think with.

Paul's own tale, on the other hand, which draws attention to the conventions by breaking them, enters, holds and expands our imaginations (and Aunt Isobel's) with its concrete actuality: its subversive language/images and intent. When Aunt Isobel suggests that the little man 'lived in a bluebell wood, among the roots of a dear old tree' in a 'dear little house, tunnelled out of the soft, loamy earth, with a bright blue front door' and that he had 'a little pipe made of straw ... a little hollow straw through which he played jiggety little tunes. And to which he danced', we know this is a conceit. Paul counters, 'I thought he lived in the potting shed,' which he then describes. He tells us more: 'How sort of big his hands and feet looked and how he could scuttle along. Like a rat'; about his 'creaky sort of voice, like a frog'; about his family history: 'He isn't used to talking. He's the last one. He's been all alone for years and years ... he had an aunt and she died about fifteen years ago. But even when she was alive, he never spoke to her.' While Paul's tale may not be true, his choice of detail makes it *feel* true. When Paul tells us how he captured, tamed ('with food mostly') and used the little man to satisfy his curiosity about the natural world ('I'd take him out and let him go down rabbit holes and things, on a string. Then he'd come back and tell me what was going on') and how he is now in a cake tin with holes in the lid in the very bedroom we're all in, we 'know', in Paul's sense, that this 'must have happened'. There is a reality here that is patently missing from Aunt Isobel's stories. That reality (truth might be another way of thinking of it) lies in the integrity of the transaction between teller and told. We have four of these transactions here: three placed within the story (between the unnamed author of Aunt Isobel's 'read' story and Aunt Isobel and Paul, between Aunt Isobel as teller and Paul as listener, and between Paul as teller and Aunt Isobel as listener) and one without (between Mary Norton as storyteller and ourselves). If we assume that authors and readers expect things of each other — very little in the case of the unknown fairy-tale author and Aunt Isobel; a great deal in the case of Mary Norton and Paul — then what we are considering here are the kinds of world we, as creators and selectors, are inviting readers to inhabit and, in Wayne Booth's terms, the kind of company they may keep.[23]

Mary Norton offers us more than one world. There is the primary world of the bedroom where we at once feel at home because we've been here too. It's a safe, secure world that we recognize. Then we have the patently transparent story-worlds Aunt Isobel offers us and Paul's trenchant alternative. Mary Norton is asking us to examine the insides of those worlds and to decide for ourselves whether we agree with Paul's criteria for selecting a story. Not only is she asking us to try on, as it were, different kinds of storying for size: she also wants us to consider the question at the heart of this text — what might this story *do* for its reader? Aunt Isobel's stories enchant her ('Really this was quite a pretty story') but bore us. Paul's shocks and shifts our thinking. Mary Norton's does more. While, for instance, we may agree about the need for truth/reality in stories, would we have chosen quite the same means of making our point about stories being 'real' as Paul? Just as Paul harnesses the little man and shows a lack of feeling for his plight, not perhaps atypical for a boy of his age (although it is countered in stories like Raymond Briggs' *The Man* and Lynne Reid Banks' *The Indian in the Cupboard*), so too does he consciously, on the one hand, and unthinkingly, on the other, cause a disjunction in his kind, well-intentioned aunt's world. For example, when he tells her why the little man never spoke to *his* aunt:

'He didn't like her,' said Paul.
    There was a silence. Paul stared dreamily at the window: he saw it had begun to snow. Aunt Isobel sat as if turned to stone, her hands idle in her lap. After a while, she cleared her throat.
    'When did you first see this little man, Paul?'

Paul is no innocent and his actions prompt readers to think and question, from their own experience, what is happening in the worlds of this story.

We encounter two kinds of fantasy world here. One is a traditional fairy-tale world, shorn of all grit and reduced to a clichéd cardboard travesty (although, interestingly, the inspiration of Aunt Isobel's 'told' tale provides us with a hint of intertextuality, however unimaginatively used). The other is a miniature version of our own world with which it eventually merges. It's a 'what if' world that we recognize from our own play.

In all these worlds we encounter narrative time and a subtlety in its deployment which runs counter to the general assumption that 6- to 9-year-olds prefer stories that work solely on the basis of 'what happens next'. While we do have what-happens-next time here, we have other time too. We shift in and out of story time: once-upon-a-time; invented-but-in-the-past time mixed with flashback time, becoming now-cake-tin time. We have emotional time too: warm-indoor-safe time shifting midway through Paul's tale into snowy-cold-perhaps-dangerous time.

Mary Norton's construction of her text and the stories within the overarching story allow us another experience of time. We enter 'Paul's Tale' midway through the story Aunt Isobel is reading. If you recall, hers makes a languid beginning (a risky beginning). Indeed, for the first four pages, we, like Paul (and this is, of course, the point), are itching for something to happen (for a different story maybe?) but we have to tolerate uncertainty and slowness (like Paul, we, metaphorically speaking, distract ourselves with feathers and hot-water bottles) before it does. Even then, every time we think we know what kind of story we're in, Mary Norton changes gear, always pausing, slowing down time before the shift. For example, just before Aunt Isobel picks up the cake tin before the denouement:

> The door was ajar. Timidly Aunt Isobel pulled it open with one finger. There stood the cake tin, amid a medley of torn cardboard, playing cards, pieces of jigsaw puzzle and an open paintbox.
> 'What a mess, Paul!'
> Nervously Aunt Isobel stared at the cake tin and, falsely innocent, the British Royal Family stared back at her, against a hazy background of Windsor Castle. The holes in the lid were narrow and wedge-shaped, made, no doubt, by the big blade of the best cutting-out scissors.

This is one of those stories which illuminate the process of artistic making: the way writers find forms to match what they want to say. We have an overarching story and three stories within it — all told in different language and each revealing its teller's character and intent. We're exploring here the varieties of ways in which stories can be told and 'language stretched to reconstruct, remake, extend and understand our own experience of living in the world'.[24] We relish not only the story but the questions it makes us ask about storying by its juxtaposition of tale within tale. This is a story that would survive, as Joan Aiken once put it, in a 'wind tunnel', for it has something new to offer at each re-reading, including that 'legacy of past satisfactions' that James Britton identifies as coming with 'an increasing sense of form'.[25]

When Jack Ouseby suggests that the fundamental questions which any debate on reading must address are 'What kind of books? What kind of reading? What kind of readers?', he is asking us to consider the question which this chapter raises. 'When it comes to selecting stories for children,' he asks, 'is our commitment to those books which will nourish and sustain the imagination or are we happy to put before them the threadbare, the mediocre, the second best?'[26] Too often, once children have mastered print, we leave them to get on with reading independently themselves. Left to their own devices, we know that children may take their first tentative steps with what they know, and what they know may well be 'mediocre, second best'. We, on the other hand, offer them series upon series, not individual book upon individual book, selected for what it may do for the individual reader. By not attending critically to fiction produced for 6- to 9-year-olds, transitory though it may be, we neglect the 'potential reader'.[27]

The literary journey is not a linear one but it *is* a cumulative one, building on previous reading experience, preparing for future more demanding literary experience. If 6- to 9-year-olds are to stride out as readers rather than be left running on the spot or, worse still, dropping out altogether, it is our responsibility to keep them gently and firmly on the move by selecting stories to share with them or to be read on their own which offer them adventures in print which are also growing points. That is what 'Paul's Tale' does for us as selectors and for 6- to 9-year-olds as readers.

Notes

1 Mary Norton, 'Paul's Tale', in *The Last Borrowers Story: Poor Stainless,* Viking/Puffin, London, 1994, pp. 55–80.
2 Margaret Meek, 'What counts as evidence in theories of children's literature?', in Peter Hunt (ed.), *Children's Literature: The Development of Criticism,* Routledge, London, 1991, p. 176.
3 Margaret Meek, *Learning to Read,* Bodley Head, London, 1982, p. 137.
4 Eve Bearne, 'Myth and legend: the oldest language?' in Morag Styles, Eve Bearne and Victor Watson (eds), *After Alice: Exploring Children's Literature,* Cassell, London, 1992, p. 145.
5 J. A. Appleyard, *Becoming a Reader: The Experience of Fiction from Childhood to Adulthood,* Cambridge University Press, Cambridge, 1990, p. 83.

6 *Ibid.*

7 Peter Hunt, 'Questions of method and methods of questioning: childist criticism in action', *Signal 45* (1984), pp. 186–7.

8 Elaine Moss, 'Feeding the artist (literacy through literature: children's books make a difference)', *Signal 64*, 1991, pp. 15–16.

9 Michael Rosen, 'Raising the issues', *Signal 76*, 1995, p. 33.

10 Peter Hunt, 'The decline and decline of the children's book?', unpublished article kindly supplied by Nancy Chambers.

11 Nancy Chambers and Elizabeth Hammill, 'Reading new books', *Signal 67* (1992), pp. 68–9. Some of the ideas about series publishing expressed in this paper were first explored in 'Reading new books'.

12 Michael Rosen, 'Raising the issues', *Signal 76*, 1995, p. 44.

13 Julia Eccleshare, *Children's Books of the Year 1993*, Andersen Press Limited in association with the Children's Book Foundation, London, 1993, p. 6.

14 Peggy Hicks, 'Fiction for 7 to 9', in Nancy Chambers (ed.), *The Signal Review of Children's Books 1: A Selective Guide to Children's Books 1982*, The Thimble Press, Stroud, 1983, p. 25.

15 Margaret Meek, *How Texts Teach What Readers Learn*, The Thimble Press, Stroud, 1988.

16 Jenny Gilbert, 'Will reality bite back?' *Independent on Sunday*, 26 June 1994, p. 35.

17 Madeleine Lindley and a team of reviewers, *Children's Books of the Year*, 1994 Edition, Young Book Trust, London, 1994, p. 45.

18 'Reviews', *Books for Keeps* No. 76, September 1992, p. 10.

19 Margaret Meek, 'Curiouser and Curiouser', in Nancy Chambers (ed.), *The Signal Selection of Children's Books 1989*, The Thimble Press, Stroud, 1990, p. 53.

20 *Ibid.*, pp. 52-3.

21 Jets were first published simultaneously by A. & C. Black and Collins Young Lions in 1988.

22 Elizabeth Hammill, *A Signal Summary: Updating the Signal Bookguide Fiction 6 to 9*, The Thimble Press, Stroud, 1992, p. 3.

23 Wayne Booth, *The Company We Keep: An Ethics of Fiction*, University of California Press, Berkeley, 1988.

24 Meek, *op. cit.*, p. 16.

25 James Britton, 'The nature of the reader's satisfaction', in Margaret Meek, Aidan Warlow and Griselda Barton (eds), *The Cool Web: The Pattern of Children's Reading*, The Bodley Head, London, 1977, pp. 107–8.

26 Jack Ouseby, 'Reading and the imagination', in Colin Harrison and Martin Coles (eds), *The Reading for Real Handbook*, Routledge, London, 1992, p. 35.

27 Margaret Meek, 'What counts as evidence in theories of children's literature', in Peter Hunt (ed.), *Children's Literature: The Development of Criticism*, Routledge, London, 1990, p. 178.

Other series and books mentioned in this chapter

Series: Gazelles (Hamish Hamilton, London); Blackbirds (were published by Julia MacRae Books, London); Kites (currently published by Viking, London); Banana Books (Heinemann, London).

Books: Children's Books of the Year (published annually since 1970 by the National Book League, Children's Book Foundation and Children's Book Trust, London); Arnold Lobel, 'Frog and Toad' books — *Frog and Toad Are Friends* (World's Work 'I Can Read' series, Kingswood, Tadworth, Surrey, 1982), and others in series; Edward Marshall, ill. James Marshall, 'Fox' books — *Fox in Love* (Bodley Head, 'Bodley Beginners', London, 1983), and others in series; Kevin Crossley-Holland, ill. Alan Marks, *Storm* (Heinemann, 'Banana Books', London, 1985); Jan Mark, ill. Sally Holmes, *The Twig Thing* (Viking, 'Read Alone', London, 1988) and ill. Paul Howard, *Taking the Cat's Way Home* (Walker Books, 'Six to Eights', London, 1994); Bob Wilson, *Ging Gang Goolie, It's an Alien* (A. & C. Black/Armada, 'Jets', London, 1988); Andrew Matthews, ill. Tony Ross, *Dr Monsoon Taggert's Amazing Finishing Academy* (Methuen, 'Read Aloud', London, 1989); Shirley Hughes, *Chips and Jessie* (Bodley Head, London, 1985); Roger McGough, ill. Tony Blundell, *The Great Smile Robbery* (Viking Kestrel, London, 1985); Raymond Briggs, *The Man* (Julia MacRae Books, London, 1992); Lynne Reid Banks, *The Indian in the Cupboard* (Dent, London, 1980).

CHAPTER 2

'You're Not Wasting Your Money on That!' — a Bookseller's View

Kate Agnew

Kate Agnew presents the radical view that 'it is not developing technology that threatens the book, but the widespread inability of adults to guide children to books that they will enjoy reading'. This chapter provides a bookseller's view of how adults and children behave when engaged in the tricky business of negotiating their choices of suitable books to buy. 'Negotiating' is the appropriate word, for it is clear that adult perceptions of children's books differ significantly from those of the young readers they are buying the books for. Kate Agnew supports her case by analysing the criteria that adults consciously or unconsciously use. She has observed that they seem to adopt a kind of educational puritanism when buying books for their children, insisting upon 'educational value', that there should not be too many pictures and — above all — that every book purchased can be seen to contribute to their children's 'progress' in reading. Children, on the other hand, seek enjoyment, and Kate Agnew believes adults need to be taught to understand and value a childist view of reading — just as we have come to acknowledge the validity of a feminist or a Marxist one. Older children have ways of bypassing this parental insistence on utilitarian and educational reading, but the views and preferences of younger readers are mostly disregarded — with potentially damaging effects upon their understanding of what reading can do for them.

Much of the decision-making about what children read is done by adults. Where adults are not actively selecting a particular book for a particular child, they are often at work behind the scenes; classroom book boxes are almost always chosen by adults; libraries and bookshops are stocked by adults; and information about children's books often comes from adult sources.

Probably most of us who are interested enough in children's books to be reading this book are all too well aware of the pitfalls we can encounter when recommending books for children. We are unlikely to select books that we do not have some knowledge of, whether first-hand, from a personal recommendation or from a review. We do try to put some thought into what we choose, and, as is frequently the way with adults who try their best to help, we get it wrong sometimes. What we don't always do, though, is to accommodate the views of children in our critical analysis of the books they are reading.

To anyone working in a bookshop, where financial as well as literary criteria are at work, the dominant role that adults play in selecting children's books is clear:

'Don't buy that one, you've read it already.'
'You'll have finished that in five minutes.'
'Leave those books. They're for babies.'
'I want you to get something that'll keep you busy for the holiday.'
'You're not buying that here. We can get that anywhere.'
'You're not wasting your money on that.'

All these comments, variations on which can be heard almost every day, are a clear reflection of the difference between what children want, and what adults will buy (or to a lesser extent borrow). As adults we are older and wiser, more aware of the constraints of money and the demands of time, both in terms of choosing a book and in terms of the length of time it takes a child to read it. These factors are undeniably important when it comes to choosing books, but all too often the end result seems to be that children end up with books that, at worst, they do not want to read, and, at best, will be a struggle for them to get into. As adults we tend to select holiday reading for children that will 'take a bit of getting into', thinking not only that this will be good for them educationally, but also that it will keep them going through the holiday. It is interesting, then, that the holiday reading matter we choose for ourselves is likely to be written by authors like Mary Wesley or Jeffrey Archer, and unlikely to take very much 'getting into'.

In other areas of the children's market, retailers are told to be aware of the value of 'pester power', and they are continually told of the increasing financial power held by children and young adults. It seems, though, that children's choice of what to read, particularly under the age of 11, is more dominated by adults than their choice of any other entertainment, or of what to wear, or even of what to eat.

Children over the age of 11 tend to have more spending power, and make their own decisions about what to read more often than younger children. Their new-found spending power lies behind the success of series like Point Horror,[1] designed for children who are old enough to have money of their own to spend, and priced with pocket-money in mind, they are books that can be selected easily without adult help. Readers know roughly what to expect from the stories, and a certain amount of adult disapproval adds wonderfully to their enjoyment.

Adult censorship can be the making of a book, and it is significant that the crazes for books which sweep through schools are so often for books which adults disapprove of. The adult disapproval is part of what makes the craze, but there is more to it than that; these crazes all too often reflect a fundamental difference in the things that children and adults value in a book. Some years ago Judy Blume's *Forever*,[2] which discusses a young girl's first experience of sex in detail, appeared regularly in the bestseller charts; in May 1991[3] the paperback fiction bestsellers for children over 11 included two Terry Pratchett books, along with *The True Confessions of Adrian Albert Mole*, and *Forever*, again. In November 1994[4] the top five included three Point Horror novels, one Terry Pratchett and Anne Fine's *Madame Doubtfire*. Both lists would clearly have been very different had adults predominantly been responsible for the choice of the books. At least one Bedfordshire school has banned its pupils from reading horror novels, not only in schooltime, but at home as well. What better way to promote reading?

There are few books, though, that represent such a successful invasion into the pocket-money market, and anything that isn't to be purchased with a child's own money inevitably has to go through a channel of adult approval.

This is particularly true in the pre-teenage years, where it is already clear that there is a difference between the reading matter children select for themselves, and that which adults choose for them. In 1994 Cambridgeshire libraries conducted a survey across the county asking children to tell them what their all-time favourite books were. The results have been made into an extremely interesting work which is prefaced by an even more interesting disclaimer:

> It is not the aim of 'A Book a Day ...' to provide a comprehensive list of what is considered to be the most worthy or the 'best' books available for children, but to give children the opportunity to tell us what they enjoy reading. There are some books included which would perhaps not be the first choice of adults, and there are no doubt some significant omissions too.[5]

Sure enough, the list of children's all-time favourites includes books that adults would be unlikely to think of; *Jurassic Park*, for example, or *The Addams Family*. In the picture book section there are many old favourites, *Happy Families* and *Mr Magnolia* for instance, included alongside more recent publications like Bernard Ashley's *Cleversticks* or Marcus Pfister's *Rainbow Fish*, but across the list as a whole there is a notable absence of the recent prize-winners that adults would have been likely to choose. There are none of the Smarties overall winners for 1991, 1992 or 1993, and none of the *Guardian* winners for the same period; only one of the Whitbread winners for these three years appears, and none of the Carnegie prize-winning books, yet adults choose these books for children *because* they have won prizes.

A survey carried out by Puffin in 1994[6] showed that a high percentage of children's books, particularly for children below the age of 11, are chosen by their parents. The survey also shows that children have little more influence over the choice of book bought for them when they are 9 than they did at the age of 2; a very surprising finding when one considers how much influence children exert over the purchase of toys and/or clothes by the age of 9 or 10.

Having said that, however, it is still true to say that children do exert a strong force in the market-place, and that if a book fails to be read in classrooms it rarely lasts for long on the publisher's backlist. Perhaps it would be more true to say that adults control frontlist purchasing, while children have a greater say in the backlist, not least because backlist books are, by definition, paperback, and therefore more likely to fall within pocket-money or book token spending. Paperbacks have a lower unit price than hardbacks and therefore have to sell more copies to cover their costs. In addition to this, backlist paperbacks rarely receive any review coverage. Publishers, therefore, need the books to be sold into families as well as schools and libraries, and are dependent on the playground grapevine to recommend the book to new readers. So children do, after all, have some influence over publishing decisions.

If adults are to continue exerting such a strong influence over their children's reading, then the decisions they are making must be good ones; we all know too many children who have been put off reading by being given books that are too boring, too old or too young, or which were forced upon them inappropriately as part of a school assignment.

As adult readers we value different things in literature from those valued by children, and perhaps our attention span and powers of concentration may be longer, so that 'difficult' books are more accessible to us; they may well be shorter too, so that we get tired of the adventures of the Famous Five before their intended readership does, or so that we cannot face reading the same bedtime story for the thirtieth time.

However, it has long been acknowledged that the best children's books can be read and enjoyed by children and adults alike, at many different levels. Children are aware, if not always consciously so, of the demands of plot and character, of the complex relationship between pictures and text, and of the complex range of meanings conveyed by different styles of writing.

Adults' and children's views differ because the approach of adults is analytical. *They* forget to take into account the enjoyment that children get from reading a book. No wealth of critical acclaim or analysis is going to make a children's book last if the book itself is not something that children will enjoy reading, and re-reading.

While children's guidance as to what to read often comes from suggestions passed round the playground, adults are more likely to base their choice upon what has been reviewed in the papers, not least because this is one of the few available sources of information about children's books for adults who have little time to read them for themselves. Magazines like *Books for Keeps* publish up-to-date reviews, many of them by teachers who are working with children and talking to them about their books every day. Although such sources of information are invaluable, many of the reviews published in less specialist publications are written by adults who are used to analysing adult novels, and who forget the different needs of children's books. The end result is often an analytical review that recommends books to adults rather than children. Ian McEwan's *The Daydreamer*, for example, received critical acclaim with many favourable reviews; Andrew Davies described it in the *TES* as a 'wonderful book which will be enjoyed by anyone from about seven years upwards';[7] in the *Sunday Times* Nicolette Jones describes it as 'a celebration of the awakening longings that infuse the lives of all children entering adolescence'.[8] Few children have yet commented favourably on it, however, and although this may be in part because, as a hardback, it has not yet been widely read, I think a more likely reason is that the descriptions of childhood are for adults to recognize in retrospect. The view is very much that of an adult looking back upon the beginnings of adolescence rather than a reflection of the feelings of children themselves.

The book begins:

> When Peter Fortune was ten years old grown-ups sometimes used to tell him he was a difficult child. He never understood what they meant. . . . It was not until he had been a grown-up himself for many years that Peter finally understood.[9]

The Daydreamer is, as the critics say, a good book, but a book in which the adult stance is implicit in the language of the first chapter.

Is it possible, then, for us to choose children's books more effectively? Is there some kind of critical checklist we can work through in order to 'know' that a book will work for a particular child? The problem about trying to produce some kind of critique for judging children's literature is that we all assume that we know what factors are important *just because we have been children ourselves*. But to read a children's book as a child is extraordinarily difficult when one is used to bringing adult critical faculties to bear. Perhaps the easiest way would be, like Peter Pan, to never grow up! But given that most of us have, more or less, grown up, is there any way that we can learn to read texts as children? To some extent, I believe there is.

Reading as a child is something that many readers do from time to time, most commonly when we return to a favourite childhood book in order to re-read it as an adult. Opening the pages of an old favourite can take us back to childhood as quickly as Proust's forgotten scent. We can open the pages of *Anne of Green Gables* and long for auburn hair and puffed sleeves, or dip into *Swallows and Amazons* and long to be camping out on Wild Cat Island, despite the fact that our adult selves tell us that actually it is all somewhat unbelievable, not to mention terribly sexist that Susan is always left to do the cooking and be motherly.

In re-reading these old favourites most of us have little trouble in reading both as a child and as an adult. The problem seems to come when we are confronted with new texts. Can we then read these as a child, or does the adult, analytical interpretation always have to dominate?

The first step towards learning to read as a child is to accept that it is a valuable activity, and that the young reader has a valid perspective. If we can have a Marxist reading of a text, or a feminist one, why shouldn't we also have a child's — or childist — reading, and just as feminist and Marxist readings can stand alongside other readings, why shouldn't a child's or childist reading be allowed to stand alongside other critical analyses of children's literature? There is an exact analogy: just as women's experience may lead them to value more highly plots and subject matter that may be dismissed as being of limited interest by male readers, so too adult readers may dismiss the plots of children's books as being too trivial, despite their value to a child reader.

Children are aware of whether a book is well written. They dismiss ill-thought-out plots too, and characters in whom they cannot believe. They enjoy the sounds of words, even where they cannot enjoy their meanings, as anyone who has read poetry to a class of young children will know. So to read a text as a child is not to ignore its literary quality.

However, the thing that is of most importance to them is whether they have enjoyed it. But it still seems to happen too often that the first priority of adults when choosing a book for a child is not the child's enjoyment. The Puffin survey mentioned above also asked parents what criteria were most important when they chose books for children. The replies were very revealing: 93 per cent of them mentioned 'educational value' as their highest priority, and 86 per cent mentioned age range. Illustrations were also considered important (84 per cent), but knowledge of the author came much lower down the list of priorities (38 per cent).

The mother of a 9-year-old said to me recently, 'She's not really reading. She's only reading picture books.' As far as the child was concerned she was happily reading, easily able to change from reading picture books one minute to E. Nesbit the next. The important thing to her was that she was still getting pleasure out of books; it didn't matter what kind of books they were. To her mother, however, she wasn't reading because the books she chose did not 'stretch' her.

So, if we are to encourage children to enjoy reading, we have got to give them books that they will enjoy, and in order to do that we have to learn to read and value books as they do. Perhaps first we have to try to suspend our adult preconceptions of what a book ought to be or do, and of what constitutes literary merit. We need to listen more to children too, to value what they have to say about books and to learn what books they enjoy and — even more — which ones they have hated.

Almost always, when I am trying to recommend a book for a child in the shop, I will ask them not only what books they have liked reading, but also what they have hated. Many of them are surprised by this question; often it is not something they have been asked by an adult before, and so they are unused to the idea that it is acceptable to dislike some books. Not only is it acceptable, though, it is actually a very positive move towards finding books that children will enjoy. Interestingly, it is a question that children are usually better at answering if their parents or teachers are not within earshot, perhaps because these may be the adults who have provided the disliked books, but more probably because they are used to being allowed to describe books only in a more positive light, and therefore talking about books they have disliked is somehow rather wicked.

We all find it much easier to enjoy things if we are not being told to do so, and children, too, will start expressing their honest opinions about books only if they are allowed to criticize as well as praise. It is much easier for adults to remember how to read as a child if they can discuss reading with children who are honest in their opinions. I think we need to teach children that books are not sacred texts; they have value only if readers value them.

As adults we are aware that books are 'good for us', and, in a nation that is becoming increasingly dominated by competition and performance league tables, adults are very concerned that their children should be reading the 'right kind' of books. Not only should children be reading suitably educational books, but they are also encouraged to read the right kind for their age, so that a book they may have enjoyed at 7 becomes too babyish, in the adult's eyes, at 9, however much the child may still be enjoying it.

Ironically, this is at a time when educational tools are seeking to become more entertaining in order to ensure their share of the market. The use of CD-ROM is spreading in schools and at home, and the debate about the future of books has received widespread publicity. However it is not CD-ROM in themselves that threaten the future of reading — when asked about the book versus CD-ROM debate on BBC's *Blue Peter* recently, one child commented succinctly that you can't take a computer to bed with you — but the widespread inability of adults to guide children to books that they will enjoy reading.

This is not to say that children only enjoy reading 'lightweight' fiction, such as the Point Horror series; children can and do enjoy a variety of reading matter that includes series fiction, classics and picture books, non-fiction, comics, the backs of cereal packets, etc. The problem is not that children choose to read only a limited range of books, but that as adults it is we ourselves who tend to try to constrain their reading into a very narrow band. We are obsessed with the concept of progress in children's reading as well as being limited by poor criteria in selecting children's books. This conviction that children's reading matter ought to change consistently as they get older often works against children's enjoyment of reading; too often 8- or 9-year-old children in the shop are happy to be browsing through picture books, while their parents are hurrying them onto chapter books. This is partly because the adults in question don't have time to look through picture books when they are convinced that they will end up purchasing a chapter book, and also partly because the adults don't want to buy a picture book, since they are convinced that it represents less value for money. There are, more often than not, fewer words to a page in picture books than in chapter books, but, as we know, children can and do read picture books many times, and at many levels; a book like Anthony Browne's *Piggybook*,[10] which children can read at different levels as they grow older and their understanding of the adult world changes, is a case in point. The number of times children re-read favourite books often dispels the 'value for money' argument, and it is certainly not one that enters the equation in public libraries. Yet conversations with librarians suggest that, even in libraries, adults are often reluctant to borrow picture books for children over the age of 7.

This concept of progress goes on being applied right up to the teenage years, despite the fact that as adults we almost all enjoy a wide range of reading material that encompasses magazines and newspapers, 'lightweight' books, and 'serious' novels. Too often we forget that children need a similar variety in their reading matter; something to tax them is stimulating sometimes, but something easy and fun to curl up with after a busy day at school can be just as important if reading for pleasure is to compete with the vast range of leisure-time activities available to children. When choosing books for children we have to consider and understand what they value in a book and what purpose that book has to serve, as well as the educational and financial criteria that we value as adults. Only then can we decide which books constitute a waste of money, and which provide valuable and entertaining reading matter.

Notes

1 Point Horror series published in England by Scholastic, London.
2 Judy Blume, *Forever*, Gollancz, London, 1976.
3 *Books in the Media*. Bestseller List for Children's Books (11 +), May 1991.
4 *Books in the Media*. Bestseller List for Children's Books (11 +), November 1994.
5 *A Book a Day Keeps the Boredom Away: 365 Favourite Books Chosen by Children*, Cambridgeshire Libraries Publications, Cambridge, 1994.
6 *Puffin Survey. Children's Books, a Parent's Guide*, Puffin Books, London, 1994.
7 Andrew Davies, *Times Educational Supplement*, 7 October 1994.
8 Nicolette Jones, *Sunday Times*, 2 October 1994.
9 Ian McEwan, *The Daydreamer*, Jonathan Cape, London, 1994, p 7.
10 Anthony Browne, *Piggybook*, Julia MacRae Books, London, 1986.

CHAPTER 3

Is a Series Reader a Serious Reader?

Jenny Daniels

In Jenny Daniels' chapter we encounter the voice of one young reader who clung tenaciously to The Famous Five at a time when she was experiencing a number of difficulties in her life. The chapter develops into a persuasive account of how this kind of series entices and supports insecure readers. Transcripts of Emma discussing her reading demonstrate that this young reader was capable of liking the characters at the same time as judging them, and that she recognized the class and gender assumptions in the Malory Towers stories, while still enjoying them. Only by understanding such paradoxes of literacy can we begin to understand that reading such a series is not necessarily passive or uncritical. The chapter moves on to a consideration of currently available popular series for older readers, and here the voices of the readers show two things: their shrewd grasp of marketing and publishing as well as narrative practices, and their indignation at the way their tastes are set aside in school.

In this chapter I want to examine what we mean by a 'series reader'. The term itself carries with it certain cultural assumptions about the value and status of people who admit to their preference for series. I want to look at reading patterns and reading behaviour of series readers in order to question that assumption and to place the reading in cultural, and particularly educational, contexts. The word 'serial' carries with it connotations of something less than acceptable, especially when it is used in relation to popular fiction or communication. For many people, it is associated with 'serial killer', a macabre phenomenon that seems to have captured the imagination of late-twentieth-century readers. How do such cultural phenomena occur? The *Oxford English Dictionary* describes series as 'a number of things following or connected with each other'. A 'serial', on the other hand, is a story or film presented in separate parts. A serial killer is someone who kills repeatedly in a pattern which identifies a particular obsession or perversion.

What do these somewhat confusing terms tell us about reading and our understanding of reading behaviour? I want to argue that someone who reads 'series' is often regarded by the literati as somehow deficient, not a proper reader by the standards of the cultured. Children are peculiarly sensitive to the way in which their reading is viewed by adults. The patterns of choice that children establish in the early stages of reading are therefore extremely important in determining their view of themselves as readers and the material they are likely to turn to. In this chapter, I want to look at the way in which a series works to entice its young readers to repeat the experience. What is it that is held together or connected in a narrative text which encourages repetition? What are young readers looking for? I then want to look at the way children make choices about books. What role do teachers, parents and publishers play in this scenario? Finally, I want to argue that series readers *are* serious readers, that they are solemn and thoughtful, sincere, not casual. They are, to use the much abused term, 'real readers'.

The enormous numbers of 'series' books (for adults and children) currently available in bookshops indicate how popular they are with publishers. They also raise some concerns as to the framing of choice that might ultimately restrict readers (see Chapter 1). I am conscious of the many new reading schemes which introduce particular characters and develop the readers' knowledge of them through the characterization in the texts. The *Oxford Reading Tree*[1] is a good example of the way in which Rod Hunt's characters have an immediate appeal to young children. Their funny and credible antics present a world in which young children feel safe, a world that may be idealized, but one which they *want* to relate to. It is one of the better examples of fostering this series approach with children. When the characters are placed in different situations, the reader can use prediction with increasing accuracy, developing confidence and fluency as a reader. Many young children express their delight in 'knowing' Kipper or expressing a preference for Chip. Rod Hunt invites children into a world which is recognizable and fun.

Being able to recognize familiar characters in books can form a pattern of reading with very young children which gives them confidence in their early efforts. This 'knowing' of the characters in books is a vital part of early literacy and is established from a young age. Indeed, many children will be familiar with characters from television such as Postman Pat and Fireman Sam. They come to school with a plurality of readings of such characters, for example from viewing (either the television programme or video), books, comics, toys marketed under franchise, puzzles, T-shirts, trainers and all kinds of stationery. This lays down a pattern of expectation which can rapidly transfer into reading behaviour. While it is tempting to dwell on this particular stage, I want to concentrate on newly independent readers and how they establish themselves in a literate environment.

At the risk of raising howls of 'not again', I want to look at Enid Blyton and her contribution to literacy and reading. The role of her books in education has gone through a variety of responses, from undiluted accolade to rigorous exclusion. She now occupies an uneasy seat somewhere between liberal tolerance and political indifference. What cannot be in question is her continuing popularity with young readers, despite the racism and sexism she is undeniably guilty of. This is all old ground now. Rather than rehearse some of those arguments yet again, I want to look at one young reader in relation to Enid Blyton in detail. I hope to show the development of Emma's reading skill and the way in which Enid Blyton played such an important part in encouraging critical readings.

Emma: a case study in determination

Emma always enjoyed stories and the pleasure of being read to. As a young child she had a strong sense of rhythm and loved music. Nursery rhymes were always a particular delight and she would spend hours thumbing through a Hilda Boswell collection which contained both traditional and newer versions. She also heard many regional rhymes from her grandmother and extended family. The act of reading seemed to be a serious event for her. It demanded adult attention and, in the early days, did not include a younger sister. Favourite bedtime stories were often highly moral in tone. For example, the tale of 'The Little Red Hen' caused considerable concern when the unwilling helpers were refused a piece of the freshly baked bread. Despite its obvious moral conclusion, Emma took strong exception to the selfishness of the Little Red Hen. Although not realizing it at the time, she was already 'reading against the grain' of the text and recognizing that she had the right to argue with the author and the moral.

After starting school a few months before her fifth birthday, she contracted whooping cough and subsequently missed two terms. Being read to formed an important part of her rest and recovery, though she showed little interest in reading for herself. By the time she returned to school her classmates were firmly entrenched in the Ginn reading scheme. Emma hated it, not least because she was trailing behind them. The quality of the text and illustrations was hardly likely to encourage her. What emerged was a pattern of sharing books and being read to at home contrasting with an increasing disillusion about reading in school. In neither case was she showing any attempt to read independently. At 7½, she was sent to a remedial teacher for extra help on Tuesdays. She now tells stories of feigning illness on Tuesday mornings and the indignity of having to 'sound out' individual phonics six inches away from someone who suffered badly from halitosis! At almost 8 she was given a book about going to ballet class.[2] It was a simple story with delicate illustrations by Rachel Isadora. Emma could relate to it in many ways, being a dancer by this time. The central pages showed the five classical ballet positions and the correct French terms underneath. This was the turning point for her — she quickly became a reader, albeit of French initially.

By the end of Year 4, Emma had read every Famous Five book[3] which Blyton had written. A few had been found in the house — old crimson hardback editions from the 1950s. These were soon joined by a huge number of paperbacks bought at jumble sales or given by friends. They were lovingly read, re-read, and organized on shelves. Very few were swapped or left the house once they became part of the collection, but it was the reading of the books and not the books as artefacts which attracted her. During this period reading played a crucial part in Emma's development and identity. Like so many children, she had been aware of the importance that reading occupied in the minds of parents and teachers. Her own rather tenuous grip of what reading actually entailed had been hampered by illness and insecurity. The Famous Five invited her into a safe, old-fashioned world where children engaged in adventures and emerged triumphant by the last chapter. The characters in the book were more than known; like old friends, they were reassuring, predictable, even at times tiresome. Something special had connected in her mind which made Emma want to repeat the reading experience. What is there in the Blyton books which 'connects' to make such a series so popular?

In Emma's case, she loved the four characters and the exciting child-centred world that they lived in. The fact that adults are either stupid or villainous (and usually both) was a great attraction. The clear moral codes of conduct and behaviour enforced her own understandings of how she thought the world should be. Even the significance of food in the stories was re-enacted in her own life and still forms an important anchor for stability and continuity. Above all, she was reading, and, like many anxious parents and teachers, we were content initially that she was at least reading independently. When this became her only reading matter (other than books for information) there was concern that an undiluted diet of Blyton was limiting and possibly harmful. In the politically aware times of the mid-1980s, the overexposure to the racism and sexism in the Famous Five books seemed potentially damaging. As parents we had never actively encouraged her reading of Blyton, probably feeling more than a passing embarrassment at the number of 'unsuitable' books around the house. (Indeed, many friends and colleagues had commented disparagingly about the number and variety.) We never bought a Blyton book (to salve a liberal conscience!) but that was no serious deterrent. However, we did buy an audio cassette tape of *Five Go to Kirrin Island*.[4]

The intention was to occupy both children during long journeys on motorways. It was then that we discovered how important the stories were to her — the wish to repeat the tape as soon as it had finished, the insistence on reverential silence as Jane Asher enunciated the text so beautifully. We later discovered that the absence of any illustrations added to the pleasure.

Our patience with Blyton, and Emma, was wearing thin! One way of countering the experience was to parody the voices and characters. A French boy introduced in the story, Pierre le Noir, was nicknamed 'Sooty' by the Famous Five. This provided the adults with hilarious entertainment, mimicking the accents (both French and English) and conducting impromptu scripts for the next unlikely event. Cups of coffee in the motorway cafe were bought with 'lashings of cream' and served by Mrs Penruthluns. Emma remained totally impervious to all the ribald comments — if anything, it only served to make her more determined to repeat the Blyton experience. She watched a film made by 'The Comic Strip' team, *Five Go Mad on Mescalin*. The satire is particularly heavy and unmistakable. She thoroughly enjoyed the film, but it did not act as a deterrent to the reading!

What we failed to understand was the nature of that reading experience for her. Like so many millions of children, before and since, she was not being inculcated into right-wing dogmatism. Nor was she becoming a passive and uncritical reader. Enid Blyton stories told her that she *was* a reader — that she could do this strange activity that parents and teachers get so concerned about, and in the doing of the reading, she could identify with an exciting and child-centred world. When Emma was 10, we taped a conversation about books and Blyton in particular. I wanted her to explain why she liked the Famous Five so much.

> *Emma*: I think Enid Blyton plans it all out in her head before she writes it down. It's easy 'cos you can read it in your head.
>
> *Me*:   What about the Famous Five? Do you know what's going to happen in those?
>
> *Emma*: It's a similar kind of thing. They are walking along a hill, or get into an adventure in a cave or something.
>
> *Me*:   Mmnnn ... and ...
>
> *Emma*: And they go into a cave and find mysteries set out for them and they meet up with people they have met in other series.
>
> *Me*:   Mmnn ...
>
> *Emma*: So there are people they get to know as you get to read the different books.

Emma is conscious of how she reads the books and the patterns that she actively seeks. The expectation is high — and Blyton never fails to deliver the goods! Her comments about 'reading it in your head' make it clear that she distinguishes between the reading she may be asked to do in school, and the private reading she uses with the Famous Five books. She trusts the Blyton format in that her predictions about characters and events are always proved right. This leaves her free to experiment with new words and sentence constructions which she encounters in her reading. Blyton is never likely to confront a reader with anything radically different, so that a young reader gains confidence by essentially repeating the experience. When 'old friends' are incorporated into different narratives, it has the effect of strengthening that confidence.

In this next section Emma tries to explain the effect of the Blyton books:

Emma: She gets to the point right at the beginning of the book, like ... some other books I find it difficult and it takes me three chapters to get into it — and I can't do that — it bores me. I think she bases it on schools and mysteries and there are lots on Malory Towers and St Clare's and Famous Five. I quite like them but some are very, very scary. Like ... I read the first chapter of number eight Secret Seven, and it was just aaargh ...

Me: What was so scary about them?

Emma: I think she puts too much adventure in them really. Only it was scary because there were strange lights and people were running around in the night ... ugh ... yeuck! I think she puts too much in them 'cos you don't get people running around like that in real life, do you?

Me: No, I suppose not ...

Emma: She just goes round and round in circles.

Me: Does that actually stop you reading all the books though?

Emma: Not really. You think that something else is going to happen, but it never really does.

Emma: Some of them ... now ... They're boring ... Malory Towers[5] — not like my school at all. ... She bases them all on posh people — the upper class. They all go to boarding school and it's very fa la la. ... I think people who are snobbish are stupid.

Me: And yet you enjoyed reading them?

Emma: I enjoyed reading them 'cos it gave me an idea of what those kind of people are like. They think they're OK but they're not really. They all talk in a funny way. I know they're based in the 1940s ... but ... I'd rather have Judy Blume or Gene Kemp.

Me: What's the difference between those and Blyton?

Emma: Blyton is a posh snob. Mmnnn. ... She tries to get through that it's good to go to boarding school. Gene Kemp hasn't written so much, but it's a much more satisfying feeling.

Emma knows what it is she wants from a reading experience; she recognizes that Blyton can quickly capture her attention and tell her 'how it goes' in the first few pages. Again, the reassurance must be highly motivating, given that the world can be a threatening place for a child. The tone of Emma's voice as she asks about night-time activities is on a rising note of anxiety. Fear of the dark and mysterious events become the focus for unspoken fears. She recognizes the limitations of the narratives when she expresses the hope that something else may happen — but it never does. I would argue that inexperienced readers are prepared to settle for a thinly layered text at this stage of their reading development. When they subconsciously feel more confident in scanning the words, they can then recognize the unsatisfying nature of the text.

Emma uses the stories for emotional reassurance; hence her revisiting the books at times — again, perfectly natural reading behaviour. At the point that they become 'boring', she has made enormous strides as a reader. She can test out the reality of the story against her own life experience. Emma recognizes the class divisions portrayed in Blyton's books — the 'posh' people, as she describes them. She knows that Malory Towers is 'not like her school at all', but that the characters gave her an idea of what 'those kind of people are like'. This is not a reader who accepts the text unquestioningly. Emma is behaving as a *critical reader*; she is 'reading against the grain'.

She is not unusual in this respect. Like all young readers, Emma is constantly hypothesizing, testing out what the world should be, and how she can use her reading to help the process. Like so many Blyton fans, she can deliver a searing criticism of social mores — but it does not detract from the pleasure of the book. Her comment about Gene Kemp signifies a level of reflection which is very sophisticated. Why does Kemp provide a 'satisfying feeling'? Surely it is because her books do have more depth, more bite to them? Emma will go on to be a confident reader, using her reading skills across a wide range of education. She has learned to read 'not so much about different people, but to read about people differently'.[6] Blyton, we have to accept, has been instrumental in helping this.

I would argue, then, that a series reader is a serious reader. While Blyton may be the most popular with children, she is condemned by teachers and educators — and often by parents. Once in a pattern of reading set by a series, many children want it to continue. There are certainly enough series on the market to satisfy their demand. Increasingly they have a gender bias, for example Sweet Valley High[7] or the R. L. Stine horror stories.[8] There is some concern that these books can become like an addiction, that they enslave young readers, preventing them from experiencing a wider range of texts. I now want to look at choice in relation to children's reading behaviour, and the way in which publishers operate in determining the range of books available. We might first look at how experienced readers *choose* what to read.

One small, unremarkable piece of information collected by the makers of the *Bookworm* programme on BBC was the way in which adults choose books in public libraries. Confronted by the enormous range of books available, most library users turn to the 'recently returned' shelves. What does this tell us about choice? One assumes that readers use libraries, but why do they have such difficulty in selecting what to read? What strategies do any of us use when it comes to charting our literary courses?

I suspect that all readers experience similar difficulties. Our instinct is to repeat the pleasure provided by the first encounter with a book which captures our imagination. A series encourages this; hence the popularity of the romance genre or the detective story. The books are produced to an agreed format and marketed under a distinctive cover. We do not have to agonize over which shelf to turn to first; our actions are gently guided by the beckoning row bearing a number of the very books we know we like. If it is a particular author we have enjoyed, then most readers will automatically look for other books by her or him. Young readers will employ similar tactics. I want to move on and report some of their voices and attitudes, showing how they contrast with many teachers' assumptions.

Children's voices

What is remarkable about the many conversations I have had with young readers is their ability to *reflect on* and *articulate* their own reading behaviour. Yet many made it clear that they had never talked about reading and their choice of books, either with a teacher or with friends. Perhaps this silence results from an attitude which assumes that once the skill of reading is acquired, then readers must fend for themselves. In large classes and with demands from other curriculum areas, it is easy to see how this can happen. Reading may well be an integral part of the school day, but curriculum demands result in an emphasis on information reading. There is less time to give conscious attention to reading, particularly fiction. It is often at this point that series reading becomes a useful support. Conversations with children about reading also show just how important it is to them. They will go to extraordinary lengths to *find* a particular book. They quickly learn to read the cover and the blurb on the back of the book. A series reader will be clued in by a distinctive cover design, often a logo which simplifies the process and also gives it an adult feel. Children build reading into their physical as well as emotional world. Many talk about the pleasure of bedtime reading, the thrill of reading clandestinely under the duvet, the give-away squeak of the loose floorboard announcing an irate parent. Others make reading places, in old furniture or favourite bushes in the garden. Some of the reading places described by both children and students have been extraordinary, and obviously real.

The following extracts are from a mixed group of Year 4, 5 and 6 children — three boys and three girls. The two older girls, Sue and Clare, read the Sweet Valley High[7] and Babysitters[9] series. The younger girl, Chloe, was firmly entrenched in Famous Five, and Russell, aged 9, was finding the whole idea of choosing books problematic — his reading ability was such that any radical challenge to his idea of himself as a reader caused anxiety. A similar phenomenon occurred with the two older boys, Steve and John. They were both good readers, but found choice difficult. All the children described patterns of reading which were *not* practised in school. Their comments indicate only too clearly how, as teachers and parents, we fail to recognize how serious they are as readers.

Me: So you read these books in bed late at night before you go to sleep — when no one is watching you — or sometimes early in the morning. Do you ever bring them into school?

Steve: I don't bring mine!

John: No.

Russell: I have a couple ...

Chloe: I only bring mine into school when it's really exciting and I don't want to finish it in bed.

Russell: I've got one in my drawer from ages ago.

Me: What about Sue's Sweet Valley High and Babysitters books? I expect the boys don't read any of those? Have you seen any of them?

John: I've seen them ...

Steve: I've read one Babysitters one, but didn't like it ... I wouldn't touch Sweet Valley High ...

Me: Why not?

Russell: 'Cos it's for girls, man! It's all kissing ...

Me: You don't like it but you've never looked at it?

Russell: I looked at the back cover and at the introduction ...

Sue: It's about boys as well as girls — it's not all girls' stuff. There's girls in Famous Five.

The discussion then went on to a heated debate on the merit of the stories in Sweet Valley High and Babysitters. The girls knew their texts thoroughly — they could argue on the basis of plot, characterization, narrative technique and the response of the reader. It also shows how the boys and girls are divided in their perceptions of books. The transcript shows how, for these children at least, reading is important, divided between home and school. Their own choice of reading at home is the result of careful selection; they are in control of when and where the reading happens. Generally the books are not taken into school, and it is interesting to speculate why. My rather directed question to Sue about the Sweet Valley High books was prompted by her very sceptical expression. Sue knew that the books would be frowned on in a school context, but she was not prepared to articulate it at that point.

It did raise an issue for the boys, though. Steve acknowledged that he had looked at them. John admitted to reading a Babysitter book, though he said he did not like it. Russell angrily interrupts, "Cos it's for girls, man!' The use of 'man' both asserts his maleness and at the same time appeals for male support. Up to this point, Russell had shown himself to be a wide and critical reader. All three boys are struggling to express personal reaction set against an awareness of social opinion. The confusion established in their gendered reading is forcibly expressed. What followed was a fascinating discussion of the way in which they were each drawn to books by the cover and the blurb, and their consciousness of the gender orientation involved in making their choice.

> *Russell*: A lot of the books in the library are not very interesting, so I put them back.
> *Steve*: I look at the front cover.
> *Me*: With a series, like Sweet Valley High. ... You know the shape, the colour. ... Do you always look for those, or would you try something different?
> *Sue*: Well, things about the same cover ... with, like Babysitters, they have a club sign on it. And yet one book I've got has these two girls talking on the front. That was really good, but it wasn't a series. The cover attracted me 'cos it looked like Sweet Valley High.

They all show awareness of marketing tactics and the way books can be packaged to attract them. In Sue's case, she was prepared to try a book on the assumption that it would provide a similar read to her usual series. Russell goes on to recount, with a degree of passion, how he was 'taken in' by the blurb on a book which bore no relation to the actual narrative. Publishers are beginning to grow wise to the perspicacity of their young clientele.

Teachers have an important role to play in helping children to become discriminating readers. A later part of the discussion revealed frustration about the poor range of books available, and teachers' attitudes to 'good' literature.

> *Me*: Do you use the school library?
> *Chloe*: No ... they're boring books that you know you don't want to know.
> *Steve*: I think that the books in the library should be all kinds of books — not just interest books. They're all information books. In

class 6, they've got nothing there ...
Sue: All the girls read Babysitter books, but there's only one copy and they all read it, like, fifteen times. It's the only good one in the library.
Me: Have you read any books by Philippa Pearce or Gene Kemp? Do you know any of those names?
Chloe: Yes ... but I don't read them. Mummy doesn't like me reading all these series books — so she sometimes makes me read something else.
Sue: Yeah ... My mum says, 'Give up on the Babysitter books — you've read them all — they're all the same.' But they're not all the same, they're based on the same characters but each one is a totally different story.

The transcript does not do justice to the impassioned tone of their voices. The scorn expressed about the kind of books in the library and adult intervention in their choice of books was remarkable. It continues later in the discussion.

Russell: We do have reading groups — but we can't choose what we read.
Me: But if it was Sweet Valley High or one of the books that you all enjoy ...
Sue: But we wouldn't be allowed to read any of them.
Chloe: *We have to do plays and they're really stupid.*
Russell: They say things like 'You should have seen me while I was alive.' Not very scary at all!
Me: Not like the R. L. Stine stories!

The views expressed by this particular group of children were echoed by many more. They were all serious readers, appreciating what the texts had to offer and actively seeking out material not readily available. Most importantly, they registered and silently resented the heavy-handed and intrusive attitudes from adults (parents and teachers). Both Sue and Clare had felt pressure from mothers to read 'something else'. Their parents wanted to encourage wider reading, but the intervention has precisely the wrong effect. The children's anger was articulated on the tape, certainly representing 'voices off'.

In this chapter I have tried to show that, contrary to popular belief, a series reader is a serious reader. With Emma we are able to see how she makes a popular series like Famous Five work to her advantage. By behaving like a reader, she becomes a fluent, critical reader. The text has 'taught what she wants to learn'. The children who rely initially on series are conscious of the disapproval they invite. Yet they can vigorously defend their reading and reflect on its effect. We need to listen to the voices which may contradict our own preferences about good books. As

Margaret Meek succinctly points out, 'instead of condemning some children's stories as unsuitable, adults need to take time to help children talk about what they read so that they learn to express their judgements, however tentatively at first'.[10] The children included in this chapter had passionate views about their reading, but knew that school was not the place to make judgements on particular books. Most of all, they demonstrated that a series reader is solemn and thoughtful, sincere, and certainly not casual.

I would like to thank Emma for her commentary on Blyton: she continues to challenge my assumptions, and is still my best critic! My thanks go also to the many schools who have made me welcome, particularly Meldreth Primary School and the children mentioned here. All names, apart from Emma, have been changed.

Notes

1 *The Oxford Reading Tree*, Oxford University Press, Oxford, 1989.
2 Rachel Isadora, *My Ballet Class*, Picture Lions, William Collins Sons and Co. Ltd, 1983.
3 Enid Blyton, The Famous Five series, Knight Books. First published 1944 by Hodder and Stoughton.
4 Enid Blyton, *Five Go to Kirrin Island*, Hodder and Stoughton, London, 1946. Cassette tape, Hodder Children's Audio, 1984.
5 Enid Blyton, Malory Towers series, Methuen, London, 1951.
6 Margaret Meek, *How Texts Teach What Readers Learn*, The Thimble Press, Stroud, 1988, p. 29.
7 Francine Pascal, Sweet Valley High series, Bantam Books, London, 1990.
8 R. L. Stine, Point Horror series, Scholastic Publications, London and New York, 1990.
9 The Babysitters series, Hippo Books, Scholastic Children's Books, London and New York, 1991.
10 Margaret Meek, *How Texts Teach What Readers Learn*, The Thimble Press, Stroud, 1988, p. 30.

CHAPTER 4

Revenge of the Teenage Horrors

Pleasure, Quality and Canonicity in (and out of) Popular Series Fiction

Charles Sarland

We are all aware of the canon of literature, and we know that it is ill-defined, culturally constructed and always changing. Alongside it, there exists another canon, also ill-defined, culturally constructed and always changing — an alternative canon of popular literature, constantly negotiated by young readers sharing and informally discussing their unofficial readings with one another. This canon has its discourses, its enthusiasts, and its critics, and in this chapter Charles Sarland gives us an insight into the ways these critics talk and think about the works they discuss. His chapter brings the voices of these readers to us. The critics are schoolchildren; the texts are works in the Point Horror series. He shows us that these young critics know that the criteria for judging quality are bound up with the emotional satisfaction that reading can provide. They understand about character, structure, suspense, narrative perspective and their own role as reader. He confronts the difficulties, admitting that as an adult there is little in these fictions which he can find interesting. He does not require adult readers to surrender their preferences; but he invites them to attend to what young readers have to say about their own reading.

What makes a good book? Or a good film or television programme, come to that? Or a good footballer or tennis player? Why do we choose the wallpaper we choose? Or the dress, or shirt? What makes us say to a friend, 'Oh, you must read that/see this/watch the other'? These are important questions in our cultural lives. In answering them we negotiate some of our most crucial relationships: who our friends are, even who our partners are. We make discriminatory judgements about the qualities, values and pleasures of our leisure activities, and we like to argue and debate those judgements with others who share our enthusiasms. There is nothing exclusively adult about such discriminatory judgements; children and young people make them all the time.

In *Signal 73* I discussed the Point Horror series, which were being read by some 12-year-olds I talked with. I analysed some of the themes and structures of the books, and attempted to show how they related to some of the youngsters' concerns. Now I want to look at the criteria by which that same group were making discriminatory judgements about what they read. The bulk of my evidence comes from our discussions of Point Horror, but occasionally I trawl more widely for their views on other books.

It may surprise some readers that a debate about 'quality' and canonicity should relate to material widely regarded as 'non-quality', but it is my case that in making such distinctions as adult readers we fail to acknowledge a whole range of discriminations the youngsters are making with regard to just such material. Furthermore, I shall be arguing that the grounds of their discriminations are remarkably similar to ours, so much so that I suspect we need to re-examine our judgements in the light of theirs.

Pleasure and quality

When I was working on the research for *Young People Reading*,[1] and in the process of writing it, I deliberately avoided discussions of quality. I was faced with the evident enthusiasm of young people for pulp horror and other forms of popular literature and video, and everything I had read on the subject assumed that these were degraded products, lacking any quality whatever, and that the purpose of education was to teach young people to denigrate them, and to enjoy instead literature deemed to be of quality. With the exception of Donald Fry,[2] no one had seriously tried to analyse what young people might be getting out of such reading, and accounts of what it had to offer were hard to come by. In *Young People Reading* I suggest that we all engage in debates about quality, though some of us may be concerned with the relative merits of the Chippendales and Patrick Swayze, while others may be exploring the contesting attractions of *Nostromo* and *Middlemarch*. Whatever the focus, I had plenty of incidental evidence of children and young people making judgements about quality, even though I had not gone about collecting it systematically.

Questions of pleasure and the criteria for quality are inextricably tied up with each other. When I ask the youngsters what they like about Point Horror, and what makes the books good, and as they get beyond the one-word answers — 'excitement' — they start to give me the criteria for their judgements. These are simultaneously accounts of pleasure and descriptions of how they make judgements of quality, and they use the criteria both when praising the books they like and when criticizing those they don't.

Somebody once said that only children and professors of English re-read books. Maybe so, but the rest of us revisit other art forms all the time. We listen to the same piece of music over and over, whether it be Luciano Berio's *Sinfonia* or Michael Jackson's *Heal the World*, and with the advent of video some of us view the same film over and over — children certainly do. I ask the girls why they re-read.

> *Alison*: Sometimes you just feel like reading some book ... and you go and look around, if you, oh I love that book, I'll just go and read that ...
>
> *Liz*: Yeh, 'cause you get a book you know you'll like, so, say if you're going somewhere, on a trip or something, rather than get one you haven't read you'll get one that I really like, so ... I'll know I'll enjoy it.

What is at stake here is emotional satisfaction: 'oh I love that book'. The girls re-read what gives them pleasure. A lot of my own re-reading and revisiting of other art forms is of the same order. When I rewatch *Psycho* or *Victor Victoria*, or when I re-read *Carrie's War* or Arthur Ransome, I am revisiting known pleasures, known emotional satisfactions, as well as often discovering new ones. The re-reading of children and young people is no different.

In addition, however, there is a continuity between the pleasures of re-reading and the pleasures of reading for the first time. Thus, as I currently read Winifred Holtby, or the Conrad I never read as an undergraduate, or watch Michael Jackson's *Moonwalker* or Leos Carax's *Les Amants du Pont Neuf*, I recognize those same pleasures, those same emotional satisfactions. That is the starting point, the baseline. We read for pleasure. The pleasures will be varied and diverse, but once reading gives us no more pleasure, we will stop. The only exceptions to that rule may be people who must read for a living, but for the rest of us, and particularly for the young, pleasure is what reading is about.

For the young, however, schooling messes up all that, and literary studies have, alas, been the tool used in school to do the messing up.

Traditionally, literary studies have taken a hard line on pleasure, specifically by creating hierarchies of pleasure, some being held more worthwhile than others. More recently, literary studies have tended to ignore pleasure altogether. The hierarchy of pleasures was based on the personal-growth, personal-response model of English teaching. The Bullock Report insisted that the way to personal growth was through the reading of great literature, and English teachers have for a long time seen it as their job to try to bring pupils to the pleasures of that same 'great literature'.

The problem is that the rhetoric and the practice of the personal-growth model were very different, for too often what actually happened was that many pupils both learned to discount their own pleasure and failed to gain the pleasure promised them from reading Dickens, or *Jane Eyre*, or, if they were younger, *Carrie's War* or *The Battle of Bubble and Squeak*.[3] I would argue that a generation of school students has actually been taught to hate the classics by the very process that was meant to engender a love of them.

Teachers and others have not been unaware of this problem, and the personal-response model has come under attack from a number of quarters. Some feminists, for instance, have started to explore the pleasures of reading popular romance, pleasures that traditionally have been effaced in school to the extent that a generation of girls has come to learn that it barely counts as reading, let alone as literature. A second attack has come from the media studies people, who, as they penetrated the English teaching establishment, discovered that the supposed purpose of media studies was to teach pupils to despise television and the popular arts in general.

Critiques from such perspectives demonstrated clearly that the traditional, supposedly child-centred approaches to English teaching had, in fact, created a hierarchy of pleasures, based on a simple equation: the more people liked something, the less worthwhile the pleasure. When questions of quality were addressed, there was a remarkable alignment, for the books liked by the few were always classified as quality, whereas books liked by the many were regarded as rubbish.

One way of trying to solve this problem is to explore with the young what gives them pleasure, what that pleasure consists in, and what criteria they use as they share their pleasures, both by asseverations of quality — this book is good — and by the generation of canons — these books are good. Traditional criticism will not help us here, since it starts from the premise that some books, notably formula fiction, are trash.

My project, then, is to establish the criteria exercised by the youngsters in their judgements of the quality of what they read.

Structure and pacing

When I start to question the youngsters about why they like Point Horror, one of the first things they talk about is structure. This takes two forms. The first relates to the development and resolution of emotional engagement across the whole of the book. That engagement is expressed in terms of suspense. The second concerns the ebb and flow of tension within the writing. The two overlap.

Here are the girls, first of all talking about the development and resolution of suspense. They are setting up criteria and using them to criticize *The Waitress*.

Me: You say it's not so good.
Liz: No.
Alison: No.
Me: Why not?
Mary: It looks good.
Alison: 'Cause like there's no, with all of the other ones there's like a mystery and you're sort of building up to the big bit ...

They continue:

Liz: And you think something's going to happen ...
Alison: And so you know something's building up to happen like someone will die and the murderer will come to them and you're trying to work out who did it and what mystery of how they died ...
Liz: It's silly, it's boring ...
Alison: But with *The Waitress* it's like a couple of notes saying, be careful or you might have an accident.

The Waitress does not build up suspense as it ought. Other books are more successful. Being scared is part of it:

Alison: But then *The Lifeguard* I was reading, that's all about, he's drowning them, and I was reading it in the bath!
Me: (Laughs)
Alison: So I was really freaked out, and I was really freaky, so I just had to sit down and finish it to get my nerves away.

We continue:

Me: You find them quite frightening, do you?
Alison: Yeh, and that's what makes me read them I think, 'cause it's quite fun. 'Cause once you read it then you sort of think 'I've got to know what happens to stop me being scared.' And you think, 'Oh that was excellent' at the end of it. You just have to read them.

The more the girls talk, the more they bring out the crafting of the story, the ways the plot is structured and suspense is developed. In the first place there has to be unpredictability:

Alison: I think the more unpredictable it is the better, unless it's something like someone who hasn't been in the story much.

In most of the books in the series, the successive climaxes have variety and an escalation of threat. Where this does not occur, the girls are critical. In *The Boyfriend*, for instance, the character of the boyfriend returns three times in zombie make-up, and there are at least three false murders with three false knives. Each time it is 'just a joke' designed to get the heroine to change her ways.

> *Mary*: I was getting scared. And when it said 'just a joke', I thought, oh well that's a load of rubbish now.
> *Alison*: Yeh, it's a bit of rubbish.
> *Mary*: But it was still quite good.
> *Alison*: But then you read on and then it's just a joke again. And that isn't so good.

In a couple of the books a specific structural device is used — the introduction of an anonymous first-person narrator who is the murderer. This narrator only has a page now and then, interspersed through the main narrative, but the device seems to be particularly effective for these readers. It is used in *The Lifeguard*, and in describing the book Alison tells me not so much the story as the way the story is told, emphasizing the effectiveness of this change of narrator.

> *Alison*: ... you're sort of just reading about the girl, and you suddenly get a chapter that's on the lifeguard, and he's like 'how could he be so stupid leaving the body like that for them to just see' ... and you know it's the lifeguard because it's written in funny writing, and it's just like a page long or something ... and then you really want to get to the next one of the lifeguard. There [she shows me] there, it's just like that long ... a page and a bit ... just to give you an idea of what he's thinking.

In *Funhouse*, another title highly rated by both the girls and the boys, something very similar occurs, with the added complication that the interspersed sections include the murderer's discovery of a diary and his progressive revelation of its contents as the book proceeds. These first-person interruptions read like diary entries themselves, and it is this, I think, that James is specifically referring to:

> *James*: ... and the thing I found best was ... one chapter was what's happening ... every other one was a diary of the person who was doing all that, and it said like, you know 'Tess knows that I'm doing it' and stuff. It's really clever.

The use of threats can be similarly effective. Mary tells me about one book, title unspecified, where the threat takes the form of a poem:

> *Mary*: That's what made me really ... read the rest.
> *Alison*: It sort of makes you excited and want to read on, and you want to know what's happened, even though you don't know any of

the characters ... like you can read the first page and if it's got a poem you can sort of think 'Ah who's done it, who wrote it, who's it to?', and you just want to know everything.

You might think that the nature of this sort of thriller means that the reader is swept on mindlessly by the headlong chase of the plot. Unquestionably, for these readers this is an important source of emotional satisfaction, but in their accounts the youngsters show that their reading is far from mindless. The very fact that many elements of the stories speak directly to interests and concerns of these readers in ways they can immediately understand means that they are both aware of and appreciative of how the book is put together. Not only that, they don't give simple and-then accounts but speak again and again of the crafting and the structure. John offers further insights into the question of quality, when he talks about the pacing of the narrative:

James: I think it's good if the plot doesn't take ages to actually happen, but it just builds up and then calms down like John said earlier on.
Me: But that's about the pace of the story, isn't it?
James: Yeh.
John: Yeh.
Me: Make it go faster and slower and both ...
John: Yeh, in a really good bit you read, and then you get quicker and quicker and quicker and quicker, and then you sort of take a breather, and then it starts going slow, and then it gets to a really quick, and then ...
Me: And do you need that? Supposing it was quick all the way through, would that be just too much?
James: Yeh, it wouldn't be ...
John: Yeh, it needs to be like, it has to have good sharp important bits in it. ... And then there's, you've got to have the not so important bits to tell you what's going to happen, like, which have got nothing to do with the story, just to calm down a bit.

The boys seem to be suggesting that a book that was all climax would not do. Books need an ebb and flow of excitement and respite, of engagement and contemplation, of action and explanation.

The first set of criteria, then, by which these youngsters are judging the quality of what they read, concerns the crafting of the book in order to develop suspense. Unpredictability and surprise are important, as are variety and escalation of threat. Shifts of narrative point of view contribute, as do anonymous threats dropped into the story at appropriate intervals. The books have to be written in such a way that the reader can play the game of outguessing the protagonist, and the pacing of the narrative is vital to retain the reader's interest.

Narrative perspective and character role

The narrator of any book offers a perspective upon the characters. Most Point Horrors are narrated from an anonymous third-person point of view, focused through the understandings of the protagonists. Thus, ostensibly, we only know what they know, suspect what they suspect, and so on. The narration itself, and the reading process, is such that there is always a gap between the characters' perceptions and the reader's. The reader is enabled to take a more objective view of the characters than they are themselves. In the thriller genre the protagonists are always caught up in situations over which they do not have complete control and in which there are others who know more than they do. The narrator need make no overt demonstration of this superior knowledge, but the very fact that conventional third-person narration is both omniscient and cast in a virtual past means that the narrator knows what the protagonist does not. This is certainly true of the Point Horror series.

In addition, in popular fiction the role of the character is more important than characterization. And while we learn quite a lot about the thoughts of the protagonists, such thoughts are only offered either as analysis of what the character knows or as a prelude to action — very rarely as a psychological development. The characters think in order to do. The role of the protagonist is to be both victim and detective. This aspect of all thriller and detective heroes and heroines as learners, gaining cognitive control over their social world, has particular resonance for young readers. In a sense the role of victim and the role of learner are mirror images of each other and mutually interdependent, for not knowing puts you at risk and implies that someone else does know. It is this aspect that the youngsters commented on. In telling me about it, Alison also makes a comment about pacing.

> *Alison:* I like the way they're easy to read, and they introduce you to the characters straightaway. There's no waiting to find out about the characters. 'Cause it's like someone's watching her and sort of following her round telling you about all her actions, and so you can easily tell what she's like and that. So you get to chapter five and realize suddenly that she's scared of things. It's obvious from the beginning.

James makes a similar comment:

> *James:* I think something good is when they've got someone clever, someone that you know is cleverer than the person, the star, like Hannah ... who's doing it ...

Alison is talking about *The Lifeguard* and James about *Funhouse*, both examples of specific alternative perspectives being written into the text.

But in the very structure of the genre there is always an omniscient narrator, who knows more than the victim/protagonist. And I get a sense from Alison's and James's comments that they share that omniscient stance as readers. The books always involve clues and threats, and the protagonists go through a process of doubt about whether they are imagining things. The reader knows that they aren't and is thus invited to be omniscient, alongside the narrator, and outguess the protagonist.

For all that they primarily function as roles, the characters have to have enough individuation to engage the reader's interest. (James here, and above, uses 'star' to mean protagonist, an interesting and symptomatic example of his ease of movement between visual and written fictions.)

> *James*: The reader has got to know what the star is like, exactly, you've got to really go into depth about how he thinks, and then you know what kind of person it is ... and so you feel you know how they feel when things like that are happening. And also the person who's doing the bad things, so you feel that you know him.
>
> *John*: Yeh, like in the book ... at the beginning you've got to like explain and show what the people are like. And sometimes the, even like in this *[The Boyfriend]*, it seems like you actually know the person after they've explained them to you.

In addition there needs to be a variety of characterization:

> *Me*: What makes a good story then?
>
> *John*: Um ... the way it happens, how the people are all like different in different ways.

This is indeed a feature of the series: apart from the protagonist there will be three or four main characters, generally male, all of whom will be suspects. While all will be attractive, one will be strongly built, another slim, or one will be dark and tall, another fair and boyish. One will seem kind, another stand-offish. One will be a footballing hunk, another a swot. They are thus clearly differentiated by looks and by some personality trait.

Two further criteria of quality have emerged. The first, linking narrative omniscience with the role of protagonist as victim/investigator, invites the reader to out-investigate the protagonist. The second, the variety of characterization, also generates interest for these readers.

Beyond Point Horror: realism and characterization

At various points in our discussion, I asked the youngsters to think about books other than Point Horror and to tell me about other things that made a book good. They told me that it had to be realistic; it had in some way to be like their own lives. Here are the boys raising the issue of realism and, along the way, coming out with impeccably politically correct views about *The Turbulent Term of Tyke Tiler*,[4] a book both are enthusiastic about.

> Me: How does the fact that you discover that she's a girl, at the end, change the story?
>
> John: In the way that you, you're thinking, oh this boy Tyke is doing this and doing that, sort of thing you'd expect some boys would do, like mucking around with another boy and playing games and not hanging around with all the girls and that, and then it changes the story by finding out that Tyke's a girl, and that just changes it all ... so you didn't expect a girl to have done that ...
>
> James: Yeh, it makes you see the realism of the fact that you can get girls who er ...
>
> John: Yeh, you think, it's really like ... thinking of some boys being sexist really ... and then you find it was a girl you feel a bit awful that you're a bit sexist about it.

Critics of *Tyke Tiler* have claimed that it is mechanical, that Tyke is simply written as a boy and then switched at the end. Others report that many readers never follow the switch at all, since it involves a fairly alienating shift of narrative perspective. These boys code the book as 'realism', however, and for them it works very well. Realism is an important factor for the girls, too, and character is important in that context.

> Liz: Stuff that's more true to life like that, and like *Are You There God? It's Me, Margaret*,[5] it's more like true, like what some people would be going through.
>
> Alison: Yeh, I suppose ...
>
> Mary: Those Adrian Mole, you know those ones ...
>
> Alison: ... they're like a boy who's about thirteen, and he's an intellectual, so they're not boring.
>
> Liz: That's funny.
>
> Alison: So they're true to life, but not boring. They're like interesting, true to life, like an interesting character's life.

The girls contrast Point Horror with 'stuff that's more true to life': Blume and Adrian Mole.[6] Point Horror itself is clearly not social realism in the accepted sense but thematically, in the portrayal of adolescent social relations and the negotiation of trust and friendship, the series handles issues that are very real in their readers' lives. Such 'realism' feeds through to the readers' perceptions of character too, for what may seem to older readers to be merely stereotyping within the genre is perceived by these less experienced readers as fully rounded characterization. For example, and as I have noted before, a number of the protagonists are spoiled brats. None is worse than Joanna, heroine of *The Boyfriend* by R. L. Stine. For once Stine makes explicit play of the fact that she is spoiled, and for John this constitutes part of the attraction of the book. In the opening scene Joanna has stood her boyfriend up and is secretly gloating over his discomfort as he waits for her in the shopping mall:

John: ... and she's feeling really good about it ... She's being really mean and feeling good about standing him up and everything.

Me: Now, do you like the girl, the character of the girl, or not like the character of the girl?

John: Don't really. She's, as it says, she's spoiled, and all she keeps doing is boasting about her BMW and everything. She's boasting about everything she's got and she hasn't really got any friends that much 'cause of what she's like. You feel sorry for her in a way but in another way you think that she's just spoiled and it's her fault how she's acting, and it's her fault that she got into all the mess.

Me: Now you said when you read the back that you thought it had a spoiled girl in it, and you thought it would be interesting to read about a spoiled girl?

John: Yeh, probably be interesting to see what really were meant by 'she was spoiled'. ... I just wanted to know what she was like, as a spoiled girl ... and how she got muddled up in between two boys.

John here is surely exercising what Harding calls detached evaluation in the spectator mode. He might be talking about my reading of the character of Isabel Archer in *The Portrait of a Lady* or indeed of Emma Woodhouse in *Emma*, two noticeably spoiled protagonists who also get muddled up, though in their cases it's between *three* boys.

We have, then, two further criteria of quality. Books have to be realistic, to be seen by the youngsters as like their own lives in some way. Furthermore, books need to have characterizations that are interesting to them in their own right. Once again, the youngsters' notions of realism and ours are likely to be very different, since we have the hindsight of experience and they don't.

To sum up, these 12-year-olds, in judging the books they read, are particularly aware of the crafting of the storytelling and of its structure, the shifts in narrative perspective, and the articulation of genre conventions such as clues, threats, and the succession of perilous situations. They are aware both of the build-up and the resolution of emotional tension across a whole story as well as the importance of its ebb and flow. They want variety of detail, unpredictability of plot, and differentiation of character. Furthermore, the cognitive game of out-guessing the protagonist and the play of victim versus seeker of knowledge have particular relevance for them.

The list does not end there: the youngsters also like books that dramatize their concerns with impending adolescence. Choosing friends, learning to become independent, coping with being not quite a child but not quite an adult, dealing with the disruption of emerging sexuality and its containment or lack of containment within the family and the social group — all these emerged from readings of Point Horror.

Not all these criteria are needed to identify a good book. One does not look to psychological thrillers for social realism or to a Henry James novel for a rollercoaster ride of suspense and its resolution. But it is clear enough to me from my conversations with these youngsters that a number of them have to be in place for a title to enter the canon. This brings me to the final section, for what these youngsters are doing, of course, is laying down the ground rules for the construction of canons.

The social construction of canons

Canons are constructed when a group of people agree on criteria of judgement. Particular critics at particular times encapsulate particular sets of criteria and identify a canon explicitly. F. R. Leavis did it in *The Great Tradition*[7] and Fred Inglis does it for children's literature in *The Promise of Happiness*.[8] Over the years the examination boards have generated a canon by implication, by the continuous use of a limited number of authors and texts. The booklists in the April 1993 proposals for the rewrite of the orders for English in the National Curriculum have explicitly created a canon.

With contemporary fiction, the literary establishment and awards like the Booker Prize and the Carnegie Medal provide signposts. 'Reputable' modern authors like William Golding or Margaret Atwood do not take long to appear on A-level lists and in university syllabuses, and there is presumed to be a continuity of criteria by which literature is judged to be good. All of this is arrived at by social negotiation among the arbiters of taste. Canons are socially constructed.

Different social groups will construct different canons, in some cases mutually exclusive canons. Indeed, part of the process of constructing canons will be identifying texts that fall outside the canon. In these postmodern times it is hardly surprising to find a variety of canons reflecting the cultural pluralism of modern society.

Children and young people also engage in the social construction of canons, which involves a number of factors, including the views of their peers, their older siblings, their parents, and the publishing and video industries. The discussions I have had about Point Horror give some indication of the phenomenon.

Point Horror was sweeping this particular class as a craze. Within the class there were four main sources of information and influence: Mary, one of the girls in the study; friends outside school; older siblings and their friends; and the operation of the commercial market.

> *Me:*   How did you get to hear about Point Horror, how did you start ...
> *Alison:* Mary brought them.
> *Liz:*   Her [indicating Mary].
> *Alison:* Well, my stepbrother gave my sister *The Lifeguard* for Christmas, and then Mary lent me a book and I thought 'Oh that's really good.'

So where did Mary get them?

> *Mary:*   Well I was just in W.H. Smith's, I was, I didn't have any books left, and I went in there, and there was things like all the Judy Blume books and all the Point Horror books, but these ones looked more interesting and I looked on the backs and it sounded really good. So I got *The Cheerleader* but I didn't really get into that much.
> *Alison:* Yeh, that wasn't a very good one.
> *Mary:*   But then I decided to get *The Boyfriend* 'cause it sounded quite good and, um, Laura, this girl that I know, she read it before me and she said that was really good, so I read it.

There is, then, an interplay of critical judgement, enthusiastic recommendation and the social processes of living and working with your friends. With James the decision-making process is currently going on, over *Black Milk* by Robert Reed.[9] It has initiated a personal debate for him in which his own taste, his mother's views and the recommendations of a friend are all featured. The debate comes down specifically to questions of bad language, always an important sociocultural marker.

> *James:*   The thing about *Black Milk*, though ... it was a bit too, it had a bit too much swearing and violence, it was a bit ... I don't think my mum would like it.
> *Me:*   You don't think your mum would like it?
> *James:*   No. Peter Bridge gave it to me.

There are nice distinctions to be made:

> *Me:*   And your mum wouldn't like it ...
> *James:*   Well she, she probably wouldn't mind that, she wouldn't mind, um, she wouldn't mind if it said like things like may, can I say this?
> *Me:*   Yes, you can.

James: Crap, and things like that ... but when it came to the F word ...
she might get a bit, she might think I don't want you reading
that, and stuff ...

James begins to apply his own criteria here too:

James: Mmm. It was ... I think they um kind of, they started to um ...
er ... put the, put the swearing in just for the sake of it.

Later the boys elaborate:

John: If the book's just got a few swear words in it, which like
someone gets hit, they say 'oh shit', or something like that ...
then there's not that bad, but if someone's got something in, in it
where they're just swearing for the sake of it, I don't like it
much.

James: Yeh, it's somehow a bit, a bit meaningless ...

Deciding which social group you are going to join, and which cultural
canon you will espouse, and establishing the criteria by which you will
judge the quality of that canon, are all interlinked social processes. James
is debating between his mum's taste and his friend's. What is watched on
the video or the presence or absence of a video in the house — these are
important cultural markers. The debate about swearing is part of the
more general debate about the policing of language, and also about action
and violence in cultural artefacts.

A number of interpenetrating factors enter the social negotiation of
canonicity for these youngsters. There is, first, the role of a central and
influential figure within the peer group. Then there are the influences of
other peers, and older siblings and their peers. The operation of the
market is crucial too. If the stuff wasn't sitting in W.H. Smith's by the
shelfload, Mary would not have picked up on it. Parents too have a role to
play. Underlying the discussions and recommendations are the critical
judgements already discussed.

The lists

The April 1993 proposals for English in the National Curriculum[10] have
already been revised, but they provide an indicator of the thinking that
underlies one side of the debate. They insist throughout on the promotion
of literature of 'quality' and 'depth'. What they mean is 'those writers and
texts which are of central importance to our literary heritage', and while
wide reading is explicitly not discouraged, it must be monitored. 'Pupils'
voluntary reading activities should be reviewed to assess their abilities and
to ensure that each pupil is developing effective reading strategies.' It is
clear that these strategies are to be applied to texts of 'quality' and 'depth'.

The following canon is suggested for Key Stages 3 and 4 (ages 12 to 16): *Treasure Island, Huckleberry Finn, Little Women, Robinson Crusoe,* Hardy's Wessex tales, *Jane Eyre, A Christmas Carol, Gulliver's Travels, Silas Marner, A Tale of Two Cities, The Mayor of Casterbridge, Wuthering Heights, Pride and Prejudice, The Moonstone, The Red Badge of Courage.*

In my discussions with the youngsters they mention a number of titles which are being read by their own peer group, by older siblings and by their parents. These include visual fictions (film and video), and in their talk the youngsters move effortlessly between the forms. Compiling lists from these sources is instructive, and nowhere is there an overlap with the National Curriculum.

What the proposals do, it seems to me, is to demonstrate the institutionalization of a 'great divide' between reading for pleasure and the study of literature. Enlightened teachers will take children across the boundary as they have always done, but to do so they will find themselves increasingly having to defy both the letter and the spirit of the National Curriculum.

Conclusion

Teenage is a time of independence from, yet dependence on, the family. This statement may be hackneyed but is true of most people's experience. Point Horror dramatizes the conflicts in book after book after book. Because the youngsters know what it is all about, because they don't have to struggle to understand the content, they are in a position both to appreciate the pleasures of, and to start discriminating about the quality of, what they are reading. In this they are no different from me in my experience of reading Conrad, whom I struggled with for years and whose qualities I am only just beginning to appreciate, because suddenly I understand the content. Before that I was as incapable of a discriminatory reading of Conrad as I was of crossing the Atlantic by flapping my arms.

There are continuities and discontinuities between the youngsters' reading and mine. The continuities suggest that there is something in common to be found in the satisfactions gained when different people of different ages and with different interests and backgrounds read and/or view diverse canons; the discontinuities suggest the reasons why those different canons appeal to different groups. I can show what I mean with a couple of examples from Point Horror.

First of all, there are common criteria. The Point Horror evidence suggests that the youngsters find satisfaction in structure, character and the connection between the action of the novel and the development of human relationships. There are continuities here between the youngsters' readings of the series and my viewings of, for example, Hitchcock, where I delight in the crafting of the storytelling, am engaged by the characters, and find that the development of the human story is appropriately objectified by the unfolding of the thriller plot. Hitchcock is an apposite example, since *The Birds* is specifically referenced in one of the books, and *Psycho* implicitly in another; but I could say the same for *Pride and Prejudice*, where the unfolding of the human story is appropriately objectified in the unfolding not of a thriller plot but of a Beauty and the Beast fairy-tale plot.

The discontinuities, by contrast, will lead me to choose one canon, and the youngsters to choose another. For example, although both the youngsters and I are interested in characterization, the characters in Point Horror affect us differently. For me they are shallow, self-centred, and represent most of what is worst about modern consumer society. They play out stereotypical dilemmas of what it means to be a teenager surrounded by the most unlikely family and social situations, live through events guaranteed to mess up permanently the most stable and well-adjusted personality, and all they do is shrug, smile and go off on a shopping spree. I cannot find any reasons whatever to be interested in them. Yet for the youngsters they are vivid realizations of the definitional dilemmas of a state they are yet to embark upon. I am a 49-year-old academic; they are 12, and goodness knows what they are going to be when they grow up. Additionally, I am a male, and the predominant enthusiasm for Point Horror comes from girls. What is strange is that there are any continuities at all. Alison even shares with me an admiration of the work of Philippa Pearce: one of her favourite books is *The Way to Sattin Shore*.[11]

I have explored a corner of that complex cultural process that is the experience of pleasure and the judgement of quality in the reading of books and the watching of films. My point is that, in a diverse society with a complex and diverse entertainments industry, pleasure and those judgements of quality will manifest themselves in diverse ways, none more diverse than in the pleasures of children, who are always into anything that is new, that looks as if it might appeal, and who exercise their judgements and deploy their criteria for pleasure with considerable aplomb. If we want to know what they think, we have to talk to them, and if we do, they will have something to tell us.

Acknowledgement

My thanks go to the staff and pupils of Bignold Middle School, Norwich, for giving me access to the school and allowing me to collect the evidence upon which this chapter has been based.

This chapter is a slightly altered version of an article which first appeared in *Signal 74*, in May 1994. Reprinted with permission of the publisher, Thimble Press, Lockwood, Station Road, Woodchester, Stroud, Glos, GL5 5EQ.

Notes

1 Charles Sarland, *Young People Reading: Culture and Response*, Open University Press, Buckingham, 1991.
2 Donald Fry, *Children Talk about Books: Seeing Themselves as Readers*, Open University Press, Buckingham, 1991.
3 Nina Bawden, *Carrie's War*, Gollancz, London, 1973; Philippa Pearce, *The Battle of Bubble and Squeak*, Deutsch, London, 1978.
4 Gene Kemp, *The Turbulent Term of Tyke Tiler*, Faber, London, 1977.
5 Judy Blume, *Are You There, God? It's Me, Margaret*, Gollancz, London, 1978.
6 Sue Townsend, *The Secret Diary of Adrian Mole*, Methuen, London, 1982.
7 F. R. Leavis, *The Great Tradition,* Penguin, London, 1948.
8 Fred Inglis, *The Promise of Happiness: Value and Meaning in Children's Fiction,* Cambridge University Press, Cambridge, 1981.
9 Robert Reed, *Black Milk*, Orbit, London, 1990.
10 Department for Education, *English for Ages 5 to 16, Proposals of the Secretary of State for Education and the Secretary of State for Wales*, HMSO, London, 1993.
11 Philippa Pearce, *The Way to Sattin Shore*, Kestrel, London, 1983.

Point Horror titles referred to in this chapter: Richie Tankersley Cusick, *The Lifeguard*, 1988, 1991; Diane Hoh, *Funhouse*, 1990, 1991; Sinclair Smith, *The Waitress*, 1992, 1992; R. L. Stine, *The Boyfriend*, 1990, 1992. All are published by Scholastic, London; the first date in each case refers to the original publication in the USA.

PART II

Voices from the Past

The idea of reading as a conversation between the reader and the writer, through text, is a familiar one. We are used to the notion that literature — in this case children's literature — speaks to the reader and, increasingly, we are getting hold of a sense that the 'meaning' of any text exists in the dialogue which goes on between reader and text. What is often forgotten is that there are many other clamorous voices speaking through, about and to the texts which we, and children, read. The conversation isn't just between a reader and a text but between readers and writers throughout ages and across cultures. Other sections of the book eavesdrop on some of these conversations between readers; this section begins by listening to some of the voices from literature of the past and moves towards considering how these voices might be heard in the future. Among the engaged, sometimes familiar and comforting, sometimes exhortatory, dialogues between readers and texts, however, there are other voices, less concerned, perhaps, with the pleasures of reading. These are the voices of 'those who know best' introducing a note of compulsion rather than satisfaction. The different chapters examine what some of the commentators, interpreters and originators of a range of texts have to say.

It seems that there is no escape from the idea that literature for children is meant to 'do a job' of some kind. Looking back into the history of children's reading reveals preoccupations with a tension between 'instruction and delight' which parallel some of the debates going on now. Linked with this apparent opposition is the idea of texts offering health or harm to readers. It should come as no surprise, perhaps, that these matters have accompanied children and their reading throughout time, but acknowledgement of recurrent or residual themes arising in debates about texts for children does not mean that because 'it's the same old story' the tensions can be accepted uncritically. The fact of the matter is that it's *not* exactly the same old story. Just as stories themselves shift and reshape through time, reflecting the preoccupations of the tellers, so do the commentaries on those texts and the kinds of public debates which go on about them.

John Rowe Townsend, an experienced historian of literature for children, opens the section by tracing the relationships between parents and children as they are reflected through fiction for children and young people from the seventeenth century onwards. From the strong central features of admonitions to obey the dictates of parental authority and appeals to rational behaviour in children through to the disappearance of parents from fiction or the introduction of faulty adults, emerges a kind of tolerance between the generations. As John Rowe Townsend points out, in this part of the twentieth century young readers are 'expected to face in fiction the harsh realities of life' alongside adults, rather than being placed in the earlier position of coming to terms with some hard truths through adult intervention. This careful delineation of changing relationships between the generations as depicted in books for children is a reminder that texts necessarily act as representatives of the cultural mores of the time. In the second chapter David Whitley also considers how 'the moral certitudes of respectable adulthood' have been reflected in children's fiction. He chooses, however, to examine this through the changing uses of Aesop's fables as the basis for introducing children to social conduct — and conflict. Taking 'a great leap backwards in time', David Whitley argues that despite the 'supreme adaptability of the fable' which has meant that children seem to have read them with pleasure throughout the ages, these tales have been unaccountably neglected in more recent educational and literary debate. In examining some of the different voices which have told the fables, he suggests that these are narratives within which children, too, can find their own voices.

In another journey into the past Morag Styles echoes the shift from the didactic and improving towards a more open and playful use of texts. In tracing a history of poetry written specifically with children in mind, she describes some of the landmarks as well as identifying some writers on the margins of the way. While outlining the work of some poets with an urge to improve and educate, to make the young devout, Morag Styles finds other, somewhat neglected poets, who captured a sense of what children might enjoy and who presented a world more on the eye-level of a child. Moving into this century, she offers a reminder of De La Mare's vividness and Milne's sad little voice before considering the seriously funny voices of 'urchin verse' and the gritty tones of other modern poets for children. Although idealization of the child and a sense of precious innocence may not be overtly presented in poetry written for children now, this tough and resilient poetry reflects the authentic voices of children in their everyday experience. The recent explosion of energetic and iconoclastic poetry does not mean that poetry from the past is neglected, however; far from it. As Morag Styles points out, poetry, including that from the past, is 'currently undergoing a boom in sales'. In the present 'positive climate for poetry' she reminds us that we hear many voices from all ages.

Janet Bottoms similarly identifies the clamour of many voices as she examines what is said — and done — about using Shakespeare with children. Since Shakespeare is considered one of the most significant voices from the literary past of Britain, it is no great surprise that 'those who know best' use his works as a site for dispute. While politicians insist on children 'doing' Shakespeare as part of their 'cultural heritage', writers and academics argue about the suitability of the texts for children — or the children for the texts — and teachers wonder how they are to fulfil the competing demands of the English curriculum. Janet Bottoms questions the whole idea of cultural heritage, arguing that culture cannot be seen as a fixed notion but that it is better interpreted as a site for the renegotiation of meaning. This view of remaking links with her theme of 'playing with' rather than 'doing' Shakespeare. She argues that children can explore Shakespeare's texts individually and together because Shakespeare is a poet and dramatist who allows spaces for readers/players to fill with their own voices. In recounting the responses of different children who have been encouraged to grapple with the texts, she argues that far from offering Shakespeare to children as something which has fixed meaning, they can create their own interpretations rather than having to take on those of others.

The final voice in this section is that of the writer Jan Mark, whose chapter aptly rings with her own ironic humour in this careful study of literature from the past. Whilst she examines some shifts in attitudes towards texts for children, Jan Mark summarizes the main threads of argument in this section — literature used as propaganda or pleasure. However, she reminds us that it's not a simple opposition — in the words of John Locke it *is* possible to combine 'instruction with delight'; the example of Louisa May Alcott proves that propaganda can also provide a good read. In considering how contemporary writing will be read in the future, Jan Mark argues that those authors who trust the reader, who are uncompromising and unpatronizing, are likely to be the ones whose works will remain as satisfying and enduring texts for children. The best writers for children, she says, 'recognize the transience of childhood'; it is the adults who find this difficult to take, not the young readers. In looking towards the twenty-first century, she reminds us that the same debates about the messages carried in books for children will be carried out then. 'Voices from the past' will include our own and will be argued with by new generations. Quite rightly.

CHAPTER 5

Parents and Children

The Changing Relationship of the Generations, as Reflected in Fiction for Children and Young People

John Rowe Townsend

Much of the earliest printed material used to instruct and admonish children was not fiction, but once the tradition of creating 'organized recreational literature' for children was established, there was even greater scope for inculcating 'family values'. At first, children's fiction may have reflected some of the harsher attitudes of parental authority, but this gradually shifted towards literature which depicted a much warmer view of family life. Even later, children's stories got rid of the grown-ups, or revealed them as fallible. John Rowe Townsend wonders whether this move towards a harsher realism, alongside the appeals of modern youth culture, will mean that books for older children and teenagers will be set aside in favour of other popular cultural forms, or books written for adults. Whatever the outcome, it is certainly true that earlier representations of family life which tended to revere the authority of parents have been replaced by portrayals of more relaxed and equal relationships between parents and children. There is much greater evidence of toleration of difference. In this trend, John Rowe Townsend finds hope.

The Heavy Curse of God will fall upon those Children that make Light of their Parents ... The Curse of God! The Terriblest Thing that ever was heard of; the First-born of Terribles! ... Children, if you break the fifth Commandment, there is not much likelihood that you will keep the rest ... Undutiful Children soon become horrid Creatures, for Unchastity, for Dishonesty, for Lying, and all manner of Abominations ... And because these Children are Wicked overmuch, therefore they Dye before their Time ... Children, if by Undutifulness to your Parents you incur the Curse of God, it won't be long before you go down into Obscure Darkness, even into Utter Darkness: God has reserved for you the Blackness of Darkness for ever.[1]

The quotation is from *A Family Well Ordered*, by Cotton Mather, published in 1699. Cotton Mather was a tyrannical New England divine of the Puritan hellfire-and-damnation school, and a fairly obnoxious specimen of it; but his tone of voice can readily be found in English writings of his day. You can hear it, for instance, in John Bunyan's grim and threatening *Book for Boys and Girls* of 1686 ('Death's a cold Comforter to Girls and Boys/Who wedded are unto their Childish Toys' &c.). And even in the *Divine Songs* of Isaac Watts, a gentler soul, in 1715, there are dire warnings of the consequences of disobeying one's parents:

> Have you not heard what dreadful Plagues
> Are threaten'd by the Lord
> To him that breaks his Father's law
> Or mocks his Mother's Word?
>
> What heavy Guilt upon him lies!
> How cursèd is his Name!
> The Ravens shall pick out his Eyes
> And Eagles eat the same.
>
> But those that worship God, and give
> Their Parents Honour due,
> Here on this Earth they long shall live,
> And live hereafter too.

Neither the *Divine Songs* nor *A Family Well Ordered* was fiction, of course. Literature that was meant specially for children, from the dawn of printing to that time, was overwhelmingly instructional or admonitory. There were plenty of tales, songs and ballads around, but they were for general circulation, not for children particularly, and indeed they came in for a good deal of condemnation. There is a well-known quotation from Hugh Rhodes, author of a *Boke of Nurture*, published around 1550: 'Keepe them [your children] from reading of fayned Fables, vayne Fantasyes, and wanton Stories and Songs of Love, which bring much Mischiefe to Youth.' And, a century and a half later and a continent away, Cotton Mather was still harping on the same theme: he complained of the corruption caused by 'foolish Songs and Ballads, which the Hawkers and Peddlars carry to all parts of the Country'.[2]

Organized recreational literature for children can hardly be said to exist before the middle of the eighteenth century; but although the 'good godly books' of the Puritans were not fiction and certainly not meant to be fun, all histories of children's literature have something to say about them; and quite properly, because the moral stories which dominated 'official' children's fiction until well into the nineteenth century were rooted in some or all of the same attitudes. Children must obey and take instruction from their parents; the aim of such instruction was to instil religion and morality and indeed, for many writers, to save souls from hell.

Cotton Mather, it will be noted, put the Fifth Commandment — 'Honour thy father and thy mother' — at the head of the line: 'If you break the Fifth Commandment there is not much likelihood that you will keep the rest.' Nor was he exceptional in doing so. There was no doubt in the Puritan mind, or in most others, that wisdom and therefore authority were vested firmly in the older generation. Indeed, it was widely held that children were limbs of Satan, soaked in original sin which must be wrung out of them by beatings and exhortation.

In the Georgian era, attitudes to children changed considerably. Naturally such changes are piecemeal, varying between regions, classes and individuals. But among the more enlightened a new view was replacing the old fundamentalism; children began to be seen not as already corrupted by original sin but rather as blank pages on which the right messages were to be written. A good deal of mellowing was inspired by the philosopher John Locke, who has been described as the inventor of the child.[3] In his *Thoughts Concerning Education*, Locke argued that children should be taught by kindness rather than the rod and should 'play themselves into that which others are whipp'd for'.[4]

John Newbery, pioneer of the children's book trade and one of the most endearing of eighteenth-century figures, was an admirer of 'the great Mr Locke', and based his successful publishing philosophy on this concept of 'instruction through delight'. It was, however, continually impressed upon Newbery's young readers that they were to be good; and the first requirement for goodness was obedience. Dedications of Newbery children's books are to 'great and little good Boys and Girls' or to 'all little good Boys and Girls' (though standards were relaxed in some later titles: *Goody Two-Shoes* in 1765 was inscribed 'to all Young Gentlemen and Ladies who are good or intend to be good').

The nature of goodness is made clear in the story of Tommy Trip (in Newbery's *Liliputian Magazine*, 1751), who rescues a little boy from Woglog the Great Giant and takes him home to his parents:

> Upon the road he charged him to be a good Boy, and to say his Prayers, and learn his Book, and do as his Papa and Mamma bid him, which this little Boy has done ever since; and so must all other little Boys and Girls, or no body will love them.

This is a considerably milder sanction than hellfire. The eighteenth century was not much given to religiosity. It was the Age of Reason. Morality could be allied with reason, and both with self-interest. Virtuous behaviour, it was repeatedly pointed out, paid off. In the latter part of the century, the English followers of Jean-Jacques Rousseau, notably Thomas

Day, the author of *Sandford and Merton* (1783–9), and Maria Edgeworth, in *The Parent's Assistant* (1796) and *Early Lessons* (1801), urged upon children the need to act on rational principles, and pointed out the disasters that could result from failure to do so. By implication, parents should stand back and let their children learn by experience. In Maria Edgeworth's famous story of 'The Purple Jar', which was included in both the collections named, Rosamond's mother allows her to have the jar of coloured water from the chemist's window in preference to new shoes, with the result that her shoes deteriorate to such a degree that she can 'neither run, dance, jump nor walk in them'.

The formidable Sarah Trimmer condemned what she called 'Rousseau's system', but the eighteenth-century emphasis on reason and even on material interest can still be found in her *History of the Robins* (1786). I have always liked the reasonable tone in which a little boy's mama in this book impresses upon him the relative positions of children and parents:

> Remember, my dear, that you depend as much on your papa and me for everything you want as these little birds do on you; nay, more so, for they could find food in other places, but children can do nothing towards their own support; they should therefore be dutiful and respectful to those whose tenderness and care they constantly experience.[5]

In this case the child is offered a rational argument for behaving itself. In general, however, immediate and unquestioning obedience — to parental authority, not to reason — was required and was, as Gillian Avery has observed, 'the foundation stone of both Georgian and Victorian nursery discipline'.[6]

By the early nineteenth century, the old, fierce religious teaching was making a comeback; indeed, it had only gone a little way underground. Its most ferocious exponent was Mrs Sherwood, whose famous *The Fairchild Family* appeared in 1818. The Fairchild children, Henry, Lucy and Emily, are forever doing naughty things and being punished by their parents and warned of the dire consequences of their conduct. 'Henry,' says Mr Fairchild at one point, 'I did not punish you because I do not love you, but because I wished to save your soul from hell.' Another time, when Henry has refused to learn his lesson, has been flogged by Mr Fairchild and is still recalcitrant, Mr Fairchild informs him as follows:

> Henry, listen to me: when wicked men obstinately defy and oppose the power of God, he gives them up to their own hard hearts; he suffers them to live, perhaps, and partake of the lights of the sun and of the fruits of the earth, but he shows them no mark of his fatherly love or favour; they have no sweet thoughts, no cheerful hours, no delightful hopes. *I stand in place of God to you, whilst you are a child.*[7]

The attitudes of the author are obtrusive, and one would think them forbidding, yet *The Fairchild Family* was reprinted and read to bits for something like a century from its first publication; and this can only have been because naughty Henry, Lucy and Emily were in fact much more like actual children than the impossible goody-goodies who came to infest so much of Victorian children's literature. In fact I think it is true to say that *The Fairchild Family* was a key book of the nineteenth century in being the first major family story.

Another landmark in the same direction was Catherine Sinclair's *Holiday House* (1839).[8] Miss Sinclair had the refreshing aim of portraying 'that species of noisy, frolicsome, mischievous children now almost extinct, wishing to preserve a sort of fabulous remembrance of days long past, when young people were like wild horses on the prairies, rather than like well-broken hacks on the road'. This remark brings one up with a jolt if one has read many old children's books. No doubt such a species existed; no doubt also there was a considerable gap between children as they really were and children as they were supposed to be. Children had been presented in the seventeenth century as creatures of unearthly piety or as limbs of Satan, in the early eighteenth century as blank pages to be written on, and by the Rousseauites as either wise children or foolish children. In books they were either good or bad examples to others. One would have to look rather hard to find between covers a child who could be described by such adjectives as frolicsome and mischievous. The Fairchild children probably come nearest to those Catherine Sinclair wished to portray, but to Mr Fairchild, and presumably to Mrs Sherwood as author, they were children whose immortal souls were perpetually in peril. The important point about Catherine Sinclair's children, another Harry and Lucy, is that they are not wicked children, but *naughty* children. There is all the difference in the world.

The naughtiness of the children in *Holiday House* is quite impressive: at one point Harry plays with a candle — which he's been told not to — and nearly burns the house down. Laura cuts off her own hair and disgraces herself and her family by appearing, contrary to instructions, before a company of 'fine people' in a torn old gingham frock. The children are forgiven most of their misdemeanours because they are good at heart. None the less, after the affair of the gingham frock, Laura's grandmamma, Lady Harriet, tells her she will be severely punished: 'Parents are appointed by God to govern their children as He governs us, not carelessly indulging their faults but wisely correcting them.'

Harry's and Laura's father, by the way, is conspicuously absent, having gone abroad to get over the death of his wife, and apparently taking no interest in his children. But he retains the status of God's deputy. And in America, Elsie Dinsmore, heroine of a series of hugely selling children's novels in the 1860s, and probably the greatest prig in literature, when told that she could do some forbidden thing without her father's knowledge, declares that she 'cannot disobey Papa, even if he should never know it, because that would be disobeying God, and He would know it'. Mr Dinsmore bullies Elsie abominably, but this does not alter the ground-rule that Father is always right. At least, Father is always right in fiction for and about middle-class children. In the growing body of nineteenth-century fiction for and about the poor, it could be a different matter. Here the motto was often 'A little child shall lead them'; and children who, though neglected and uneducated, had achieved amazing levels of piety rescued their brutal drinking or gambling parents (usually fathers) and brought them rejoicing to love of the Lord. Alternatively, parents in such fiction were often dead, or died in the course of the story. There was a great wave of 'waif novels', of which few are now remembered and none, I think, read.

The great change comes with the rise of the family story. *The Fairchild Family* and *Holiday House* were precursors, but the books that really established the family story comprised the series by Louisa May Alcott that began with *Little Women* in 1868. This has remained the greatest of them all in reputation with the general public, both in the USA and UK, though there were other popular and well-regarded family stories by such late Victorians as, in this country, Mrs Ewing and Mrs Molesworth. With benefit of hindsight we can see that the stiff stereotype of authoritative parent and obedient child had to become relaxed and relatively flexible before a story so greatly loved as *Little Women* could appear. A relationship of ruler and subject had to be replaced by one in which affection rather than awe was the heart of the matter. The family story would not work in an atmosphere of chilly grandeur. The key characteristic is always warmth.

We may note that in many of the most-loved family stories, such as those of Louisa Alcott, E. Nesbit and the American writer Eleanor Estes, while family solidarity is of the essence, families are not necessarily *complete*. Father or mother may well be dead; father may be away — at the war, as in *Little Women*, or even in prison, like the father in E. Nesbit's *Railway Children*, although of course he has been imprisoned unjustly. And these loved and loving families were more often than not hard-up. The lack of money not only provided a mainspring for some of the plots — as in Nesbit's *Treasure Seekers* — but, more importantly, brought out the *value* of family life, of family love and affection, which glowed all the more warmly when one realized that it was cold outside and the wolf was not far from the door. When in one of Eleanor Estes's Moffat stories a five-dollar bill is lost, this is a real crisis, and the reader knows it.[9]

In the thickly populated fields of late-nineteenth- and early-twentieth-century literature, however, it becomes more and more hazardous to pick out individual books and authors as examples; and the best books are not necessarily the best indicators of attitudes. In general, both children and parents had become more human, although it was still axiomatic that parents were wise and authoritative and that children should be obedient and respectful. In books that were not, or supposedly not, for children it could be quite another matter. Huck Finn's father was no ideal parent. Kipling in *Stalky & Co.* and Kenneth Grahame in *The Golden Age* and *Dream Days* were disrespectful of adult authority, and it is interesting that these books, though not children's literature, were in the shadowy area around its borders.

In the USA the family story featuring a poor family — as people, not as a social problem — makes quite an early appearance with *Five Little Peppers and How They Grew*, by Margaret Sidney in 1881. This was the first of a series, forgotten now but hugely popular in its day, about a family life that centred around Mrs Pepper, a poor but (inevitably) warm-hearted widow. In England it took longer to achieve the descent to a humble social level. The poor are always patronized. This is true as late as 1937, with Eve Garnett's *The Family from One-End Street*[10] and its successors. Here father is a dustman and mother a washerwoman; they have seven children and live in a little old terraced house. This seems to me to be working-class life seen from the outside, with the Dustman and Washerwoman (spelled by the author in capital letters) presented almost as comic characters. But the love, warmth and solidarity of family life come across strongly and have appealed to children over many years.

In the first half of the twentieth century there was a curious tendency — in England at least — on the part of authors to send parents abroad or otherwise get them out of the way so that the children could take the centre of the stage. In Arthur Ransome's Swallows and Amazons books,[11] grown-ups are relegated to the second-class status of 'natives', who don't really understand. Mother is privileged by being called 'the best of all natives'. Parental authority — indeed, the overriding authority of father, to whom mother must apply for permission to let the children camp on the island at the beginning of the first book — is not in doubt, but is mostly kept out of sight.

In the middle years of the present century, all seems to have been quiet on the family front. There was, of course, World War II, right in the middle of those middle years, and there were the 1950s, a decade when it still seemed to many people that the main aim was to get back to what had been normal before the war. I find it hard to bring to mind books from those years that address questions of family relationship. The chapter on family stories in Margery Fisher's admirable and detailed survey *Intent upon Reading* (1961)[12] lists few titles that are now available or even much remembered; most have fallen unnoticed by the wayside. One book that I recall from the early 1960s, and that I wish was in print, was *The Battle of*

Wednesday Week, by Barbara Willard,[13] in which a mother who has been widowed with two children marries an American widower with four, and the children are determined to hate each other. In fact they row so horribly that the parents decide to go off on holiday and leave them to it; whereupon, as you might guess, they find they can get on together after all and they appeal to the parents to come back. It's a good story, and although this is not quite the orthodox family, the book in essence is still reassuring, since the parents are all they ought to be and it's up to the children to adjust. Parents still rule, though not with a rod of iron.

In general, British practitioners of the family story were not of the quality of the Americans. Eleanor Estes with the Moffats, Elizabeth Enright with the Melendys, Madeleine L'Engle with the Austins — these were the people who were writing the good family stories, Americans all. And, good though they were, they presented a one-sided picture of family life as it ought to be: loving and mutually supportive. In fact this was seen as the great merit of the family story. It is all spelled out in the 1964 edition of *Children and Books*, by May Hill Arbuthnot, who was for many years the great guru of American children's literature.

> It is in the family that the child learns his first lessons in the laws of affectionate relationships. ... The status of the mother and father in the family circle provide a child with his first concepts of the woman's role and the man's role in life, and often determine his consequent willingness or unwillingness to accept his own sex. ... When family relationships are normal and happy, a child starts life with healthy attitudes. ... When the reverse is true, his approach to other people is often suspicious or belligerent. In either case — a happy or an unhappy home background — books can help. Stories about family life may interpret to the fortunate child the significance of his own experiences which he might otherwise take for granted ... On the other hand, children who have missed these happy experiences may find in family stories vicarious substitutes which give them some satisfaction and supply them with insight into what families can be.[14]

Obviously, Mrs Arbuthnot saw the family story as exemplary: it was to show family life as ideal, to show the child who wasn't lucky enough to have a good home what it was missing. I am sure she would not have approved of a story which showed a bad, neglectful home, implying bad, neglectful parents. She would not have thought it right to put such a thing in the hands of children. In Britain a year later (1965) Gillian Avery was to write:

> For years now, realism has been the fashion on the stage and in fiction, but those who write specifically for children write with a set of taboos that held good in the days of L. T. Meade and Evelyn Everett Green. They omit (instinctively, not consciously, one feels) all unpleasant traits

in a child's personality; all crudeness and coarseness. Their children hardly seem to have a physical nature, beyond a good appetite. Family relationships are smooth, Mother is always right, Father never irks his sons.[15]

Both these extracts make it sound as if nothing had changed, nothing would ever change, and everything in the (fictional) garden of childhood was lovely. As a matter of fact, I think Gillian Avery was a little behind the times, since a few cracks were beginning to appear in the façade. I can claim to have produced one of the cracks myself with my book *Gumble's Yard*, in which the setting was a northern slum, the adults were a shiftless unmarried couple, and the children were left to fend for themselves.[16]

As the 1960s went on, there was to be a collapse of accepted assumptions on a much broader scale. The 1960s were the decade of the wind of change, of Black Power, of the rise of feminism, of the Vietnam War, of increasing rejection by the young of the values and mores of their elders. Along with this went a rapid acceleration of what had been a fairly slow and manageable trend: the loss of self-confidence of the parental generation. In a changed and turbulent world, parents were no longer sure of their own wisdom and competence. The unwritten social contract between parents and children, under which the parents jointly provided care and the children gave, if not total obedience, at least a willing allegiance and co-operation, was under pressure from both sides. On the one side were more divorces, more broken or one-parent families, more adults prepared to put their own interests first. On the other side, a distinctive youth culture was developing in which it no longer seemed the natural aim of the adolescent to become an adult as soon as possible. Younger children were growing, not directly towards adulthood but towards the new status of teenager.

Authors could not and did not ignore the new world they were moving into. Increasingly, children were expected to face in fiction the harsh realities of life. The two-parent, white, middle-class family ceased to be taken for granted. Not only did divorce and desertion become common-place; parents slid down the moral slope. In young adult books particularly, they were more and more likely to be useless or even vicious, reaching rock-bottom probably in the collection of appalling parents who inhabit the novels of the American writer Paul Zindel.[17]

In Britain the change has been less drastic than in the USA; nevertheless the atmosphere has altered so much since the early 1960s that unsmooth family relationships hardly need to be remarked upon. A great deal has been written about Alan Garner's *The Owl Service* (1967),[18] but it has not always been noted that the parents of the young people in the story are largely the source of their troubles. Gwyn, the clever Welsh boy with an outsize chip on his shoulder, can say to his mother, 'Oh, drop dead, you miserable cow!' Roger's father Clive will sacrifice anything for a quiet life;

Alison's mother Margaret, who never actually appears, exudes selfishness and snobbery from somewhere just off the edge of the page. Considered in the limited aspect of parent–child relationships, *The Owl Service* could well be called an un-family story; here is a group of adults and young people all together under one roof but with no solidarity whatever, nobody getting on with anybody else, all of them simmering together like a nest of wasps. The parents in *Red Shift*[19] a few years later are a disaster for the young couple at the centre of the story.

Another well-known book of the same period as *The Owl Service* is *A Pair of Jesus-Boots*, by Sylvia Sherry (1969).[20] The hero Rocky O'Rourke lives in the back streets of Liverpool with an inadequate mother, a stepfather away at sea, a stepsister who's a little strange in the head, and an older brother in prison. The un-family story again; and Rocky, although unquestionably the hero, is rough, reckless and destructive, without any respect for the law or any sense of right and wrong. His main ambition is to 'do a job', like elder brother Joey. Rocky, in fact, has attractive human impulses and will come good in his own way, and he does get some help from grown-ups — the stepfather when at home and an ex-professional footballer with a weakness for the bottle — but there's no feeling in this book of an accepted, acceptable order of things into which parents are duly bringing their children up.

The lack of harmony between children and parents, of loving security in family life, has even been projected back to times before World War I in an excellent book, *The Children of the House*, by Brian Fairfax-Lucy and Philippa Pearce, which was published in 1968 and reissued in 1989 as *The Children of Charlcote*.[21]

This is a story about four children who live with their parents in some grandeur, yet are deprived of affection, deprived even of decent food and clothing; and there is an unforgettable scene in which the parents go away on a brief visit and the children dance for joy on the marble floor of the great hall in celebration of their absence. What warmth there is in these children's lives comes from the pitying servants, not from the father and mother. I myself find the book shocking, almost frightening; against such a background a sense of parental neglect, of the harm that people can do to their children, shines out with fearful bleakness. And, in these days when we are being made aware of what goes on behind closed doors, of what children suffer silently because they are weak and have no redress or because, as we now know, they often believe the guilt must be their own, a story like *The Children of Charlcote*, based on real life in a real stately home, must make us wonder uneasily what may have happened through the centuries that the eye never saw and the heart could never grieve at. Is it possible that the conventional façade of family life, as presented in children's fiction and as approved of by such personages as Mrs Arbuthnot, was unwittingly helping to conceal from view all kinds of nasty things that went on in the real world?

In real life we have become used, in the last quarter-century, to the divorced or feckless or alcoholic parents, the unorthodox households of various descriptions, the early pregnancies, the tearaway young males, the ramifications of the drug traffic. It is a reasonable contention that, since modern life contains all this, children's books must face it, as otherwise they lose all credibility. It's hard enough already for books to hold their own against the competition of television and video cassette and the peer pressure of an insistent youth culture. Here are some questions that are raised. Are books for older children and teenagers becoming a lost cause, too slow and too solitary — in that reading is something you do by yourself — to stand up against the noisier and more vivid attractions of modern youth culture? Should authors and publishers accept that children's books will soon be virtually restricted to picture books for the very young and not-too-demanding storybooks for beginning readers and primary-age children, since the great majority of older children and teenagers will either have rejected books in favour of pop culture or have moved over to adult books? In asking these questions, I am not implying any answers; but it seems that young adult fiction in particular is having a hard time at present, both here and in the USA.

Even in books for younger age groups, one notices that there are now a great many departures from the traditional family pattern of parents and children. Look along the shelves in bookshop or library and you will soon find examples. Here are just two or three recent ones. In Jan Mark's *The Twig Thing*,[22] which is a Read Alone book, specifically designed for a child's first solo reading, and first published in 1988, we have a father and two little girls moving into their new home — a rather seedy old urban house. What is interesting about this story is what isn't in it: namely, mum. Not only is mum not there; she isn't even mentioned. Has she died, have she and dad divorced or separated, has she simply run away, and if so why? Has the break-up only just happened, and is dad setting up a home with the children for the first time, or was it so long ago that the little girls have forgotten they ever had a mother? No information is given.

I suppose the assumption is that this is just the way it happens to be; a motherless household is an ordinary thing, part of the scenery. I know that when my own children were small, some thirty years ago, they would have asked, round-eyed, 'Where is their mum?' Do today's children ask that question or do they just take it in their stride?

Another recent book by a well-known writer is Anne Fine's *Flour Babies* (1992).[23] The central character here is a boy who is rather a thug but for whom the author wins sympathy. What interests me is that all through the book the boy is obsessed with the father who walked out on his mum soon after he was born; then at the end he realizes that the obsession is pointless. Father has gone for good and is irrelevant to his life. 'My father is just one more person on the planet who doesn't know who I am. That's all he is. And only the people who know you really count.' The way forward for him is acceptance. If your father has upped and gone and taken no interest in you, well, that's the way the cookie crumbles.

Of books I've looked at recently, the most striking from this point of view is Jacqueline Wilson's *The Suitcase Kid* (1992).[24] The narrator, Andrea, is 10. Her parents have divorced, and quarrel in her hearing every time they meet. Andy spends alternate weeks with them, and whichever she's with she has a long bus journey to school instead of getting a ride. They both have new partners; from being an only child, Andy now has five-and-a-half step-siblings, and she's determined not to like them or the step-parents. At every opportunity she proclaims the wish to be back with her own mum and dad in the old home; she is sullen and unco-operative, her schoolwork is neglected and she plays truant. But in the end it comes right: she makes a friend of her stepbrother on mother's side, she loves the baby to whom father's new partner gives birth, and she's reconciled to her situation. Well, she'd better be, since it's never going to be unwound. But if you stand back and look at it dispassionately, it seems that this child has had a rotten deal; it isn't surprising she's disturbed. And just as she has acquired step-parents and siblings willy-nilly, so also of course have the step-siblings themselves — they've all got step-parents now, and they've got her. They didn't ask for her any more than she asked for them. The respective parents have done what *they* wanted to do, and the six children have to like it or lump it. Is that fair play between the generations?

In this book Jacqueline Wilson, rightly, is not taking sides; she just tells the story, which is quite a convincing one, and as reader you form your own view of the matter. The late Roald Dahl, in his own idiosyncratic way, took the side of children against adults. I used to say, apropos of the avuncular style often used in the pre-Dahl past when writing for young children, that it made me think of ageing uncles going down on their creaking knees to play with the kids on the carpet and achieving nothing but a loss of dignity. With Mr Dahl you have something different: a kind of cocking a snook at the adult world, as if he were pretending to be a cheeky and very articulate 10-year-old.

I haven't read all Mr Dahl's books for children, but when I heard that my granddaughter was having *Matilda*[25] read to her at school I bought a copy and learned how Matilda was treated as a scab — a scab on the skin, not a blackleg — by her nasty parents, Mr and Mrs Wormwood, and how she punished her father by such devices as replacing his hair-tonic with her mother's platinum-blonde hair dye, extra strong — to say nothing of how she humiliated her dreadful headteacher Miss Trumbull. It's meant to be funny, of course, and I'm sure it gets lots of laughs. I am not disposed to explode with anger at Mr Dahl; I don't suppose any child thinks his stories describe life as it really is; but I can't help feeling that from an adult point of view he was something of a fifth-columnist, though adults didn't seem to notice it.

At the older reading level, I haven't found much evidence that parents are being put back on the pedestal from which they were dislodged thirty years ago. A recent Carnegie Medal winner, Robert Swindells's *Stone Cold*, drives headlong into the issue of young people's homelessness. What the story is actually about is the 17-year-old narrator's experiences on the streets of London, and it's a gripping account, but in the present context I'm concerned rather with the family situation that leads into it. The boy's father ran off with another woman three years ago, but

> that's not why I ended up like this. No. Vincent's to blame for that. Good old Vince. Mum's boyfriend. You should see him. I mean, Mum's no Kylie Minogue — but Vincent. He's about fifty for a start, and he's one of these old dudes that wear cool gear and try to act young and it doesn't work because they've got grey hair and fat bellies and they just make themselves pathetic. And as if that's not enough, Vince likes his ale. I suppose Dad must've been a bit of a bastard in his way, but at least he wasn't a boozer. You should see the state Vincent's in when he and Mum come home from the club ... And the one thing that really bugs me is the way he leers at Mum and comes out with this very suggestive stuff about going to bed and rounding off a decent night.[26]

And so on. The author is not suggesting, of course, that all parents are like that. But certainly the pedestal has collapsed, and fictional family life has moved a long way from the sanitized institution described by May Hill Arbuthnot and Gillian Avery a generation ago. Personally, I don't want parents to be on a pedestal; I'm sure that a more relaxed, more equal relationship than the authoritarian one that still tended to exist in my youth is an improvement, and more likely to result in harmony between the generations. But my main concern here has been to trace how attitudes are reflected in children's fiction rather than to comment on the attitudes themselves.

I'm going to finish on a note of hope for the parental generation. I've just been re-reading *Goggle-Eyes*, published in 1989 by Anne Fine, who is not noted for being an unduly conventional writer. Here the protagonist, Kitty, is the child of a divorced mother, who is rather scatty and active in progressive causes, and has had a number of boyfriends. Now Mum has a new man in her life: Gerald. Gerald is thoroughly conventional and conservative and all the things that modern progressives abhor. Kitty finds him a pain. And yet, as her narrative goes on, it becomes clear that he's shrewd and sensible, has his own sense of humour, and in fact is just what Mum and Kitty need. At the end Kitty finds that, although he hasn't yet come round to the progressive causes, he's 'soothing, amiable and steady — easy to have around. I'm used to him, I suppose. He's part of the furniture. I honestly believe, if he and Mum got married, I wouldn't mind.'[27]

Well, Kitty is telling her story by way of consoling another child who resents the prospect of a stepfather, so you could say she's upholding the new mores of society in which a mother's boyfriends and/or a change of parents are quite to be expected and you have to come to terms with them. It wouldn't have done for Mrs Arbuthnot. What I find interesting and likeable is that although I feel fairly sure the author herself is in sympathy with Mum and the progressive causes, the quality most noticeable at the end of *Goggle-Eyes* is *tolerance*. While people with differing views and of different generations can get on together, all is not lost.

Notes

1 Quoted by A. S. W. Rosenbach in the introduction to *Early American Children's Books*, Southworth Press, Portland, Maine, 1933.
2 *Ibid.*
3 Penelope Mortimer, 'Thoughts concerning children's books', *New Statesman*, 11 November 1966. Reprinted in S. Egoff, G. T. Stubbs and L. S. Ashley (eds), *Only Connect*, 2nd edn, Oxford University Press, Toronto, 1980.
4 John Locke, *Thoughts Concerning Education*, §149–156, in J. L. Axtell (ed.), *Educational Writings of John Locke*, Cambridge University Press, Cambridge 1968 (and many other editions).
5 In Mrs Trimmer's *Guardian of Education* (1802–6), quoted by F. J. Harvey Darton, *Children's Books in England*, 3rd edn, Cambridge University Press, Cambridge, 1982.
6 Gillian Avery, *Nineteenth Century Children*, Collins, London, 1965, p. 206.
7 Mrs Sherwood, *The Fairchild Family*, first published 1818.
8 Catherine Sinclair, *Holiday House* (with an introduction by Barbara Willard), Hamish Hamilton, London, 1972. First published in 1839.
9 Eleanor Estes, *The Moffats* (1959), *The Middle Moffat* (1960), *Rufus M.* (1960), The Bodley Head, London.
10 Eve Garnett, *The Family from One-End Street*, first published by Frederick Muller Ltd, London, 1937.
11 Arthur Ransome, *Swallows and Amazons* and eleven succeeding books, first published by Cape, London, 1930–47.
12 Margery Fisher, *Intent upon Reading: A Critical Appraisal of Modern Fiction for Children*, Brockhampton Press, Leicester, 1961.
13 Barbara Willard, *The Battle of Wednesday Week*, Constable, London, 1963.
14 May Hill Arbuthnot, *Children and Books*, 3rd edn, Scott, Foresman & Co., Chicago, 1964, p. 5.
15 Avery, *op. cit.*, p. 227.
16 John Rowe Townsend, *Gumble's Yard*, Hutchinson, London, 1961.
17 This paragraph and the one before it summarize a fuller account in Chapter

16 of my study of English-language children's literature, *Written for Children*, 6th edn, Bodley Head, London, 1995.

18 Alan Garner, *The Owl Service*, Collins, London, 1967.

19 Alan Garner, *Red Shift*, Collins, London, 1973.

20 Sylvia Sherry, *A Pair of Jesus-Boots*, Cape, London, 1969.

21 Brian Fairfax-Lucy and Philippa Pearce, *The Children of the House*, Longman Young Books, London, 1968; reissued as *The Children of Charlcote*, Gollancz, London, 1989.

22 Jan Mark, *The Twig Thing*, Viking Kestrel, London, 1988.

23 Anne Fine, *Flour Babies*, Hamish Hamilton, London, 1992.

24 Jacqueline Wilson, *The Suitcase Kid*, Doubleday, London, 1992.

25 Roald Dahl, *Matilda*, Cape, London, 1988.

26 Robert Swindells, *Stone Cold*, Hamish Hamilton, London, 1993.

27 Anne Fine, *Goggle-Eyes*, Hamish Hamilton, London, 1989.

CHAPTER 6

Aesop for Children
Power and Morality

David Whitley

It's probably true that all fiction offered to children is meant to 'teach' in some way, but fables have the special feature of highlighting this teaching function by offering explicit moral lessons. Their genesis in a culture of unequal power, however, means that they are also capable of including subtle political nuances. Perhaps for these reasons, they have been used as vehicles for a variety of moral and political views by their editors and presenters, at times losing all their moral challenge, in other versions offering complex representations of morality. In looking with fresh eyes at a genre which, although ever present in children's reading, seems not to have enjoyed much analysis in educational terms, David Whitley suggests that fables offer children a chance to grapple with some big issues. However, while giving young readers a chance to tackle matters of moral decision, justice, authority and the consequences of social acts, fables are well-rooted in everyday experience. The very flexibility of the fable is, he argues, its greatest strength, making the form a powerful vehicle for children to forge their own emergent meanings. However, it's not enough just to recognize the lessons taught by the fables; we have to learn how to use the lessons they teach.

Children need imaginative forms where they can explore the operation of power in the world within which they are growing up. They also need to develop an ethical understanding which will allow them to assess the operation of power in the world and the range of responses available to them. Few genres of literature offered to children bring these two strands together with more force or clarity than the Aesopic fable. And yet, though children continue to read Aesop with pleasure in a variety of forms, the genre has been curiously neglected in educational and literary debates. Writers on children's literature have acknowledged the importance of the fable in historical terms, but fairy-tales and folk tales have received far more sustained attention and analysis. And fairy-tales, in general, are much more widely used in the classroom. By some curious quirk of history the most overtly didactic form of children's narrative would seem to have elicited least interest from educationalists concerned with literature. In reflecting here on the fable in the context of children, power and morality I want to suggest that there is more life in the old dog Aesop than is currently recognized. We may do well not to sideline the form which has, for most of the past two millennia, been considered central to children's pedagogy. First, however, we need to think carefully about the particular qualities of this form.

What are these qualities? Although a number of writers, from Chaucer onwards, have exploited a potential within the Aesopic fable for more extended literary development, in its most familiar form the fable is a short, spare narrative, delivered with emblematic clarity. Its themes are the most basic, primary issues in human experience — death, food, survival, strategies for defence, betrayal and one-upmanship. In the sharp, clear definition which they give to these universal themes, fables voice concerns which are not of any one particular time or place; the lesson, the 'moral wisdom', they embody seems detached from any particular cultural perspective.

So far, so good. But here two major problems begin to emerge for anyone wishing to advocate children's more sustained engagement with fables in the modern world. The first of these relates directly to the issue of power and is evident in the earliest recorded instance of the fable in Western literature. This occurs in the epic *Works and Days* of the Greek poet Hesiod, who may have lived as early as the eighth century BC. The story which Hesiod interpolates into his epic narrative begins: 'And now I will tell a fable for kings even though they are wise.' He proceeds to tell the story of a hawk's relentless demonstration of its power over a helpless nightingale:

> Thus spoke the hawk to the speckled necked nightingale as he seized her in his claws and carried her up among the clouds — and pitifully did she whimper as the crooked claws pierced her through. The hawk then spoke to her masterfully: 'Simple creature, why do you cry aloud? One far mightier than yourself now holds you in his grip, and you will go wherever I take you for all your singing, and I will make a meal of you if I choose, or I will let you go. Foolish is he who would match himself against those who are stronger; he is robbed of victory and suffers pain as well as shame.'[1]

The moral wisdom wrung out in this earliest of written fables would seem to be that the vulnerable should accept that their fate is controlled by forces far more powerful than themselves. This attitude of resignation to the terms of an implacable and often cruel fate (which is ideologically aligned to an extreme form of political quietism) is common in the very early literature of the ancient world. It derives in part from economies in which substantial proportions of the population had slave status and consists in a compelling recognition of powerlessness. But it also connects with a substantial number of stories within the traditional Aesopic corpus — 'The Wolf and the Lamb', 'The Eagle and the Tortoise', 'The Town and Country Mouse', for instance — which can be read as instances of the foolishness of claims for equality and justice, or of the painful consequences awaiting those who attempt to move beyond the horizons within which they are currently circumscribed. It connects also with what is perhaps the central problematic of the fable tradition, where the perspective on power is generally from the bottom end of the hierarchy looking upwards, but where the moral wisdom advocated often meshes with the ideological interests of those at the top.

This begins to look less hopeful as a literature suitable for youngsters whose imaginations need to test the boundaries of power and powerlessness in their own age and context. What value can fables formed within the sinews of what Hegel called the master–slave dialectic have for the modern world? The problem seems to be compounded by the ways in which images of power and powerlessness explored in these stories are linked to an overtly moralizing tradition. The famous fable of 'The Frogs Who Wanted a King' provides one of the most striking examples of this tendency. In the Penguin Classics version this fable is rendered as follows:

> The frogs were tired of having no one to govern them, and sent a deputation to Zeus to ask for a king. He saw how simple they were. So first of all he just dropped a block of wood in the pond. For a moment they were frightened by the splash and dived to the bottom. Then, since the wood stayed quite still, they came to the surface, and in the end they became so contemptuous of it that they jumped up and squatted on it. Thinking it undignified to be ruled by such a thing, they approached Zeus again and asked him to change their king; this one, they said, was too easy-going. Losing patience with them, he sent them a water-snake, which devoured as many of them as it could catch. This fable teaches us that we are better off with an indolent and harmless ruler than with a mischief-making tyrant.[2]

This popular fable has been read in a number of — often highly conflicting — ways during the long history of its retellings.[3] The moral at the end could be seen as an attempt to stabilize these potentially divergent meanings within a single, coherent perspective. Yet both the form (the overtly didactic context for narrative performance) and the content (do we really want to encourage our citizens of the twenty-first century to accept 'indolent and harmless' rulers with patience?) of this version of the moral would seem to sit very uneasily with the attitudes and assumptions underlying good pedagogic practice in the modern world.

Can anything redeem the fable for our own times then, or should we now leave it alone, rendered mute by historical change, strangled by the attitudes inherent in its origins? Herodotus once wisely observed that the way up and the way down are one and the same; in a similar vein, I'd like now to suggest that the way forwards may be, initially, to take a great leap backwards in time. For something rather odd happened to the Aesopic fable back in the eighteenth century and some of the paradoxes associated with the way it is currently perceived seem to me to derive from its evolution during this period.

Prior to the eighteenth century, although the fable had been used as a pedagogic tool, particularly in the teaching of Latin, it was not seen primarily as children's narrative. Indeed, it has been argued that in the seventeenth century its use within the realm of public oratory became strongly politicized; and the range of extended literary versions in the vernacular attests to its status as a serious form of adult entertainment.[4] But when a separate category of children's literature began to take shape in the middle part of the eighteenth century, the terms on which Aesop's fables would be included were crucial and have, to a large extent, informed the position the fables have in the popular imagination to this day. To highlight the most important and symptomatic developments that took place at this time, I want now to look briefly at some of the changes made to one of the most famous early collections of the fables by the novelist Samuel Richardson.

Making Aesop safe for the nursery

Although Jean de la Fontaine had set new standards for the fable as a work of literature in the volumes he produced in France in the late seventeenth century, it was the native tradition which was initially more influential in Britain, and Sir Roger L'Estrange's lavishly illustrated folio edition, first published in 1692, provided the model for many eighteenth-century imitators and successors. Samuel Richardson certainly considered L'Estrange's version sufficiently important to republish it in 1740, editing, changing and expurgating the original text with great care and thoroughness. His purpose, as he announced in his preface, was to 'reduce the work to such a size as should be fit for the *hands* and *pockets* for which it was originally designed'.[5] He would, in other words, reproduce it in a form more suitable for children. But it was not only the size and price of the collection which he thought it necessary to adapt to the needs of 'smaller hands'. Richardson's edition reformed the earlier work to 'give the *exceptionable reflections* a more *general* and *useful* turn'.[6] Richardson toned down L'Estrange's text by altering or removing some of the racier language and editing out some of the more licentious stories. But the *reflections* to which he took particular exception were those which invested the fables with strong political meanings, and these he tried to neutralize or turn around by giving them a much more generalized ethical, and often pious, inflection.

L'Estrange was an ardent royalist, a supporter of the claims of the Stuart dynasty and an advocate of the divine right of kings in its absolutist form. Such a political position was anathema to Richardson and, in his task of making the book safe for the nursery, he needed to expurgate the politics, as well as cleansing the moral tone. L'Estrange, for instance, gives a very different twist to the popular fable of the frogs from that in the Penguin Classics version, by appending the following reflection to the tale:

> By which, the frogs are given to understand the very truth of the matter, as we find it in the world, both in the nature, and reason of the thing, and in policy and religion; which is, that *kings are from God*, and that it is a sin, a folly, and a madness, to struggle with his appointments.[7]

This fable had long been a battleground for interpretation between those who wished to use it to back up positions ranging between democratic and antipopulist extremes. Endowed with L'Estrange's ultraconservative flourish, it certainly would not do for Richardson, who set about trying to neutralize the invective, refashioning it in terms of the most generalized of pious injunctions. Richardson's revised conclusion that 'God certainly knows what is best for us, and a resignation to his providence is the surest way to obtain his blessing',[8] was unlikely to have antagonized any of the political constituencies of his age. The point I want to draw attention to here, though, is that Richardson, in trying to make the fables safe for children, does not simply reverse the political orientation of his acknowledged source. This indeed had been done earlier in a popular collection put together by Samuel Croxall in 1722. This edition was shaped in conscious antithesis to L'Estrange's, offering a context for reading the stories designed to be more congenial to Whigs and libertarians than to Tories.[9] Richardson does not try to assert an alternative political context, however: rather, he tries to take the politics out of it altogether, searching for an ideal language of high moral tone which will win universal assent. Richardson himself does not take this project to its logical extreme; he includes a range of fables which he judges to *compel* 'a Political Turn' wherein, he states, 'we have, in our Reflections ... always given that Preference to the Principles of LIBERTY'.[10] However, as the universalizing moral strand becomes more all-encompassing in the hands of his successors, the fable, reformulated for children, is no longer an adjunct of debate and potential controversy. It is more a benign introduction, later an *aide memoire*, to a set of universally acceptable maxims that constitute the moral certitudes of respectable adulthood. In turning away from more troubled sites of disputed knowledge towards the serene waters of maxims that are distanced from any particular context or apparent special pleading, the fable loses its function in the active making of ideologies and instead becomes itself a kind of reified ideological form.

Thus, in making Aesop 'safe for the nursery', in removing it from the arena of debate and controversy, the form became associated with a version of childhood and education within which story was seen as a pleasing, readily memorizable pathway towards the unexceptionable moral wisdom of adults. But in becoming safe, the fables also became unchallenging for the classroom. Fables acquired the status of proverbs — sanctioned by custom, part of the stock of common culture, but essentially unexciting. They were hardly the first port of call for those seeking to develop qualities of active reflection or critical engagement with the world.

This was never the whole story, of course. The fables themselves were too varied and sharp-edged to fit neatly into a single perspective. Moreover, the figure of Aesop himself, the disfigured slave underdog who used his stories to survive and gain an edge in life, continued to preside over the fables in the West, even though, after the eighteenth century, his mythologized biography was no longer used as the standard preface to all major collections. Still, there continued to be a sense that the fable was a mode in which potentially dangerous or offensive thoughts could be expressed without incurring the direct wrath of those implicated, particularly those in power. Hans Christian Andersen gave a fairly anodyne version of this idea when he suggested:

> Years and years ago, someone thought up a clever way of telling other people the truth without being rude. You made up a good story, often about animals. It might seem funny but it was serious underneath. They called it a fable. The animals did some clever or silly things. But they were really the clever and silly things people do. So you might listen to a story and say to yourself: 'That fable's about me!' But no one *said* it was about you so you didn't need to get angry.[11]

This gives the fable an interesting, if somewhat domesticated, function as a relatively safe channel for social improprieties. But there remained others who could exploit the subversive potential of the form further.

This sketch may perhaps now provide enough of the history of the fable to suggest some of the reasons for its present, somewhat atrophied, status and for the more challenging potential this disguises. I want to pause now to draw a few tentative conclusions before proceeding to look at some more recent reworkings of the form, alongside the ways in which children may appropriate and respond to it. What then does this brief review of the history of Aesop suggest? I would like to propose three main areas of concern.

Aesop's fables have traditionally been combined with a 'moral' application

Some twentieth-century anthologizers of the fables have reacted against this tradition by simply abandoning the moral postscripts to the tales. But, though this may be more congenial to twentieth-century aesthetic taste, it misses the point that these tales essentially examine social conduct and conflict: and that in doing so they inevitably connect with other kinds of discourses — ethical, social, political — which seek to evaluate human conduct in the world. Aristotle claimed that the usefulness of the fable lay in relation to the arts of persuasion, particularly popular oratory, where its advantage lay in providing analogies that could succinctly highlight the significance of events: the advantage of fables 'are comparatively easy to invent', he suggested, 'whereas it is hard to find parallels among actual past events'.[12] Certainly the fable opens out into the ways of the world in a much more direct form than does, say, the fairy-tale. These are stories designed to be used within the world — whether to satirize, to persuade or to expound. The fable is, profoundly, the narrative of praxis.

Writers who have produced collections of the fables have generally sought to influence the way they will be read, to promote particular kinds of interpretation

This practice has been more overt than is the case with most other kinds of narrative. Aesop's mediators have repeatedly sought to exert authorial power in relation to the stories' meanings. When fables came to be written as a distinctive form of children's literature, this power tended to be used to promote the most generalized — and 'safe' — of injunctions as accompaniment to the narratives. But this is by no means the only way the fables have been turned; indeed, the attempt to make fables safe could be construed as symptomatic of a historically quite specific anxiety at a time when a new kind of readership — particularly among children and women — was being created in the eighteenth century.

Fables would seem to offer particular kinds of power to readers who know how to use them

This notion is inscribed in that 'metafable' — the life of Aesop — which was the standard preface to all earlier major collections.[13] Aesop's life shows, again and again, how he uses his ability to tell apt stories at timely moments to gain an authority and influence otherwise inconceivable for a slave. The model of Aesop himself suggests that the interpretation of the fables is not a matter to be settled in the armchair of a study. Rather, interpretation depends upon the context within which the fables are uttered. If you can find the appropriate fable at a critical moment you may be able to alter — quite radically — the view which people take of a situation and their consequent actions. Any reader of a fable is also a potential reteller and Aesop's ability to 'read' situations through fables and hence to influence events from the apparent margins of power would seem to propose a model for all those with access to the fable tradition. The power which this implies is potentially available to all readers of the fable, and this is perhaps also a corollary of the unusually insistent form in which authors have sought to direct their audiences' understanding of these tales. Like some sacred texts, these stories have not been felt to be safe to pass on to readers without an accompanying commentary. May this not imply anxiety as to what readers could do with them if left undirected?

Fables for our time

Armed with a more active and powerful sense of the fable's potential as a storytelling form, we may now be able to look at its use in our own time with fresh eyes. How have contemporary writers responded to its challenge and appeal? Perhaps the first point to make is that, despite being ousted from its status as the primary narrative resource in the classroom, there has been no fall-off in the number of versions published for children. Moreover, the form would seem to cross linguistic and cultural boundaries; Aesop's fables are produced in an extraordinarily wide variety of different countries and have some claim to the title of a world literature. There is plenty of life in the old dog still here, then. But what have more recent writers for children made of both the potential and the problems I have suggested are inherent to the tradition? There is, of course, a great deal of diversity, but I shall try to pick out one or two developments which seem particularly germane to the issues I have been exploring.

I began with the problem of power and powerlessness in the fables: how a significant number of the stories voice the concerns of the apparently powerless but in doing so seem to reinforce the claims of the powerful to be entitled to act without measure or restraint. One solution to the problem of what to do with such stories, which seem to fit uncomfortably with the developing consciousness of young citizens in modern societies aspiring to some form of democracy, is simply to leave them out. The Aesopic corpus is very large and any modern reteller of the fables must interpret the tradition in the first instance through a very active process of selection. An example from the work of Naomi Lewis, however, suggests that there are other ways of dealing with this issue. We do not have to simply leave out of account what is uncomfortably alien, reactionary or 'other'. In retelling the story of the 'Tortoise and the Eagle', she invokes the tradition distinctively by bringing Aesop himself into the frame of the fable:

> One came to Aesop saying, 'Well, master-servant, here is a tale. Now what do you make of it?'
> This was the tale:

> A tortoise with a restless mind longed for a different view of the world. 'I know it only at earth level, a few steps here, a few steps there, and *that* for me is a day's journey.' He begged the eagle to teach him how to fly.
> 'A foolish notion,' said the bird. 'Quite preposterous. You are not made for flight.'
> 'Then carry me in your claws, so that I can see the world from above, even if only this once.'
> The eagle picked up the tortoise then, at a great height, let him drop, to perish on the rocks below.

> Aesop's reply:
> I could read this several ways,
> Some of blame and some of praise.
> No single answer fits the case.
> The lowly born should know their place?
> You cannot wish beyond your range?
> It's all ordained; things cannot change?
> Or — greatly wishing is no vice?
> But every wish demands its price?
> No vision can be wholly lost?
> The dream fulfilled is worth the cost?[14]

Here the interpretive frame is exploited in a very thorough way as a provocation to thought. The initial set of ideas offered to ground a reading of the fable are rooted in an image of social stability which came to be supplanted by more democratic ideals. The ideas which follow — couched in the language of vision, desire and the imagination — owe much to the ethos of Romanticism. This careful balancing of pre-democratic and post-romantic ideas then shapes, but refuses to close off, the reflective space within which the reader is invited to consider the fable. The interpretation, in other words, does not adjudicate between rival claims of the inner world (imagination/wishes/dreams) and the outer world (stability/social order). And if wisdom here is rendered equivocal, if the unacknowledged force of the reply is directed towards the moral relativism of the modern world, then this would seem to reinforce the power of the reader in seeking resolution of the issues embedded in the story, rather than to suggest there are no sides to be taken here.

Even more radical ways of working with the tradition are suggested by the work of Mitsumasa Anno. In *Anno's Aesop*[15] the fictional mediator who interprets the tales for the reader is not Aesop but a figure derived from the beast subjects of the tales themselves — a talking fox. Anno brilliantly exploits the paradoxes inherent in the fables' humble origins by making his fox interpreter acute, imaginative and non-literate. Versions of the original Aesop's fables are now framed in the most elaborate manner, not only through visual illustrations which often operate at several levels, but also through the fox's commentary. The fox purports to be reading the original fable to his son but in fact makes up a series of stories only obliquely related to the themes of the original. Voice in these fables is thus rendered polyphonic and the intertextual weaving and slippage is often extremely complex, even though the stories themselves remain clear in outline. Perhaps the most radical development here is the degree to which the reader's interpretive power in relation to the story is supported — indeed enhanced — through the example of the fox. The fox's wild sallies into the fable form are inspired by the fool's licence: interpretation through the more sober mode of moral exposition remains a possibility (the addendums to the original fables are largely retained) but the dominant mode of engagement with the tales is through the opportunities they offer for reinvention, for a carnivalesque rechannelling of themes.

In thus reappropriating the form within the framework of an oral, pre-literate culture, Anno makes pictures as central as text for establishing the range of meanings generated by the fables. The fox, in this book, would seem to be using Anno's illustrations as cues in constructing his own versions of the fables, and the illustrations themselves are richly layered in terms of possible implication. It may well be the case that after the interpretive framework for the fables was rendered more generalized and safe for children in the eighteenth century, the work of making available diverse and challenging readings became more the burden of the illustrators. If this is so then Anno certainly exploits this potential more fully than many. In the fable of 'The Wolf and the Crane', for instance, the Aesopic version is placed alongside a coloured illustration of an elongated wolf with hugely extended jaws, into whose opening a crane is seen boldly, if injudiciously, inserting its head and beak. The story tells how the crane helps the wolf by extracting a bone which had stuck in the wolf's throat. When she claims some reward for her action, the crane is told roundly that she should think herself lucky the wolf refrained from closing his jaws and eating her. The moral reflection states uncompromisingly that the 'weak cannot demand justice from the strong'. Yet this grim political realism is counterpointed by a larger image, which spreads across both pages connecting the Aesopic fable with the fox's version. Here the form of the elongated wolf and intrepid crane is repeated; but the wolf is transformed into an alligator and the crane to an alligator bird, which feeds safely in the alligator's mouth because it offers the reciprocal

These birds are called alligator birds. They eat what gets stuck between the alligator's teeth. This keeps the teeth clean and at the same time the birds get enough to eat. It's a very good arrangement for all of them. But one day along came a wily crane who was planning to play a mean trick on the wolf. He showed the wolf what good friends the alligator and the alligator birds were. Then he said, "My dear friend, I'm a dentist. Let me clean your teeth the way those alligator birds are cleaning

'The Wolf and the Crane', from *Anno's Aesop*, © Mitsumasa Anno. Reproduced with permission.

The Wolf and the Crane

A wolf once got a bone stuck in his throat. So he went to a crane and begged her to put her long bill down his throat and pull it out. "I'll reward you well," he promised. The crane did as she was asked, and got the bone out quite easily. The wolf thanked her warmly and was just turning away when she cried, "What about that reward of mine?" "Well, what about it?" snapped the wolf, baring his teeth as he spoke. "You can go around boasting that you once put your head into a wolf's mouth and didn't get it bitten off. What more do you want?" So the wolf got what he wanted and the crane was cheated of her reward.

The weak cannot demand justice from the strong.

the alligator's teeth." You see, the crane had always had a grudge against the wolf. Now the crane planned to fool the wolf into thinking he was a nice, helpful friend. Then, when the wolf opened his mouth, the wicked crane was going to poke the soft part of his throat with his sharp beak. *Ouch!* Well, the wolf pretended to believe the crane. But do you think he was fooled? Not at all. He was just waiting for his dinner to come right into his mouth by itself!

benefit of a kind of natural toothbrush. The image of a natural order constituted by the exploitative power of violence is replaced — though not cancelled out — by an image of weak and strong creatures serving each other's needs interdependently. Ecology replaces hierarchy as the dominant interpretive mode for the illustrations as the images grow larger, even though the force of the original fable remains strong. The images in this fable compete for space: the dominant ideas about social organization and power which inform the Aesopic version are made to relate to opposing possibilities implied in the image of the alligator. What at first sight appears to be a linkage established through parallelism — two aggressive predators each stretched out along the page in elongated form — turns out on closer examination to be a juxtaposition of opposing ideologies. The disparity between form — apparently similar — and underlying meaning — strikingly opposed — is a particularly subtle device which invites the reader to reflect on the implications of the story at many levels. But it is also wholly in keeping with the diversity of the fable tradition, for the Aesopic corpus contains a good many stories which assert the value of animals' dependence on one another, even though there are rather more fables seeming to enforce recognition of the inevitable dominance of the powerful. In a sense, Anno has simply brought these two aspects of the tradition together.

Children and the power of retelling

Anno's Aesop promotes a particularly active engagement by the reader in discerning the fullest possible context within which these tales may signify. But evidence that children can still find this form vivid and meaningful within their own terms must derive from the use they make of it themselves. I would like to conclude with an example of a child's writing, undertaken in the classroom and inspired loosely (in the best tradition of Anno's fox!) by a version of the fable of the 'Town Mouse and the Country Mouse' written in the fifteenth century by the Scottish poet Robert Henryson. Here then is the 9-year-old girl's tale:

The Two Mice
Once upon a time there were two golden brown mice called Sally and Cally. They were sisters but Cally lived with their Dad. Sally lived with their Mum. Their Mum lived miles away from Dad Mouse. Cally has only seen her sister once in her life time, but she still writes letters, but Sally never writes back. Once she wrote back a run away plan. This is what she wrote: [a map giving details of a meeting point for the escape is inserted into the narrative at this point]. Something terrible went wrong, they did get there, they did meet but a cat came and took Cally. Even if Cally's only seen her sister once, she is my twin sister, so Cally kicked

and scratched until the cat bled. The cat let go. Cally started running home and shouted out 'I'll do you a favour one day.'

This story was composed by an unconfident writer, who invested a great deal of time and care in putting her brief narrative together. The compactness of her story — so characteristic of the fable form — is extremely effective and would repay considerable scrutiny and formal analysis. But the point I wish to draw attention to here is the apparent ease with which a fifteenth-century narrative about mice who are sisters has been transformed into a fable for our own time. What is so impressive is not so much the reconsidered context, although the focus on families which have split up is both a striking and relevant contemporary theme, which may perhaps have had personal meaning for the child concerned. But it is the way this theme has been worked with which is even more impressive. It is as though the qualities and form of the traditional fable have enabled this child to find a voice which is straight, direct and strong on a topic which might easily have become choked by sentiment and the desire to make everything come out right. The fable's essential toughness enables the longing for family connection to be accepted with full force without being sentimentalized. The twin sister mice are differentiated: one is a verbalizer whose faith and emotional need are registered indirectly through the image of the letters she keeps writing to her sister without ever receiving a reply; the other expresses herself through action, issuing the potentially dangerous invitation to meet and proving the strength of her blood connection through the fury of her violent intervention with the cat. But once the connection has been so powerfully demonstrated, the reality of lives which must be lived apart continues to be asserted. The mice separate with an open acknowledgement of interdependence and debt: 'I'll do you a favour one day.'

This child's story demonstrates the supreme adaptability of the fable. The force and directness with which it can be made to apply to a range of situations as these come to be culturally defined is, arguably, the greatest strength of the form. Aristotle was right in perceiving the fable to be a form deriving from the power of analogy in persuasive thought, centrally caught up in the ways in which we speak about the world and judge actions within it. The tradition of telling fables, at its best, is connected to the contest for ideas as well as the most fundamental aspects of human feeling and motivational drives. Through the figures of animals and the associations they bring with them, big issues such as the relative claims of democracy and hierarchical structure can be tested against each other; yet the fable keeps its feet firmly on the ground, working within a framework of basic human instincts and desires. The form in which fables are communicated has always been important and we have been fortunate, in recent years, to be served by an increasing range of imaginative adaptations that have understood in depth the best qualities inherent in this tradition. The point is now not only to read but also to learn, once again, how to use them.

Acknowledgement

Thanks are due to children from the Spinney School, Cambridge, and their teacher Hannah Curtis.

Notes

1 Lloyd Daly, *Aesop without Morals*, Thomas Yoseloff, London, 1961, pp. 12–13.
2 S. A. Handford (translator), *Fables of Aesop*, Penguin Classics, Harmondsworth, 1964, p. 44.
3 For a full discussion of the range of political positions this fable has been used to support, see Annabel Patterson, *Fables of Power*, Duke University Press, London, 1991.
4 *Ibid.*, especially pp. 81–109.
5 Katherine Hornbeak, 'Richardson's Aesop', *Smith College Studies in Modern Languages* (1937–8), **19**, p. 33.
6 *Ibid.*
7 *Ibid.*, p. 38.
8 *Ibid.*
9 'There is no question but that Croxall's *Fables of Aesop and Others ... With an Application to each Fable* was designed not only to compete with L'Estrange, but to discredit him as one who had distorted his classical originals, and imposed upon them a political interpretation that was not only offensive to Whigs and libertarians, but incompatible with the fable's origins.' Patterson, *op. cit.*, p. 143.
10 Samuel Richardson, *Aesop's Fables*, S. Richardson, London, 1751, p. xi.
11 Hans Christian Andersen, 'What's a Fable', quoted in Mark Cohen (ed.), *The Puffin Book of Fabulous Fables*, Penguin, London, 1989, p. 9.
12 Aristotle, *Rhetorica*, II, 20. Quoted from W. D. Ross (ed.), *The Works of Aristotle Translated into English*, vol. XI, Oxford University Press, Oxford, 1946, p. 1394.
13 For a full discussion of the functions of the 'metafable' of Aesop's life see Patterson, *op. cit.*, pp. 13–43.
14 Naomi Lewis, *Cry Wolf and Other Aesop Fables*, Methuen, London, 1988.
15 Mitsumasa Anno, *Anno's Aesop*, Reinhardt Books, London, 1990.

CHAPTER 7

'Every Child May Joy to Hear'
Poetry for Children from John Bunyan to Michael Rosen

Morag Styles

In this journey through the history of poetry written for children, Morag Styles takes time not just to point out some of the well-known and lovingly remembered 'landmark' poets from the past but to pause occasionally to pick out new features in the landscape. The 'small revolution' represented by Ann and Jane Taylor as they bend their poetry towards what children may enjoy — as well as what may do them good — takes the eye towards other poets like Christina Rossetti who have often been neglected in anthologies and collections. At the same time, Morag Styles reminds us of just why Robert Louis Stevenson is still so greatly loved and remembered as a poet who talks directly to children (and to the children within the adults we now are) and of de la Mare's appeal to 'the young of all ages'. Another reminder, however, is of the toughness and passion of many messages carried in favourites old and new. In coming towards the present and the end of the journey, pointing to the current popularity of poetry which meets young readers on their own ground, Morag Styles offers us refreshment in her confidence about the healthy climate for children's poetry now.

In this chapter I want to take the reader on a journey into the past, picking out what I think are some of the most significant landmarks in poetry for children from the seventeenth century to the present day. The journey is an idiosyncratic one, and, to make it manageable, I am going to avoid lingering too long on well-known poets, while being forced to neglect others. After the sifting process, some key genres, some distinctive voices and some previously overlooked poets demand attention. I hope the reader will find the route an interesting one and that I have provided enough signposts to show the way through the different trends and developments which make up this broad brush-stroke history of poetry for children.[1]

A garden of verses?

It is possible to get a taste of how poetry for children has changed over the centuries by considering the titles of some of the better-known collections. *Country Rhimes for Children* by John Bunyan (1686) is my starter text.[2] First of all, it locates juvenile poetry in the natural world ('country rhimes'), which poets have continued to do until the present day, though less obviously so since the 1970s. A quick glance at some further titles should convince the reader of this point:

> *The Butterfly's Ball and the Grasshopper's Feast*, 1807
> *Sketches from Natural History*, 1834
> *The Children's Garland*, 1862
> *Marigold Garden*, 1887
> *Peacock Pie*, 1913
> *The Cherry Tree*, 1959
> *Of Caterpillars, Cats and Cattle*, 1987

From Bunyan on, rural themes have always been a popular subject for poetry. I cannot recall an anthology for children before the 1970s (pure humour apart) that does not include reference to nature. It remains a popular theme and one that most poets deal with at least some of the time. It is not in the least surprising that the natural world should be well represented in poetry for children. After all, it is possibly the most frequently used topic in adult poetry and the one which is often considered suitable for children. All of us are strongly affected by the time of year, time of day and the state of the weather, and long, sooner or later, to get out in the countryside or glimpse the sea. And poetry, especially since the Romantic movement, has charted this affinity between human beings and nature. The change in the latter part of the twentieth century is that many poets for the young are interested in the daily lives of ordinary children who mostly live in cities. So nature poetry is now becoming 'green'. Concerns about the environment, disappearing species, pollution and the loss of rural habitats are well reflected in contemporary poetry for children.

Little poems for little people

Bunyan wrote his 'country rhimes' *for children*. For 300 years it was commonplace to emphasize the youth of poetry's readership, as the following titles demonstrate:

> *A Collection of Pretty Poems: 'For the Amusement of Children Three Feet High'*, 1770
> *Poems on Various Subjects for the Amusement of Youth*, Kilner, 1785

Original Poems for Infant Minds, Taylor, 1804
Little Poems for Little People, Claude, 1847
Songs of Childhood, de la Mare, 1902
When We Were Very Young, Milne, 1923

The stress on the smallness of children and how young they are tends to put the adult writer in a superior position, looking down, however benevolently, on little people who need protecting and guiding. This was even more pronounced in poetry whose main intention was didactic.

A Looking-Glass for Children, Cheare, 1672
Divine Songs 'Attempted in Easy Language for the Use of Children', Watts, 1715
Hymns in Prose for Children, Barbauld, 1781
Hymns for the Nursery, Taylor, 1806
Pretty Lessons in Verse for All Good Children, Coleridge, 1834
Hymns for Little Children, Alexander, 1848

The daughter of one of the most famous Romantic poets is still writing 'lessons' (though pretty ones) for 'good' children in 1834. Indeed, the desire to improve, educate and make the young devout is perhaps the strongest current in children's literature until at least the middle of the nineteenth century.

But the most didactic, severe or religious poets realized they had to entertain and amuse children, if they were to succeed in getting their message across. In his preface to *Country Rhimes for Children*, John Bunyan makes it clear he knows that if children are to imbibe the medicine, their palates must be sweetened first.

> Wherefore good Reader that I save them may
> I now with them the very Dottrill play
> And since at gravity they make a Tush
> My very Beard I hide behind the Bush
> And like a fool stand fing'ring of their toys
> And all to show them they are girls and boys.[3]

Mentioning toys was not at all unusual, because another thread that links 300 years of poetry for children is that of the pretty, playful, song-like and sometimes exotic, as the following titles suggest:

Mother Goose's Melody, Anon, 1760
The Pied Piper of Hamelin, Browning, 1842
A Pomander of Verse, Nesbit, 1895
The Merry-Go-Round, Reeves, 1955
The Children's Bells, Farjeon, 1957
This Way Delight, Read, 1957

But entertainment and music was not enough: poetry for children required metaphors which stressed richness and lasting value, as in *The Children's Harp* (1850), or *The Golden Staircase* (1910), or Palgrave's *The Golden Treasury* (1931). There have been quite a few 'treasuries' of poetry for children since then.

Streets and sidewalks

Turning to recent poetry is almost shocking after the stress on decorum, diminutive and delights of an earlier period. Any list of titles after 1974 shows the gap that has emerged from the earlier period.

> *Wouldn't You Like to Know?* 1977
> *Rabbiting On*, 1978
> *Revolting Rhymes*, 1982
> *Where the Sidewalk Ends*, 1982
> *I Din Do Nuttin*, 1983
> *I Like That Stuff*, 1984
> *The New Kid on the Block*, 1986
> *Salford Road*, 1986
> *There's an Awful Lot of Weirdos in This Neighbourhood*, 1988

The differences are plain to see. There was no mention of youth except for a 'new kid on the block' with connotations of streetwise, 'tough guy' kids. There was certainly no religion or morality. Nothing rural was alluded to; in fact, the location has moved to the 'block', 'sidewalk' or 'road'. Humour was in, especially the vulgar, grotesque and ugly; anything 'pretty' was out. The language became cheeky with regular use of what some critics describe as slang. Perhaps the new poetry indicated a shift in power — it was sometimes subversive, and certainly child-friendly, and adult authority was often questioned. Might it not have been time by the second half of the twentieth century for poets to start taking some account of children growing up in cities? And black children and working-class children too? Some critics seemed to feel that the nursery door had been flung wide open and the furniture thrown out in the street. Before considering that proposition, a little meander is necessary to investigate how we got to the street from the garden.

The paths of virtue

Until the fun of Lear and Carroll in the middle of the nineteenth century, poetry for children was largely didactic. (There are some significant exceptions to this rule which I will identify as I go on.)

Here's the misnamed Abraham Cheare, a good Puritan and true to his period:

> My pretty child, remember well,
> You must your ways amend;
> For wicked children go to hell,
> That way their courses tend.[4]

Cheare, like Bunyan, had a serious purpose in writing for the young and also spent time in prison for his beliefs, but his poetry for children is unrelievedly punitive. It is not hard to imagine Abraham's wagging finger and his threat of 'hell-fire and damnation' if young readers did not heed his warnings. There is absolutely no space left for readers to bring their own experience to bear and make their own minds up, and certainly none whatsoever in which to play. Nathanial Cotton, though writing nearly a hundred years later, is as bad.

> That toys our earliest thoughts engage,
> And different toys maturer age.
> That grief at every stage appears
> But different griefs at different years.
> That vanity is seen, in part,
> Inscribed on every human heart.[5]

Although Cotton is regarded as one of the few good poets for children of the eighteenth century, there is little here to please the young. A better poet and a kinder one straddled the two centuries: Isaac Watts wrote his *Divine Songs: Attempted in Easy Language for the Use of Children* in 1715. He was a humane, Nonconformist minister who also worked as a tutor for children and composed some of the best hymns ever written. 'Jesus shall reign where'er the sun' is one of the many still popular today. Watts's poetry is described by a later editor as 'an early and outstanding attempt to write verse for children which would *give them pleasure* but at the same time point and urge to the paths of virtue'.[6] Watts showed his understanding of children and poetry in his preface:

> what is learnt in verse is longer retained in memory and sooner recollected ... There is something so *amusing and entertaining* in rhymes and metre, that will incline children to make this part of their business a *diversion.*[7] [my emphasis]

Watts's verse was extremely popular in his own lifetime and continued to do well until the beginning of this century. He was gloriously parodied by Carroll in his Alice books more than a hundred years later, but his ear for rhyme and rhythm and his gentleness with his young audience deserves our admiration. His best-known 'song' includes the following verses:

> How doth the little busy bee
> Improve each shining hour,
> And gather honey all the day
> From every opening flower!
>
> In works of labour or of skill
> I would be busy too;
> For Satan finds some mischief still
> For idle hands to do.[8]

With Carroll's witty pen this became:

> How doth the little crocodile
> Improve his shining tail,
> And pour the waters of the Nile
> On every golden scale.
>
> How cheerfully he seems to grin,
> How neatly spreads his claws,
> And welcomes little fishes in
> With gently smiling jaws.[9]

Another eighteenth-century poet who wrote for children while languishing in prison for debt was Christopher Smart, who wrote his *Hymns for the Amusement of Children* in 1772.

> *Hymn for Saturday*
>
> Now's the time for mirth and play,
> Saturday's an holiday;
> Praise to heaven increasing yield,
> I've found a lark's nest in the field.
>
> A lark's nest, then your playmate begs
> You'd spare yourself and speckled eggs,
> Soon she shall ascend and sing
> Your praises to the eternal king.[10]

Devout, yes, but it's also a celebration of religion, childhood and nature, and Smart has a sense of what children might enjoy. Anna Barbauld was more severe: 'But it may well be doubted, whether poetry *ought* to be lowered to the capacities of children, or whether they should not rather be kept from reading verse'; yet she wrote *Hymns in Prose for Children* (1781), which is full of poetic prose! 'The golden orb of the sun is sunk behind the hills, the colours fade away from the western sky, and the shades of evening fall fast around me.'[11] There is no space in which to discuss the devout verse of Charles Wesley or Cecil Frances Alexander, who wrote 'Gentle Jesus', 'There Is a Green Hill', 'Once in Royal David's City' and other well-known hymns.

Opening up the nursery

At the beginning of the nineteenth century two sisters began a small revolution in poetry for children. Ann and Jane Taylor's first collection, *Original Poems for Infant Minds* (1804), broke the mould. Harvey Darton comments: 'They were original as no previous poems for the young had been, in that you can see the authors, as it were, talking lovingly and naturally to real flesh and blood middle class children whom they knew.'[12] Their scope was fairly wide, encompassing the cradle song, moral tales in verse, nature poems and family life. The best-known poem from this collection is Jane Taylor's 'The Star'. Before the reader dismisses it as lightweight and sentimental verse, try reading it as if it had never been encountered before.

> Twinkle, twinkle, little star,
> How I wonder what you are!
> Up above the world so high
> Like a diamond in the sky.
>
> When the blazing sun is gone,
> When he nothing shines upon,
> Then you show your little light,
> Twinkle, twinkle, all the night.
>
> As your bright and tiny spark,
> Lights the traveller in the dark –
> Though I know not what you are,
> Twinkle, twinkle, little star.[13]

The poem looks at the world with the wondering eyes of a child. The language is simple, but the images are memorable: a diamond in the sky, a tiny spark lighting the traveller's way, a faint twinkle in the sky when the sun has gone down. There were other poets trying in quiet ways to soften the harsh lessons for children which dominated their literature in the first decade of the nineteenth century. Roscoe's *The Butterfly's Ball and the Grasshopper's Feast* (1807) set off a myriad of imitations of fantastic, narrative poems about various animals and insects. The authors often tried to inject a bit of realistic natural history, including the author of the best of the sequels, Catherine Ann Dorset. *The Peacock at Home* is at least as good as Roscoe's original.

> Description must fail, and the pen is unable
> To recount all the lux'ries that covered the table.
> Each delicate viand that taste could denote,
> Wasps a la sauce piquante, and flies en compote;
> Worms and frogs en friture for the web-footed fowl,
> And a barbecued mouse was prepared for the owl;
> Nuts, grain, fruit, and fish, to regale every palate,
> And grounsel and chickweed served up in a sallad.[14]

Romantic visions

Of course, this kinder poetry did not come out of the blue. Its roots are in the Romantic movement. Attitudes towards childhood and nature were fundamentally challenged by the Romantics and were enormously influential in shaping writing for and about children. We cannot underestimate the enormous shift of ideology that Romantic poets were expressing. The most famous statement about childhood is by William Wordsworth in the poem entitled 'Intimations of Immortality' from *Recollections of Early Childhood*. Nothing would ever be the same again, though literature for children took some time to be convinced.

> There was a time when meadow, grove, and stream,
> The earth, and every common sight,
>   To me did seem
>   Apparelled in celestial light,
> The glory and the freshness of a dream.
> It is not now as it hath been of yore; –
>   Turn wheresoe'er I may,
>   By night and day,
> The things which I have seen I now can see no more
>
>   · · ·   · · ·   · · ·   · · ·   · · ·   · · ·
>
> But trailing clouds of glory do we come
>   From God, who is our home:
> Heaven lies about us in our infancy!
> Shades of the prison-house begin to close
>   Upon the growing Boy...

These quotations from the poem sing the same song: the equating of childhood with wisdom and joy; the loss of a pure affinity with nature on reaching adulthood; childhood innocence as a state of grace. Wordsworth, Coleridge, Keats, Shelley and Byron are the famous names of the Romantic movement. There were others, of course, whose influence is often neglected or ignored — Charlotte Smith who wrote *Elegiac Sonnets*, which now looks like early Romantic poetry, ten years before *Lyrical Ballads* (1795) and Robert Burns, writing 'Romantic' songs and poems in the 1780s and 1790s, to name but two. Perhaps the fact that Burns was a working-class Scot and Smith a woman has something to do with their marginalization as heirs of the Romantic movement? Scholars usually mention another famous precursor, William Blake, whose *Songs of Innocence* (1789) raised children's poetry to a new dimension. Harvey Darton writes: 'a great imaginative writer had ... broken into the narrow library that others were toiling so laboriously to fill for children ... they never dreamt of knocking at the gate of heaven or playing among the tangled stars.'[15] The first poem in *Songs of Innocence* ended with these lines:

> 'Piper, sit thee down and write
> In a book that all may read.'
> So he vanish'd from my sight,
> And I pluck'd a hollow reed,
> And I made a rural pen,
> And I stain'd the water clear,
> And I wrote my happy songs
> Every child may joy to hear.[16]

Here was a poet interested in writing a 'book that *all* may read' and which '*every child* may joy to hear'. Blake was an original, out on his own, a visionary genius, a radical, a man of passion and compassion. *Songs of Innocence* challenges the prevailing notions of his day. Blake is a great landmark in poetry for children, but as his contribution is assessed in countless other texts I will not dwell on it in this chapter, except to mention that his poetry was not published in a conventional edition until the middle of the nineteenth century. Once that happened, he quickly got incorporated into edited anthologies of poetry for children and continues to prove popular today.

'There was an old man with a beard'

In the middle of the nineteenth century a British poet, Robert Browning, and two Americans, Henry Wadsworth Longfellow and Clement Clark

Moore, published long, narrative poems which have been on the children's list ever since: *The Pied Piper of Hamelin* (1842), *The Song of Hiawatha* (1855) and *The Night before Christmas* (1844), respectively. But it was two brilliant humorists who changed the face of poetry for children in the Victorian period: Edward Lear and Lewis Carroll (Charles Dodgson). As the nineteenth century also ushered in Christina Rossetti and Robert Louis Stevenson, it can be seen that it was a momentous period for children's poetry, though thinly populated in comparison with what was going to come.

'Between 1865 and 1875 the entire course of juvenile poetry was altered by two bachelor writers who had little in common except an elfin lightsomeness and a love of other people's children,' writes John Mackay Shaw in his massive compilation, *Childhood in Poetry*.[17] The actual year when Edward Lear published *A Book of Nonsense* was 1846; the other bachelor was, of course, Lewis Carroll. Before them was another great humorist, Thomas Hood, but space does not permit me to discuss his work here.

Lear was first and foremost an artist who struggled all his life to earn a precarious living as a professional painter specializing in landscapes and birds. The nonsense verse came about as a refuge from the trials and irritations of his life — epilepsy, lack of funds, an eccentric personality and regular bouts of severe depression. When he was well, there was no one livelier than Lear, but, like many of those writing after him who chose to express themselves primarily in nonsense, Lear felt somewhat alienated from society. The urge to comment sardonically on the conventional world and escape from its restrictions is evident in the melancholy, though greatly amusing, verse:

> My life is a bore in this nasty pond
> And I long to go out in the world beyond![18]

Friendship with children and writing for them gave him a welcome respite from his problems.

Lear made the limerick form his own and brought nonsense verse to a head, exploring its possibilities with an inventiveness and playfulness which was quite stunning, equalled only by Lewis Carroll. Lear was also a talented musician and this ear for musical language is one of the reasons why the verse is so good. He drew gloriously quirky pictures to accompany many of his poems. *Nonsense Songs* was published in 1871, the same year as the brilliant 'Jabberwocky' and 'The Walrus and the Carpenter' appeared in *Alice through the Looking Glass*, which Harvey Darton described as 'the spiritual volcano ... the first real liberty of thought in children's books'.[19] Carroll was also an accomplished parodist:

he plays memorably with Jane Taylor's 'Twinkle, twinkle, little star':

> Twinkle, twinkle, little bat!
> How I wonder what you're at![20]

In the twentieth century, only Mervyn Peake and Shel Silverstein have come close to these two masters of nonsense. Interestingly, both were also artists and illustrated their own work. In 1896, Hilaire Belloc's first book of cautionary verse, *The Bad Child's Book of Beasts*, sold out of its first print-run in four days. By the last decade of the nineteenth century it had become possible to make fun of the moralists who dominated children's literature for so long. The fact that *The Bad Child's Book of Beasts* was so instantly popular says something about the capacity of children to recognize a good thing when they see it, and Belloc continues to sell well today. Fifty years before that, Heinrich Hoffman had produced *Struwwelpeter* (1845) in much the same vein, although the macabre illustrations which accompanied this darker text terrify some younger and older readers, including this writer!

Love me, my baby

In 1872 an outstanding writer entered the field of poetry for children when Christina Rossetti published *Sing-Song*. It came out to rave reviews, such as that in *The Athenaeum Magazine*, which described it as 'some of the saddest as well as the sweetest verses of our time'.[21] Rossetti is one of the few women poets of the nineteenth century to make it into the children's canon. (It is a great regret to me that I have to ignore many talented women poets whose names deserve attention in this chapter.) Jane and Ann Taylor require a further mention, as they are likely to have influenced Rossetti. Their gentle poems of motherly love in *Original Poems for Infant Minds* seem direct precursors of *Sing-Song*. Before the Taylors' seminal collection, most poetry for children was uninterested in exploring loving relationships between mothers and children. Now affection between mother and baby was openly and tenderly expressed in poetry written specifically for children, often mirroring the inconsequential, tender, rhythmic talk that adults often use with babies.

The Baby's Dance

Dance, little baby, dance up high,
Never mind baby, mother is by;
Crow and caper, caper and crow,

> There little baby, there you go:
> Up to the ceiling, down to the ground,
> Backwards and forwards, round and round.
> Then dance, little baby, and mother shall sing,
> With the merry gay coral, ding, ding, a-ling, ding.[22]

In Rossetti's poems her eyes are always on the baby in the mother's arms, looking up into her eyes, as she murmurs sweet nothings.

> Love me, — I love you,
> Love me, my baby;
> Sing it high, sing it low,
> Sing it as it may be.
> Mother's arms under you,
> Her eyes above you
> Sing it high, sing it low,
> Love me, — I love you.[23]

The sheer musicality of her nursery rhyme book, the quality of the writing, the range and variety, the baby/mother-centred nature of the poems and the fact that the poems have lasted and are still enjoyed by many children makes it outrageous that *Sing-Song* is not easily available to buy today. Jane and Ann Taylor and Christina Rossetti reflect their age in placing women with children in the nursery. But they also tried to find ways of expressing emotional significance and fulfilment for them at a time when these were limited, and that deserves our admiration, I think.

A Child's Garden of Verses

Now we reach 1885 and Stevenson's great collection, *A Child's Garden of Verses*. I believe Stevenson was doing something that no other poet achieved before him, and that few poets have achieved since; he captured, as honestly as it is possible for an adult to do, what it feels like to be a child.

> And does it not seem hard to you,
> When all the sky is clear and blue,
> And I should like so much to play,
> To have to go to bed by day?[24]

A *Child's Garden of Verses* is an almost flawless book: of the sixty-four poems in it, there is hardly a weak one and many are outstanding. It changed for ever the possibilities of how children could be written for and about in poetry. W. H. Garrod, Professor of Poetry at Oxford University, took the same view: 'This genre Stevenson created.'[25] Harvey Darton agreed with Garrod:

> But before Stevenson, save for a chance line or two, hardly a verse had been written as a child, given word-skill, might have written it ... the substance is in the fabric of a child's mind — the child who was always in Stevenson.[26]

Stevenson admitted to Edmund Gosse in March 1885: 'there is something nice in the little ragged regiment ... a kind of childish treble note that sounds in my ear freshly; not song, if you will, but *a child's voice*'.[27] Stevenson was an only child and a sickly one. He did, however, have a nurse, the famous Cummy, to whom *A Child's Garden of Verses* is dedicated, and who looked after him devotedly and gave him a taste for fantastic stories. She was also a religious bigot who frightened the impressionable child half to death with tales of hellfire and damnation. The dual themes of sickness and isolation and night-time fears strongly pervade the poetry, and we know from the letters and conversations of the adult Stevenson that Cummy was clearly both a comfort to the invalid and a source of religious terror and guilt. Something of this dread is captured in the second section of 'North-West Passage'.

> All round the house is the jet-black night:
> It stares through the window-pane;
> It crawls in the corners, hiding from the light,
> And it moves with the moving flame.
>
> Now my little heart goes a-beating like a drum,
> With the breath of a Bogie in my hair;
> And all round the candle the crooked shadows come
> And go marching along the stair.
>
> The shadows of the balusters, the shadow of the lamp,
> The shadow of the child that goes to bed –
> All the wicked shadows coming, tramp, tramp, tramp,
> With the black night overhead.

However, the most powerful impression that comes out of *A Child's Garden of Verses* is the sense of a child's absorption in the world of play and how play is intimately bound up with the imagination. 'Child's Play', an essay by Stevenson, shows him to be an acute observer of children's play.

While we grown people can tell ourselves a story ... a child ... works all with lay figures and stage properties. When his story comes to the fighting, he must rise, get something by way of a sword and have a set-to with a piece of furniture, until he is out of breath. When he comes to ride with the king's pardon, he must bestride a chair ... need for overt action and lay figures. ... He is at the experimental stage; he is not sure how one would feel in certain circumstances; to make sure, he must come as near trying it as his means permit ... play is all.[28]

This is one of the finest accounts of children's compulsion for play, which is one key to the collection.

> *A Good Play*
>
> We built a ship upon the stairs
> All made of the back-bedroom chairs,
> And filled it full of sofa pillows
> To go a-sailing on the billows.
>
> We took a saw and several nails,
> And water in the nursery pails;
> And Tom said, 'Let us also take
> An apple and a slice of cake;' –
> Which was enough for Tom and me
> To go a-sailing on, till tea.
>
> We sailed along for days and days,
> And had the very best of plays;
> But Tom fell out and hurt his knee,
> So there was no one left but me.

This is so simple and so true to life. There is no extraneous detail; it is simply told, and therein lies its charm and authenticity. This is a near-perfect account of how children recognize the boundaries of the fantasy world they create, yet how imagination allows them the escape route of adventure. To juxtapose such impossibilities is the prerogative of childhood. Stevenson seems more able than most to express experience as a child might in straightforward language and *in a child's voice*.

Knocking on the moonlit door

As we approach the twentieth century, it is fitting to begin with, perhaps, the most famous poet for children writing in the Romantic tradition, Walter de la Mare. His delicate, harmonious poetry presented an idealized, uncomplicated, but beautiful and memorable view of the world which was lyrically explored in melodious writing. His first book of poetry, *Songs of Childhood* (1902), showed that a talented new voice was willing to write not just for the young but out of a deep conviction that childhood held the key to wisdom. De la Mare was also a wonderful storyteller, and this talent is captured in unforgettable narrative poems such as 'The Listeners'.

> 'Is there anybody there?' said the Traveller,
> Knocking on the moonlit door;
> As his horse in the silence champed the grasses
> Of the forest's ferny floor;[29]

He looked at the world with the wondering, appreciative eyes of a small child and therein lies the charm of his poetry and its limitations. Even his biographer, Theresa Whistler, a lifelong friend, describes his writing as sometimes 'exhausted, blood-thinning and sentimental'. Yet 'it stands time and trouble, it carries the tang of authentic, spiritual experience — however elusive, fine-spun and minor keyed the stuff in which de la Mare may deal'.[30] That seems to me a fair summary of his work for children too. De la Mare had an eye for detail and the vividness of his writing brings alive a person, a place, a rural scene, a nightscape. But it is only truthful to a point, by ignoring what is ugly or messy or difficult. De la Mare's vision of the world (the 'minor key') radiates with sensitivity, appreciation, delicacy and charm, although, for me at least, it is spoiled by his refusal to take on board the flawed, imperfect reality in which most of us live. But read him for a gorgeous holiday from everyday life.

> And in my court should peacocks flaunt,
> And in my forests tigers haunt,
> And in my pools great fishes slant
> Their fins athwart the sun.[31]

He brought to his poetry both craftsmanship and the critical pen of a perfectionist. At the same time he was deeply imaginative and intuitive. His special feeling for children (and the child within him) gives him a unique place in poetry for the young which he deserves to retain, whatever vogues or fashions follow. He also compiled a ground-breaking anthology 'for the young of all ages', *Come Hither* (1923), which is both erudite and appreciative of the humbler voices which make up the oral tradition.

When we were very young

In the first half of the twentieth century, a clutch of interesting poets wrote for children, about half of whom are better known as adult writers — T. S. Eliot, Robert Graves, Robert Frost, Edmund Blunden, James Kirkup and others. The best of those who specialized in writing for the young were Eleanor Farjeon and James Reeves, still regularly anthologized and with collections in print. Reeves was another visual poet with a lyrical gift and a sense of humour. I doubt whether lines like 'The sea is a hungry dog' or 'Slowly the tide creeps up the sand' will ever go out of favour. The same is true of Eleanor Farjeon, whose range is wide and whose joyful, rhythmic style will surely always find an audience in the young: 'Cats sleep anywhere/ Any table, any chair.' There is no space to do justice to these poets, but I hope to tempt any reader who does not know their work to go and read them.

I will, however, pause to defend A. A. Milne, who has been smeared too often with the damning epithet of 'whimsy'. It must be acknowledged that there is not much interest in upper-middle-class nurseries with old-fashioned nannies any more, and that some of Milne's verse is precious and dated. Most of it isn't. And my touchstones are young children in inner-city, early-years classrooms who still love the poems because they are good. Milne was an excellent poet of light verse with a talent for rhyme and metre. He was also very funny and sometimes looked at the world as convincingly from a child's point of view as an adult can. Who can forget that dreadful bully, James James, Morrison Morrison, Wetherby George Dupree; or Bad Sir Brian Botany who 'bopped them on the head'; or the 'two little bears who lived in the wood/ And one of them was bad and the other was good'; or Mary Jane's loathed rice pudding. The poems ring because Milne was a master within a limited canvas. Sometimes there is the lament of the neglected child:

> 'If I'm a little darling, why don't they come and see?'
> I think to myself,
> I play to myself,
> And nobody knows what I say to myself;
> Here I am in the dark alone.[32]

Perhaps he understood his son, Christopher Robin, on whom the poems are based, better than the latter thought. The sad little voice in some of the poems suggests that Milne may have realized only too well his limitations as a father.

Urchin verse

John Rowe Townsend coined the term 'urchin verse' as 'family life in the raw with its backchat, fury and muddle, and instead of meadows ... disused railway lines, building sites and junk heaps' in *Written for Children*, his critical history of children's literature.[33] Townsend is describing a genre which was then new but which has dominated children's poetry since the 1970s. Gone are decorous descriptions of family life. Gone are romantic evocations of a beautiful world shared happily with the animal kingdom. If animals are around in urchin verse they are likely to be scruffy mongrels lifting their legs at lamp-posts or parrots shouting rude remarks or some straight talking about the fact that we kill and eat animals. Kids are fighting, contradicting grown-ups, getting one over on their teachers, etc.

So while nature will always be one of the great themes of poetry, the street and the ordinary home and school lives of children began to be seen as worth exploring in verse. Michael Rosen, probably the best-selling and most notorious of urchin versifiers, published his first book, *Mind Your Own Business*, in 1974, which heralded the new 'streetwise' school of poetry. Some critics exclaimed that it wasn't poetry. Rosen had the impudence to write in the vernacular (some of the time), in a very free 'free verse', about fighting with his brother, missing his mum's Spanish onions when she was away, memorizing the oral text of his dad's scoldings and mourning the loss of a filthy old shirt. Surely, this wasn't the subject matter or the language of poetry! Idealization and innocence have gone; the poetry reflects the sometimes awful, sometimes wonderful, crazy, riotous, boring, fragmented, disappointing and tedious moments of childhood. It could be argued that what the 'urchin verse' poets offered young readers was not slight or joky, but empowerment by writing about children's concerns in the sort of language children actually use.

One of the criticisms of this poetry is that it is superficial and lighthearted, reducing itself to the level of children at their worst. This is true to a certain extent, as the inclination of this particular group of poets (see below) is to enjoy the sort of pranks children play, to poke fun at propriety and to see the things from the 'underdog's' viewpoint. But that does not mean that the poetry is slight or that they ignore challenging issues or painful experiences. In fact, I would argue that poetry for children has always addressed serious concerns. I don't just mean that in the past much of it was moralistic. I mean that poets and anthologists for children have regularly tackled substantial issues, believing that their readership was interested in and capable of understanding them. It was not uncommon to find topics like slavery, poverty, cruelty and injustice in poetry for children before and during the nineteenth century. There are many such poems by Blake: 'Holy Thursday' is a good example. Lucy Aikin included the powerful 'Against Slavery' by William Cowper in one of the earliest anthologies, *Poetry for Children* (1801). The Taylors wrote poems about emancipation of slavery in their collections. Felicia Hemans' 'Casabianca' is about the self-sacrifice of a child ('The boy stood on the burning deck').

Contemporary poetry for children, including so-called urchin verse, has a passionate and angry side too. It deals sharply with child abuse, bullying, racism, the humiliations of old age and childhood, death, war, nuclear weapons, neglect, unhappiness, illness and much more. What then *has* changed over the centuries? The everyday experiences of ordinary children have become the subject matter for poetry. The language of that poetry is unlikely to be heightened and includes regional dialect, Creole, Patois and the idiom of the street. But this should not be exaggerated. Standard English is still widespread, and conventional verse forms and regular metre are still commonly used. Although there is plenty of experiment with free verse, traditional forms still hold their place. In the last decade, quite a number of collections have been published reflecting, at last, multi-ethnic Britain. Editors have also started to compile anthologies by women writers, who are still under-represented in most poetry books.

A category like 'urchin verse' encapsulates a broad range of poetry being written for children today. Many poets don't fit into such a catch-all category — Adrian Mitchell, James Berry, Grace Nichols, Gerard Benson, Philip Gross, John Mole, Richard Edwards, Libby Houston, Berlie Doherty, Wendy Cope and others. And those who might — for example Roger McGough, Brian Patten, Adrian Henri, John Agard, Jackie Kay, Allan Ahlberg, Benjamin Zephaniah, Gareth Owen and Judith Nicholls — have their own distinctive voices.

The two poets for children of the latter half of this century who stand out in different ways, because their verse is strong and because they don't fit into any of the categories, are Ted Hughes and Charles Causley. Both are equally well known for their adult writing. Causley is a poet and anthologist of distinction. He is difficult to pin down, as his work is subtle and varied. There's the ring of the storyteller, the feel for musical language, often a hint of something mysterious or even sinister that is left unexplained. His poetry is rooted in folklore, often deriving from his native Cornwall, and steeped in the oral tradition of ballads and the ancient magic of words.

> Nightingales' tongues, your majesty?
> Quails in aspic, cost a purse of money?
> Oysters from the deep, raving sea?
> Grapes and Greek honey?[34]

This is the beginning of the title poem from his earliest collection, *Figgie Hobbin*. Causley is still writing with great authority, more than twenty years on. It would be a sad day if his poetry ever went out of fashion.

Then there's Ted Hughes, Poet Laureate, a nature poet who turns his back on Romanticism by making his readers face realities about the animal world — cruelty, harshness, sex and death, as well as beauty and awe. Hughes doesn't compromise for the young: he gives them an honest account, as he sees it, with little held back, but delivered with 'affection'.

> Writing for children one has a very definite context of communication. Adult readers are looking for support for their defences on the whole. . . . One can communicate with children in a simple and whole way — not because they're innocent, but because they're not yet defensive, providing one moves with affection.[35]

Hughes has written some of his best poetry for children, the finest of which is in *What Is the Truth?* I cannot view a fly as just an irritation after encountering Hughes' searing metaphors: 'The fly is the sanitary inspector . . . little Michelin men hoovering up the rot and the goo . . . a knight on a black horse.'[36] It is too strong for some tastes, particularly for those who prefer to apply rose-tinted spectacles to childhood, but he offers poetry of power and potency to readers who can manage it.

It is now clear that poetry has been undergoing a boom in sales in this country, both for children and adults. Perhaps the fact that in Britain poets have regularly worked in classrooms for the last twenty years has something to do with it. Could it be that some of those adults buying poetry today learned to love it at school? And was that interest in poetry engendered by much-maligned teachers and the poets themselves? The practice of putting successful writers in classrooms on a large scale is unique to Britain. Organizations and companies who have poured money into these ventures for many years deserve our thanks. So do committed groups of people across the country, such as the amateur enthusiasts running festivals, teachers and publishers collaborating on book weeks, local arts associations organizing community events, librarians, booksellers and the like, who have done so much at a difficult time to promote the arts in general and poetry in particular. What we have now is a positive climate for poetry. And traditional poetry is still widely available and enjoyed. Michael Rosen's recent video, *Count to Five and Say I'm Alive*, documents children the length and breadth of this island reciting their favourite poems. Along with the 'urchin versifiers' and other contemporary poets, what they select are poems by Shakespeare or Shelley or Stevenson or Tagore. Although there is still much to achieve, voices from the past and present who need a wider audience, and prejudices to be addressed, it is true to say that poetry for children has never been stronger.

Notes

1 I am considering poetry written for children between the ages of about 5 and 12 mainly in Britain, but with some reference to USA and Europe.

2 This text has been troublesome to bibliophiles, being hard to trace and variously titled as *Divine Emblems* and *A Book for Boys and Girls*, as well as *Country Rhimes for Children*.

3 John Bunyan, *Country Rhimes for Children*, London, 1686.

4 Abraham Cheare, *A Looking Glass for Children*, London, 1673.

5 Nathanial Cotton, *Visions in Verse*, London, 1751.

6 J. H. Pafford, introduction to facsimile edition of *Divine Songs*, Oxford University Press, London, 1971.

7 Isaac Watts, *Divine Songs, Attempted in Easy Language for the Use of Children*, printed for M. Lawrence at the Angel in the Poultry, London, 1715.

8 *Ibid.*

9 Lewis Carroll, *Alice's Adventures in Wonderland*, Macmillan, London, 1865.

10 Christopher Smart, *Hymns for the Amusement of Children*, Sleator and Williams, Dublin, 1772.

11 Anna Barbauld, *Hymns in Prose for Children*, London, 1781.

12 F. J. Harvey Darton, *Children's Books in England*, Cambridge University Press, Cambridge, 1982, p. 179.

13 Jane Taylor, *Rhymes for the Nursery*, Darton and Harvey, London, 1806.

14 Catherine Ann Dorset, *The Peacock at Home,* John Murray, London, 1807.

15 Harvey Darton, *op. cit.,* p. 179.

16 William Blake, *Songs of Innocence*, first published 1789.

17 John Mackay Shaw, *Childhood in Poetry*, Vols 1–5, Gale Research Company, Detroit, 1962.

18 Edward Lear, 'The Duck and the Kangaroo', from *Nonsense Songs and Stories*, first published 1894.

19 Harvey Darton, *op. cit.,* p. 260.

20 Lewis Carroll, *Alice's Adventures in Wonderland*, London, 1865.

21 Review in *Athenaeum Magazine*, 6 January 1872, p. 11, quoted in Jan Marsh, *Christina Rossetti*, Jonathan Cape, London, 1994.

22 Ann and Jane Taylor, *Rhymes for the Nursery*, Darton and Harvey, London, 1806.

23 Christina Rossetti, *Sing-Song*, George Routledge and Sons, London, 1872.

24 Robert Louis Stevenson, from 'Bed in Summer', in *A Child's Garden of Verses*, first published 1885.

25 W. H. Garrod, *The Profession of Poetry*, Oxford University Press, London, 1929, p. 184.

26 Darton, *op. cit.,* p. 315.

27 Robert Louis Stevenson, in a letter to Edmund Gosse, in Bradford Booth and Ernest Mehew (eds), *The Letters of Robert Louis Stevenson*, Yale University Press, London and New Haven, 1995, p. 56.

28 Robert Louis Stevenson, 'Child's play', *The Cornhill Magazine*, 38, 1878, in *R. L. Stevenson, Essays and Poems*, ed. C. Harman, Dent, London, 1992.

29 Walter de la Mare, from 'The Listeners', in *The Listeners and Other Poems*, first published by Constable, London, 1912.
30 Theresa Whistler, *Imagination of the Heart: The Life of Walter de la Mare*, Duckworth, London, 1993.
31 Walter de la Mare, from 'Tartary', in *op. cit.*
32 A. A. Milne, *When We Were Very Young*, Methuen, London, 1924.
33 John Rowe Townsend, *Written for Children*, Penguin, Harmondsworth, 1965.
34 Charles Causley, *Figgie Hobbin*, Macmillan, London, 1970.
35 Ted Hughes, quoted in L. Paul, 'Inside the lurking-glass with Ted Hughes', *Signal*, **49** (January 1986).
36 Ted Hughes, *What Is the Truth?* Faber, London, 1984.

CHAPTER 8

'What's a Cultural Heritage When It's at Home?'

Playing with Shakespeare in the Primary School

Janet Bottoms

Why should children read Shakespeare anyway? Not by compulsion, Janet Bottoms argues, but because playing with Shakespeare is fun. But even 'fun' isn't reason enough; children deserve the chance to use their personal and cultural experience to enter the 'gaps' in the dramas in order to forge and shape their own meanings. This does not suggest a loose liberality with some of the ideas offered in the plays, but a robust engagement with the text itself recognized as representing a fictional world. While children may well bring their personal experience to bear on the plays, this does not mean that they should be encouraged to blur the distinction between the fictional world of the drama and their everyday realities. Most particularly, Janet Bottoms urges that children should be given the chance to see Shakespeare's language as something which can be pleasurably played with. In questioning the notion of 'cultural heritage', Janet Bottoms argues that far from offering Shakespeare as a repository of received cultural meaning, the 'ultimate meaning of any work is in the response it inspires'. The children's voices which bring this chapter to a close provide rich evidence of just what those responses might be.

Shakespeare bulks so large in our national consciousness (whatever shape he may take) that any attempt to discuss his place in school is bound to be affected by echoes of 'voices off'. There are the voices of politicians, prescribing Shakespeare as the 'cultural heritage' of every child — to be wrapped up and presented to them at 14, whether or not they choose ever to look at it again. There are those who would make of him a 'site of contestation', where oppositional readings can strip the veil of 'universality' from the hierarchical, Eurocentric values beneath; and there are the Shakespeare lovers, who would protect him from all whose capacity they do not think large enough to 'comprehend' him fully — whether for his sake or their own is not always clear.

When, if ever, one may expect to reach a 'full comprehension' of Shakespeare is a matter of some disagreement. For a group of university teachers the introduction of compulsory Shakespeare at 14 'would risk permanently alienating a large number of children from the pleasurable understanding of classical literary works',[1] while a teacher who is happy to use him with this age group argues that to introduce him any younger involves 'so many compromises that I can hardly claim to be dealing with Shakespeare's plays'.[2] As for bringing him into the primary school, this has been described as 'mere hocus-pocus', a 'dubious ... vogue for getting children to chant and play with passages from Shakespeare taken out of context the meaning of which they can only guess at'.[3] Finally — not a 'voice off', this one, but very much a desperate voice from within — there is the primary teacher who hears colleagues' enthusiasm but, in view of all the other curriculum demands, doesn't feel justified in spending the time on Shakespeare.

In the face of all this, is it really possible to argue that Shakespeare not only can but should be brought into the primary school? Given the limitations of time as well as of the children's experience, can the primary teacher be said 'to be dealing with Shakespeare's plays' — and what, anyway, constitutes 'dealing with' Shakespeare? I prefer to think of 'playing with' Shakespeare — an activity which is neither meaningless chanting nor performing a play under the direction of a teacher who can explain the 'meaning'. (Some children can learn surprisingly long roles and enjoy doing it, but inevitably in such a production a few will get the large parts while others are left feeling unimportant and uninvolved.) Playing is exploring, individually and communally. It is an intensely valuable activity, as every teacher of young children knows, and to play with Shakespeare is not to learn '*the* meaning' but to discover meanings, to re-create them, experiment with them, build and grow through them, making something new. This, after all, is what Shakespeare did with his source materials, and his texts also were subject to revision in the playhouse. Such experiment and re-creation is truly playing *with* Shakespeare.

Two questions have to be faced immediately: why bring Shakespeare into schools at all; and is the primary age a suitable one at which to introduce him? One immediate answer lies in the mounting evidence that young children *enjoy* working with Shakespeare. When they talk about it, the word which comes through again and again is 'fun'. 'It's fun to do.' 'It's a good story.' One teacher, after her first tentative experience, told me that she was convinced that this is the best age for introducing Shakespeare because the children are still young enough not be too self-conscious about acting, and yet mature enough to discuss the important issues: they are 'like very young, naive adults who want to learn an awful lot'.

Obviously, 'fun' is not in itself a sufficient reason for taking classroom time, and neither is 'catching them young' for Shakespeare before they can decide he is 'boring'. However, if learning to read involves acquiring the ability to interact with the text; to fill in the 'spaces' between the words where meaning is composed by the reader; to 'travel through the text', as Iser puts it, 'unfolding the multiplicity of interconnecting perspectives which are offset whenever there is a switch from one to another',[4] then there is real educational value in playing with Shakespeare, for the obvious (and yet sometimes overlooked) reason that he is both a dramatist and a poet. In both of these capacities he leaves many more 'spaces' to be filled than are left by a more consistent, narrative voice speaking from a single, clearly premised point of view. If we add to this the fact that his plots are common to many cultures, frequently the stuff of folklore, and concerned with basic family relationships or with tricks and 'jests', we can see why children find them easy to relate to. They combine accessibility with the safety which comes from being set in a fictional world, in another place and time.

Texts and contexts

The world of the play can be understood in more than one way. On one level it is the world of a story, and can be presented to the children as just that. Shakespeare tells 'good stories', a fact which can be recognized without reference to the name of the storyteller. Moreover, they have been shaped by a dramatist into episodes which focus on conflict, whether external (between one or more characters) or internal. They give powerful expression to morally complex or conflicting viewpoints, which invite from the 'hearers' both an empathetic and a critical response. As Bruner says:

> Story must construct two landscapes simultaneously. One is the landscape of action, where the constituents are the arguments of action: agent, intention or goal, situation, instrument, something corresponding to a 'story grammar'. The other landscape is the landscape of consciousness: what those in the action know, think or feel, or do not know, think or feel.[5]

In exploring Shakespeare's stories, through activity and discussion, children can both learn something of the 'story grammar' — the way stories are constructed — and develop a greater imaginative awareness or consciousness. This is their primary context.

There is another kind of context, however — the context of the children's own previous personal and cultural experience. Even young children do not come to a story without experiences and opinions of their own through which to give it meaning. The teacher may choose some of these as the interpretive context or 'point of entry' into a play, presenting the children with a problem situation to be discussed and its outcome predicted, or introducing it through reference to some theme, such as war or jealousy, to which they can relate. It is the energy of the narrative action which carries a play along, but — placed in the right frame or context — it is also accessible to children as a way into a deeper understanding of their own world. Whatever the chosen point of entry, it is this choice which is every teacher's key to opening up the world of the play in a way which is valuable to a particular group of children at a particular stage of their development. At the same time, the distinction between the world of the play and the personal world of the child should always be preserved. It is also very important that the characters of that play world remain within it.

This is sometimes forgotten by adults keen to make the play 'relevant', or to encourage a total imaginative engagement with it by introducing the characters or their dilemmas into the everyday world of classroom or home. Until children have learned how to distinguish fact from fiction, and especially where the signals given to them by the teacher are ambiguous, there is a danger that this will confuse or distress rather than liberate them. This is apparent in an account of work with one class of 7- to 8-year-olds who were introduced to *King Lear* through visits by actors 'in role'. As the children 'became immersed in Lear's world . . . they moved from watching the Fool or the mad Lear on the heath to wanting to *be* the characters and take on the language and action for themselves', but while one child said 'I like *King Lear* — it's my best subject,' another held back from going into the hall where the sessions took place, saying 'it's horrible'.[6] A few boys also opted out of any involvement or interest in the discussions or developing story-line, worrying their teachers by what was felt to be their lack of participation but which was probably, rather, a healthy resistance. Those same boys were later completely gripped by *Macbeth* when they were given the opportunity to explore the text through the drama process and fewer demands were made on their suspension of disbelief. In using such material, it is of the first importance that the encouragement of imaginative empathy is combined with a clear preservation of fictional distance.

Suiting the action to the words

One difference between a play and a story is that the latter is usually presented in the past tense and from a fixed perspective, while a play evolves in a continuous present. Several different characters, each one a discrete centre of consciousness, are physically present to the audience who, to a greater extent than the listener to a story, are engaged *along with them* in a constant process of evaluation, prediction, and renegotiation of the meaning of events. The classroom is, of course, very different from the theatre, yet it is in a very similar mental process that the teacher should seek to involve the children, and there are various methods, drawn from the techniques of 'active storytelling' and the rehearsal exercises of the theatre and described elsewhere, which can be used for this purpose.[7]

Given the constraints on classroom time, the teacher who employs such strategies as these must obviously be selective in the choice of scenes or situations to explore. There is no reason to feel that it must be the whole play or nothing, though it is important that what is selected should still be understood in the context of a whole narrative. Fortunately, this is not difficult with Shakespeare, since his plots are basically simple. The demands of his theatre led him often to plait several distinct stories together, but it is relatively easy to unplait them. 'Playing with' *The Tempest*, for example, might involve concentrating on the story of Prospero's revenge, or the relationships of Prospero, Caliban and Ariel, while quietly dropping one or two other of the multiple strands which make up the whole play. Though it may be argued that an understanding of the interconnection of the several plots of a play is intrinsic to a full 'reading' of it, any interpretation is bound to be selective and partial, and with children of primary age it is better, I believe, to explore one or two of the story-lines fully than to falsify the emotional complexity of relationships and dilemmas by adopting a single narrative perspective.

However, concentrating only on character and action is still not making full use of the tremendous resource which Shakespeare offers. 'Shakespeare's stories', divorced from the language through which he conceived and 'bodied' them, are not Shakespeare — they are something other and generally less rewarding or stimulating. Much of our ability to think imaginatively and creatively is dependent on the habit of metaphorical thinking, or making new mental connections — in short, of being *surprised* by what language can do. It is this which makes the highly figurative, phonically interesting language of Shakespeare's plays so valuable in education. Not merely do children *not* find that they cannot understand it, but the sounds, the rhythms and the sheer newness of the 'intricate word weaves'[8] appeal to them strongly. The only important qualification to the argument for using Shakespeare's own language is that it should never be presented in the form of textbooks. In the first instance it is much better not to present it in written form at all, but orally, in small units which can be grasped by individuals and then put together with others to produce dramatic sequences or choral effects.[9] Words and movement — physical movement expressive of the words, or physically created shapes expressive of images — are the key to the ability of young children to take possession of the language for themselves, enabling them to reach a communal and personal understanding which may sometimes be deeper than that of many adults reading alone in their studies. As Margaret Meek says:

> Poetry is never better understood than in childhood when it is felt in the blood and along the bones. Later it may be intricately interpreted, explained and demonstrated, as something made of language.... Poetry is also about language as *plaything*.[10]

This should not be seen as 'getting children to chant and play with passages from Shakespeare taken out of context the meaning of which they can only guess at'. There is a great deal of evidence that, if they are encouraged to enter the 'play world' through the appropriate doors, children understand more than adults expect, and many who are not seen as fluent in the formal classroom demands of literacy can show an understanding of complex ideas. To deny this is to deny meaning to the experience of children such as 9-year-old Ben, with a low recorded reading ability, who commented, 'At breaktime I have a big bunch of Shakespeare in my head. It keeps going round in my mind.'[11] 'Meaning', after all, is not something fixed and inherent in the text; it is performative, constituted by the interaction between the 'reader' (any reader) and text. The recognition of this should also be empowering to teachers who are afraid that they might not be able to convey '*the* meaning' of Shakespeare to their pupils.

Playing and meaning

I was privileged, recently, to discuss with a group of children what Shakespeare meant to them, following a performance of 'their' *Macbeth*, the culmination of a term's work on the play.[12] Several of the strategies mentioned above had been employed by the teacher in the course of this, and their script was a combination of Shakespeare's and their own, as voices off contributed a subtext of 'thoughts' to the words of the Macbeths in several key scenes.

Before beginning work themselves, the children had been shown the cartoon video version in the *Animated Tales* series,[13] but claimed that they had not understood it, and since the work I watched showed how well they did, in fact, understand the play, I asked them what they had found difficult. 'The witches ... like the cackling and that,' was the answer. Their own performance had been completely devoid of cackling — the witches being fey and tantalizing rather than grotesque — so I asked why they thought the witches cackled. 'To show they're *evil*,' answered one child, with relish, but another, clearly speaking out of her own experience of playing the part, interrupted to explain: 'We're not evil in a way but we are, but we tell the future.' 'They're quite nice but they're horrible as well,' commented a third. Those children might lack an adult critical vocabulary but through 'playing' Macbeth's questions and reactions they had come to comprehend the ambiguous nature of Shakespeare's 'weird sisters'.

A discussion of the murder of Duncan followed, in which they were eager to explain to me some of the psychological complexities and moral dilemmas at the heart of the husband–wife relationship in the play:

> 'Actually it wasn't Macbeth's fault, it was actually Lady Macbeth's fault.'
> 'I made an excuse up that he reminded me too much of my own father and everything, and in the end he gave up and did it. I had the daggers ready.... In the end I killed myself because I was getting so furious ... because I thought I had all blood on my hands.'
> 'That's because she thought ...'
> 'She had a breakdown, and she thought she couldn't even wash off a little spot of blood ...'
> 'And she thought it was going to stay there for ever ...'
> 'Out, out.'
> 'Out damn spot ...'
> 'And in the end she killed herself because she thought everybody would think it was her.'
> 'It wasn't actually Lady Macbeth, it was Macbeth.'
> 'In some ways he was [evil] and in some ways he wasn't, like the witches ... then some time on in the play he was.'
> 'He was nice but — he wanted to be nice, but then he became evil.'

While the language of the play clearly resonated in their minds, it was also possible to see how they interacted with Shakespeare's text, filling in the 'spaces' and interpreting them through their own understanding of human relationships and motives. We discussed the scene in which Lady Macbeth reads the letter from her husband — a scene in which they had worked out a 'dialogue' between the text and their own subtext of her thoughts — and I asked whether it hadn't been Macbeth's idea to murder Duncan:

> 'No.'
> 'No, it was my idea.'
> 'It was actually her idea ...'
> 'She was so anxious to be queen ...'

'I wanted to be queen, I couldn't wait, because once he wrote the letter to me, and I found out in there, and then we did the dialogue ...'
'That's where I was in, I was in the dialogue.'
'I thought of becoming really rich and to rule the country.'

I asked whether they thought Macbeth didn't want to rule the country:

'Well, he did, but he liked ...'
'He liked Gilbert too much ...'
'He liked Duncan.'
'... and he wanted to wait for him to die of old age.'
'Yea, but then he had to kill him because otherwise Lady Macbeth would have, well ...'
'Because I would have done it.'
'... would rather have *divorced* him.'
'Because I would have done it myself, and he was worried that I'd get hurt or something.'
'Like if I might have woke up and I might have killed her.'
'Blackmail ...'

The whole discussion showed how the children could move in and out of the roles which they had developed, identifying with them and yet preserving an objectivity — a recognition of the difference between actor and role. In addition they were becoming conscious of certain narrative patterns, as was made clear to me when one told me that the bit he liked best was the 'gun fight' — hastily amended to 'sword fight' — at the end.

Undoubtedly these children understood what they had been doing, and understood some of the problems — the nature of the witches, for example — which exercise adult critics. They were quite clear about the need to explore the text stage by stage, and how understanding grew out of this exploration:

'If you just went to the story, and tried to make a play, you wouldn't understand it or anything — you've got to do it bit by bit, you can't just go straight onto the play.'

However, they were also sure that it was worth doing — they had enjoyed it. When I asked them why they thought *Macbeth* was a good story, and why they had found the work 'fun', I was told:

'He [Shakespeare] makes it up, and you have to ...'
'He mixes stuff up that don't make sense but they do.'
'Yea ... he says old words, Scotland words and you don't understand them, but then, but if you were back in that time you would — we're learning about Macbeth and history, you see, and you feel like you're there ...'
'Actually, there — it makes you think about it.'

Margaret Meek puts it in a very similar way when she describes literature as:

> literate *activity* that can bring everyone a fuller enjoyment of life, beyond usefulness, beyond, even, the worthy notion that it is nourishment that makes us grow. It is its own kind of deep play. For all that the books I have called literature at various stages of my growing old have joined me to the history and language of my forebears in ways that plumb my very depths, and taught me who I am, for all that they have also added wondrously, immeasurably to my understanding of human kind, myself and the world, I think of them as something I have *enjoyed* in the richest sense.[14]

A personal heritage

'Literature', according to another definition, 'does not merely enable the reader to apprehend the imaginative vision of the author, but also teaches him to exercise the same imaginative vision in himself'.[15] Over the last four centuries 'Shakespeare' has been a continuous inspiration to other artists in words, music, painting or the dance, and this, too, is a tradition in which primary children can join with their own drawing and designing, music, dance, modelling, and writing — the result of active, physical and oral explorations of Shakespeare's words. The ultimate 'meaning' of any work of art is in the response it inspires. Young children may be less good at putting their understanding into words, but the quality of the work produced in many classrooms is perhaps the final proof of its value.

Playing with Shakespeare, then, is the entry into the story and world of 'the play', with all its connotations of philosophical and ethical issues, explored through a variety of strategies — prediction and retrospection, improvization, physical and oral activity, and creative response. It is also a recognition of the limits of that world, and where or how it touches upon one's own, gained through reflection, discussion and involvement in a community of 'players', each one bringing to it his or her own perspective. The meanings that readers and audiences have found in Shakespeare have varied from age to age. This is, after all, the nature of a 'classic' — not that it 'conveys universal values'[16] in any fixed sense, but that many people at different times, and of different cultures, find something that stimulates or challenges them, something that is significant to their understanding of their own personal or social values. We need not fear to bring Shakespeare into the modern, multicultural classroom if we teach our children, and are ourselves willing, to enter into that dialogue with the text which involves both listening and reacting, questioning, disputing, exploring — even rewriting.

It has been said, repeatedly (and almost as often questioned or refuted), that Shakespeare is part of 'our' culture. As Jerome Bruner has pointed out, however:

> A culture is constantly in process of being recreated as it is interpreted and renegotiated by its members. In this view, a culture is as much a *forum* for negotiating and renegotiating meaning and for explicating action as it is a set of rules or specifications for action. Indeed every culture maintains specialized institutions or occasions for intensifying this 'forum-like' feature. Story-telling, theater, science, even jurisprudence are all techniques for intensifying this function — ways of exploring possible worlds out of the context of immediate need ... It follows from this view of culture as a forum that induction into the culture through education should also partake of the spirit of a forum, of negotiation, of the recreating of meaning. But this conclusion runs counter to traditions of pedagogy that derive from another time, another interpretation of culture, another conception of authority — one that looked at the process of education as a *transmission* of knowledge and values *by* those who knew more *to* those who knew less and knew it less expertly.[17]

Too often, in the view of educators (and politicians) Shakespeare has been associated with the 'transmission of knowledge and values', though actors have always known that this is not the way a play works. 'Shakespeare's plays,' as Adrian Noble says, 'are points of departure, not goals to be achieved.'[18] They are points of intersection between a historically produced text, a developing tradition of interpretation, the personal, familial and cultural history of every person in the theatre or classroom, and the communal experience developing from that intersection which, in turn, becomes part of each individual history. *Teaching* Shakespeare may be perceived as transmitting to or imposing one group's values and tastes on another: *playing with* Shakespeare, on the other hand, is a continual negotiation and renegotiation of 'meaning', an activity to which we may hope that some at least of our children will continually return as they grow, adding further dimensions to their understanding, though possibly never entering as unselfconsciously into the world of 'play' as they did in their early years. *This* is their cultural heritage.

Notes

1 Letter from 21 university teachers, *Times Higher Education Supplement*, 20 November 1992.
2 Neil King, 'Starting Shakespeare', in R. Adams (ed.), *Teaching Shakespeare*, Robert Royce, London, 1985, p. 57.
3 Sean McEvoy, 'The politics of teaching English', *English in Education* (Autumn 1991), 25, p. 76.

4 Wolfgang Iser, *The Act of Reading: A Theory of Aesthetic Response*, Routledge & Kegan Paul, London, 1978, p. 118.

5 Jerome Bruner, *Actual Minds, Possible Worlds*, Harvard University Press, Cambridge, MA, 1986, p. 14.

6 Described by Sarah Gordon in her unpublished MEd dissertation, 'Play out the Play: A Study of Active Approaches to Primary School Shakespeare', Cambridge University Institute of Education, Cambridge, 1989, pp. 63–4.

7 See, for example, Lesley Hendy, 'From drama into story: strategies for investigating texts', in M. Styles, E. Bearne and V. Watson (eds), *The Prose and the Passion*, Cassell, London, 1994; and S. Gordon and C. Geelan, *IBM Young Shakespeare: Macbeth*, English Shakespeare Company, 1993.

8 Victor Nell, *Lost in a Book: The Psychology of Reading for Pleasure*, Yale University Press, New Haven, 1988, p. 63.

9 'People understand words at a much simpler level than we have come to expect — a more intuitive level. So, we have to find ways to get them not only on our tongue, but to make them part of our whole physical self' (Cicely Berry, *The Actor and His Text*, Harrap, London, 1987, p. 22). For examples of work in school inspired by these ideas see Gordon and Geelan, *op. cit.*; and Peter Reynolds, *Practical Approaches to Teaching Shakespeare*, Oxford University Press, Oxford, 1991.

10 Margaret Meek, *On Being Literate*, Bodley Head, London, 1991, p. 182.

11 S. Gordon, *op. cit.*, p. 97.

12 My thanks to the children of Year 4 (1992–93), Duxford County Primary School, Cambridge, and to their teacher David Jones, for allowing me to watch and discuss their work with them.

13 *Macbeth*, abridged by Leon Garfield and animated by Soyuzmultfilm Studios, Moscow; in the series *Shakespeare: The Animated Tales*, Shakespeare Animated Films Ltd and Soyuzmultfilm, 1992; distributed by Island World Communications.

14 Meek, *op. cit.*, p. 182.

15 Christopher Butler, 'What is a literary work?', *New Literary History* (1973), 5, p. 20.

16 *English for Ages 5 to 16: National Curriculum Proposals, June 1989*, DES and Welsh Office, London, 1989, Chapter 7, para. 16.

17 Bruner, *op. cit.*, p. 123.

18 Adrian Noble, quoted in *The Independent*, 11 July 1992.

CHAPTER 9

The Way We Were

Jan Mark

Jan Mark gave this chapter as a talk at the opening of the conference. Its wide-ranging scope and scholarship is coupled with the kind of narrative energy and allure which makes her such a compelling writer. In taking a sideways look at nostalgia she not only aptly rounds off this section, but points forward to some of the issues which are raised in the final section of the book. She reminds us that what is new today can quickly become translated into 'the dull thud of the cliché' but that 'we shall all look quite good bathed in the rosy glow of yesteryear'. It all depends on where you're standing. These pleasurable digs at moral attitudes about children's literature and declining standards are matched by a thorough examination of shifts in attitudes towards texts for children. Whatever is written for children will carry the unmistakable features of its age; whatever will endure from current writing to be read with gusto in future ages presents an intriguing set of imaginings. Whatever the future of particular writers who are popular now, Jan Mark is clear that the most valuable writing does not patronize or draw moral conclusions, but speaks to young readers with respect, 'trusting their percipience'.

One of my heroes is the slightly melancholy figure of Augustus Henry Lane Fox, who, but for a series of happy chances that placed him where he most needed to be, might have ended his career as he began it, an assiduous but undistinguished army officer. Unlike the general run of nineteenth-century innovators, the engineer adventurers-such as Stephenson and Brunel and their kind, he was a miniaturist with an infinite capacity for taking pains. Thus, given the task of testing the new Minié rifle that was to replace the musket as the staple weapon of the British army, he noted that although the homicidal capacity of the new gun might be revolutionary, there was nothing revolutionary about the weapon itself. The rifled barrel was only an *improvement* on the smooth bore, as the breech-loader was to be over the muzzle-loader, the musket had been on the arquebus, and the arquebus on the crossbow. The whole history of ballistics can be traced back to the slingshot, which itself is only an extension of the human arm. A convert to

Darwinism, Lane Fox believed that artefacts developed in the same way as species, by 'evolution not revolution'.

In order to observe this process more closely he began systematically to collect firearms; when on a providential posting to Southern Ireland among antiquarians, who at the time were little better than grave-robbers, it was this same attention to the apparently insignificant that led him to excavate for detritus rather than for treasure, and to discard nothing as negligible, unworthy of notice: thus he turned archaeology into the exact science that it has become today.

His persistence was rewarded. In later life he inherited the title of Baron Pitt-Rivers, along with an estate on the Wiltshire–Dorset borders that encompassed some of the richest archaeological sites in the whole country.

General Augustus Henry Lane Fox Pitt-Rivers was a kind of presiding genius while I was researching and compiling *The Oxford Book of Children's Stories*. This collection was intended from the outset to be an archive, demonstrating the progress of the children's short story from its beginnings as a vehicle for moral and educational precepts, to its present form in which it is identical, in all but viewpoint, to its adult sister.

The undertaking was a form of archaeology; much detritus was sifted, and nothing discarded out of hand as negligible. Much treasure was included in the final selection, but more was left out. Treasure is easily recognized; it shines. In its place I offered material that by no means glowed with a gemlike fire but, as with an archaeologist's potsherd or bone splinter, cast light upon its period, often obliquely, because it was atypical of what one might have expected. As a result there is, in my own personal Pitt-Rivers collection, enough material to compile perhaps three other books of comparable length.

There was no attempt made to forecast what this particular medium — the short story — might become; all that was offered was the suggestion, an unarguable one, I would have thought, that the present generation of writers is as surely destined to go out of date as its predecessors, since its work, like that of its predecessors, is inevitably affected by contemporary attitudes to children and childhood, and inevitably informed by the worldview extant at the time of writing.

This is not necessarily a worldview that we now share. The Oxford book, and an accompanying article in *Signal* magazine, drew flak from some reviewers because I was perceived to be accusing certain writers of xenophobia, bigotry or anti-Semitism — even traducing them.[1] Neither word seems to me apposite. There was no question of accusing or traducing, since the evidence was overtly hoisted on a high mast, in full public view, with no attempt at concealment. This was what I *was* drawing attention to; the fact that attitudes we now consider abhorrent were once regarded as perfectly normal, healthy, even commendable, and that writers who, ahead of their time, also found them abhorrent, tended to have been overlooked; that enlightened liberals of the eighteenth century, such as Aikin, Barbauld and Day, failed to make a lasting impression on an increasingly imperialistic society. This trio would have had hard words for Captain W. E. Johns, the creator of Biggles, who said of himself, a touch disingenuously:

> I teach a boy to be a man, for without that essential qualification he will never be anything. I teach sportsmanship according to the British idea. One doesn't need blood and thunder to do that.[2]

Leaving aside any debate on exactly what the present British idea of sportsmanship may be, consider the following comment:

> Captain Johns's socio-political attitudes are those one would associate with a not-unduly intelligent Empire-builder of the late Victorian 'white man's burden' period. The white man's superiority is always heavily underlined. Biggles speaks calmly of 'the value of labour in the tropics, particularly white labour, which is always better than native work'. The word 'natives' appears with unfailing regularity (even 'Wogs' for Arabs occurs) and they are always little more than animals.[3]

This was written in the late 1950s. The quotations are from a book called *Young Writers, Young Readers,* in which various educationists expressed forebodings over the likely effects of schoolchildren's reading habits. What, for instance, would become of boys who read Biggles? The writer of the above could not foresee that five of them would grow up to be Monty Python and to seal the fate of Biggles, thereafter, as a standard British joke. A generation of adults concerned to protect their young from Quentin Tarantino and Oliver Stone have little to fear from the shade of Captain Johns, although we may yet live to see *Reservoir Dogs* become regular Bank Holiday viewing at teatime on BBC1. Look what happened to *Jaws*.

It is worth pausing to think about this, for there is a tendency, particularly prevalent among critics, to believe and to insist that whatever opinion or appreciation currently obtains *must be the right one.* Children look at photographs of their parents wearing modes of a slightly earlier time and, knowing nothing of the speed at which fashions change, imagine that the way people dress now is the right way, the proper way, and that they used to dress differently because they did not know any better. Poor benighted creatures, they believed in their ignorance that flares, hipsters, platform soles and kipper ties were the right things to wear because no one had discovered how to make anything different. As any fool knows, the thing to wear is a baseball cap turned arsy-versy, billowing jeans and trainers that resemble surgical boots. This is right. It is proper. It will never change.

We can forgive them, for we know that when everyone wore flares, hipsters, platform soles and kipper ties they looked very ordinary *because* everyone wore them. Today's wannabee gangsta will encounter the same incomprehension from his own children who, as yet unborn, are nevertheless programmed already to roll around on the floor in hysterics at the age of 13, having seen a photograph of Dad at the same age. They will never believe that he chose to look like that. I do not feel that we should extend the same leniency to critics who cannot come to terms with the knowledge that one day they will be superseded.

The urge always to go one better is endemic in the assessment of the creative arts. Who has not seen adverts like these? 'Makes *Lady Chatterley's Lover* look like *Little Women*.' 'Makes *Apocalypse Now* look like a vicarage tea-party.' 'Makes *Reservoir Dogs* look like *Breakfast at Tiffany's*.' None of this tells us anything but that the reviewer is inadequately equipped with a comparative faculty. He has probably never been to a vicarage tea-party (has anyone?), has read only the dirty bits in *Lady Chatterley's Lover* while at school, and has never read *Little Women* at all. (But he *has* seen *Reservoir Dogs*.) His only concern is to make sure we know that giant strides have been made, barriers vaulted, taboos breached — 'this makes *The Witches* look like *Winnie the Pooh*'.

One might be inclined to call this interesting condition neolepsy, except that the sufferer is less enthralled by the new than by *now*. Now we've got it right, at last. An extension of this myopia is the failure to recognize a breakthrough or innovation if it does not have an immediate effect. It is particularly true of the field of children's fiction, where the readers upon whom it has the greatest impact, children, have to grow up and become writers themselves before the innovation is developed and enters the mainstream.

I would suggest that one of the reasons why children's fiction dates more rapidly than the adult variety is that children, as inexperienced readers, are drawn to texts that approximate to their own vernacular. Writers who are praised for their realistic dialogue and the accessibility thereof are often using a language as artificial as anything in Congreve — it simply *looks* like the way people speak. The first title in the Oxford book is 'Celia and Chloe' by Sarah Fielding, innovative because it is a very early example of a children's story with a plot.[4] The plot is instantly recognizable to anyone familiar with photo-romances, but it takes considerable reading skills to extricate it from its eighteenth-century syntax. Adults can do that. Adults continue to read and enjoy the plays of Shakespeare, thus conferring upon them classic status, because they can see that his characters are not solely of the sixteenth century, that people have always behaved like that, and that people have always talked like that because, once shorn of its quaint oaths and similar gadzookery, the nuts and bolts of the English language have stayed remarkably constant.

Comparably, there is nothing distinctively medieval about Chaucer's pilgrims. They have medieval jobs; aside from that, one could find a similar assortment of tourists, crooks, yuppies, chancers and career clergy at any point in history, up to, and beyond, tomorrow. It is difficult to enjoy the same recognition of many characters in children's fiction, because they are always at the mercy of adults who have their own notions of what children ought to be. *Little Lord Fauntleroy* is a case in point.[5] Cedric Errol is an interesting and attractive child, basely betrayed by his author, who dotes on him like a fond mother boasting to aunts, thereby rendering him deeply suspect. We think now, of course, that we have got it right at last. Let us come back in a hundred years, shall we, and find out?

In the early years of children's fiction, children appear as figures who commit sins and make mistakes in order that older and wiser persons may point out the error of their ways for the purposes of future improvement. Over a couple of centuries writers became more inclined to allow them to appear as people rather than as puppets, but they remained none the less children as observed by adults of their generation, unacknowledged by the children of the next and by the adults of the next on behalf of the children. Many writers involved in the creation of juvenile fiction are exercised by a healthy fear of going out of date, and yet nothing goes out of date faster than the up-to-date; the shock of the new becomes the dull thud of the cliché.

Authors can inflict this damage on themselves, clinging compulsively to a bright idea until it asphyxiates in a stranglehold. It comes as something of a surprise to read the first of Enid Blyton's Famous Five books, before the eponymous Five atrophied into a series.[6] The set-up is convincing enough; unfunded scientist whose theories earn him no money to support his wife and child; the knowledge of this failure exacerbating an already explosive temper which has been inherited by his only daughter, whose own surly solipsism is the result of isolation. She has almost no contact with other children and uses all of her scant pocket-money to pay someone else to look after the pet that she is not allowed to keep at home. Her awakening to the rewards and pleasures of sociability upon contact with her three cousins could have provided *one* fascinating novel, but alas, after fame and fortune attended Uncle Quentin, George went to boarding school and Timmy the dog became the fifth of the Five, book after book continued to rely upon the original scenario, now a threadbare formula, while Quentin's rages and George's precarious sexual orientation began to look like psychiatric case histories. Another great British joke was born.

But a well-loved series acts as a kind of comfort-blanket; the certainty of more of the same is hugely reassuring to unadventurous readers. As adults fasten like lampreys upon a saga, avidly watching generations pass, children love series in which everything and everyone stays exactly the same for ever, the very antithesis, in fact, of real childhood, where everything inexorably changes, and every painfully acquired grasp of the rules is rendered obsolete as the rules are altered. Even very young children can be heard speaking wistfully of some lost Golden Age, 'When I was little. ...'

The best writers for children were, are, those who recognize the transience of childhood. The very purpose of the original and much-derided moral tales was to assist in the eventual production of an adult, not a perfect child. If one considers childhood as a vehicle gathering speed, with someone at the wheel who cannot reach the pedals or the gear lever, then one might think of an adult as a child who has learned to drive. But in even one lifetime the traffic builds up, the roads become more dangerous, the demands made of the vehicles become more complex, the signs and signals more confusing. In my Pitt Rivers mode I felt the highest regard for the writers who had noticed this and adjusted the brakes, tuned the engine and tightened the steering. Even so, the work of many has been dismissed as period pieces instead of lauded as vital components in a process. Yet no one derides George Stephenson for building The Rocket rather than Eurostar, or Edison for inventing the phonograph instead of turning his talents to the technology of the compact disc.

Here is Blyton again:

> There was once a little girl called Tilly, who told tales all day long. I don't like tell-tales, do you? Well, nobody liked Tilly!
>
> 'Mummy, Peter pushed me today! Mummy, Ann dirtied her frock! Mummy, Pussy has been lying on your best cushion! Mummy, the postman dropped one of your letters in the mud and dirtied it — I saw him!'
>
> That was how Tilly told tales all the day, and people got so cross with her! Ah, but wait! She didn't know the tell-tale bird was about![7]

To the average infant teacher who deals with around thirty Tillys five days a week, none of this will sound especially depraved, but it earned Tilly a place in *A Book of Naughty Children*, which also comprised such wilful malignancies as nail-biting and pigeon toes.

Approximately one century earlier an anonymous contributor to the *Magazine for the Young*, who may possibly have been Charlotte Yonge, created a serial story about a village school. This establishment, run for working-class girls, doubled as a Sunday School, so there is a noticeable religious content to the episodes, but their charm lies in the strong and sympathetic drawing of the schoolgirls, including another tell-tale:

'If you please, Miss, there are Ellen Wild, Honor Walton and Emily Morris, and a lot of them all at play with the boys upon the hill.'

This was said in a little shrill voice by Elizabeth Kingsley, with her eyebrows set up, and her eyes open, as if she thought it most wonderful and amusing to have such a thing to tell of two of the steadiest girls in the first class.

'I am sorry for it, and sorry you are in such a hurry to tell,' replied Miss Dora, in a grave voice which checked Elizabeth, who went back to her place, not, however, without a sort of pleasure in the thought of the fine uproar there would be when Miss Edith came in and was obliged to speak to the girls in fault. Not that Elizabeth was an ill-natured girl, far from it, she was always ready to help other people, and was trying to remember to give up her own will. But she liked the amusement, the excitement of other people being scolded; even the being sorry for them was pleasanter than having nothing new, and above all she liked to have something to say.[8]

In a later episode there is an outbreak of petty thieving in the school. The girls are extremely free with their accusations until the culprit is discovered and turns out to have been a likely suspect all along — with hindsight. But it was evidently far more gratifying to discuss *un*likely suspects. The irrepressible Elizabeth and her friend Kate are surprised by their own reactions when the truth is known:

'I don't know why,' said Elizabeth Kingsley, 'but it makes me feel very sorry. I cannot think how it was that I thought it would be rather — that I should rather like it if Emily Morris had been found out.'

'I know just what you mean ... One felt anxious and angry then, and only wanted to have it cleared up; but now one only feels shocked and sorry.'

'Aye,' said Elizabeth, 'but I thought then I should rather like to be shocked. Was not that very odd, Kate?'

Kate had something of the same feeling herself, but she did not understand it, and so she only said 'Yes'.

Certainly Elizabeth and Kate and their friends are given some fearfully pious lines to deliver, but we can still enjoy an admiration for the author in respect of her generally successful attempts to write about real children with real problems, coming to terms with the gulf that exists between what they think and what they know they are supposed to think. Always sympathetic, never censorious, even towards the expelled thief — she can even risk allowing Kate to doubt openly if expulsion was the wisest course of action. One of her most attractive scenes is saved until last; on hearing that one of their teachers is to marry, Elizabeth and some of the older girls organize the whole school into making a patchwork quilt as a wedding present. It is done in the utmost secrecy, which is pleasurable in itself, and they look forward in an agony of excitement to the day when they can give the present and, of course, enjoy hearing their work praised. The event is, predictably, a let-down:

> Mrs Howard did really notice several of the patterns, and said how very pretty they were, and she asked those who stood near to show her their portions. She was plainly very much pleased, and yet Rose was rather disappointed that she did not call up more people to look at it. There was Miss Howard to be sure, and Mr Howard ... and he said it was a great piece of work and nicely done, and they must have been very much pleased to do it, but he did not praise them as Rose, Elizabeth, and even Kate expected .... He said twice over, too, that they must be very good clever little girls, and it was very odd that this was what Caroline Wallis and Emily Morris dwelt upon most of all, though they had done little more than a very few of those easy joinings on the border which had been devised for the little ones.

I remember it so well; I was there, and so were you, and so were all of us. The author's breakthrough here has been to refrain from drawing a moral conclusion. There is no need; the circumstances speak for themselves, and she has had the wit to know when to stop; when to trust her readers' percipience. Everyone in childhood has shared the disappointment of Rose, Elizabeth and Kate, the profound injustice of what adults regard as scrupulous fairness. No doubt the little girls are morally enhanced by not getting what they feel they have earned in the way of extravagant praise, but there is no authorial intervention to remind us that they were the better for it. They did not *feel* better; this is the real message.

This is a point at which one might look forward over a hundred years to the novels of Noel Streatfeild, in which talented children were routinely snubbed and belittled by peers, parents and teachers, in case they became swollen-headed. Just how they were expected to become self-critical without ever learning to appraise their own levels of excellence was an issue that Streatfeild sidestepped by making them ineffably gifted, immune to outside influences. Only the meek deserved encouragement. Fortunately, few of them showed any signs of intellectual brilliance, where consistent denial of their capabilities would have proved truly disastrous.

The history of human achievement in any course of endeavour is punctuated by breakthroughs — Streatfeild's own *Ballet Shoes*[9] is one, the first genuine career novel — but in science and technology the gains are usually immediately apparent and acted upon. Observe the short but startling career of the computer, for instance. In areas of creativity they are less apparent. A whole generation may pass before anyone acts upon them, and the effects are by no means permanent. A hundred years after the events at Langley School the worst aspects of the moral tale are still with us in the lustreless and superficial stories of Blyton. Writers, early writers especially, and especially early writers for children, tend to become bywords for what they failed to do rather than for what they achieved, and often on the basis of hearsay rather than experience.

Only a few months ago a columnist in *The Guardian* stated that Louisa M. Alcott made Jo March, the heroine of *Little Women*, abandon her literary career in order to get married.[10] Elsewhere it has been written that readers have never forgiven Alcott for not 'allowing' Jo to marry the rich, handsome and adoring Laurie, bestowing on her instead the consolation prize, a middle-aged academic; for not sending Jo to Europe instead of Amy, since it is Jo's lot in life to suffer disappointment. For a start, Alcott had no real interest in a heroine to whom things came easily; she preferred protagonists who were up against it, as she had been all her life. But one only has to return to the books to see how critics may wilfully miss the point if it suits their argument. Jo's literary career is going nowhere when she marries; later it takes off spectacularly. Moreover, far from denying Jo the glittering prize of a marriage with Laurie, Alcott makes it clear that this clever, independent girl refuses to marry a man she loves only as a friend, having been brought up by a mother who has already advised her daughters that it is better to remain single than to endure an unhappy marriage simply because marriage is expected of a girl. Jo eventually marries for love; Alcott leaves us in no doubt at all that it is Laurie who has got the consolation prize, and knows it.

Mrs March's views on marriage cannot but remind us that she herself is saddled with possibly the most useless husband in fiction, and her eldest daughter, Meg, who at 17 marries the first man who has asked her, later refuses to let her own daughter make the same mistake in the last book of the series, *Jo's Boys*.[11] This book also features the trials of Nan, the medical student, fighting off the attentions of her childhood sweetheart in order to devote herself to her work. She has neither time nor inclination to be a wife. Finally her obduracy succeeds. The childhood sweetheart finds the nice airhead he deserves and Nan, unimpeded, storms on ahead to become a doctor and, we learn at the end, to remain single.

Alcott is taken to task for her moralizing, and she did have an unfortunate habit of interrupting narrative to buttonhole the reader face to face, but she was not writing solely to entertain; she was writing polemic, as a propagandist for feminism, for women to work, or wed, or do both according to their personal inclinations. There is no profit in denying her status as an innovator simply because much of her work fails to satisfy contemporary taste. The fate of girls whom her message had passed by is detailed in E. M. Delafield's novel of 1932 (although set possibly 20 years earlier), *Thank Heaven Fasting*, a terrifying account of what befell a young woman whose only asset was marriageability (i.e. virginity) and who forfeited her reputation by acting indiscreetly *once*.[12] Sixty years before, when Meg March went to a dance dressed like a tart and got drunk, her mother was not particularly dismayed, being far more outraged by the suggestion, overheard at the same house party, that she was deviously planning an advantageous marriage for her daughter.

If Jo is an unusual departure from the conventional portraits of teenage girls in the mid-nineteenth century, her mother is altogether remarkable. An incident that might have furnished a startling scene in *Little Women*, had that book opened earlier in Jo's life, is referred to in *Little Men*, where Jo, now a mother herself, reveals that her own mother hit her only once, during her childhood, for losing her temper.[13] Jo recalls turning upon her and crying, 'You're mad [angry] yourself. You ought to be whipped as much as me.' The mother thought about the justice of this, and apologized.

Another later writer who made a conscious effort to break the mould was Eve Garnett with *The Family from One-End Street*. The said family were the Ruggleses, Jo and Rosie, and their seven children. The book opens in a way that ensures the reader is in full possession of the facts:

> Mrs Ruggles was a Washerwoman and her husband was a Dustman. 'Very suitable too,' she would say, though whether this referred to Mr Ruggles himself, or the fact that they both cleaned up after other people, it was hard to decide.[14]

Actually, Mrs Ruggles is speaking of neither her husband nor their respective jobs, but reassuring the reader that it is very suitable to write a book about the family of a washerwoman and a dustman who are bringing up their family on the breadline or, as Winifred Holtby said of the Hollys in *South Riding*, 'in the fear of the Lord, the sanitary inspector and the Poor Law Authorities'.[15] *South Riding*, although rewarding for a young reader, is an adult novel. It is instructive to compare the treatment, by the respective authors, of the Holly and Ruggles families, not least in the matter of birth control.

In *Written for Children*, John Rowe Townsend pointed out:

> There is a warm sense of family solidarity ... Nevertheless it seems to me to be too condescending to be altogether commendable. Mr and Mrs Ruggles are seen from above and outside. Even their names, and the choice of their occupations ... make them seem slightly comic. People from higher up the social scale are terribly nice to the Ruggleses; and the Ruggleses know their place.[16]

This is irrefutable, but reading the book as a child I did not notice it, any more than I noticed that Streatfeild's Fossil family were the kind of people who would employ my mother to do the cleaning. On the other hand we owe it to Garnett to applaud what she was trying to do, and succeeded in doing; removing the menials, however comic, from the sidelines to centre field; giving them leading roles instead of bit-parts. They have a past and a present; definitely they have a future. Unlike the ubiquitous waifs of late-nineteenth-century fiction they may be poor but they are not destitute; they are not victims. They are helped, but they are not rescued. The second eldest child, Kate, goes to grammar school on a scholarship, and while Jo Ruggles dreams of keeping a pig in the back yard for short-term gains, Kate aims to go to agricultural college and improve the quality of life in general. Jo and Rosie may resemble a comedy duo on the halls, ever ready to burst into a song by Albert Chevalier, but as characters in a children's book they fulfil the roles of any parental couple from any social stratum, those of mother and father.

One might also contrast Garnett's depiction of the way in which middle-class people treat the Ruggleses with a book that came out the year before *One-End Street*, 1936, the same year as *South Riding*, incidentally: *More about John and Mary*, by Grace James. Differences are apparent from the outset:

> John and Mary were staying with their Granny at Smockfarthing when John's seventh birthday came round. These lucky young people had two happy homes, one in the great city of Rome, and the other at their Granny's farm ... in Berkshire.[17]

Lucky indeed. Towards the middle of the book they have the opportunity to be terribly nice to someone from lower down the social scale. The creature is fed before they take it out:

> The sun was so warm that when Tim Baines came, Mrs Dyer brought one of the milking stools into the yard and put it beside the round wooden table, scrubbed so white and clean where the separator and churn stood airing. Mrs Dyer spread a sheet of *The Times* over the table because of grease spots, and she brought Tim Baines a big plate of Irish stew with lots of potatoes and gravy, which she kindly and thoughtfully told him to eat with a spoon. He finished every scrap and also a baked apple and cream. One of the nursery windows overlooked the yard, and the children were so much interested in the sight of Tim Baines eating his dinner that they could hardly be persuaded to eat their own.

Good as a zoo, really. Grace James shows a considerable understanding of children and childhood, but Tim Baines scarcely counts as a child. He appears to be on the same level as a yard dog as far as the children are concerned. Whatever the shortcomings of the Ruggles family, paradigm of the deserving poor, Garnett paved the way for people like them to star in their own stories (a fact we take for granted, now) and, eventually, to write them. There is some pressure on writers these days to boast about their disadvantages in order to be taken seriously, like Monty Python's 'four Yorkshiremen'.

Even so, four years after the Ruggleses made their first appearance, Enid Blyton in *The Twins at St Clare's* had something to say about the lower orders getting above themselves. A shopkeeper who has made his pile sends his daughter to St Clare's, a private school, in the hopes of turning her into 'a lady':

> 'Good heavens, Sheila, where were you brought up? Haven't you learnt by now that decent people don't say "Didn't ought to!"? My goodness, you talk about your servants and your Rolls Royce cars, your house and your lake and goodness knows what — and then you talk like the daughter of the dustman.'[18]

This is quite a Shavian speech by Blyton's unexacting standards, but never mind the quality, feel the width. Sheila's base origins are also betrayed by the fact that she does not wash her neck, and you could find yourself in *A Book of Naughty Children* for that omission. It seems not to have occurred to the girls, or to the author, that after a year in the superior environment of St Clare's, Sheila has learned precisely nothing, in class or out of it. The novel is, in the main, harmless pap, a pallid pastiche of every other girls' school story ever written; it is just unfortunate that Blyton chose a dustman's daughter as the epitome of low life. Jo Ruggles the dustman might have to go cap in hand to the vicar for help in clothing his family; his daughter was going to make her own way.

Back in 1960 the essayists in *Young Writers, Young Readers*[2] had Blyton on their hit list along with Captain W. E. Johns, nativity playwrights, contributors to comics (*Eagle*, for instance, now a respectable collector's item) and tabloid journalists, admittedly not then the wolverines and rottweilers of current obloquy. A survey of reading habits is preceded by an anthology section of writing by children, apparently unaffected by the frightful rubbish they had been reading. In spite of this, the Poet Laureate, C. Day Lewis, in his foreword, felt it necessary to exhort parents and teachers 'to try to ensure that our children's minds are not cramped or stereotyped by an exclusive diet of shoddy, conventional, "popular" reading'.[19] And as standards declined — standards are always declining; it is their nature — what became of that lost generation of readers? Why, they became us. And here we are, 35 years on, just as worried, with standards having declined even further, more meretricious garbage being published every day, and the BBC, heretofore a bastion of quality, reduced to crowing over its having secured the rights to Little Noddy. No one reads any more; this is a well-known fact. They are all plugged into computers. People who write on walls cannot even spell four-letter words.

Thirty-five years from now, I suspect that things will be pretty much the same, and we shall all look quite good, bathed in the rosy glow of yesteryear, compared with the ghastly tripe that will be written and read in 2030. With luck the true greats will have been recognized and given their due. The prime innovator of our own times, William Mayne, frightens the grown-ups; they do not want to engage with his uncompromising style, his intellect and his wit, and for that reason withhold him from children. It is much easier to promote the works of Roald Dahl, who makes rude noises and uses daring words like 'knickers'; much easier to share his own view of himself as the great iconoclast, the *dernier cri* in children's fiction.

Those of us who read Mayne when younger learned that there was no need to observe special requirements when writing for children. You may write exactly what you want to write, and in any way you see fit; the kind of freedoms taken entirely for granted by adult authors. His influence, largely unacknowledged, has been considerable. It is fascinating to contemplate what history will make of Dahl.

Notes

1　See, for example, Jan Mark, *The Oxford Book of Children's Stories*, Oxford University Press, Oxford, 1993; and Jan Mark, 'The Patrick Hardy Lecture', *Signal*, 73, January 1994.
2　D. R. Barnes, 'Captain Johns and the Adult World', in Boris Ford (ed.), *Young Writers, Young Readers*, Hutchinson, London, 1963 (revised edition) p. 115.
3　*Ibid*. p. 118.
4　Sarah Fielding, 'Celia and Chloe' in *The Governess*, Andrew Millar, 1749.
5　Frances Hodgson Burnett, *Little Lord Fauntleroy*, first published 1886.
6　Enid Blyton, *Five on a Treasure Island*, first published by Hodder and Stoughton, London, 1942.
7　Enid Blyton, 'The Tell-Tale Bird' in *A Book of Naughty Children*, Methuen, London, 1944.
8　Anon., 'Langley School', in *Magazine for the Young*, 1848.
9　Noel Streatfeild, *Ballet Shoes*, first published by J. M. Dent, London, 1936.
10　Louisa M. Alcott, *Little Women*, first published 1868, and *Good Wives*, first published 1869.
11　Louisa M. Alcott, *Jo's Boys*, first published 1886.
12　E. M. Delafield, *Thank Heaven Fasting*, Macmillan, London, 1932.
13　Louisa M. Alcott, *Little Men*, first published 18.
14　Eve Garnett, *The Family from One-End Street*, Frederick Muller, London, 1937.
15　Winifred Holtby, *South Riding*, Collins, London, 1936.
16　John Rowe Townsend, *Written for Children*, revised edn, Penguin, Harmondsworth, 1983, p. 187.
17　Grace James, *More about John and Mary*, Frederick Muller, London 1936.
18　Enid Blyton, *The Twins at St Clare's*, Methuen, London, 1941.
19　C. Day Lewis, Foreword, in Ford, *op. cit.*, p. ix.

PART III

Classroom Voices

Other parts of the book have looked at what happens when readers get into conversation with writers or when readers talk together about their reading. The chapters which follow take account of these conversations, but introduce new voices — some from different cultures, others entirely imaginary. Most particularly, though, the voices of the classroom become stronger. All of them are talking from different viewpoints about stories and how they offer meeting points, and points of departure on new journeys, for readers and writers of different ages, cultures and experiences. In entering the domain of the classroom particular issues arise; for example, how can children best be encouraged to draw on 'the myriad voices which surround their lives' as Holly Anderson puts it? And how might children be encouraged to take more risks and to experiment more freely as readers and writers? All of the chapters in this part of the book consider the role of the teacher in promoting and extending children's language and literacy, suggesting more deliberately considered kinds of intervention in the process of children becoming satisfied readers and writers. The meeting point — the conversational focus — is story.

Throughout this part of the book a strong central thread is the importance not only of acknowledging children's cultural experience, but of taking full account of how the cultural contexts of home and school intersect. Another is the sense that, given the chance to show it, children often know much more about the complexities of different genres than we might acknowledge. Noticing what children can do and say about and with story is essential; it can mean teachers becoming better listeners as well as good talkers. Whatever the implications, the different chapters offer both challenge and practical example of just how the dynamic between reading, writing and talking can be energized. Geoff Fox opens by suggesting that teachers need to learn how to teach children to read the rich resources of picture books. He argues that because picture books are complex texts, they offer both pleasure and the success of effortful interpretation to readers of all ages. In a wide-ranging chapter, Geoff Fox suggests that reading picture books can pre-figure the analytical demands of more developed or mature reading — both in school and out. He looks back at earlier picture book makers and reaches forward into readers' futures to emphasize the need to pay continuing and conscious attention to the process of pictorial reading — including reading 'in the gaps'.

Many of those gaps, those invitations to link one text with another, one set of experiences with the experience of the story, can only be filled as the developing reader gathers more and more reading experience. At the same time, if children are genuinely to be able to read between lines and peek into the gaps, nooks and crannies of books, they don't just need experience of a range of other texts, but a sense that their personal and cultural experience is something which has relevance in their development as readers. They also need learning contexts which value and authentically take account of the cultural experiences of home and community. So what about those children for whom reading is not yet a practised and satisfying activity? The kinds of questions raised by Geoff Fox become both more urgent and more demanding of teachers when young readers are approaching texts written in a language which they cannot yet use fully, drawn from a culture whose codes they don't yet know how to negotiate. Brigid Smith points to the need for 'stories in which readers can find themselves'. For her — and of the children and teachers she has worked with both here and in the Indian subcontinent — these are children's (and teachers') own stories made into books for themselves and others to read. Arguing for 'contextually based learning', she describes how a dictated story can be 'a serious vehicle for learning in many aspects of literacy'. Her work in Andhra Pradesh leads her to the belief that in order to help developing bilingual pupils in schools in the UK, we also need to understand the different ways of taking on literacy reflected in children's homes and communities. This means looking carefully and critically at how we teach and how we offer children new learning experiences.

Lesley Hendy's chapter on drama as a means of language development echoes this sense of an urgent need to reappraise the contexts offered for learning. Where Brigid Smith describes the bridge between a child's personal cultural experience and the learning requirements of schooling by looking at developing readers, Lesley Hendy looks at how a bridge can also be offered through fantasy and role-play. Children need 'active and compelling experiences in contexts that are familiar' if they are to develop as confident, assured and ambitious language users, and she describes how this can be made possible through story linked with drama. In active storytelling, the teacher becomes a guide towards language and conceptual development, helping children to practise making judgements, offer opinions and develop critical awareness of how narratives can be made and remade. Teacher intervention becomes a modelling process for reflecting on learning as the teacher enters the imaginative world on the children's own terms. Using children's capacity to engage seriously and productively in role-play helps the teacher to adopt a new role of careful and attentive listener.

The value of role-play for learning is central to Holly Anderson's chapter, but here the focus shifts towards children's writing. Using a range of examples of children's texts, she argues that 'role-play and writing in role are legitimate games to play in the classroom'. Holly Anderson's starting point for looking at stories is unusual: she uses non-narrative writing and specifically letter writing to open an argument which draws together the threads of the other chapters. While story is so important in learning, there are constant tensions for teachers related to traditional teaching practices and to curriculum requirements for children to develop narrative and non-narrative writing. Although narrative is a powerful communicative act, in the classroom it can become sterile and devoid of meaning if used as a mere recounting of experience: the do-it-then-write-about-it kind of task. How then to teach the use of non-chronological forms while preserving the vitality of narrative? How also to ensure that children are actively involved in negotiating, making and reflecting on their own learning? For Holly Anderson some answers emerged as she looked at children writing letters at home and in the classroom. Children first meet letters in their homes and communities; there are social and cultural reasons for writing letters. This makes writing letters a potentially powerful way of encouraging children to write in non-chronological forms. But the potential for building on home experience and using imaginative possibilities for playing with language came to light when Holly Anderson began to combine letter writing and role-play. By entering into the story world of play, children in Key Stages 1 and 2 managed to write effectively in non-narrative form, drawing on different genres which reflected the range of their reading and personal experience. In this way the 'myriad voices' of writers, readers, teachers and children, over time and across cultures, entered the classroom. The chapters which follow suggest that listening to them carefully might tell us a thing or two!

CHAPTER 10

Reading Picture Books ...
How To?

Geoff Fox

This chapter began as a talk after dinner on the first evening of the 'Voices Off' conference; it was an informal occasion and one which invited participants to become involved. Geoff Fox maintains this conversational tone as he invites the reader to join him in a discussion of some ideas inspired by his observations of readers and picture books. As in the best of ruminative, exploratory conversations, this chapter covers wide ground, moving backwards into the history of picture books and looking forward to what very young readers of the present day might be able to do with their reading in the future. Much of this, Geoff Fox argues, depends upon sensitive and thoughtful teacher intervention. We still have a lot to learn about how picture books can be read, and this chapter shows how developed readers — as they read backwards and forwards in a text, both literally and in memory or recall, as they read between the lines and in the gaps in narratives — are using the very techniques and approaches to reading which picture books can so readily teach. The question is: having noticed this, what can we do to help young readers become conscious of, and develop further, the versatile and flexible modes of reading offered by picture books?

Glimpses of *Gorilla*

To begin with, consider three cameos, all of them involving Anthony Browne's picture book, *Gorilla*:[1]

- A parent–teachers' association meeting in a Torquay primary school, one evening of book week. There are just enough copies to go round the 60 or so in the group, one between two. By the time I've issued the last book, the class is more or less out of control, and my planned instructions are superfluous. Some of the parents exploring the books together have never met before, but there is animated talk everywhere

— not about whether their children would enjoy the book, but about the book itself.

- A class of Year 3 B.Ed. undergraduates pores over *Gorilla*. They share details as they discover them, celebrate the wit, and move back and forth within the book, setting images alongside each other (such as Hannah's chilly breakfast with Father, and Hannah's midnight feast with Gorilla). They go back to the beginning and start the book again. Next week, in another course, the same students spend a couple of hours considering Carol Ann Duffy's elusive poem, 'Small Female Skull'.[2] Their behaviour — mental, verbal and even physical — seems almost identical to the way in which they read *Gorilla*.

- A skilled sixth-form teacher is beginning her two-year English Literature A-level course at a further education college. Twenty students wait for a challenge worthy of their As and Bs at GCSE. They are issued with a copy of *Gorilla* apiece. There is a whiff of rebellion — they hadn't analysed *To Kill a Mockingbird* to bits and completely understood 'Dulce et Decorum Est' for this. 'I'd like you, if you would, to read this text and, when you're ready, talk to your neighbours about it in any way you choose.' After 10 minutes they are absorbed. Eventually, the teacher draws together their ideas about the book and how it is crafted. These, she suggests, raise many of the questions about literary texts the group will be looking at over the next two years. The session provides a 'marker', a series of reference points, for the weeks which follow.

All three groups enjoyed a concentrated and often hilarious engagement with the book. Discussions were punctuated by sudden bursts of pleasure, as some fresh detail was pointed out: the 'Mona Gorilla'; Hannah ballroom dancing on the lawn, balanced on her gorilla partner's feet; the gorilla-head newel post at the foot of the banisters. But beneath the shared enjoyment, what was going on?

We have learned much in the last twenty years about what happens inside readers' heads when they encounter novels and poems. For the most part, we have understood readers' processes by close observation and by asking them to report their own reactions to novels and poems. Often, their idiosyncratic comments surprised us, and new insights about how reading 'worked' began to inform how literature was taught, particularly in secondary schools and in higher education. In its earliest manifestation (the Cox version), the National Curriculum drew heavily on what we had learned.

The processes of 'reading'[3] picture books are not so well charted. Because many of the readers of picture books are young, it is less easy for them to manage the self-awareness needed to say what happens when they meet a book and when a book meets them. It is an intractable area, as I confirmed when, in preparation for the lecture at the Homerton conference on which this chapter is based, I spent half an hour with each of a dozen 9-year-olds. I asked them first to read Anthony Browne's *Hansel and Gretel*[4] on their own (though in my presence) and then talk with me about the experience. As far as I could tell, all of them were missing much of the detail and patterning of the book — how its crafting *is* its content; just as a sixth-form teacher might feel his or her students were missing much of what a novel offered if they read merely for plot and character.

In this chapter I want to attempt a description of what picture books might contribute to the long-term growth of a reader. I want to suggest that the mental activities of a reader absorbed in a picture book have much in common with the processes which mature, highly competent readers employ as they read other kinds of texts, such as novels and poems. If this is so, it may be that we have available to us in picture books a means of fostering development in reading which is more potent than is usually recognized. If we knew more about these areas, I suspect our teaching might be shaped by a keener awareness that we are laying down quite specific foundations for the long-term development of a reader.

Some preliminaries

First, I want to acknowledge the work of others in this relatively unmapped territory. My most influential guides have been Margaret Meek,[5] Perry Nodelman,[6] Jane Doonan,[7] Margaret Mackey,[8] David Lewis[9] and Maurice Sendak.[10] I shall draw directly on their work, since I need to use their thinking to move towards some practical possibilities in the classroom.

Secondly, I have chosen to use a number of well-known picture books to exemplify this discussion. In making familiar choices, I thought that readers of this chapter would probably know the context of the specific illustrations I shall mention. Where others have already commented on these illustrations, I have not hesitated to make use of their insights.

Lastly, I want to invite you, the present reader, to engage in a brief activity which is closely parallel to one which the listeners at Homerton College seemed to find useful at a similar stage of the discussion. The purpose is simply to ask you to check your own experience of the field I am exploring. If you are willing to play, this is the activity:

- Please recall a picture book you met for the first time quite recently; or, alternatively, track down one that you've been meaning to read, and read it as you usually would.
- When you've done that, could you jot down what you did when you read the book? If you need no further prompting, please do not read on until you have jotted. But if my request is not clear, such questions as

'Did you spend time on the cover?' and 'Did you read words first or pictures?' might indicate what I'm interested in: as precise a description as possible of the reading process.

- Having done that, you might try two or three questions, in addition to those in the last paragraph. Did you read the title page? Did you re-read the book — and if so, why and with what results? Did you move about within the book, comparing one image with another? What impact, if any, did the shape of the book, the layout on the page, the typefaces, the texture of the paper, make upon you?

More of this interrogation might alienate you beyond recall; perhaps further questions will be suggested by the discussion which follows.

The shaping possibilities of picture books

We have come to see reading as a dynamic exchange between writer and reader as each unique experience of a text is created. A kind of fluid balance — somewhat in favour of the author — has to be maintained in this interplay; as readers' responses to poetry and prose were closely examined, it was tempting to lose sight of how novels and poems shape their readers' activities. Margaret Meek's invaluable *How Texts Teach What Readers Learn* reminded us just how picture books, as well as novels and poems, do exactly that.

I want now to describe some aspects of reading behaviour which picture books invite. For the sake of clarity, they appear here as separate activities, but of course they are not in practice. Readers, after all, can do several things at once.

Looking forwards, glancing back

To take a familiar matter first, we know that picture books often require young readers to ask the basic question, 'What is going to happen next?' There is a lively host of characters moving at one pace or another from left to right across the pages of picture books (in Western cultures, at least) — and half-way off the right-hand edge in some cases. Rosie the Hen, heroine of *Rosie's Walk*,[11] is a classic example; Pat Hutchins's pictures insist that we turn the page to find out just what disaster will next befall Rosie's pursuer, the fox. As Perry Nodelman notes:

> Picture books are filled with pictures that show an action just before it reaches its climax ... a quick glance through any group of picture books might suggest that the entire population of the human universe spends most of its time with one foot in the air; in this storytelling medium, the evocation of action is of the essence.[12]

But it doesn't stop there. Almost all readers, and listeners, learn to ask what happens next in a story, simply by being around in the world with their ears and eyes open; but *Rosie's Walk* not only asks you to look forward, but invites to look backwards too, if you want to savour the taut anticipation of the fox and his (it *must* be a male) series of bathetic catastrophes. You need also to check what the minor characters are up to — just what were those frogs (which we now see leaping in consternation) doing on the last page? Many an undergraduate reader has not learned that some novels, and most poems, *expect* you to look backwards as well as forwards. Without mentally, and sometimes literally, glancing back through the story, the reader of a detective fiction, for example, would soon become disengaged from the riddling game the writer proposes. Then there is the matter of irony. Without the ability to recall earlier events, dialogue or authorial comment, readers of the novels of Jane Austen or Fay Weldon might find them tedious, if not trivial. Given the freedom to say so, indeed, a number of undergraduates will confess to exactly that experience of Austen at A-level. A reader who loses sight of Marlow and his listeners on the Thames barge as night falls on the estuary in the opening pages of *Heart of Darkness*[13] surely also loses much of the bleak self-knowledge he achieves through his 'inconclusive experience' in pursuit of Kurtz, or the recognition that one 'interminable waterway' inevitably leads to another.

There is more to be said on this, particularly about the reading of poetry, but two or three further examples, left undeveloped, must suffice for now. Without a willingness to range back and forth in the book, what would a reader make of, say, Milan Kundera's *The Unbearable Lightness of Being*,[14] or Penelope Lively's *Moon Tiger*?[15] And, though you may not be sure whether you are looking backwards, forwards, both or neither, where would you be with Martin Amis's *Time's Arrow*?[16]

Between the lines

One of the characteristics of able readers at work (or, better, at play) is their capacity to meet the challenge of what Wolfgang Iser called 'the telling gap'[17] left by the author for the reader to fill; or, to echo the title of this book, to listen to the 'voices off' — to enjoy what is *not* said, to collude with the author in creating that part of the text which does not appear physically on the page. A rationale for the criticism of all kinds of children's books might be developed using this notion as perhaps its most fundamental criterion. What kind of gaps does a writer leave for the reader to fill? Blyton, say, requires her reader to fill hardly any 'telling gaps' in terms of narrative — what's there on the surface is what there is. Alan Garner, in sharp contrast, asks his reader to work hard 'between the lines', or 'off the page' if you like, to enjoy the different levels of meaning embedded in *The Owl Service*,[18] whilst the gaps in his *Red Shift*[19] are so extensive that all but the most able and persistent readers might well disappear down the cracks.

Anthony Browne, John Burningham or Maurice Sendak, to take well-known examples among contemporary makers of picture books, consistently leave spaces for readers to fill; indeed, in Burningham's much-loved *Come Away from the Water, Shirley*[20] and *Time to Get out of the Bath, Shirley*[21] the literal gap between left-hand and right-hand pages has to be spanned by any reader if they are to grasp the two worlds Shirley inhabits. In their gleeful subversions of traditional tales (*The True Story of the Three Little Pigs*[22] and *The Frog Prince Continued*,[23] for example), Jon Scieszka and his illustrators barely allow readers a breather in the games they must play between the lines. All of these creators of picture books are becoming favourite subjects of adult readers with an eye for the postmodernist.

There is nothing new, however, about leaving spaces for the reader to fill in picture books. Randolph Caldecott (1846–86) was an expert at posing questions, and implying answers, in his illustrations. Caldecott well knew, no doubt, that such gaps tend to draw readers more closely into a book as they become, in effect, joint creators of the text. For Maurice Sendak, 'Caldecott is an illustrator, he is a songwriter, he is a choreographer, he is a stage manager, he is a decorator, he is a theatre person; he's superb'.[24] Sendak draws attention to Caldecott's closing illustration to 'Bye, Baby Bunting'[25] (we have already been invited to fill

some surprising gaps, for although Daddy *goes* a-hunting, he is evidently so unsuccessful that he ends up at a Hare and Rabbit Skin Dealer's in order to fetch Baby a rabbit skin). The final picture is full of questions. What is the baby to make of this extraordinary situation? Sendak wonders if the baby is thinking, 'Does something have to die to dress me?' Understandably, the rabbits seem equally pensive. And does that demure but oddly detached mother have a thought in her head about this disturbing encounter?

The companion story in Caldecott's original book was 'Hey, diddle, diddle'. Here, the handsome young dish sweeps the easily impressed spoon off her feet (to the chagrin of several other young dishes, upon whom his choice has not fallen — they are left, literally, 'on the shelf'). Though the rhyme may conclude with the pair's elopement, Caldecott does not. Father Knife and Mother Fork (we must infer, as we fill the gap Caldecott's picture implies) have hunted the couple down and a comprehensive thrashing leaves the dish in pieces as the spoon is led away by her parents. The chorus of grief-stricken young dishes is left to bewail the waste of so eligible a serving platter. He should have stuck to his own kind.

This reading 'between the lines', or even *beyond* the lines, this juggling with inferences, is an all-important, and intensely pleasurable, aspect of the art of reading. Chaucer knew that well. When he says of the Cook as they ride together towards Canterbury,

> But greet harm was it, as it thoughte me,
> That on his shyne a mormal hadde he,
> For blankmanger, that made he with the beste.[26]

readers who know a juxtaposition when they see one may feel certain that the hands that are scratching the pus-filled sore will, in the next minute, be plunged into the mixing bowl preparing that superlative blancmange. Readers who miss such implications are nonplussed by authors' games of this kind, or simply read past them.

The art of reading between the lines might begin, for the fortunate reader, with the picture book. Does a teacher, or a parent for that matter, simply hope that, if child and book are brought together, this process will begin? Of course, in some cases, it does; the maker of the picture book may well 'teach' an alert reader how a book is to be read so clearly that things develop without further assistance. But do primary teachers set out consciously to develop children's ability to read between the lines of picture books, as secondary teachers might do with students reading novels or poems?

Sharing secrets of detail

When I work with secondary students, and with undergraduates, it is clear that there are those who find it difficult to 'select the appropriate gear' as readers; to find a mode of reading suited to a particular text. A passage from a novel or a poem which asks to be read closely and reflectively may be approached at the same speed, say, as a Jeffrey Archer.

Picture books in which the illustration extends the words require close scrutiny, if their secrets are to be enjoyed to the full. Some may merely demand perseverance and keen eyesight. Leslie Brooke's retelling of *The Three Bears* (1905)[27] asks rather more of its readers. Here the bear motif is found throughout the illustrations, and each discovery offers the attentive reader fresh satisfactions — a secret found is a secret shared. Bears appear as decorations beneath the mantelpiece, and there are embroidered bears in the bedspreads, and carved heads of bears on the bedposts. The house is decorated with verbal and visual puns: 'Thyme is Honey: Save It' advises a framed motto on the wall. The Great, Huge Bear's bed carries the pattern of the Great Bear constellation in its footboard; hanging beside the fireplace is a portrait of a distinguished soldier, Major Ursa DSO (somewhat disconcertingly sporting his bearskin helmet); while on the bedside table, Little, Small, Wee Bear has left a half-read copy of *Tom Bruin's Schooldays*. Raymond Briggs[28] plays a similar game, for on Fungus's library shelves are such classics as *Far from the Madding Bogey*, *Memoirs of a Bogey Hunting Man*, and *Anne of Green Bogeys*. In the same vein, the Ahlbergs' Jolly Postman books[29] reveal fresh, minute delights over many re-readings.

The childlike exclamations of pleasure from the adult groups we met at the outset of this chapter came, perhaps, as they found an extra doorknob on the front door before Hannah and her Gorilla embark on their fantastic night adventure, or the topiary gorilla lurking outside in the

garden — there are scores of such examples in Browne's books, some of which might not be noticed until after a dozen or more readings.

The kind of reading which picks up such detail is an acquired art, yielding an enjoyment in the nuances of language which literature teachers, at any level, want for their students. Picture books might well enable a reader to begin to acquire the art.

Stories within stories

A necessary dimension of mature reading seems to be a belief in the stories which lie behind the story on the page — a sense that although we happen to be following *this* story, we might just as readily be following others which are happening off the page. Some picture books depend upon much the same implication of other stories behind the story, glimpsed within the detail of their illustrations.

Anno's wordless series of journeys to different countries (and through different kinds of narratives, some historical, some literary, some belonging to the visual arts) will serve as an example. The reader finds Anno himself somewhere, usually with his horse, travelling through every picture. Numerous separate incidents are taking place about the page. Some of them are 'free-standing' stories, complete in themselves, unique to Anno's book; but others have their roots elsewhere. In one opening of *Anno's Britain*,[30] for example, there are glimpses of stories which readers may already know. Here, in his washerwoman's weeds, is the escapee Mr Toad, wheedling his way onto the canal barge; several inches across the double-page spread, the same Mr Toad takes his ease over a picnic with Ratty, while Mole feeds the horse, grazing near their gypsy caravan. In the upper left-hand corner, Constable's hay-wain sets out to cross the ford.

The recognition that stories are connected is an important one for developing readers. Novels they may meet much later in life, such as Julian Barnes's *A History of the World in 10½ Chapters*,[31] depend upon a reader's awareness of intertextual connections. Close attention to particular picture books may provide a beginning of this kind of awareness.

Patterns within a book

Some recent picture books have made increasing use of recurring motifs or visual patterns within themselves. This is almost inevitable in stories which depend upon repetition (Rosie on her walk, for example), but there are more subtly embedded patterns. Sendak's Max,[32] intent upon one kind of mischief or another, makes a tent in his own home (before his voyage to the land where the wild things are) with what seems to be a curtain slung over a rope of knotted handkerchiefs. Inside is a three-legged stool. After the wild rumpus, wanting to be where someone loved him best of all, King Max sits wistfully inside his tented pavilion, on his three-legged stool.

Anthony Browne allows images to reverberate throughout a book; some of them even recur (gorillas, brick walls, cages, for example) from one book to another. In *Hansel and Gretel*, triangular and conical shapes abound: three-cornered mouseholes, chateau roofs and fir trees all foreshadow the menace of a witch's hat (which never fully appears). In the same way, the imprisoned lives of the children, and their father, are implied through the use of numerous vertical 'bars', from the stripes on the dresses of Gretel and her doll to the cage in which Hansel is locked up by the witch. The children make their way back from the forest early in the story to be met by a scowling stepmother (mouth turned down at the corners in a triangle reinforced by the frowning lines of her cheeks and her hair-line, all framed by the conical shape of a fir tree reflected in the glass of the cottage door). A similar image greets them when they arrive at the witch's house: same mouth, same lines furrowing the cheeks, same hair-line — but this time net curtains and the leading on the glass provide the frame. In Susan Jeffers's *Hansel and Gretel*[33] the stepmother and the witch differ facially — but one has a scarf and the other a blouse made from identical material.

Adult readers, and playgoers, also need to be aware of motifs and patterns — Graham Swift's use of water and circularity in *Waterland*,[34] the Thames in *Our Mutual Friend*,[35] the ubiquitous beast references in *King Lear* — whilst the interplay of echoing images (their similarities and their shades of difference) threads through the experience of poetry.

Fantasy and metaphor

Some adolescent readers find playful engagement in fantasy and metaphor particularly difficult. The 'series' novel, from Mills & Boon to the currently popular Point novels, may bear a tenuous relation to daily life, but they depend upon the illusion of everyday reality, much as *Neighbours* and *Coronation Street* pretend to be about suburban Sydney and urban Manchester. For readers unable to move beyond the doubtful security of this kind of reading, the risks of psychological play involved in such texts as Ursula Le Guin's Earthsea quartet[36] or Margaret Atwood's *The Handmaid's Tale*[37] will prove several steps too far.

Picture books might have accustomed such earthbound, hesitant readers to adventurous mental play within narratives from an early age. The early steps along this path can seem risky. A 4-year-old 'paused' the story as Sendak's Max stepped into his private boat to ask her father: 'This is, it *is* just a dream, isn't it?' Just checking. Once safely launched with Max, she could get caught up in all the rumpus she fancied.

Sendak himself talks of *The Tale of Peter Rabbit*[38] as a metaphor for the lifelong conflict between rules and independence; a notion which may be best kept at a manageable distance through metaphor whether you are 5 or 55. Thinking by means of metaphor is often necessary in reading picture books; and, clearly, it is also necessary in the pleasurable reading of most poetry and many novels.

Form and content

The relationship between form and content was one of the areas the sixth-formers in the third of my initial cameos had hardly begun to think about. Their GCSE teaching tended to focus upon the 'facts' of story, not about how it was told, whether the form was prose or poetry. Even undergraduates on courses about the novel, given the freedom to be honest, will still protest that all this *analysis* tends to get in the way of enjoying the story 'for itself'; and in their talk and critical writing, there is a constant impulse towards retelling the events of a plot.

It may be that earlier awareness of how works are crafted would have persuaded them that you can't talk about content without form. Picture books provide clear areas for discussion of this matter. In choosing a shape for the book, why does Barbara Cooney, the illustrator of Donald Hall's *Ox-Cart Man,*[39] prefer 'landscape' to 'portrait'? The pioneer farmer has to make long journeys each year along the New England trails to trade his goods, and children are well able to see that the shape of the book reinforces the distances he must walk and the changing rhythms of the countryside and seasons he passes through. Why does Sendak move gradually from small pictures with large white margins in *Where the Wild Things Are* to three double-page spreads with no margins and then back to small pictures and, finally, no picture at all to accompany that comforting 'And it was still hot'?

Why do writers and their publishers choose glossy paper rather than matt? Why this size or style of typeface rather than another — or why, on occasions, different typefaces within the same book? Why ivory paper rather than white?

Even in junior school classes, it is a short stride from talking about the shaping of a picture book to the shaping of a poem on the page. Yet it is discussion of this kind (the effect of a particular sonnet form or the verse pattern of a ballad) which older students find difficult to the point of resentment.

Hearing the soundtrack

Some readers, even at undergraduate level, seem to struggle to 'hear' the words on the page. Their own reading aloud suggests that they do not distinguish the voices of characters within a novel or indeed find appropriate voices for different modes of narration, even when there seem to be clear enough indications provided by the writer.

Picture books might offer a valuable start in this process of sounding a text on the inner ear. Caldecott is once more a prime example. Maurice Sendak draws attention to the illustration in which the Queen of Hearts and the King of Clubs dance, feet barely touching the floor, in the foreground, while well 'upstage' a counterpoint is beaten out upon the bottom of the tart-stealing Knave as his master administers some vigorous punishment.[40] The young royals watch the beating while their parents watch the dancers. The reader simply *must* learn to hear so distinctive a soundtrack. In fact many young readers, unselfconsciously playing about with different voices with a sympathetic adult reading along with them, do 'hear' picture books exceptionally well. It may be that they *lose* this ability, possibly even while they are being 'taught to read' through less dynamic texts.

If this is so, it is a sad waste of an opportunity, for the vivid characters who populate picture books regularly 'speak' through the pictures rather than the words, requiring the reader to give them a voice.

Reading picture books, reading poems

I have tried, in the last few pages, to show how reading picture books may be the beginning of a continuum leading to the reading of complex prose fiction. I have mentioned poetry rather more briefly, and yet in some ways the reading of picture books and the reading of poems seem remarkably parallel. Some of the processes of reading poems might be described in brief (though I hope not too crudely) in this way:

- Different poems require to be read in different registers. Being able to find an appropriate register is very much the key to reading poetry.
- Consider two examples, the ballad and the sonnet. The verse form of a ballad keeps the reader driving on to find out what happens next, though even here the economy of the telling leaves spaces between the lines (why *was* that 'eldern knicht' at the king's right knee so quick to recommend Sir Patrick Spens as the best sailor to set out into those North Sea gales? Sir Patrick certainly knows he's been set up). A sonnet, and much modern free verse, by contrast, asks you to 'walk around' inside and outside a poem in a kind of spiralling mental movement, allowing sense to develop, often in the spaces between the words. Some readings are retained and some discarded, as you wind among the lines.
- Images must work together and illuminate each other — sometimes shifting as you contemplate them, more like mobiles than pictures side by side in two dimensions.
- As one walks about the poem, the music, the rhythms and the patterns become more distinct, and make more sense together.
- One reading may not be enough; the poem is differently experienced on subsequent meetings — especially if time elapses between them. Fresh details emerge to readers willing to perceive them.

All of these processes could be equally applied to a full reading of a picture book. Clearly, the best preparation for reading poetry in the secondary school is the frequent positive experience of poetry in the primary school. But picture books may well have a part to play in preparing readers to engage with complex poems which do not yield their richness at a single meeting. The picture book reader who is aware of what might lie between the lines, of how images work, of how the patterning makes its impact, and who recognizes a book which needs re-reading, is well equipped to meet the demands of tightly crafted poems. Accomplished readers of picture books are unlikely to be mystified and alienated by such poems.

How to ...?

So *how* might children (and perhaps all of us) best read picture books? And how might children be 'taught' to read picture books better? We need to tread cautiously, since we know from research and experience that each reader's reading style is unique in its finer preferences.[41] Moreover, it may be that some children *already* read picture books rather better than print-fixated adults; 6-year-old Michael caught me by surprise when I asked him (probably merely as a getting-to-know-you gambit), 'Do you like reading picture books with a grown-up?' 'Not really,' he said, 'they don't know how to read the pictures.'

Jane Doonan has helped many of us to read picture books with greater awareness and consequent pleasure. In *Looking at Pictures in Picture Books* she sets out her own practice as she meets a new book.[42] Her approach is underpinned by her training in both art history and English literature. As she picks up a new book, she carefully notes the cover, the title, the names of author and illustrator, the book's size and shape and so on before she moves on to a close look at the title page. What expectations are already set up? Then, she does a couple of skim readings to satisfy the basic urge to 'know what happens'. A slower reading follows, allowing details to emerge. Next, there is an unhurried page-by-page exploration — do words and pictures match, or do they have separate lives of their own? She might then focus 'on the language alone — its rhythms and word order and tone', and then she re-reads 'to pull it all together'. Return visits may follow after a passage of time.

I asked undergraduates who had spent three or four sessions thinking about half a dozen picture books to devise a model of how they might approach a new picture book (whilst acknowledging that any book might demand its own unique mode of reading). They did not know *Looking at Pictures in Picture Books*, but nevertheless came up with processes remarkably similar to Jane Doonan's.

Developing young readers in practice

Clearly, the sharing of picture books is common enough in primary schools; perhaps more so with infants than with juniors. I wonder, however, whether practice has been evolved which is informed both by an understanding of what picture books ask readers to do, and how children respond to them. If such teaching *is* widespread, then it does not seem to be much written about;[43] and we need both information and guidance.

What might such work look like in the classroom? Any attempt to develop children's reading of picture books might begin by looking at what 'good readers' do, as far as we can generalize; we might then be able to devise work which enhances, or even introduces, those habits of reading. We might, for example, encourage them to read in ways derived from Jane Doonan's approach outlined above. Again, it has become common practice for secondary teachers to ask students meeting a new poem to 'jot around' the words on the page; ideas, connections, patterns, questions, things they notice and want to come back to. Two young Canadian teachers told me that they transferred this approach to picture books with exciting results. With the originals close at hand, their 7-year-olds jotted around photocopies of the illustrations in response to the question, 'What do you see?' Subsequent discussion moved towards speculation and interpretation on the basis of close observation. (The class had previously used much the same strategy in a course introducing 'Great Paintings of the World'.) Children whose classrooms surround them with picture books are well able to sustain lengthy, searching discussion without the physical presence of a teacher, though they may be equipped with guideline questions; a model worth imitating is provided by a videotape[44] produced by the University of Brighton, which shows a group talking fascinatingly about *Gorilla* for perhaps 20 minutes.

There is space here for a single example of whole-class teaching. A BEd student, Tracey Seagrove, was recently on her final teaching practice in Truro with a class of 9-year-olds.[45] The teaching 'unit' which follows eventually absorbed about a day and a half.

- Tracey began by reading the sentence which comprises the entire verbal text of *Rosie's Walk*: 'Rosie the hen went for a walk across the yard around the pond over the haycock past the mill through the fence under the beehives and got back in time for dinner.' The turning page dictated pauses in the reading.

- As luck had it, none of the children knew the book. Each of them was asked to make a pencil drawing to illustrate one episode of Rosie's constitutional, and after a second hearing of the story, they set to work. One Rosie was about to tuck into roast chicken for dinner.

- Six copies of the book were then passed out. There was indignation on all sides. 'You never said anything about the fox!' 'How were we supposed to know the fox is chasing her?' 'Is that a Walk, or is that Rosie a dead hen?' They look more closely at the book.

- Some interesting, often theoretical, discussion followed, partly initiated by the teacher. How is this story 'carried'? Not just by the words — the pictures work just as hard in telling the full story. What do *readers* have to do? How has Pat Hutchins invited them to do whatever they have to do? The notion of 'filling telling gaps' was thoroughly explored, and the children were increasingly 'on the inside' of the authorial process, as far as that is ever possible. At the very

least, they knew more clearly how readers play their parts in creating a
text.

- It was almost lunchtime. But, said the class, we could do that! So
'Godfrey's Walk' was conceived. They settled on a mouse pursued by a
cat, just as Rosie is pursued by her fox. The words are very similar to
Pat Hutchins's words. Originality is not the issue here — they are
following the time-honoured practice of how writers have learned to
write. Malcolm Bradbury, joint architect of the renowned Creative
Writing MA at the University of East Anglia, notes that the teaching
and practice of creative writing 'benefit most from the deep knowledge
of the resources and the many varied means of writing and from the
analysis of the work of others, above all the great practitioners, and of
the nature of the writing process itself'.[46]

- Anticipating that cats can be tricky, Tracey found some photographs
and pictures to serve as models. When the class returned after lunch,
some decisions about consistency between pictures were taken — a
black-and-white cat couldn't suddenly be transmogrified into a tabby,
for example.

- Adventures parallel to Rosie's were decided upon and episodes
allocated to teams of illustrators. As Godfrey emerges from his hole,
and sets out upon his walk (left to right across the page, of course), the
cat lurks in waiting. What Godfrey and the reader notice is the
mousetrap just outside his hole. We know the cat will not be so
circumspect, and sure enough, in the next picture, the luckless feline is
on tiptoe with pain, the mousetrap clamped over its paw. The children
noticed that Rosie's adventures are often watched, and reacted to, by
other smaller animals; in 'Godfrey's Walk' a flurry of birds, ladybirds,
butterflies and assorted bugs take flight when the cat encounters a
ferocious dog.

- As they created their book, the 9-year-olds had a specific audience in
mind. The following morning, not without trepidation, they went
down the corridor to submit their completed work to the reception
class.

- Success. The infant teacher wanted to keep their book so that her class
could look at it again. They decide to make more books, each to
feature a couple of the infants in starring roles.

At one level, this is a straightforward piece of teaching. What impresses
me, however, is that it is informed throughout by the teacher's own
theoretical understanding of how picture books work; and, increasingly,
by the class's understanding of how they work, too. There is little direct
instruction, but the framework of the lesson ensures that ideas are
explored obliquely; and there is surely no doubt that the children who
carried out this work have become that much more skilled, more
committed, as readers of picture books.

And, my argument runs, they are that much further along the road to becoming readers of other kinds of texts.

What more do we need to know?

Rather a lot. We need to know much more about what readers of picture books actually do; we need to find ways of discovering their processes which are not distorted by the artificial contexts of formal research. We need to know how to help parents who read with their children to learn *how* to read with them; they might also be alerted to the long-term potential of picture books in developing the art of reading.

Within school, it would be very helpful to know what primary teachers, and maybe their secondary colleagues, are already doing in terms of theorized teaching of picture books. We might then look to share and develop more, readily manageable, classroom activities which promote enjoyable close reading; sometimes, perhaps, by helping children to understand the crafting of picture books. For example, many children may need to learn such arts as reading words and pictures working together.

If the budget allows, would it be worth making more use of sets of picture books in ways derived from our understanding of the processes of fluent readers? If I had to be marooned on a desert island with a primary class and no more than one suitcase of teaching materials, I suspect I'd pack a set of *Gorilla*.

Notes

1 Anthony Browne, *Gorilla*, Julia MacRae Books, London, 1983.
2 Carol Ann Duffy, *Mean Time*, Anvil Press, London, 1993.
3 I use the term 'reading' a picture book for want of a better word. Alternatives seem clumsy, but I mean to include the processes of looking at pictures, and also connecting words and pictures.
4 Anthony Browne, *Hansel and Gretel*, Julia MacRae Books, London, 1981.
5 Margaret Meek, *How Texts Teach What Readers Learn*, Thimble Press, Stroud, 1988; and *On Being Literate*, The Bodley Head, London, 1991.
6 Perry Nodelman, *Words about Pictures*, University of Georgia Press, Athens, 1988.
7 Jane Doonan, *Looking at Pictures in Picture Books*, Thimble Press, Stroud, 1993.
8 Margaret Mackey, *Picture Books and the Making of Readers: A New Trajectory*, National Council of Teachers of English, Urbana, IL, 1993.
9 David Lewis, 'The constructedness of texts: picture books and the metafictive', in *Signal* 62, 1990.
10 Maurice Sendak, *Caldecott & Co.*, Rheinhardt Books/Viking, London, 1989.

11 Pat Hutchins, *Rosie's Walk*, The Bodley Head, London, 1968.
12 Nodelman, *op. cit.*, p. 160.
13 Joseph Conrad, *Heart of Darkness*, first published 1908.
14 Milan Kundera, *The Unbearable Lightness of Being*, Faber & Faber, London, 1984.
15 Penelope Lively, *Moon Tiger*, Andre Deutsch, London, 1987.
16 Martin Amis, *Time's Arrow*, Cape, London, 1991.
17 Wolfgang Iser, *The Act of Reading*, Routledge & Kegan Paul, London, 1978.
18 Alan Garner, *The Owl Service*, Collins, London, 1967.
19 Alan Garner, *Red Shift*, Collins, London, 1973.
20 John Burningham, *Come Away from the Water, Shirley*, Cape, London, 1977.
21 John Burningham, *Time to Get out of the Bath, Shirley*, Cape, London, 1979.
22 Jon Scieszka and Lane Smith, *The True Story of the Three Little Pigs*, Viking Kestrel, London, 1989.
23 Jon Scieszka and Steve Johnson, *The Frog Prince Continued*, Viking, New York, 1991.
24 Sendak, *op. cit.*, p. 24.
25 Randolph Caldecott, *Hey Diddle Diddle and Baby Bunting*, George Routledge & Sons, London, 1882.
26 Geoffrey Chaucer, 'Prologue' to *The Canterbury Tales*, 385–387.
27 Leslie Brooke, *The Three Bears*, Frederick Warne & Co., London, 1905.
28 Raymond Briggs, *Fungus the Bogeyman*, Hamish Hamilton, London, 1977.
29 Janet and Allan Ahlberg, *The Jolly Postman*, Heinemann, London, 1986, and *The Jolly Christmas Postman*, Heinemann, London, 1991.
30 Mitsumasa Anno, *Anno's Britain*, The Bodley Head, London, 1982.
31 Julian Barnes, *A History of the World in 10½ Chapters*, Cape, London, 1989.
32 Maurice Sendak, *Where the Wild Things Are*, The Bodley Head, London, 1967.
33 Susan Jeffers, *Hansel and Gretel*, Dial, New York, 1980.
34 Graham Swift, *Waterland*, Heinemann, London, 1983.
35 Charles Dickens, *Our Mutual Friend*, first published 1864–5.
36 Ursula Le Guin, *A Wizard of Earthsea* (1968), *The Tombs of Atuan* (1972), *The Farthest Shore* (1973) and *Tehanu* (1990), Gollancz, London.
37 Margaret Atwood, *The Handmaid's Tale*, Virago, London, 1987.
38 Beatrix Potter, *The Tale of Peter Rabbit*, first published 1902.
39 Donald Hall (pictures by Barbara Cooney), *Ox-Cart Man*, Viking, New York, 1979.
40 Randolph Caldecott, *The Queen of Hearts*, George Routledge & Co., London, 1881.
41 See, for example, Norman Holland, *5 Readers Reading*, Yale University Press, New Haven, 1975.
42 My skeletal outline does scant justice to the thoroughness of the approach, which is fully described in *Looking at Pictures in Picture Books*; see Note 7.

43 An exception is *Not So Simple Picture Books*, by Pam Baddeley and Chris Eddershaw, Trentham Books, Stoke on Trent, 1994.

44 Muriel Robinson and Carole King, *Creating a Community of Readers Part 1* (videotape), University of Brighton, Brighton, 1993.

45 I am grateful to Tracey Seagrove for permission to quote her work at this length.

46 Malcolm Bradbury, 'To begin at the beginning', *Independent*, 30 December 1994.

CHAPTER 11

'That One Horse'

Making and Reading Stories across Cultures

Brigid Smith

How can teachers find texts which will support the development of readers who are in the process of getting to grips with English? Even if books are beautifully produced and otherwise inviting, they can be inaccessible to children whose cultural experience does not match the images and references portrayed in them. Brigid Smith's experience led her to use children's (and teachers') own stories as bridges to future satisfying reading experiences. Most particularly, she argues that 'when children's culture and background is seriously celebrated in text they can enter a new discourse' and so extend and increase their command of the newly acquired language. This has implications for styles and approaches to teaching and learning, and in describing her work with teachers in Andhra Pradesh, she emphasizes the importance of 'understanding the pedagogy of a culture'. This is critically important, not just in international settings, but in our own schools, if teachers are to give genuine respect to the cultural and personal experiences which young readers bring to the texts and contexts of the classroom.

I want to explore some issues to do with telling and reading stories, including stories which are made in a partnership between a competent writer and a developing composer and reader. These issues arise as the result of my own recent experiences in making stories with both teachers and children in different cultural settings. My conviction that using children's own stories as reading texts can be an important element in learning to be a reader has already been well documented,[1] but can this conviction be sustained when teachers are working across cultures? Although my own experience of asking the cross-cultural question is a recent one, in fact questioning the usefulness and validity of using children's own stories as texts for learning to read is not new. Holdaway suggested that the consistent use of children's own grammar and vocabulary as a text for reading would result in dull and limited texts.[2] It is certainly a question asked by many teachers, and they often choose children with limited literacy experience, or limited English, as examples of those who might find the process difficult or might produce texts that are not 'good enough'.

In some ways questions such as these are missing the point about the place of dictated stories in the process of learning to read. These stories need to be recognized as 'bridge' texts rather than texts with a specifically 'remedial' function. They span the gap, for some children a huge gap, between the child's ability to talk and their ability to read and write formal texts. They have a valid place in the talk–writing continuum in the overlap that occurs between talking and writing.[3] For some children they can also bridge a cultural gap between what is available in printed texts and stories that might reflect their own lives, experiences and interests. Teachers of Traveller children know that they have to use dictated stories if these readers are going to be able to read about their own life experiences in a story. Teachers of English as a Second Language (ESL) have similar difficulties in finding materials that are both relevant and easy enough for their children to read. Some of the best texts in both these areas have been produced by the language experience approach. The fact that they often contain dialect in both construction and vocabulary can be regarded as a positive benefit in the bridging process. The evidence suggests that as children learn to read they also learn to move towards the more formal constraints of Standard English in printed texts.[4] The extensive use of scribed stories with older learners, particularly adults, underlines the importance of this way of learning to read. These learners' interests, life understanding, psychological needs and knowledge of storytelling can all be used to support the mechanical processes of reading. It is when these aspects are celebrated in print that readers can find themselves in the story, a drive towards reading which Margaret Meek reminds us is often overlooked.[5] The liberating power of this sense of self is celebrated in the opening passage, written by a student who is learning to read, in a Canadian adult literacy publication: 'It is the people whose arms are open as wide as their minds and as deep as their heart that make the stars shine as bright as the Northern Lights.'[6]

The recognition of what the reader brings to the story seems particularly important when texts are a means of introducing and sustaining a second or third language for a child. Printed texts are often stilted and limited, in both vocabulary and concept, and it is difficult to find texts that are a cultural 'fit'. However, it was when I began to work with a Bangladeshi child that the reality of these difficulties became clear to me. My limitation is my monolingual capacity, as is the case with many non-specialist teachers working with ESL children. I searched the library and bookshops for suitable storybooks and realized then how great the problem of matching child and book can be. If the age and sex of the child in the story was right, the mother wore the wrong clothes, or the context was wrong, or the story was stilted. Beautifully illustrated books with photographs of home countries were mainly addressed to English readers and had suffocatingly patronizing texts. The truth of John Agard's poem about birthday cards not having black boys 'like me?' was echoed: 'Why no books with a boy like Mohan?' Dual language books were no help, as neither Mohan nor I could read Bengali.

In the end I learned a great deal from the help that I did have. Instead of the usual partnership that generates a scribed story we needed a triangular relationship. Three of us, Mohan (aged 7), Mustakin, his cousin (aged 9) and myself formed a language triangle which enabled us to produce a number of stories.

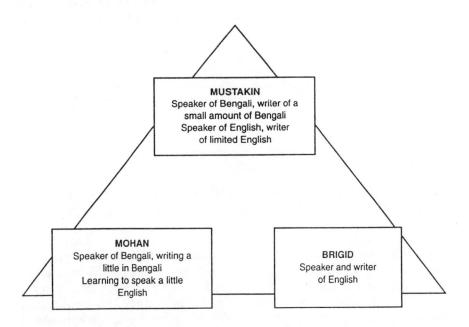

It is clear here who is linguistically deprived! Our aim was to produce some reading material which Mohan could read and that he would find interesting. At first our talk together was constrained, the boys trying to find out what kind of story I would like them to tell. Then I asked the question that provoked our first story: 'Have you ever been back to Bangladesh?' They had, and Mohan had been back recently for a number of months. The talk flowed freely, Mustakin translating what Mohan was saying for me. We decided that our first story would be about this visit. Mustakin talked with Mohan, and then translated into an English sentence which I wrote down. Together we then read the sentence. The formal opening is typical of a reading book:

> One day Mohan and Mustakin went to Bangladesh.
> They went by an aeroplane.
> It was snowing.

The repetitive second page also has the quality of a rather stilted 'reading' book, but something interesting has happened to the narrator's voice:

> We had lots of food on the aeroplane.
> We had bread.
> We had sandwiches.
> We had apples.
> When we wanted to get off we had tea and biscuits.

The next page tells how they got to Bangladesh. There they got on another aeroplane. Are they the same boys, though, who got on the plane at Heathrow?

> Then we went on another aeroplane.
> It was lovely.
> We had a monkey on the aeroplane.
> The monkey came on Mustakin's head and the monkey grabbed Mohan's mouth.
> Mohan went, 'Aaaaaah! Aaaaaah! Aaaaaaah!'
> And Mohan's mum came and Mustakin's mum came.
> Mustakin caught the monkey and Mohan caught its tail.

The story originally ended with Mustakin catching the monkey. It was Mohan, for the first time struggling to be directly involved, who insisted that *he* caught the monkey's tail.

The constraints of a culture affect the way in which children tell stories. It is interesting that the 'reading scheme' type of text, with its repetitive 'we had', and its linear progression used in the boys' first two pages changes when they reach Bangladesh. Suddenly they are centralized in the story, anarchy enters the aeroplane and the boys catch the monkey and presumably restore order. When children's culture and background is seriously celebrated in text they can enter a new discourse.

Our second story started in Bangladesh, where the twin themes of water and horses dominated both talk and stories. My own recent reading about Bangladesh village life in *Songs at the River's Edge*[7] had helped me to understand how predominant water is in the culture, and seeing children playing in irrigation tanks in hot weather and riding horses and donkeys along the dykes in Pakistan gave me some insight into the possible play arenas of village children. Our next story was about a flying horse. It was a story about Taleem and Fayeem, the cousins of Mustakin.

It was really Mustakin's story. His storytelling and language use started to fly too:

> Mohan was woosh into the water like a fish.
> He was going fast like a shark.

It was horses, too, that precipitated Mohan into telling his own story. Mustakin was the dominant person in our story-making sessions, but outside the sessions they had a more physical and equal relationship of 'bundling' and rolling on the ground together. It is this relationship that Mohan decided to celebrate in his story about 'that one horse'. Mohan arrived at our session with a beautifully coloured picture of a horse with horns (see below), and then he told his story:

> One day there was a horse.
> That one horse was very good.
> That horse one day he hurt me.
> He had big horns.
> That horse was very bad.
> He ripped Mohan's jumper.
> Mohan wanted to get Mustakin!
> The horse taked me and Mustakin to Africa.
> When we got to Africa the horse landed on a tree,
> Mustakin fell down but Mohan was safe.
> Mohan landed on Mustakin!

This story became our key reading text for some time. Here was a text in which the reader could find himself; it contained the vocabulary and syntax that he could cope with and the psychological need of the reader was met by the story. Making the story produced much talk, drawing of pictures and telling jokes. Just reading it together, however, was not going to be sufficient to support my own belief that story can be a serious vehicle for learning many aspects of literacy. Mohan needed to acquire a

knowledge of the sounds and letters of English so that he could read and write some words for himself; Mustakin needed to learn a wider written vocabulary and to acquire other strategies for reading than just 'sounding out' the letter–sound relationships.

Where did 'that one horse' take us to? First, the frequent reading aloud together helped punctuation and word recognition. Both boys began to read with intonation and meaning. If the words on the page were different to the words that they read, they began to use other strategies. They checked out their guesses by looking at the structure of the words and the letters, and their level of self-correction increased as they tried to make sense of what they were reading. They were first asked, and then asked themselves, questions equivalent to:

What would make sense?
How did the words start?
Could the prediction be checked out by grapho-phonic analysis?

The boys told a number of stories. We were able to make an alphabet of key letters based on words that had been in these stories that Mustakin and Mohan told. Each word had a picture cue and was used to practise spellings using Look, Cover, Write, Check as a technique.[8]

a	aeroplane	c	camel
	apple		cousin
b	Bangladesh		
	bad		

The words in the stories were enlarged and printed out so that they could be laminated and cut up into single words. Using the back cover of their books as the equivalent of a 'breakthrough' folder, the children could then reconstitute their stories in different ways, familiarizing themselves with the words and practising the structure of simple sentences. Mustakin began to use some of these words to start his own writing as he learned a writing vocabulary generalized from his own words. The children's books became part of the book stock of the classroom, validating them as both readers and authors, bringing aspects of their own culture to the literary life of the classroom.

Since working with these two boys I have been involved in a project in southern India (Government of Andhra Pradesh) to develop textbooks and supplementary readers. What I have learned there is the way in which the constraints and key concepts about literacy in a culture affect the kind of materials that are produced and the way in which children are expected to learn to read. The greatest need in this project was to help teachers to move from a learning model of literacy in which teaching is predominant, to one in which the learner has a role to play. It is only when there is an acceptance of this pedagogical change that the relevance of the content of reading materials becomes crucially important. If textbooks are only used for rote learning without recourse to meaning, then just improving the content does not help. At present, most language textbooks from across the developing world move from discrete learning to contextual learning. Early reading books are, in fact, script primers. They exist to teach, in dictionary order, the alphabet of the language, and rarely have text beyond the single word or phrase. However important a knowledge of letters and their sounds may be, there is now consistent research evidence to convince us that this knowledge in itself is not sufficient.[9] The developing reader needs a context for learning to read in which the purposes, discourse and structure of extended texts become familiar. Relevant, interesting stories are needed.

At first the team of Indian teacher/writers with whom I was working thought they had no stories to tell, or else that they must rehash old, familiar stories. I knew, however, that they had the ability to use language in a rhythmic and powerful way. The writing workshop took place in a remote school in a mountain area; the evenings were spent on the balcony surrounded by the sound of cicadas in the huge trees. The power supply was a regular victim of 'load shedding' in the evening, and in a deep darkness, lit only by a candle in a jar, the teachers sang. They made up songs to suit the occasion or else they used songs they had already written. The Telugu language contains its own 'tunes' implicit in the syntax of the song. It was linking this leisure rhyme and story-making activity to writing that enabled us to move forward. What was needed in the new book was rhymes and stories containing the key letters to be learned by the children. In this way children could become familiar with the letter to be learned in a meaningful and developmentally appropriate way. Using a small group of children to try out our stories each afternoon in a storytelling session, we quickly became aware of the texts which engaged the children's interest. We also realized which texts were compelling enough in content and structure to help the children to remember them and to read along with the teacher. We learned that story can be the true primer for learners.

As children respond to stories, understand them and come to share in reading extended texts, they develop the ability to discriminate sounds and letters and to segment new words. These learners will automatically use phonics to check out whether a guess is correct or not.[10] Teachers rapidly grasped the importance of pictures, story and rhyme to contextualize sounds and letters, and interest and relevance. The new Class One textbook in Andhra Pradesh, written with teachers, now exemplifies that pedagogical approach.

What has such understanding got to do with the learning of ESL children in England? It has convinced me that it is not just an

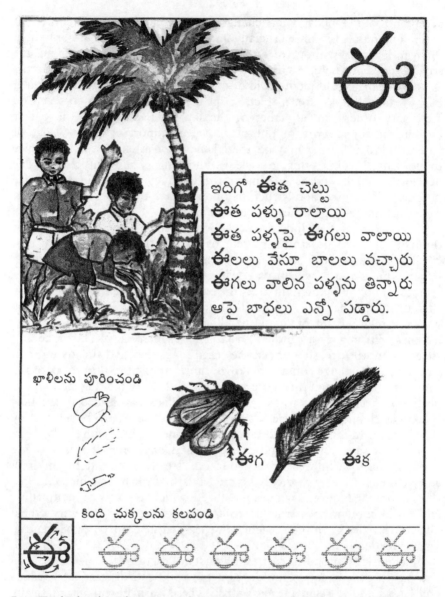

ఇదిగో **ఈత** చెట్టు
ఈత పళ్ళు రాలాయి
ఈత పళ్ళపై **ఈ**గలు వాలాయి
ఈలలు వేస్తూ బాలలు వచ్చారు
ఈగలు వాలిన పళ్ళను తిన్నారు
ఆపై బాధలు ఎన్నో పడ్డారు.

ఖాళీలను పూరించండి

ఈగ   ఈక

కింది చుక్కలను కలపండి

From 'Textbook and Supplementary Reader Development', a project for the Government of Andhra Pradesh under the auspices of the Overseas Development Agency. The material was developed with teachers as prototype classroom textbooks. Reproduced with permission.

understanding of the stories and signifiers of a culture that is important; we also need to understand the *pedagogy* of a culture. What are the learning styles of parents and other relations? What is valued as literate behaviour? What is the status of rote learning and the role of the teacher?

The school environment, the buildings (or lack of them) class sizes and multigrade teaching as well as the dominant religious and cultural pressures in a community exert a pressure on the way in which children learn. Many children in England continue to be influenced by these pressures through Saturday schools, Mosque schools and the experience and expectations of parents. In the classroom, we expect children to interrogate print and pictures, to look for multilayered meanings in texts and illustrations and to bring their own ideas, feelings and perceptions to bear on the book they are reading. This may be particularly difficult for children from some cultures, in which notions of text and authority are quite different.[11] The problem of making mistakes may have great significance in cultures where accuracy and correctness are essential and mistakes are 'shaming'. Shirley Brice Heath brought some of these issues to life in her descriptions of early language environments.[12] She also identified ways in which schools need to understand and support literacy learning within the context of early language development. The importance of these understandings is crucial in educational projects in the developing world.[13] We need to extend our concept of literacy to encompass the sociolinguistic contexts in which children learn to be language users.[14] If we believe that the construction of meaning through interaction with texts is a key component of becoming literate, then the context for that meaning has also to be taken into account.

In order to work effectively with learners of English as a Second Language, teachers may need to know about more than just festivals, clothes and food. The language of children, its cultural importance and constraints, is important. In some countries the alphabet of a language is sacred, and 'playing games' with letters can seem inappropriate. In many cultures children do not play with toys in any quantity; their social life is firmly cemented in the shared activities of their family and friends, and they do not need a 'play' world in the same way as children whose lives are seen as separate and different from adults. Many children feel familiar with rote learning and memorizing; we can capitalize on this with shared reading, using verse and rhymes and giving visual memory strategies for learning to read.

There may be many learning triangles, similar to the one that I shared with Mohan and Mustakin, that could be implemented to help children with very little English. Parents, relatives, grandparents and other members of a community who have some spoken English can help provide the bridge that can then be built into a text. Telling stories across cultures raises many issues and can give insights to teachers. The story itself can then be the vehicle for wider literacy learning.

Stories in which readers can find themselves, stories in which the cultural settings are familiar and relevant, are essential if children are going to find reading interesting and meaningful. It is important, though, to acknowledge all aspects of culture and to see where our pedagogy fits with the knowledge and understanding of other cultures. If we do not do this we may find that our beautifully crafted books are not seen as important and that children are being 'taught to read' in alternative settings with much less relevant materials.

Notes

1 B. Smith, *Through Writing to Reading*, Routledge, London, 1994.
2 L. Holdaway, *The Foundations of Literacy*, Heinemann, London, 1979.
3 Smith, *op. cit.*
4 Smith, *op. cit.*, p. 94.
5 M. Meek, 'Prolegomena for a study of children's literature', in M. Benton (ed.), *Approaches to Children's Literature*, Southampton University Department of Education, Southampton, 1980.
6 'Opening words', in *Literacy*, British Columbia, 1993.
7 K. Gardner, *Songs at the River's Edge: Stories from a Bangladeshi Village*, Virago, London, 1991.
8 M. Peters and B. Smith, *Spelling in Context*, NFER, Slough, 1993.
9 See, for example, M. Clay, *Becoming Literate: The Construction of Inner Control*, Heinemann, Auckland, 1992; and U. Goswami and P. Bryan *Phonological Skills and Learning to Read*, Lawrence Erlbaum Associates, Hove, 1992.
10 F. Smith, *Reading*, 2nd edn, Cambridge University Press, Cambridge, 1985.
11 K. Parry, 'The social construction of reading strategies: new directions for research', *Journal of Research in Reading* (1993), 16(2), pp. 148–59.
12 S. B. Heath, *Ways with Words*, Cambridge University Press, Cambridge, 1983.
13 B. Smith, 'Learning to be literate in Andhra Pradesh (Southern India) and Punjab District (Pakistan)', *International Journal of Early Years Education* (1994), 2(1), pp. 77–88.
14 B. Street, *Literacy in Theory and Practice*, Cambridge University Press, Cambridge, 1984; and 'The new literacy studies', *Journal of Research in Reading* (1993), 16(2), pp. 81–98.

CHAPTER 12

'With the Wind Behind You'
Language Development Through Drama Activities at Key Stage 1

Lesley Hendy

*Statutory curriculum requirements place great emphasis on the develop-
ment of children's use of complex forms of language — both spoken and
written. In this chapter Lesley Hendy suggests that these requirements can
be more than adequately met through a revival of the recognition that
play, fantasy and the more intentionally structured opportunities for role-
play provide fruitful ground for developing a range of language
formations. Those classrooms where teachers control or direct much of
the conversation or discussion risk losing one of the most potent resources
for language development — the imaginative possibilities brought by the
stories that children themselves know and can make. In describing her
approach to active storytelling, Lesley Hendy offers a practical entry point
to activities which can 'cover the whole range of curriculum demands'. As
well as giving the children a chance to experiment and take risks, this also
involves the teacher trying out some new approaches and developing
strategies to guide, rather than dictate, the progress of language and
learning.*

Corinne Hutt, an expert on children's play, undertook some research in
the early 1980s that looked closely at language development through
'fantasy' play.[1] Her findings were remarkable. Her research revealed that
during periods of pretend play, children's utterances were longer, and
their use of adverbs and modal auxiliary verbs was significantly higher
than when they were engaged in other non-pretend activities. She
discovered that there appeared to be a greater display of linguistic
competence when children were playing in role.

In a recent OFSTED report, the following statement seems to support
Hutt's findings:

Better overall standards in literacy were achieved where the development of spoken English was taken seriously and well-planned. When this occurred, there was regular story-telling, class and group discussion and effective questioning; adults took time to talk with the pupils; *drama and role play were used effectively* [my italics] and the teacher's or other adult's spoken language was a good model for the children.[2]

I am sure that no infant teacher would disagree that language development should be a major feature of every early-years classroom, since developing children's language skills is a strong characteristic of most activities. My experience of working with young children over many years has convinced me that they acquire knowledge most effectively through playing and actively involving themselves in their learning and through talking about what they are doing. This being so, I am puzzled by the OFSTED finding, as it is not my experience that there is 'drama and role-play being used effectively' in most of the infant classrooms that I visit today. I would like to know how frequently 'drama and role-play' were used by teachers surveyed in the OFSTED report. It seems to be a sad feature of modern classrooms that there is a lack of time for teachers and pupils to engage in 'fantasy' play, despite the evidence that role-play is a very effective medium for increasing language use.

In my present role as a drama specialist, and previously as an infant teacher, I have spent some considerable time working with children and exploring in depth the potential of pretend play as a medium for developing their language and thinking. If 'make-believe' is such a productive method of extending language, and from my own experience I would suggest that it is, why is it that so many teachers are reluctant to use drama and role-play on a regular basis? Lack of time should not be the excuse, when it has been established that effective drama activities provide such good learning opportunities.

A more plausible explanation would be that teachers are not sure how to introduce drama into the classroom in a way that is 'safe' and productive. With so much statutory curriculum content to get through, it is easier to use teaching strategies that are familiar and risk-free. This attitude is understandable. However, by not introducing more interactive talk situations into the classroom, I would suggest that teachers are depriving children of opportunities to discuss, ask questions, describe things, develop and explore ideas, demonstrate what they know, and offer their viewpoint in an environment that empowers them to do so.

Classroom talk

Talk in the classroom is not always as open and impartial as we might hope. It has some recognizable features which are not always present in other situations where people speak to each other. In most talk situations outside the classroom there are rules that ensure that speakers observe the custom of turn-taking. Speakers are free to speak when they feel it is their turn. In the classroom, too often this turn-taking is arranged by the teacher with the routine of hand-raising before speaking. The right to speak is assumed by the teacher whenever he or she wishes but this is not the same for the pupils. Teachers frequently do the talking, and organized talk is a familiar feature of classroom language. Even in the freer conditions of group work the pupils' talk is often planned and has specific outcomes prearranged. The teacher is sometimes seen by the children to be someone who knows everything and has to be deferred to in all things. Very young children quickly become adapted to the culture of the classroom. It does not take them long to know that communication with a teacher is not always as straightforward as it appears to be at first. For some children, talking to an adult can sometimes be associated with being wrong or being made to feel of low-esteem. This can cause problems for the overstretched teacher. In the busy classroom it is sometimes difficult to engage these reluctant speakers in conversations of any length. Too frequently, teachers have to accept a minimum response and these exchanges, because of their brevity, are too short to be able to develop the lasting language and thinking we would like our children to acquire. As most studies of very young children reveal, it is their eagerness to solve problems and their continuous curiosity about the world that help them learn. It is important that they are given opportunities to expand and develop their language, in order to make greater sense of the world around them. This cannot be done if they find the classroom a difficult place in which to express themselves. Very young children need times when they are encouraged to talk together as well as with a teacher, in situations of their own choosing.

The stages of play

This is where 'pretend' play can be a useful method of exploring children's language development. I am often asked at what age children in the early years of schooling should be introduced to drama. My usual reply is that they come to school already knowing how to role-play. After sensory and symbolic play, role-play is the next stage of play development. Our first encounters with the world come through our senses. In the first few months of life we are bombarded with visual, aural and tactile sensations. We explore everything around us through looking, listening, touching and feeling, smelling and tasting. Everything at this stage is sensory. This is followed by the ability to make everyday objects take on what Piaget described as a symbolic representation: the cardboard box becomes the car, we crawl under the table to make a house. Finally, we are able to change ourselves and take on 'pretend' roles. Defined by Piaget as solitary play, this stage later develops into socio-dramatic play. All nursery class teachers and most reception teachers understand this important stage of development and provide a home corner in which children can 'make-believe'. Sadly, the idea of home corners in the later years of the infant school is beginning to disappear, and with it the opportunity for sensitive and planned intervention by the teacher in children's 'fantasy' worlds. Regrettably, dramatic play in the reception classroom is too often used merely to assist classroom management and to keep children occupied while the teacher is engaged elsewhere in the room. At times this is a valid thing to do; sometimes it is worthwhile to allow the children to play alone. But there are times when it is beneficial for the teacher to enter and 'play' with them.

'Pretend' playing in reception classes

Through learning when and how to intervene constructively, the teacher will be able to enter the 'play' without the children viewing the intervention as interference. By observing or playing alongside children for a while, the teacher can assess when they are ready to accept teacher into their 'make-believe' world. It also allows time for trust to develop. With no teacher intervention, the children's dramatic play is unlikely to be sustained over a period of time, becoming repetitive and rooted in what the child already knows, so that significant new learning is unlikely to develop.

Out of the home corner from reception and beyond

By providing different types of 'home' corner such as a hospital corner, a café or a travel agent's, the teacher can offer different sets of talk and learning opportunities to the children. The travel agency may have a telephone, serving to encourage speech. It may have holiday brochures to encourage reading. Paper and pencils may be available to encourage the children to write notes and 'bookings' within the context of their dramatic play. A postgraduate student recently described how she entered the class travel agency where two girls were playing behind the office desk. In role as a customer she asked about skiing holidays in Switzerland. She tells of how one of the girls very earnestly found her the skiing brochure and helped find a good holiday. The child then 'rang' the hotel in Switzerland to see if there was a free room. She asked for times, dates and method of travel, which she entered in the agency 'diary'. The student then produced a real cheque book and credit card to pay for the holiday, and the child verified the signature by matching the credit card with the cheque. The student wrote in her report:

Through this and similar episodes, I saw for myself the enormous educational opportunities afforded for children in a role-play corner. I have seen how numeracy, literacy, language development and other real-life skills had all been practised within the space of a few minutes in an enjoyable and non-threatening way.

Once we join the children at play and adopt a role within their make-believe, we can initiate or respond in order to facilitate learning. As in the example described by the student, a teacher who is in role as a customer may ask for help looking for a suitable holiday. She might ask the child to write the telephone message to Switzerland down for her so she won't forget it. Times, dates and transport arrangements also take on a significance within the context of the play. Each teacher intervention varies the learning opportunities and the possible learning outcomes. It is particularly effective if the teacher identifies and utilizes learning opportunities which arise naturally and are offered by the children themselves. It is important for children to feel some ownership of the pretend story and that their contributions to the dramatic play are valued. The teacher may enter the story as the customer, but she must treat the 'travel agent' with the same respect as if it were real life. This will help to develop the shared fiction in a more public way, as other children could overhear the conversation and be encouraged to join in. The teacher's intervention will also help the children in role as the travel agents to become more committed to their role. By using this approach we are implicitly able to signal to the children that we value their dramatic play. We indicate that it is important to us and is a respected form of activity.

Through entering children's dramatic play in this small way we are able to build up trust and commitment which can be used later when we embark on bigger group or whole class drama activities. It is only when children are able and willing to accept an adult into their imaginary play situation or environment and are able to sustain the make-believe verbally that they will accept us taking on roles within the dramatic situation.

If we as teachers are to give children opportunities to develop their thinking we must provide them with active and compelling experiences in contexts that are familiar. By using drama to develop talk we have an effective tool to extend the management of spoken language and increase children's perceptions of the world. Through good drama the pupils are put in control of their own speaking and listening, often being given the responsibility of having the knowledge, thus becoming active contributors to their own learning.

The quality of the dramatic experience is reliant on the quality of the language used by all the participants. The strength and depth of the work will be influenced by the manner in which pupils control the talking and how they handle the move from literal situations to symbolic ones. Small children are able to recognize the importance of being given 'the golden touch', for instance. During a drama where I was in role as King Midas demanding my magic golden touch, the group of 6-year-olds in role as my servants became (within the drama) very agitated and distressed at my decision and actively tried to persuade me from my course. They knew the magic touch stood for my desire for power and knew how this could ultimately harm all I loved. Their powers of persuasion were so strong, and in one case eloquent, that I had to have good arguments for refusing their advice.

When children are allowed to speak in a make-believe situation they are given a setting in which talking can occur in a natural manner. As part of the interaction of the drama, talk can take place in a shared context in which pupils can express themselves individually or as a group. By engaging themselves not only intellectually but emotionally, as my 'servants' did, they are given the combination of intellectual and emotional experience that can make learning through drama so effective.

Speaking and listening within the National Curriculum

In the new orders of the National Curriculum, the level descriptors for Speaking and Listening require children at Key Stage 1 to talk about matters of immediate interest; make appropriate responses to what they have heard; be audible; and have awareness of the needs of a listener through providing relevant detail. They are also required to be given opportunities to talk for a range of purposes. Throughout a school day, children are asked to participate in a variety of talk situations: child to teacher, child to child, child to group, and teacher to group. They are also required to undertake different types of talk which demand a mixture of skills. Some of the following types of talk show the diversity: describe, narrate, explain, persuade, express and justify an opinion, express their feelings, criticize, evaluate, hypothesize, predict, discuss points of view, make decisions.

Asking teachers to cover all these different talk situations within the busy classroom is a tall order. To acquire any of these styles of talk will require a variety of tasks and groupings so that the children can work at different kinds and levels of thinking. For example, remembering factual information requires one kind of thinking, and comprehending the information another. If we merely ask recall questions, we are giving children only one type of experience. If children are to make sense of what they know and to test and reflect on that learning, they need to be given situations in which to work that will help them to ask questions, challenge their assumptions, solve problems, make decisions and think at a deeper level. This is not easy in any classroom.

Possibilities for different kinds of talk

This is where the use of drama can be an invaluable aid to learning. Drama is one of the few ways in which it is possible to set up opportunities for these different kinds of talk to take place. Working as themselves in a story, for example, requires the participants to create past and present events, both real and imaginary; by working in role as 'the expert', children will be required to provide information, to explain ideas and to instruct others. Dramas involving conflicting interests — King Midas versus his servants — may use argument, the need to convince and persuade, and the ability to justify and defend. Stories based in the future or using a fantastic setting may require the skills of planning, predicting and projecting beyond the immediate context, and will give opportunities for creative thinking.

Through the use of these kinds of dramatic situation, small children are able to test out different kinds and styles of talk. These can be enhanced if we take on a role in the story (teacher-in-role) to act as a model and provide an example of all kinds of informal and formal speaking. The relative safety of a story provides the opportunity for practice of spoken language to be extended. It is a truism to say that spoken language can only develop through good first-hand experience. Drama can provide a variety of such experiences that might otherwise be impossible in the everyday classroom. In drama, children are given the opportunity to talk to and with anybody, anywhere, at any time.

Interactive story-making in the nursery and reception

I have found interactive story-making to be an effective introduction to dramatic activities in the early years. This is a method of engaging children in story-making where they and the teacher take an active part in the creation of a story. Many teachers do this without movement, when they ask children what might happen in a story while they are sitting together at story-time, perhaps drawing pictures on large sheets of paper to represent the various events. In a more interactive situation, children move about, acting out their suggestions with the teacher joining in. When working in this way I have sometimes found it beneficial to suggest the opening context for the story. The teacher might say: 'We are all pigs who have got to make our way in the world.' I might take on the role of Mother Pig and ask the children's help in finding my sons who have not written to me for some time. I start with suggestions of what we should do, and then undertake some task or some journey in search of our goal. Possible story starters are the beginnings of familiar fairy stories — 'The Three Little Pigs', 'Three Billy Goats Gruff', 'Cinderella.' Although this might influence the kinds of events and characters developed in the story, it is not my role to manipulate the action so that it is merely a re-enactment of the fairy-tale. I am interested in the children telling their own story, with me in it to guide, challenge ideas and facilitate when necessary. My main function is to give voice to suggestions put forward possibly by the shyer child, or to challenge ideas or solutions to problems in order to make children think and articulate in more depth.

Further structuring of stories for older infants

By Year 1 the story-making can be given more structure. The storytelling technique already described can be continued, but by introducing periods of 'time-out' to slow down the action children can be discouraged from 'plot-guzzling' — the wanting to know what will happen next syndrome. Periods of stopping the story to look at an event or a character in more depth can help to deepen language and thinking. By introducing drama strategies (many of these are suggested in the back of the old English Orders) in a selected manner, the children can be given new experiences. At this stage they will also be able increasingly to accept the teacher taking on a named role rather than just being alongside them during the story. Teacher-in-role during early storytelling sessions will be very fluid. Sometimes you will want to define who you are within the context of the story; at other times it will be difficult to identify with a specific role as the context will be more important. The children, too, will be able to take on named roles themselves, either individually or collectively. In a particular nursery class, three girls decided they did not want to join in the initial story-making and sat out of the circle under a table. As the story progressed, the 'animals' in the story needed to speak to the birds. It was at this point in the story that these girls took on the role of 'the birds', helping each other by providing information and ideas in turn, and took us on our journey.

To improve competence in speaking and thinking through the use of language, it is important to ask what kind of language the task is requiring the pupils to use and how the language can be used to explore the situations and events within the drama more fully. Can the relationship between the verbal and non-verbal parts of the drama be used to strengthen each other? Some parts of the drama will require the 'acting out' of situations suggested by the children through the use of mime and physical movement, such as moving from one place to another, the digging of holes, the making of equipment. All these actions can be discussed so that the making of things can be explained and feelings expressed about the predicaments. This short exchange between a small girl and teacher-in-role came about as the group in role as woodland animals was deciding how they could travel on a kite.

Teacher: How do you make a kite fly?
Child A: We run into the wind.
Child B: No, away from the wind.
Teacher: Which is it then? Into or away from the wind.
Child C: I've flown a kite before.
Teacher: You're just the animal we need. How do we fly the kite?
Child C: You have to run like that ... [*She demonstrates by running around the group holding her right hand up to indicate the string from the kite.*] ... with the wind behind you to make the kite go up.

Questioning in drama

The teacher must choose which contributions to pursue and which will be the most effective in achieving the language development considered appropriate. To enable this to happen the teacher needs to be ready to ask productive questions at the correct time in the action — although we do not always get this right. Children will need to be given opportunities to analyse what they know by being given a chance to express it, as in the example with the kite. They will need the chance to set and solve problems and predict outcomes if they are to produce original ideas. By asking 'What could we have done to stop King Midas getting his golden touch?' or 'What might have happened if ...?' we have the chance of drawing out both fact and feeling. There should be opportunities for children to recognize and value what they know. Through examining the validity of ideas, expressing informed opinions on issues and giving consideration to the solutions to problems, the teacher has a method of assessing what they have learned. By identifying motives and causes and by finding evidence to support their thinking, they come to trust their own judgements.

The ability to ask questions and pose problems is one of the teacher's most important functions within the drama. Through the use of effective questioning the teacher can become a gatherer and giver of information, developing a story in several ways. She or he can establish a context and involve children in the making of the narrative. Once the context and the narrative are settled, children should be moved into thinking creatively and critically about characters and situations, thereby helping to develop their curiosity and encourage research. Through talking and reflecting on actions and events, thinking can be deepened and made to be more focused. The teacher or other children can challenge existing ideas and attitudes, and children can be allowed to reflect on and to evaluate their own experience and that of others.

Working in the story alongside the children in this way allows the teacher to enter the children's world on their terms. It allows the move away from the classroom teaching style and helps the teacher adopt a new role. In that new role we are able to test existing knowledge and introduce new learning. We can challenge assumptions and attitudes and ask questions that will encourage creativity and critical thought. We can play 'devil's advocate' by posing problems and asking for decisions. We can consider group behaviour and if necessary alter it by bringing the group to new knowledge and by making them responsible for their own learning.

When asking questions it is important to frame them in different ways, using forms such as 'who', 'what', 'how', 'when', 'where', 'which', 'why' or 'if', which demand information in reply; not simply yes and no answers, but something more than what is known already. These forms are associated with 'open' questioning, and require more elaborate response from the children. If the word 'might' is used, the possible responses become increasingly open-ended; for example, 'What might King Midas be thinking?' invites more possibilities than 'What is King Midas thinking?' The second example could suggest that there is a correct answer and that we somehow should know what he is thinking, whereas the first example opens up a number of possibilities. The least effective questions are those that produce the yes/no type of answers. This form of questioning is associated with 'closed' questioning. 'Is it raining?', 'Will he come today?' and 'Are we all ready?' will produce little productive response.

While working within children's stories we are given the opportunity to use a variety of question forms which can challenge children's language in a way that might not always be possible in the classroom. In the opening minutes of a story we might want to set the scene and provide a context for our story. The 'what' and 'how' question forms can be helpful at this point. For example, as woodland animals after a storm the children were asked 'What shall we do now? Our tree where we all live has blown down in the storm and all our belongings scattered about the wood.' We might seek information to develop the narrative ('What do we know about the dark wood? I've never been there') or encourage research: ('How can we find out how the kite flies?'). During a story of mice trying to go to the moon, the children were leaving their money behind to collect later:

Boy: You know our 2ps? I know where we landed off the rainbow —
          the North Pole. If we leave our 2ps too long they will be covered
          in snow. We must put a cross by where they are so we don't lose
          them.
Boy 2:   What happens if it snows while we are away and covers the
          crosses up?
Boy 1:   We'll make the crosses with metal that the snow drops off of.

No formal questioning on the part of the teacher could have elicited such
a discussion.

Throughout this chapter, I have emphasized the importance of the
teacher's role in creating opportunities for children to speak and listen in
circumstances where there is mutual trust and respect. In his research,
Gordon Wells observed that classrooms only gave limited opportunities
for planned and reflective talk.[3] Children in these classrooms asked fewer
questions, initiated fewer conversations, appeared to use less complex
language when speaking and spoke to fewer adults than they did at home.
If we are to achieve the 'better overall standards in literacy' as advocated
by OFSTED, then we must make sure that we are using drama and role-
play effectively in the early years.

Notes

1   C. Hutt, 'Fantasy play', in S. J. Hutt, S. Tyler, C. Hutt and H. Christopher
    (eds), *Play, Exploration and Learning*, Routledge, London, 1989.
2   OFSTED (1994) *First Class: The Standards and Quality of Education in
    Reception Classes*, HMSO, London.
3   G. Wells, *The Meaning Makers*, Hodder and Stoughton, London, 1986.

CHAPTER 13

'But Ingrid Will Have Dessert'
Letter Writing as Part of a Nourishing Literary Diet

Holly Anderson

In a similar way to the previous chapter, Holly Anderson begins by identifying the demands inherent in curriculum requirements for children to handle a range of complex uses of language. Similarly, too, she looks at the possibilities of role-play for developing children's existing capabilities to put texts together. In looking at writing, however, Holly Anderson tackles some of the current debates about genre and how best to help children write in narrative and non-narrative, chronological and non-chronological forms. Three areas of children's experience and expertise combine in this chapter — their home knowledge of the social functions of letter writing and reading; their ability to engage readily and vigorously in imaginative play; and their capacity to draw on all the texts they have read (including popular forms of text) to inform their writing. Holly Anderson uses a range of children's letters to show the appetite children have for making their own meanings clear, and the depth and diversity of their literacy and language experience, and suggests ways in which classrooms can offer a diet which will further whet children's appetites for reading and writing.

Many primary teachers have encouraged children to write letters as part of the writing curriculum. Sometimes it can be an almost automatic, unthought-of inclusion in classroom life, fitted in around a range of writing offered to cover the variety asked for within the National Curriculum. I want to take this often neglected area and explore in some detail its benefits to young and inexperienced writers. Letter writing, especially when there is a real audience and purpose, provides a focus for the writer, with the added bonus of the possibility of a real response. I want to suggest that it is an even richer source of inspiration and reflection than might be supposed. I hope to demonstrate the extent to which letter writing can be used to develop children's sense of register and to allow them to experiment with a range of genres often seen as being outside their experience.

The distinction between chronological and non-chronological writing in the National Curriculum is open to challenge and has been criticized as oversimplistic. Nevertheless, this distinction has ensured that all children have opportunities to write beyond the traditionally encouraged 'story writing' in infant classrooms. In addition, the rise in awareness of the influence that environmental print and home experiences have on children's understanding of literacy within their culture has meant that teachers provide a much broader interpretation of what might constitute a varied and balanced writing diet. Classrooms are full of texts written by and for children: story and poetry books written and illustrated by young authors are on display; notices and labels around the room are often the children's, not the teacher's work; and writing corners and role-play areas exploit opportunities for children to have more control over aspects of their writing. But in spite of the increase in purposeful writing, I wonder how often children are encouraged and helped to write sustained texts which demand that they go beyond a temporally linked discourse?

Katherine Perera observes the need to consider both organization and relationship to subject matter when reflecting on the demands that a text places on its writer.[1] She suggests that a piece of writing which has to be organized by some means other than temporality, and where the reader is unknown to the writer, is likely to be at the more taxing end of the spectrum. My experience of working in primary schools is that much writing which the children are asked to do is that which can be organized chronologically. Even those experiences outside narrative are often procedural: for example, recipes and instructions, or the write-up of an experiment or activity. Non-chronological writing tends to be such things as posters, lists and captions, all requiring some thought as to the organization and presentation of the material, but without demanding that the author carefully plans a logical structure through which the ideas can be coherently expressed. I want to explore the opportunities that letter writing can offer for children to do just this. I maintain that it demands a complex management of content which has been selected by the child for a specific reason for an acknowledged reader. As teachers we have to help children to be flexible and versatile writers by offering them opportunities to go beyond both the sterile recount for a teacher who knows all about it anyway, and the 'story' which may not enable any further discovery about the complex ways of telling narratives.

My first example starts before school and shows how a pre-school child drew on her knowledge of the power of the written word. She carefully selected her facts and organized them into a suitable form with the clear intention of persuading the reader to take her needs into account. It

'Ingrid will not have fish.'

demonstrates that very young children are perfectly capable of writing argument when they feel it is necessary.

The piece of writing shown above is by a young Norwegian girl who, having learned that her mother has written to the nursery school letting them know she is allergic to fish, is concerned that she may also not be given food she does like! It reads from right to left:

> Ingrid vil ike h fisk tål ike
> (Ingrid will not have fish, tolerates it not)
> men Ingrid vil ha desar
> (but Ingrid will have dessert)

Children do not start school until they are 7 in Norway, and are not encouraged to write before that unless they themselves demand opportunities. However, at the age of 5 Ingrid was already an accomplished communicator on paper and this is but one example of what she was capable of writing when needing to convey a message. Lorentzen explains:

> The background is that her mother has written in an application form for Kindergarten that Ingrid is allergic to fish, a piece of information that Ingrid with her sense of audience worries may lead to some very unlucky conclusions as to what she will get to eat in Kindergarten. Therefore she

writes a note to the leader of the Kindergarten, referring to herself in third person, taking on the role of a person in authority, and trying to take control of and regulate her own affairs at the same time. This text also shows that small children, if they really are engaged and familiar with the authority of print, are able to carry through a written argument. Ingrid manages to write coherently and persuasively for a case of great importance to herself. The text also contradicts that small children build up their texts in an additive way, one association following the other one ... The text is a coherent sequence of thoughts, arranged deliberately and from a global consideration. But Ingrid does not yet master the elementary directional principles of our language, nor spelling nor punctuation.[2]

Written messages such as the one opposite show how young children are capable of constructing texts to present arguments, even before they are capable of managing the technicalities. This makes it even more crucial that we offer challenges to even our youngest readers and writers.

The next example also shows a similar aptitude and, in addition, has an opening salutation and closing phrase in keeping with the genre of letter writing. A Year 2 class teacher had introduced a notice board into the classroom. Initially, even though she had encouraged the children to use it, the majority of the messages and notices were written by teachers or parents. Notes such as a reminder to the teacher that the child had a dental appointment and was therefore required to leave early were typical of those on display, and the children quickly began to refer to the information there. This alone was a success, as it helped extend the range of purposeful reading material. However, after a considerable amount of time, the children also began to write their own messages and reminders, and Julie came into class one afternoon after lunch to read:

Dear mrs fuler
Hayley is riley giting up my nevs ples kud you boow
sumthing a bat it, love from HG

(Dear Mrs Fuller, Hayley is really getting up my nerves.
Please could you do something about it, love from HG)

Both the above examples show the extent to which children can write persuasively, providing clear justification for the requests (demands!) they make to the reader of the text. Each child is confident writing a non-temporally organized text and has a clear sense of how both audience and purpose affect the choice of vocabulary and syntax.

Letter or message writing is a powerful way in which children can show their capabilities in constructing an argument, and this could therefore be used by teachers to greater advantage. Certainly, in terms of emphasis on written texts, children from quite different backgrounds seem to have experience of written messages at home. Shirley Brice Heath found that both the children from Trackton and Roadville (the two separate but neighbouring communities she studied in the USA) saw their elders write messages and letters, thus ensuring that these formed part of their literate traditions.[3] Teachers may well exploit what knowledge children bring with them to school and encourage letter writing as part of the writing experience from the beginning; and there is a strong case for the way in which real correspondence helps introduce and extend children's knowledge of written structures. However, such letters, important though they may be in overall writing development, still may not provide many real purposes for writing the sort of discourse found in the two examples of work shown so far in this chapter.

This, it seems to me, is the dilemma: how to get children to write the sort of letters and messages which would require them to use argument and persuasion, but which are at the same time likely to be beyond their own experiences and therefore would not arise naturally. So often, in trying to introduce the vital elements of purpose and audience into the children's writing, the invented 'real' purpose is just as false and sterile as the 'lesson on how to' would be. Children are not fooled by being asked to write all about themselves to a fictitious pen-pal — the teacher is identified as both instigator and audience and, instead of having any intrinsic interest in the task for its own sake, the children perceive it as yet another way of being asked to practise the art of writing. How can teachers give real meaning to a school-centred task? It was while I was working with groups of very young children on encouraging independence in writing that I was, without realizing it at the time, finding ways in which some of these dilemmas might be addressed.

As a language advisory teacher in the late 1980s I worked with many Key Stage 1 teachers, exploring ways in which we could encourage children to take more risks when writing. The National Writing Project had, for many teachers, challenged the copy-writing model of learning to write, and furthermore the National Curriculum requirements meant children had to write independently for assessment purposes. However, children who had expectations of 'correctness' found it extremely difficult to abandon the copying under/word-book approach, and teachers found that it was not enough simply to encourage children to 'have a go', with the familiar supports removed.

Nigel Hall's book *Writing with Reason* provided some ideas, where children wrote letters in response to the messages that the ladybird on display in the classroom had 'written' for the children.[4] My china cat, quickly christened Flora in recognition of her flower-covered coat, accompanied me into a reception class of children doing a topic on 'The Owl and the Pussycat'. While I worked with groups of children, others told stories into the tape recorder with Flora sitting beside it; Flora, they

Lapboards,
London Road,
Newport,
Near Saffron Walden,
Essex. CB11 3PS

Dear children,

My name is Flora and I have come to visit you today at your school. Do you have any pets? What are their names? Write back and let me know.

love

Flora

were told, loved listening to stories. Even more were keen to respond to the letter that Flora had brought in with her to school and I came away with letters from most of the class, all willingly and independently written. Some were drawings with kisses underneath, but many were attempts by the children to write messages. The children knew that Flora had neither written her letter, nor would read their replies, but somehow the activity was an extension for them of the imaginative and fantasy play so beloved of young children and central to their learning. They drew upon their knowledge that, in real life, letters are read aloud to others and replied to, or acted upon, in some way. By introducing a 'real' and tangible audience in Flora I had, as far as possible, replicated the social and cultural reasons for reading and writing letters. In addition, Flora had entered into their world of storybook, fairy-tale, fantasy characters and in

Dear Flora

bc 12 S R w e

and my f N is 28036P

my N is Jennifer

I h g a Dog

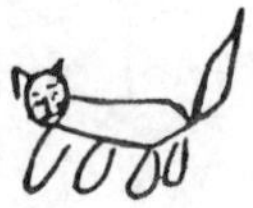

and 3 cas

and a nav RaBt

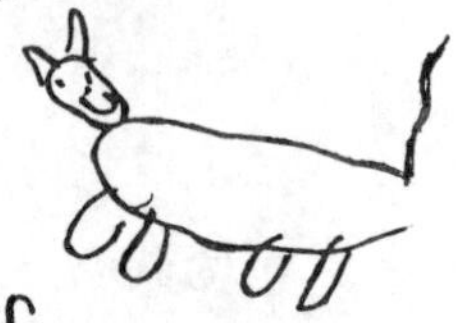

love fRom Jennifer

xxxxxxxxxxxxxxxxxxxxxxxxxxxxxxxxxxxxxxxxxxxxxxxxxxxxxxxxxxx

Dear Flora

10 Court 15 Sxxxx Road Wxxxx Essex

and my phone number is

my name is Jennifer

I have got a dog

and 3 cats

and I would like another rabbit

love from Jennifer.

Jennifer's letter to Flora and her teacher's transcription

so doing she had liberated the children so that they felt able to take risks, safe in the knowledge that Flora would not be judgemental in her response.

From then on, I used Flora on several occasions, often continuing the correspondence after I had ceased visiting the school. I could structure her letters so that the children were able to have some support in organizing their replies. Flora was, of course, always interested to hear about other animals, and one reception class wrote back in request for information about their pets.

Children were able to show in a powerful way how much they knew about the conventions of writing. Five-year-old Jennifer had taken note of the letter which Flora sent and had used the structures within the letter in her own reply (shown opposite). She mirrored the opening salutation and the ending from the original, also showing that she was aware of the need to put an address at the top (10 Court, 15 S*** Road, W****, Essex). Her phone number is added for good measure (and my phone number is . . .). Her attempts to spell show that she is aware of individual words making up a sentence and that she knows the logical, if not necessarily correct, initial phoneme. Some common words she has committed to memory (*and*, *my*, *dog*) she has attempted to spell two longer words (*another* and *rabbit*). According to Temple *et al.* she is working within the early phonemic and letter sound stages of development in spelling.[5] More importantly perhaps, she shows that she is capable of entering into a written dialogue with Flora and has given the necessary information originally requested. Jennifer felt confident in her ability to communicate with Flora, and had readily agreed to reply in writing. This enthusiasm and confidence was shown by many of the children and both pleased and surprised the teacher, who until that time had had little success in encouraging independent writing. What I was beginning to realize was that by giving children choice and ownership in writing to a fantasy character, I was giving them the support and the confidence to take risks and experiment, something which, unhappily, at school children so often feel unable to do.

The success with the very youngest children, who seemed happy to play spontaneously with writing, led me to apply this principle when working with slightly older children. Another group, this time Year 3, were liberated from the tyranny of mastering the technicalities before experimenting with what they know about writing by being encouraged to write in role. This took place within a drama lesson in which the children had discovered a notice warning of an imminent attack. Suitably 'distressed' (courtesy of a used tea-bag and burnt edges), the message read:

TO ALL VILLAGERS
Reports have reached us that Lord Donganon and his men have been sighted at Cambridge. They are less than a day's march away.

It is advised that all who read this message flee immediately to places
of safety.

The school was in a village close to a Norman stronghold. A serf from the
castle (teacher in role) just happened to be passing and indicated that,
providing the children could offer work, they might be taken in under the
protection of the baron. The children had time to write messages to their
parents letting them know what had happened and to think of suitable
jobs which might persuade the lord of the castle to employ them.
    Daniel wrote:

> Dear mum and dad
> I am going to a castle for safety reasons. Lord Donganon has been
> spotted a mile away. I am going to Mountfitchet castle. I am sorry but a
> boys got to do what a boys got to do.
> Love Daniel

Charlotte's, on the other hand, said:

> Dear mum and dad,
> I am going to a castle to keep safe. Because Donganon is coming. I am
> going to take my pencil case and my panda bear. I don't know if we're
> allowed yet.
> Charlotte

Both are wonderful examples of intertextuality, with the children drawing
on their knowledge of a variety of cultural 'texts'. Whilst the structure in
both cases shows some degree of temporal organization, with succinct
explanations given for what has happened and the resulting intended
action, each of the children wanted to extend the communication beyond
the crucial message. The boy presents a brave and challenging stance as
further justification for his actions. The girl is more hesitant about being
welcomed and appears concerned about having familiar items with her for
comfort, including this information, perhaps to relieve the anxiety of
those left behind. Both, however, present a credible attempt at a piece
of writing which needs to be carefully composed, and show a degree of
formality in keeping with the task.[6]
    The letters asking for employment, on the other hand, show quite
different features. This time the writers are not concerned with
explanations for their actions, but rather seek to persuade the reader
that they have talents which could be put to use.
    Daniel again writes:

> Dear Lord,
> I am best at cutting down trees for wood. I can pick up an axe easily. I
> can move trees easily.
> Daniel

The writer has thought of the skills that might be considered useful by the community and, important in the argumentative mode of discourse, tries to justify his statement. He can pick up an axe and he can move trees easily, and therefore he implies that he is a most suitable candidate to help with the never-ending need for wood, used both as fuel and as building material. This letter, short though it is, demonstrates that the child is able to organize his ideas, to present an argument, and to do this while at the same time meeting the criteria for letter writing. Both opening and ending are conventional for a letter to an unknown person; note how this time 'love' is omitted. The brevity of the statements, which contain all the necessary information, strengthens the formality of the register. Daniel has presumably never had to write a letter to an employer, and certainly not one who is a twelfth-century baron, but by writing in role he is quite happy to experiment and the result is a most credible attempt.

The same can be said of the next two examples, both from a Year 5 class in Sussex who, before going to a local stately home and park in which life in Victorian England was being enacted, had to write applications for employment under the housekeeper in the 'big house'. This class was used to role-play and drama being used across the curriculum; nevertheless their teacher was both surprised and pleased with the resulting letters (see pages 208 and 209).

Through the letters, the children showed an empathy and under-standing which would not have been apparent had they merely written an account of their visit on return. Such an activity would have provided a clear chronological structure (we did this, then that, etc.) and would not have demanded that the children select facts from their knowledge of Victorian life and the hierarchical administration of rich and powerful households to carefully compose and craft a piece of writing.

To some extent the central themes are defined by the task itself, with the children needing to outline the job they feel most suits their skills and to give some details about themselves. However, neither of these indicate how best they should be organized; that is left to the writer to decide and therefore, I suggest, places considerable demands on the young author. In addition, they have to decide how to persuade the reader that their claims can be taken seriously. To do this, they have drawn on elements of their invented present situation to demonstrate their declared abilities, and these need to be presented and structured within the overall piece. The choices taken also show how the children use their own historical knowledge of written form to make the final pieces of writing more authentic.

Within the letters, the relationship between the applicant and the employer has to be considered. This too places demands on the author, who must implicitly show the status of both writer and reader. Both use

Lustrells farm
Rottingdean.

14·2·1894

Dear Mrs Storey,
                 I saw your advertisement in
the local paper, it said that you needed a housema
id so I would like to apply.
My name is Beth Victoria. I am a strong
working girl. I am good at tidying as I have
lots of experience at home. I am clean and
tidy. I share a room at home so I am
easy to get along with. I like being tidy. I
am strong enough to carry the water. I do
not get home sick, I do what I am told
I think the house is beautifull.
The farm is very big so I help clean, make
the beds and lots more things.

I hope to hear from you soon.

Your humble servant.

                              Beth Victoria

Beth Victoria's letter of application for work in the Victorian stately home

the conditional tense to emphasize this inequality: 'I would like' rather
than 'I want'. Beth Victoria (her chosen Victorian name) also signs herself
'your humble servant', a clear indication of her perceived place in society.
Her opening focus is explicit, immediately giving the reason for the
writing of the letter. The next topic is about herself, and in this section
(written, as would be a text describing a universal truth, in simple present
tense) she includes a number of reasons why her application should be
taken seriously, citing specifics about her home circumstances as proof of
more general statements about her industrious nature. Her use of flattery

Two trees
Tulip farm
Rottingdean
Sussex
bn2 8Lp

Dear Mrs Story
        I would like to be an oddman at preston manor
I am strong for carrying in coal, and I am used to
chopping wood because I live on a farm, and have to
chop wood a lot. I like to work hard and one of
my favourite jobs is cleaning the floor, I would
love to do this in the servants rooms. I hope to see you
soon so that I can be interviewed for this job.

            Yours sincerely

            Peter Franklin.

Peter's letter of application for work in the Victorian stately home

('I think the house is beautiful'), while it may be an ingenious device to
add weight to the reasons for wanting this specific job, appears somewhat
misplaced within the discourse organization and interrupts the overall
cohesion of the text. However, this is still a mature and, on the whole,
well-organized and crafted piece of work, showing an appreciation of the
needs of the reader and the specific genre.

This combination of writing in role and letter writing does seem to be a
fruitful one, especially when the children have some measure of control
over the content and reason for writing. It allows children to explore the
more formal styles and registers, while at the same time providing a
degree of security by writing within a convention of which children
already have some experience. Although a letter can be chronological in
organization, more often it has to have a non-temporal structure imposed
by the writer, who chooses to select and organize the relevant details for
the particular purpose and audience. However, it appears that, perhaps
because there is an element of familiarity about the broad genre of 'letter
writing', children feel supported by this and can create their own structure

within the overall framework. Role-play gives an added element of security to the activity by providing the means through which the child can experiment and take risks, but furthermore is a vehicle through which some of the more complex features of written language can be employed. Once writing in role is acknowledged as a means by which children can be supported to write outside their experiences, the possibilities become endless. More and more unlikely scenarios can be invented to challenge the children's linguistic skills, not in a threatening but in a playful way.

The final examples I want to use were written collaboratively by groups of children in Years 5 and 6. Following on from reading *The True Story of the Three Little Pigs*[7] the children were given a number of ways in which they might respond. They were thus offered choices within a structure which had clear expectations about the outcome — that the writing was to be read, and enjoyed, by others sharing the same joke. Appreciation of both mimicry and parody feature in the enjoyment of the book, and the children readily incorporated these in their responses.

Those unfamiliar with Scieszka's version of the traditional tale need to know that the wolf's defence, when caught in the act of demolishing the third house, was that he had merely been trying to borrow a cup of sugar from the pigs in order to make a birthday cake for his grandmother, and it was a cold, rather than premeditated intention, which caused him to sneeze and blow the houses down. The final page of the book shows him in prison serving a sentence for his crimes, still hoping to borrow the sugar. One group of children, in role as the wolf who had now escaped from prison, wrote a postcard to granny (shown opposite).

What could have been a very simple task, demanding little more than a brief greeting, shows an ability to use puns, playing with words in a quite delightful way. Could any wolf granny refuse such an invitation, so carefully and persuasively written? Whereas human holiday-makers might be tempted by climate alone, the young authors felt that the way to a wolf's heart was definitely through gastronomy, so morsels to satisfy lupine tastebuds were included. This knowledge of wolves' diets based on many traditional tales was but one of the influences on the writing, others being criminal safe havens and those features which might typify Mediterranean holiday resorts. Knowledge gained from literature, television, newspapers, and both home and school experiences, was all woven together in a witty piece of work which more than does credit to the original text.

The same is true of the next example (on page 212), this time a letter from the wolf to the distraught mother of the three little pigs. The remorse shown by the carnivorous killer is quite clearly tongue in cheek and exactly captures the devious and plausible nature of the character created by Scieszka. The children are not only able to write persuasively, but to do so with irony. The formality of 'I hope you will forgive me for this terrible

Dear loving Ganny,
I am sorry about your birthday but I got
court up, get it? Please will you come and
live with me in Stew Street, Malagar? Because
of the blazing hot sun and the beautiful beachs
(My favourites is chicken beach.) This is
the best place for food. e.g omelette with chicken,
pig paella and Spanish rabbit stew. I am pleased
to tell you that I have tickets to the no
wolf disco
       From
          Dear
             Granswolf

P.S. Bring your pigsuit and I have the freshest
rabbit, next door!

Mrs M. P. Wolf
7 Pork lane
SPIZIEQ
U.S.A.
Florda

A wolf's postcard to Granny

insedent' (sic) is contrasted with, and therefore undermined by, 'Must go
my pork chops are ready for my dinner', and the final throwaway line
'P.S. I hope they taste as nice as your little porkers' leaves us in no doubt
as to the wolf's true unrepentant nature. The children's skill in controlling
these strands, bringing them together with maturity and humour, is
impressive, and by writing in role the children can play with their ideas
and practise skills without fear of failure. We can but speculate about the
models on which the children based their letter. Undoubtedly wide-
ranging, they bridge the divide between 'popular culture' and 'the literary
canon', enabling the children to use their knowledge of the type of pun
found in tabloid headlines to add the final dark and humorous twist.

The last of the three examples (on page 213) certainly goes beyond the
repertoire that would arise spontaneously through everyday classroom
experiences. In role as the wolf, the children had to write to the prison
governor asking that the sentence imposed should be reduced. An
argument is put forward, with the judge's original interpretation of the
actions redefined and challenged. A number of justifications for release

10 Wolf Way
Piggy Foot Lane
Wolfshire
EN11 9FS

Dear Mrs Porky,

I hope your coping well. I'm sitting here using boxes of tissues box after box. I sit here sobbing for what I have done. I am dearly sorry. I hope you understand that. Your sons can not write to you any more. It devastates me! I will do anything you ask of me. Your sons (the little Porkers) are not around anymore. I'm deeply sorry I hope you will forgive me for this terrible insedent. I will give you my words I will not trouble you any more. Must go my Pork chops are ready for my dinner.

Yours Sincerly
A.T. Wolf

P.S. I hope they taste as nice as your little Porkers.

A. T. Wolf's letter of apology

are given and, for good measure, flattery is also brought into play just in case the evidence alone is not sufficient. So a mixture of facts and suppositions are marshalled to come to the aid of the 'reformed character' whose plausibility is descriptively captured by the children. Using such phrases as 'ask your permission' and 'I beg your forgiveness', they clearly demonstrate an ability to write with a degree of formality in keeping with the task, at the same time as keeping up pressure to persuade.

Fox shows how argument can be contained within young children's oral narrative, and it seems as if the ways in which many children naturally act out and rehearse situations in their play can be extended to work in school which will give scope for a greater breadth and depth of activities.[8] The range of genres and registers could be taken far beyond those which are usually available to young children, who, as with our three examples, more than adequately demonstrate their linguistic skills

Cell   171
Wolf bound prison

To a marvellous prison governor,

I am writing this letter to ask your permission for an early release. I think you are a wonderful governor and have treated me kindly over the last few years. I have never known such a wonderful warm-hearted person.

The reason I would like an early release is because I am a reformed character. I have spent a lot of time on my own and this has given me time to think about what I have done but all I wanted was a cup of sugar. I didn't mean to blow the houses down. Also I didn't want to waste any food. I am so sorry!

Yours sincerely
A.T. Wolf.

P.S I beg your forgiveness.

A. T. Wolf's letter of justification

and critical abilities. What is particularly striking is the sense of play and humour which comes through so strongly in all three pieces, and how each one places quite different constraints on the writers. Dialogues between characters, or character and narrator, can provide a vehicle for discussion and negotiation. If children are capable of sustaining an argument within a genre such as narrative which is traditionally seen as chronological and therefore separate from non-temporal forms of discourse, should they not also be given opportunities to fully exploit this within other genres which might appear to lend themselves more readily to exposition, argument and persuasion? Letter writing may not, on first sight, be considered a suitable medium either. Used as an example of a non-chronologically organized text, it is likely to be exploited for realistic purposes within the classroom, and on the whole is not seen as a vehicle for imagination and fantasy in the way that narrative is. But perhaps there is more in common between the discourse structures than might initially be apparent. Both provide opportunities for children to extend their conversational dialogue through the monologue of written composition. Children's knowledge of letter writing as a means of written communication starts very early, from the moment they are helped to draw kisses on a letter to a loved relative or friend. With many books currently available using knowledge of such things as lists, messages and letters to move the plot further, children will have access to a wide range of genres in 'storybooks'. Children will use these as a basis for experimentation but will draw on an even wider range of literary experiences: fiction, news media, video games and texts traversing traditional and popular culture. The 'voices off' are all around, and children will not be confined to any one source for inspiration.

Play and experimentation are part of learning and should be given status in our classrooms. Vygotsky alerts us to the way in which play develops abstract thought.[9] Role-play and writing in role are legitimate games to play in the classroom. The children that I have worked with have all entered into the game more than willingly, showing enthusiasm and commitment. It seems as if, when they are writing in role, children's inventive and imaginative qualities are exploited in a powerful way. Moreover, letter writing provides a basis on which to move from the familiar to the unfamiliar, with children having to make choices about the tone, the style and the register to suit the specific circumstances. Awareness of audience and sense of purpose are central to these circumstances and it is because the fantasy is acknowledged, is a declared part of the activity, that it adds to the vitality of the writing. Children and teacher together enter into the contract and in doing so no one is duped. The success of the activity is dependent on creativity and playfulness, replacing what might otherwise be sterile and unproductive. Let us allow children to exploit the myriad voices which surround their lives and to have opportunities to show us they have the power to reason and argue. We must give them their just desserts.

Acknowledgements

Thanks are due to: Julie Fuller and class, Dunmow Infants School, Great Dunmow, Essex; Helen Chambers and class, Temple Infants School, Witham, Essex; the staff and pupils at Elsenham Primary School, Essex; Sandra Law and class, Saltdean Primary School, East Sussex; and Max Shailer and class, The Cranbourne School, Hoddesdon, Herts.

Notes

1   Katherine Perera, *Children's Writing and Reading: Analysing Classroom Language*, Blackwell, Oxford, 1984, p. 220.

2 Rutt Trøite Lorentzen, 'To–From: a key to the understanding of children's early writing', in M. L. Tickoo (ed.), *Anthology Series 35*, SEAMEO Regional Language Centre, Singapore, 1995, pp. 388–404.

3 Shirley Brice Heath, *Ways with Words*, Cambridge University Press, Cambridge, 1983.

4 Nigel Hall, *Writing with Reason*, Hodder and Stoughton, London, 1989.

5 C. Temple, *The Beginnings of Writing*, Allyn and Bacon, Boston, 1982, pp. 101–102.

6 It is interesting to note these different approaches to the task and to speculate how much they are dependent on the gender of the writer.

7 Jon Scieszka and Lane Smith, *The True Story of the Three Little Pigs*, Picture Puffins, Harmondsworth, 1989.

8 Carol Fox, 'The genesis of argument in narrative discourse', *English in Education* (1990), **24** (No. 1).

9 Lev Vygotsky, *Mind in Society*, University of Harvard Press, Boston, 1978.

PART IV

Voices Off

This Part refers to many kinds of 'voices off'. Anne Rowe (who, incidentally, gave the title for this book and the conference on which it is based) literally deals with voices off, as her chapter is about wordless picture books. But any notion of visual images being inferior to the written word, or just for inexperienced readers, is immediately dispelled. Anne Rowe draws on parallels with art and filmic texts, demonstrating the complexity involved in both constructing and reading these texts, something which most young children manage with delight and ease. By analysing several wordless picture books, she shows us how these texts (some of which are metafictive) substitute other languages for the written word, and challenge the reader to recreate the 'voices off' themselves, drawing on a range of visual literacies to do so.

It takes the most talented of illustrators to create picture books which invite readers to provide their own words or 'voices off' the page. Satoshi Kitamura is one such inventive and original artist who produces some of the very best, highly distinctive picture books for younger as well as older readers. He does so, he says, not by taking conscious account of children and their needs, but by using his own hunches and instincts, and seeking to understand 'what makes certain things either universal or particular'. He does, however, find children ideal readers, because of their receptiveness to the integrity of his work: 'If the work expresses itself fully, it will be received well by those who are interested in it. If the work is worthwhile to the artist himself, it will be so for some readers, both young and old.' Kitamura's voice, on and off the page, is refreshingly honest and modest, offering a fascinating commentary on some of his work. Victor Watson, appreciative of every detail (including Kitamura's 'silence'), tells Kitamura's story and insightfully, sometimes poetically, interprets his illustrations. The fusion of their different pens and voices makes this a rewarding read.

Helen Nicholson links the two writers above, as she deals in detail with Kitamura's outstanding text, *Angry Arthur*, and considers how exposure to picture books makes children 'adept at reading oral and visual narratives'. She draws parallels between the shared group readings of picture books between teachers and young children and the communal 'voices on stage' as older pupils create and re-create dramatic narratives. In a chapter that draws widely on critical theory, Helen Nicholson 'lays bare the workings of drama as an art form' in her analysis of the semiotics of performance. Using *Angry Arthur* as a model, she shows how pupils' dramatic repertoire can be extended by attention to genre, style, convention and form, and through ownership of the artistic process they can value themselves as makers of art. As everyday language is grafted with the poetic and metaphorical, pupils in performance and on stage explore the range of their own voices, as well as becoming part of an 'interpretive community'.

Matthew (Year 7) tells us uncompromisingly, at the beginning of Gabrielle Cliff Hodges' chapter, that he doesn't feel like reading because he is tired after cycling and has a headache! Gabrielle Cliff Hodges believes in listening to what pupils actually say about how and what they read, and understands their need for the comfortable and familiar. She goes on to consider the crucial role of the English teacher in guiding and challenging pupils' reading, particularly by allowing them to 'encounter the different' in a supportive context. Like Helen Nicholson, Gabrielle Cliff Hodges is concerned to foster pupils' ability to interpret and criticize texts, including those written by young people themselves, so that they are empowered as readers and willing to tolerate what may at first seem strange, difficult or unsettling in their reading. This argument is located within a framework which recognizes the centrality of the social practices of reading and peer reading networks. The crucial voices here are first of all those of the pupils expressing their views and preferences about reading. Then there are the teachers, selecting texts for individuals that demand to be read in a different way, but are not too strange, and developing classroom practices for reading where new and difficult texts can be experienced safely. Finally, there are the voices of authors such as Jill Paton Walsh, who provide 'not only a contrast with more familiar narrative landscapes, but also a vantage point from which to view them'.

CHAPTER 14

Voices Off
Reading Wordless Picture Books

Anne Rowe

Far from considering 'wordless' picture books as lacking written text, Anne Rowe requires the reader to master new languages to interpret what she calls 'sequenced picture texts'. First, she opens up the language of art and shows how the words used to describe paintings can illuminate the reading of pictorial texts: line, colour, texture, form, space, layout, etc. In the same way, some of the sophisticated techniques shared by film-makers and children's illustrators help to explain how pictorial texts are constructed: frame, angle, montage, fade, close-up, etc. Most significantly, perhaps, Anne Rowe uses an eloquent new language to describe the role of the reader or viewer – spectators (without or within), the beholder's share and insider-readers. She demonstrates how the apparently simplest and most artless of texts, those without words, are actually extremely complex, requiring the reader to 'recover' or create their own 'voices off'; and how it was small children who taught her how to read the language of pictures. She likens the reader/narrator of wordless picture books to the oral storyteller 'with the path of the narrative picked out, but with freedom for diversions to explore new tracks or revisit other vistas'.

Recently there has been a steady increase in what publishers refer to as wordless picture books, so much so that they now form a subgenre. Artists feel able to make increased demands on readers who employ a range of visual literacies to interpret wordless picture books. When I read the art of the Middle Ages, I recognize that I am standing in front of demanding picture narratives, whether these narratives are contained in traditional frames, wall paintings, altar-pieces, stained-glass windows, or complex sculptures overarching the great doors of a cathedral. The illustrators of wordless picture books continue to work in this long tradition to solve the same storytelling problems. Unfortunately, many of us have grown up in a culture where respect for the picture is minimal and certainly visual images are seen as inferior to the written word. Perhaps this is why picture book makers have moved out of their traditional illustrators' role to articulate the picture book in revolutionary ways. These artists have had to teach us how to read and interpret their work.

My own education began with Charles Keeping's *The River* and *Anno's Journey* by Mitsumasa Anno. Before that, I was still firmly in the camp of Pope Gregory the Great, who complained about pictures appearing in churches but conceded that they were appropriate for the illiterate; and I saw pictorial texts as suitable only for the most inexperienced readers. However, I now recognize that the complexities of many picture books make them available to a wide range of readers. In fact they have a 'Dickensian' audience, in that they can be read by each member of a family in individual ways, yet with the possibility that everyone can learn from them. Jane Doonan, in an article in *Signal 75*,[1] uses the term 'open address' to describe this range of response.

The Little Mouse books of Monique Felix are good examples. In *Another Story of ... the Little Mouse Trapped in a Book*[2] the hero, realizing his predicament, rushes from side to side in the book, but decides that the only solution is to eat his way out. This leads to near-disaster when the sea from another picture flows out of its frame, threatening to drown him, but for his ingenuity in fashioning the nibbled-out square of paper into a paper boat. This metafictive text intrigues many readers at different levels.

I recognize the debt I owe to children in learning lessons about picture books. Tomie da Paola also makes this point in the interview reprinted in *Bookmark*, where he is discussing *The Hunter and the Animals*.

> So it demands a little more close looking. And it's interesting that children have that ability. A lot of grown-ups miss what is probably one of the most important portions of this entire book, which is where the hunter falls asleep and the animals, who hide from him very successfully while he is trying to hunt them, change the forest.[3]

Wordless picture books?

Before any discussion of these texts, it is necessary to challenge the tag that publishers have given them. Wordless they are not, and the pre-text pages are important. Titles, for example, inform at different levels. *Vikki* (Renate Meyer) is significantly named: Victoria, victorious. It suggests her victory over loneliness caused by her exclusion from the games of her companions. I certainly need the informative title *The Grey Lady and the Strawberry Snatcher* (Mollie Bang) to make a start on this complex text. Titles name characters (*The Angel and the Soldier Boy*, Peter Collington), provide a time-scale (*All in a Day*, Mitsumasa Anno), set locale (*Window*, Jeannie Baker), suggest an intertextual reference (*The Great Escape*, Philippe Dupasquier) and sometimes misdirect (*The Trunk*, Brian Wildsmith).

After my initial reading of John Prater's *The Gift*, I felt that he had missed, with this title, an opportunity to underscore the delicious adventure of the two central characters who, pleased though they are with the present that arrives, take greater pleasure in the box in which it comes. Reflection revealed how apt the title is.

But titles are not the only words encountered. Charles Keeping, for example, uses hoardings, shop signs and graffiti to encode other messages. Jeannie Baker's *Window* explores the changes and destruction of the Australian bush during the first 30 years of the life of Sam, the central character. The 'green' message is tellingly underscored by a billboard in the final view from that window, where a 'land for sale' notice threatens a repeat of this folly.

If they are not wordless, how should I describe them? Tomie da Paola describes *Sing, Pierrot, Sing* as 'a picture book in mime'.[4] John Fiske, writing about narrative, talks of 'consequence out of sequence', which aptly describes these texts.[5] Perhaps they are better described, then, as *sequenced picture texts*.

The beholder's share

Vikki by Renate Meyer, recognized as the first sequenced picture text, is redolent of its time. It received a harsh press because it dared to repress the printed text and challenge the reader to recover it. Critics challenged the notion that such a book could be *read*. Better questions might have included: 'What do we mean by reading a picture?', and 'How can we tackle the languages in play?'

Anno's Journey and *The River* were a challenge to me when they first appeared, and I still grapple with them, but now it is as an insider reader, one who recognizes that great pictures can never be emptied of all their meanings and that each reading is part of a widening spiral of interpretation. Reading pictures is active, and meanings do not reside in the images alone. The visual text created by the artist becomes the visual work in the eyes of a reader. The work, a new network of meanings, lies somewhere between the artist and the viewer.[6] The spectator becomes a participant in the creation of meanings, to use the terminology of the critic D. W. Harding. This is what the art critic Ernst Gombrich calls 'the beholder's share'.[7] Individual interpretations are an amalgam of personal and prior visual experiences. Each viewing holds the possibility of new meanings; that is, with each new reader of the text and each fresh re-

reading of the work. The picture-book maker creates a specific universe, and some would argue that this leaves the reader/spectator with very little to do. The opposite is true. The very openness has challenged artists to use every possible means to conceal secrets right out in the open. To take an example from art history, Sassetta, the Sienese painter of the fifteenth century, wished to emphasize the magnitude of St Francis's gift of his cloak to a beggar. He painted it, therefore, with lapis lazuli blue, the most expensive colour. The secret might be hidden in an intertextual reference or the use of another conventional symbol, for example the Minotaur on the front cover of *Where the Wild Things Are* hinting at the underground labyrinths of the unconscious.

Looking in and looking at: responding to the language of art

When we look at a picture we shuttle between the transparent and opaque surface, between the art of the picture-book maker in creating a sense of reality and the craft by which that is achieved. We view the picture frame as a window frame and look through it to the 'secondary world'[8] beyond. The canvas has been hollowed out. Although we are free to enter the picture wherever we wish, we are on the lookout for significance, and artists oblige us by foregrounding key elements. There may be misconceptions but as readers we are anxious to recognize narrative, to cross the transparent threshold and to play the artist's games.

Readers can step back and re-view the opaque surface, and, given experience and support, can come to recognize the choices and the combinations the artists have made from the language of art and, at the same time, learn the language which allows readers to discuss their responses. These elements include the variety and qualities of line, colour and textures in the creation of form, and the delineation of space and the powerful organization of all within the frame. Readers respond to this surface implicitly or explicitly. The implicit awareness is part of the 'felt response' that readers experience when reading pictures. A group of primary school children, who were filmed discussing Anthony Browne's *Gorilla* as a group, make explicit responses to his use of colour to convey meanings between and beyond the lines of the text.[9] What readers learn together today they can activate tomorrow for themselves. Active readers of pictures are in dialogue with themselves, and, with experience, gain reading stamina or scope; that is, they become insider readers. As such, our readings are complex weavings within and between these surfaces. Margaret Meek talks about the 'maypole' of reading.[10] Beholders weave the ribbons or elements together according to their reading needs, the nature of the text and the patterns of their prior knowledge. These ideas are explored more fully in Jane Doonan's *Looking at Pictures in Picture Books*.[11]

To open a Charles Keeping picture book is to enter into a very individual world. Keeping argued[12] that each generation of artists should try to find an appropriate language and not rely upon the solutions found in the past. He demonstrated this commitment in *The River*, with his use of rainbow stripes of colour which did not attempt to create a realistic world, but to tap the expressive qualities of the moment. To the power of colour he added conspicuous textures of brick and wood, drawn in compulsive detail. Keeping focuses attention on the *making* of his pictures, and in that sense can be seen as a metafictive artist. He uses his pen and brush to unfold a detailed metaphor of our alienation from nature (even artificial nature if one recognizes the pollarding of the willow in the opening picture), an alienation which is resolved by the transparent qualities of glass in a modern high-rise block, allowing sunlight back into the city and the river and that tree on the far bank to be seen again.

Anno challenges us in a different way. He demands that readers draw on their prior knowledge in his texts, as much of his complexity rests on intertextual reference. His central character, a symbolic Everyman, rides through the narrative linking place, landscape, past event, literary characters and details from paintings and film in an exploration of the experiences that shape a people.

Artists know that organization of the elements of the picture is the key to conveying meaning. When creating a picture the artist recognizes that the eye will respond to a network of lines which invisibly segment its surface. The power of diagonal lines is an obvious example. Within the rectangular or landscape frame, there are two possible squares to detect. Significant detail often marks these boundaries or they can have narrative import.

The dramatic heart of the dream story of *Little Pickle*, Peter Collington's sequenced picture text, is shown overleaf. The large picture shows the crucial moment when the child is slipping beyond her mother's help, a point of no return, as she drifts out to sea, asleep, in an inflatable dinghy. This fact is revealed by the organization of the image. The line squaring the right-hand edge of the frame reveals the significance of this moment. Little Pickle's dinghy straddles this invisible line. We want to shout to wake her up. This helplessness is further underlined by the surface, which is divided vertically into its thirds — these organizational divisions are indicated by the factory chimneys. The mother is contained and isolated, trapped in her own space just as she is in the pushchair, and by sleep. The sleeping child is on her own. The last segment, ironically, contains a bollard that in other circumstances could have kept her safe.

The dramatic heart of *Little Pickle* (Methuen Children's Books, London, 1986). © Peter Collington. Reproduced with permission.

Looking-at: the influence of film language

Narrative artists are not only working in the traditions of art history, but are much influenced by the work of those other 'picture makers'. It seems natural to use film language in any discussion of sequenced picture texts. Indeed, a number have been made into very successful animated films where the books act as storyboards. There are many parallels. One, for example, is the way in which pictures are framed. The use of shots of differing spatial distance, i.e. close-up or long shot, is also common, as is the high and low angle position given to the reader. The visual literacies developed through watching film and animation allow children's illustrators to make sophisticated choices about how to tell their stories.

The influence of film is also seen in the orchestration of page layouts,

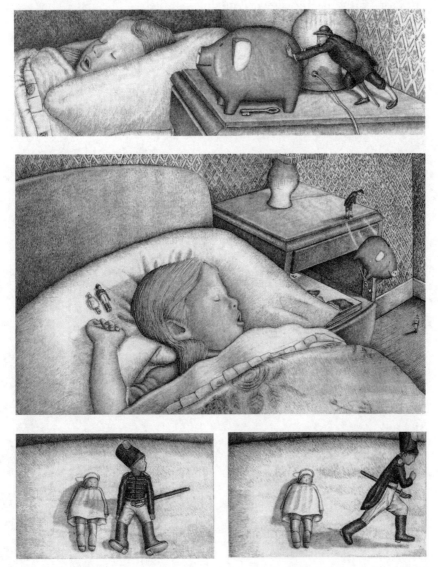

The influence of film is seen in the layout of this page, indicating continuing action. From *The Angel and the Soldier Boy* (Methuen Children's Books, London, 1987). © Peter Collington. Reproduced with permission.

so as to indicate continuance of a scene or its completion. In the illustration from Peter Collington's *The Angel and the Soldier Boy* on page 225, the boy is seen running towards the page edge, encouraging us to turn the page quickly and keep the momentum going. Artists also find some equivalence for the fade or wipe. Collington achieves this by showing his characters moving from close-up through medium shot to long shot, with the movement running parallel to the page edge (see below). To turn the page is to start a new scene.

The end of an episode is indicated by the movement from close-up through medium shot to long shot. From *The Angel and the Soldier Boy* (Methuen Children's Books, London, 1987). © Peter Collington. Reproduced with permission.

Another link between both kinds of texts is the role of editor, cutting and intercutting, so that readers or spectators are best placed to see and interpret. A close reading reveals how pictorial texts are intercut, providing different viewpoints, as on page 225, where there is a cut to point up the soldier's intervention. The final sequence of *The Angel and the Soldier Boy* is very filmic in that Collington uses a form of montage to retell, on one double spread, the return journey of his characters with the difficult and dangerous moments filling the larger pictures.

Reading the framing of the narrative

The picture maker's selections from the language of art are influenced by decisions about the organization of the book itself; I want to look at choices related to the framing of texts. Some artists decide not to physically frame their images, but allow them to bleed edge to edge. Each opening is one moment in the narrative, and the detail possible on a double spread demands a different kind of read. Some artists choose to present these double-spread pictures unframed. The unframed page draws the reader in, admirably demonstrated by Maurice Sendak in *Where the Wild Things Are*, where the rumpus goes beyond words. This book alerted many of us to the possibilities of generating meaning through framing.[13]

To frame the double spread with black line or white border is to maintain the possibility of distance between spectator and event. This can be important at moments of danger or crisis in the narrative, allowing readers an escape route. Peter Collington chooses to switch to a white-framed double spread in *Little Pickle* at the height of the storm when the tiny girl is far out to sea. The sudden double spread, and it is the only one, brings home the enormity of the danger, but we can retreat from those dangers outside the frame.

There are books in which artists employ single-page framing, but many use fractured layout where the page is broken up into a number of different-sized boxes which provide runs of sequence. The frame confines and creates tension, which in many cases leads to a breaking out of the frame. There is no room for superfluous frames, each being part of the irreducible narrative and capable of stimulating the spectator to fill in the gaps between frames, the beholder's share, with what Philip Pullman refers to as 'invisible pictures'.[14]

Close reading of a fractured layout reveals subtle manipulations and numerous invitations to the spectator/narrator for interpretation. Framing affects how we read a sequence, the order and the speed of the read. In the bathroom scene from *Little Pickle* shown overleaf the large picture invites us in. We are placed in a high position, with clues that need solving. This slows down the read in sharp contrast to the bottom three frames of that page. The can of foam is given significance with its breaking of the frame, and the eye is drawn quickly across these frames by the organization of an invisible line linking arm, elbows and Father's pointing finger. Manipulating the framing allows the artist to develop pace and rhythm in the telling and in the reading.

The frames shown also provide information about time: the use of a larger frame, with the longer time required to read it, suggests that Little

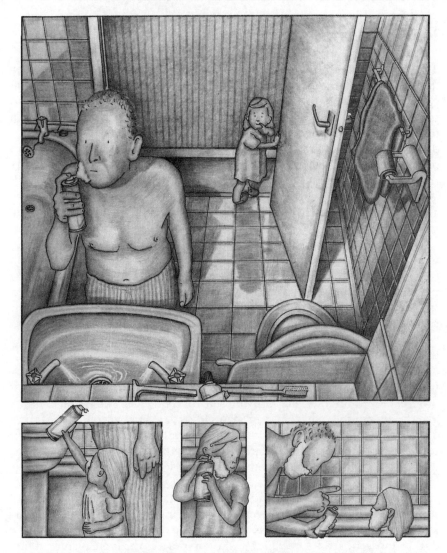

The action breaks out of the frame. From *Little Pickle* (Methuen Children's Books, London, 1986). © Peter Collington. Reproduced with permission.

Pickle spends some time watching her father shave, and that is in sharp contrast with her speedy naughtiness. The stretching of the final frame on the page hints at emotional time, which again passes slowly in uncomfortable moments.

The first frame from *The Angel and the Soldier Boy* on page 225 shows the Pirate Captain with his hands on the treasure. The central frame is an example of what is referred to, in art history, as the *pregnant moment*, or *directed tension*, where we as readers fill the gaps and complete the

Movement suggested by clever framing. From *The Angel and the Soldier Boy* (Methuen Children's Books, London, 1987). © Peter Collington. Reproduced with permission.

movement of the piggy bank to the floor. Many readers then infer that the sound of the piggy bank hitting the floor wakes up the soldier boy.

Movement can be suggested by clever framing; Angel, finding the soldier boy gone, must find a way to the ground and we see her slide down before our very eyes! Similarly, on the lower half of the page (on page 224) the panoramic view presents us with a sense of just how far Little Pickle has drifted from the shore and emphasizes the vastness of the sea. In the bottom four frames the dinghy rises into the eye of the storm, moving sharply away from the reader along a curve and into the picture's middle distance. At the same time the frames narrow as though the sea is sucking itself in to create mountains of water.

The page layout hides key aspects of the narrative, though the artist's choices may be purely instinctive, as Philippe Dupasquier suggests:

> I'm afraid it has all to do with instinct ... But there are so many elements involved in the decision that I find it difficult to explain it rationally. ... Maybe the most important factor is that your original feelings and what you actually want to say is there. If it is not satisfying enough, I usually try a different angle or a different size, or use an extra picture ... etc.[15]

Engaging the reader

In *Anno's Journey*,[16] readers are kept at a distance by the high viewpoint they are given. They see all and know far more than any of the characters. The readers can survey the visual text but their position is fixed. The figures are necessarily small; although clues are provided so that readers can piece together a coherent narrative, it is an intellectual game. They are not involved with either the characters or the events. Readers are given a watcher's role. They are the spectators-without.

Other narratives position the readers as spectators-within. This can be achieved in a number of ways. One strategy is the use of direct eye contact between the reader and one of the characters. The look recognizes that readers are beholders and invites them into closer response, in much the way a direct look to camera in a film enables a character to step out of the screen frame and make direct contact. It is the visual equivalent of 'Dear Reader'.

An air of introspection can draw the spectator in. This device is commonly used by portrait artists. Characters are shown thinking carefully about something and appear withdrawn and preoccupied, encouraging readers to identify with them and drawing them in. Readers are tempted to supply the thoughts of these characters, and by directly engaging their attention the story takes on new life.

The manipulation of what is known as the field and frame relationship influences the reader's lively involvement in the remaking of the narrative.

The artists in picture books are free to play with, or to plan for, the differing sense of involvement felt between, for example, a wide long establishing shot which gives a sense of distance and a restricted view or close-up.

After all, artists know that interpretation consumes our waking hours. Things only glimpsed are seen whole in the mind's eye. Things partially shown are recognized and completed by the viewer. This is a very broad category, containing everything from completing the partially drawn, to completing an action. Readers infer, hypothesize, and fill the gaps, drawing on particular experiences of life and of other texts.

Artists skilfully integrate knowledge about the influences of the framing. Philippe Dupasquier's *I Can't Sleep*[17] opens with an overhead view of the village, late at night. The reader is taken into one of the houses, where a man lies in bed, unable to sleep. The man gets up, and goes out into a lighted corridor and into a room, which, from the different clues presented, appears to be his studio. The likely surmise is that the

The power of a restricted view or close-up to involve the reader. From *I Can't Sleep* © 1990 Philippe Dupasquier. Permission granted by the publisher, Walker Books Limited.

man is an artist and indeed, in all probability, is Dupasquier himself. We see him in medium long-shot and note his increasing frustration. Nothing seems to go right and the artist is shown suddenly in close-up, looking in the reader's direction, but withdrawn. In the following sequences, the man moves to a corner of the room and a sense of growing depression is conveyed by the man being placed in a low position while the reader's viewpoint has moved from medium close-up to medium long-shot and has been raised from a low-level shot to a higher one. Such choices are not arbitrary, and the artist has moved readers from the position of spectator-without to that of spectator-within.

Voices off — the role of the narrator

In literary theory concerned with reader response, there is talk of implied authors and implied readers. In the sequenced picture book we are dealing with the implied narrator. Louis Marin, in an excellent discussion of the reading of a painting, quotes Beneviste: 'The events are set down as they occurred, as they gradually appear on the horizon of the story. Nobody is speaking here. The events seem to tell themselves.'[18] This seems very pertinent to any discussion of pictorial texts. The events may 'seem to tell themselves' but they are given voice by a reader/narrator. In sequenced picture texts there are narrators, the artists, who direct the telling and who will have taken up, knowingly or unknowingly, certain points of view in relation to the characters and the events portrayed. But because the tale is told in images, the narrator appears invisible and is supplanted by the reader/narrator who articulates the voices off. The individual reader re-creates the implied text which has been suppressed by the form; that is, they recover the verbal text which was translated by the artist into images and was then redundant. This new text is interestingly re-created in the vernacular of the reader and within the naturalized ideology of the individual reader, which provides increased freedom for the reader/narrator and the intriguing prospect of differing performances of the implied text because the gap between the telling and the interpretation has been narrowed.

The reader/narrator is omniscient in the retelling, seeing so much more than any character, able to voice inner feelings and following a character when utterly alone. This raises an interesting relationship between word and image. In the printed story there is, usually, a recognition that the events being related have already happened. There is, in general, confidence in the authority of the narrator because he or she knows how it all turned out and what therefore it is significant to tell. Pictures work on a running present, and in the initial read we are placed in the position of universal narrator without the authority of knowing the future, or of knowing necessarily what is significant.

Perhaps the narrator in a sequenced picture text is best visualized in the role of oral storyteller with the path of the narrative picked out but with freedom for diversions to explore new tracks or revisit other vistas.

Sequenced picture texts, alongside comics and graphic novels, are beginning to receive the close study they deserve. They reveal engaging subtleties and complexities, and since they are so good already, it will be interesting to see how these texts develop to take advantage of the growing sophistication of visual literacies.

Notes

1 Jane Doonan, 'Into the Dangerous World: "We Are All in the Dumps with Jack and Guy" by Maurice Sendak', *Signal 75*, September 1994.
2 Monique Felix, *Another Story of ... the Little Mouse Trapped in a Book*, Moonlight Publishing, London, 1983.
3 Tomie da Paola, in 'Children's writers talk about their work', in Jeffrey Aldridge (ed.), *The Best of Bookmark*, Moray House Publications, p. 91.
4 da Paola, *ibid*.
5 John Fiske, *Television Culture*, Routledge, London, 1987, p. 129.
6 Roland Barthes in *Image Music Text* (trans. Stephen Heath, Fontana, London, 1977) has a paper on the theme of work and text although the argument appears in other essays in this collection. I also link these ideas with Tzvetan Todorov's arguments in 'Reading as construction', which is reprinted in *Genre in Discourse* (trans. Catherine Porter), Cambridge University Press, Cambridge, 1990.
7 Ernst Gombrich, *Art and Illusion*, Phaidon Press, London, 1960. Discussed in Part 3.
8 Michael Benton, *Secondary Worlds, Literature Teaching and the Visual Arts*, Open University Press, Milton Keynes, 1992.
9 Video *The Community of Readers*, Part 2, Brighton University, Brighton, 1993.
10 Margaret Meek used the image in her plenary talk to the Children's Literature Conference held at Westminster College, Oxford, Summer 1993.
11 Jane Doonan, *Looking at Pictures in Picture Books*, Thimble Press, Stroud, 1993.
12 Charles Keeping, 'My work as a children's illustrator', *Children's Literature Quarterly* (1983), 8.
13 Maurice Sendak, *Where the Wild Things Are*, Bodley Head, London, 1967.
14 Philip Pullman, 'Invisible pictures', *Signal 60,* 1989.
15 Comment in a letter to me.
16 Mitsomasa Anno, *Anno's Journey*, Bodley Head, London, 1979.
17 Philippe Dupasquier, *I Can't Sleep*, Walker Books, London, 1990.
18 S. Suleiman and I. Crosman (eds), *The Reader in the Text*, Princeton University Press, Princeton, 1980. Includes: Towards a Theory of Reading in the Visual Arts.

Picture books cited in this chapter

Charles Keeping, *The River*, Oxford University Press, Oxford, 1978.

Tomie da Paola, *The Hunter and the Animals*, Hutchinson, London, 1981.

Mollie Bang, *The Grey Lady and the Strawberry Snatcher*, Four Winds Press, London, 1980.

Jeannie Baker, *Window*, Julia MacRae, London, 1991.

Philippe Dupasquier, *The Great Escape*, Walker Books, London, 1988.

Brian Wildsmith, *The Trunk*, Oxford University Press, Oxford, 1982.

John Prater, *The Gift*, Bodley Head, London, 1985.

Tomie da Paola, *Sing, Pierrot, Sing*, Methuen, London, 1983.

Renate Meyer, *Vikki*, Bodley Head, London, 1968.

CHAPTER 15

Small Portable Galleries
The Picture Books of Satoshi Kitamura

Victor Watson

The quotations in this chapter have been taken from seminars at Homerton College in September 1994, and from letters subsequently written to me by Satoshi Kitamura.

Satoshi Kitamura is not especially interested in children. He has no children of his own, and he admits that he is 'not very good with them'. He has worked with children in schools once or twice but found it very difficult to sustain their attention for more than about ten minutes. His approach was one which hard-pressed teachers will recognize: he set the children off on an activity so that he could sit back and wait for them to complete it!

Kitamura is a disarmingly frank and unpretentious person. But there is  more to this than a modest man's confession that he finds children uncongenial. When a major children's picture book maker sets himself apart from the orthodoxies that assume the willingness of writers and illustrators to visit schools and celebrate children's creativity, we should perhaps ask ourselves what this means. Shyness, perhaps. Or an anxiousness arising from the differences between British and Japanese schools. But there is more to it than that.

To begin with, there is the startling fact that Kitamura does not think about children when he makes his picture books. 'Because I like pictures, I like stories,' he said, and went on to point out — with regret — that there is in this country little interest in adult picture books. His choice of words was interesting: what he said was that there 'is no market for *everyone*'. This was not a bilingual speaker getting his English slightly wrong. He meant what he said: that there ought to be a holistic culture ('everyone') which does not 'divide adults from children'. 'People often say "children" as if they are one thing,' he explained, but he pointed out that there are as many differences of taste *among* children as there are differences *between* adults and children.

However, Kitamura does believe that young children should not be exposed to social or emotional issues which are predominantly adult, and that they should be protected from the vulgarity associated with some newspapers and television programmes. But he sees no reason why children as young as 6 should not look at the work of major artists, such as Van Gogh or Paul Klee. His thinking quietly resists one of the central assumptions of British and American culture: that children are different from the rest of us and should have separate provision.

Like most children's writers and illustrators at conferences, he was asked if he had 'the heart of a child' and if he worked for 'the child inside himself'. But on both occasions he succeeded in not giving an answer, and again we are left with the conundrum: how can we make sense of the fact that one of our most successful picture book authors denies any special interest in, or concern for, the children who find his books so absorbing? In a letter, he wrote: 'For someone who spends all his days in his tiny studio, it was nice to know once in a while that there really were people who appreciate his work.'

Is that reference to a 'tiny studio' a clue, perhaps, to a case of artistic privacy and remoteness?[1]

Satoshi Kitamura did not read many books when he was a child. But he did read comics and admits that they had a great influence on his style. At around the age of 10 he developed an interest in fine art, but he made no formal or conscious study of any particular style or art form. He was not trained as an artist, but at the age of 19 he began to do commercial work. He wanted most of all to work with stories, and a decisive point of his life was when a young cousin asked him to design a comic. He tried — but it turned out to be a picture book.

Japanese publishers were not interested in his work and he was obliged to make a living in advertising. In 1979 he came to England and for about two years he devoted himself mostly to the design of greetings-cards. He became friendly with the editors at Ernest Benn and, through them, he met Klaus Flugge, who was interested in Kitamura's work but had nothing for him to illustrate at that time. In 1981, there was an exhibition of Kitamura's work at the Neal Street Gallery in Covent Garden. It was a last attempt to establish himself in this country and he was considering whether to return to Japan afterwards. However, Klaus Flugge came to the exhibition and showed him Hiawyn Oram's text of *Angry Arthur*. Kitamura liked it so much that he spent the next two weeks working on rough sketches. When Flugge saw the sketches, he at once gave Kitamura a contract and an advance. Later, when Kitamura took the completed illustrations to the publisher's office, Flugge took a quick look and sent them straight off to the printers.

Angry Arthur (1982) was an instant success. It received both the Mother Goose Award and the Japanese Picturebook Award. *Ned and the Joybaloo* was published in 1983, and in the same year Kitamura illustrated Roger McGough's collection *Sky in the Pie*. He subsequently illustrated counting books, alphabet books, cut-out books, and more stories by Hiawyn Oram. His counting book, *When Sheep Cannot Sleep* (1987), received an award from the New York Academy of Sciences, and the Parents' Choice Illustrations Award. In 1986 he produced *Lily Takes a Walk*, the first of several story picture books which Kitamura composed and designed himself. (There is a complete list of his publications at the end of this chapter.)

Throughout this period his composition and technique were developing. He prefers to design the whole book, including the text and covers. He works mostly with water-colours, explaining that an artist using oils puts layers on the paper, but working with water-colours is more like dying the paper itself. He prefers this because he wishes to retain the texture of the paper. He is very insistent that, to him, the paper is more important than the paint. It does not matter that the published book will use a different paper; the quality and feel of the original art-paper will have contributed to the character of the artwork. Lines are drawn with water-based fountain-pen ink, partly because he likes the effect that is created when the water-paint makes the lines run. He sometimes uses poster-paint for a background and — for a gradation of colour in, for example, a sky — he will first apply water and then add the colour.

Although Satoshi Kitamura was able to give a precise and clear account of his use of colour and line, he admitted that there are some aspects of his work which are something of a mystery. For example, asked whether a book originates with an image or a story, he could say only 'Both', but he went on to explain that it is very rare for a book to begin with an entire story. 'There is usually just an idea' — and even that may lie undeveloped for several years. Another mystery is how 'emotions get into objects', as they clearly do in *Angry Arthur*. 'It just comes out,' he said, somewhat enigmatically. 'It is difficult to know how things happen.' When he was working on *When Sheep Cannot Sleep* he became interested for a while in higher mathematics — but this did not help him a bit! He returned to the picture book and at once 'all the pictures and text came into his head'. When the publisher saw the 'dummy', very few changes had to be made — but this swift and definitive composition does not happen very often. 'It's luck when [a book] gets finished,' he remarked.

The humour in Kitamura's books is very carefully worked out, and many decisions are taken consciously and deliberately. For example, the grandfather in *A Boy Wants a Dinosaur* was originally carrying a newspaper but Kitamura — with a characteristic and quite deliberate touch of mischief — changed it to a saxophone because at that time in London it seemed as if 'almost everyone with a prominent beard took up the saxophone'. However, it is clear that many aspects of his work happen unconsciously or 'half-consciously' — and that he is untroubled  by this. Speaking of Jane Doonan's account of his work,[2] he admitted that she had found many features which he was not aware of. 'There's nothing to disagree with,' he said. But 'academics analyse as if everything is done consciously. But we don't do that often.'

He is attracted by words, but he also admits to hating them at times because they seem limiting. However, since language is an effective way of telling stories, and since a sentence can be as effective as a single picture, a combination of words and images is probably the least frustrating solution. To tell a story in a limited space, both text and illustrations have to be selected; the images are chosen carefully from thousands of possible scenes in the story. If he is illustrating another writer's story, he has to read and select from the text; if it is a work of his own, he must 'read' his own thoughts and ideas in a similar way. Later he explained more fully: language can describe a sequence of events more clearly than visual images, while images more effectively depict the spatial conditions. For example, a single sentence such as 'I go to school' contains: 'I leave home, walk along the street and eventually arrive at school.' A picture can show only that I am walking somewhere, but not where I am heading for. If words are not used, at least one or two more frames are needed to complete the sequence of the journey. On the other hand, to describe in words all the features of the spatial setting would be unbearably cumbersome. We could not bear to read: 'On my way to school I saw the bakery, supermarket, lamp-posts, dustbins, a dog, an aeroplane ...' But a picture can *show* them at once, spontaneously and eloquently.

'In picture books, language mostly describes the time factor and pictures the space factor.' Another way of expressing this distinction is to suggest that words are the motor which drives the pictorial world; or that pictures are the vocabulary and language is the grammar. Kitamura offered these accounts, but warned that such convenient and attractive analogies can be misleading. As an afterthought, he suggested that there were similarities between a picture book and a map. 'In a way, a picture book is a map of an idea or a story.' A picture book is like a small portable gallery, or a library — 'A CD ROM may be smaller but it needs electricity to operate it,' he remarked.

Kitamura's method of working seems to rest on his assumption that a good idea must wait for the right moment. He is a slow worker, and he constantly goes back to ideas that originated several years previously. 'I keep forgetting everything,' he said, and he goes back to stacks of old papers and books which did not get finished. It seems that he has occasionally caused some embarrassment to his publishers by not being able to finish a book for which they may have already found buyers at an international book fair. He is unrepentant about this. He trusts his artistic hunches, and his publishers have mostly respected this. Working to commission sometimes presents difficulties; for example, he worked his way dutifully through one counting-book, but without much conviction, until he got to ten — 'then counting stopped and story started'. He could not help himself.

He has been very fortunate in his publishers. His editor has occasionally suggested small changes — such as that *Angry Arthur* should end with the boy waking from a dream. Kitamura respects his editor's intuition and judgement, and his editor has faith in his artists and authors and 'supports them like a chief among his tribe'. His publisher does not consider the likely success with children of a projected book; he is more likely simply to ask Kitamura: 'Do you believe in it?' This is why Kitamura has mostly stayed with the same publisher. He has been similarly fortunate in his collaborator, Hiawyn Oram. With *In the Attic*, he found his illustrations were moving steadily away from the writer's text, but she agreed to rewrite it to fit the illustrations. They worked well together with *Angry Arthur* too. He does not often illustrate other writers' texts and admits that this is largely because he is a little lazy and rather fussy, and, since he is a very slow worker, he has a fear of getting stuck too long with one text. When he is designing one of his own, he can leave it and return whenever he pleases.

Kitamura admits that he does not read many picture books. 'There are so many!' he said. It was only after he had completed *Angry Arthur* that someone showed him *Where the Wild Things Are*. But he does exchange ideas and what he called 'painted letters' with his friend David McKee.

Cultural differences between Japan and Britain have not troubled Kitamura very much. One difference he referred to brought vividly into perspective the cultural insularity of the USA and Europe: he explained that in the West, whenever his books were translated, the characters' names were translated too. (Arthur became Willy in the German translation, and Lily became Julie in French.) But books translated into Japanese retained the original European names, because the whole book was openly welcomed as a book from another culture. There are signs now that Britain and other Western countries are beginning to take other cultures as they are. He was surprised to find that, when he has written the text for a book in English, he finds it difficult to translate it into Japanese, his first language. Another surprise was that in this country an artist has great freedom over hair colour: in Japanese picture books, hair is always black.

A more serious cultural phenomenon was that he found early in his career that certain aspects of his work puzzled some people. There seemed at times to be something in his pictures or in the delivery of his ideas that

was not received in the way he had hoped, although readers in his own country would have had no problem in understanding. Kitamura is not distressed by this. He explained it culturally: 'There's a kind of slang — the way we talk in our circle of people,' he said. Some artists in his position seek to stress their cultural differences and to appeal to their readers as exotic. Kitamura prefers not to do that. He is more concerned to understand what makes certain things either universal or particular. He believes that this has little to do with subject-matter, or with details of either text or pictures; it is something to do with 'the way it is delivered — the execution of ideas, an integrity based on an understanding of one's own ideas and intention'.

The word 'integrity' brought him back to a consideration of children as readers. Although he had earlier said he tended not to think of them as a special and distinctive audience, he did suggest that they were in some ways the ideal readers. He does not worry about their intelligence or their reading levels, but he does value their lack of preconceived ideas, their sensitivity, the fact that things have more impact on their senses, and their receptiveness to the 'integrity' of the work. He believes it would be wrong for him to try to make his picture books easier for children on the grounds that they were less intelligent or had a shorter attention span. 'If the work expresses itself fully,' he said, 'it will be received well by those who are interested in it. If the work is worthwhile to the artist himself, it will be so for some readers, both young and old.'

Because of its apparent resemblance to comic books, Kitamura's artwork may seem simple. In fact, however, a close examination reveals a creative and subtly discriminating intelligence at work. Probably the many posters and greetings-cards he has designed were excellent training for a picture book author; they would have obliged him to design illustrations that condense a narrative situation in one  frame, or make a complex point with clarity and economy. The key word in that sentence is 'narrative' — for, although Kitamura is clearly a humorist and a cartoonist, he is essentially a maker of stories.

Jane Doonan rightly places a special emphasis on Kitamura's use of line:

The drawn (or painted) line is a direct record of the movement of the artist's hand ... His pen meets the paper once and for all, with no margin for error, no chance to reconsider. The quality of the line is fine, unbroken, and exhibits a slight tremor, which charges the drawing with energy.[3]

I would add that, through line, colour and composition, Kitamura's picture stories convey a strong impression of sound or silence. His skill with scenes of frenetic and nihilistic energy, both cosmic and domestic, is well known. In *Angry Arthur* the dark colours, the fragmented and zig-zag line, the distorted perspectives and the boy's scowling all suggest cataclysmic *noise*.

Many of his narratives progress through confusion to calm. His latest picture book, *Sheep in Wolves' Clothing*,[4] is about three sheep who plan a trip to the beach, only to find a group of wolves elegantly playing a slightly sinister game of miniature golf on the sand. After their swim, the too-trusting sheep find that the wolves have stolen and unwound their woolly coats for their business, Wolfgang & Bros, Quality Knitwear. The story has something of the appeal of a Richard Scarry picture book: the narrative is fast and bizarre. There are several genre jokes — for example, the private detective, Elliott Baa, who, complete with dark glasses, hat pulled low over his face, loose tie and a grim wiseguy expression, helps the sheep to discover the wolves' knitwear factory. With the aid of some friendly cats, the sheep take on the wolves in their own hideout. Kitamura has designed three single-page illustrations and a double spread to depict the extraordinary tangle of cats, wolves, sheep, wool, toppled furniture and spilt office equipment. In Plate 1, the design is broken down into 30 separate frames, each giving a brief filmic glimpse of a situation which no eye could take in as a whole. Disruption and noise are barely contained in the uneven frames as the fragmented narrative sequence simply stops. Over the page it will resume, as the wool — and the wolves — are sorted out; but here there is action, though in no comprehensible narrative order. A careful look at the frames reveals that in the midst of this confusing tangle of wool, wolves and cats, the sheep are carefully avoiding the violence. One of them — a football joke? — is holding up a yellow card, and his propitiatory gesture seems to be reproachfully saying, 'Come on, guys! Let's not get rough.'

Quite different artistic features can be seen in a series of greetings-cards designed by Kitamura, based on traditional rhymes. Plate 2 is an illustration of the nineteenth-century children's rhyme:

> Dickery, dickery, dare,
> The pig flew up in the air;
> The man in brown
> Soon brought him down,
> Dickery, dickery, dare.

This deceptively simple illustration is typical of his pictorial narrative skill, his sense of the comic and his attention to detail. The forms are carefully placed within the composition, with a rather stylized distant landscape of lake, hills and trees. The tree in the foreground and the clouds are used to suggest height — particularly important in a narrative about flying. And the colouring of the clouds has been chosen to match that of the pig — a joke, probably, about their contrast in weight and density. At the bottom, several birds gaze gravely upwards, their presence enhanced by intense colour — a clever detail, since in the disorderly world of this paradoxical narrative the creatures who *can* fly are all on the ground. Central to this simple narrative is the kindly gravity of Saint Francis and the apprehensiveness of the pig as they look each other in the eye. The saint's open fingers are visually linked with the open mouth — and perhaps the trotters too — of the worried pig. Saint Francis is a firm and reassuring figure, solid and brown, with his feet firmly on the ground where the pig ought to be.

Kitamura's single-frame illustrations are composed to suggest a moment of stillness in a continuing story. Each has a strong implied suggestion about what preceded this narrative moment, and they always point to, or hint at, the likely outcome. Here, the saint has clearly just entered from the left, having done his shopping at the local supermarket. The narrative future is more problematic: the leaning tree, the curved incline of the words, and the way the pig is tipping alarmingly down towards Saint Francis, all indicate that the urgent dramatic problem is not with flying but, as the poem indeed suggests, with *how this foolhardy animal is going to get safely down.*

Saint Francis' Tesco bag illustrates the artist's narrative mind at work. Kitamura explained in a letter to me that, if medieval monks were around today, they would probably carry plastic bags containing breadcrumbs, Bible, rosary, etc. A Sainsbury bag, he said, 'would not go with their ascetic image'. And he explained in some detail why other supermarket chains were equally unsuitable. This is typical of Kitamura; every small detail is carefully worked out, and the tiniest part of an image — in this case, a plastic shopping bag — can become a kind of imaginative periscope looking out at a wider narrative background *which is outside the picture.*

This illustration reveals another characteristic of Kitamura's artwork for children: its dreamlike otherworldliness. Everyone in this nursery-rhyme series is engaged intently on some bizarre activity or caught in an absurd predicament. The eccentric old woman tossed up in a basket grimly aims her broom at the cobwebs in the night sky; Doctor Foster glares ferociously at some ducks from the middle of his puddle; the hush-a-bye baby in the treetop looks anxiously out at us with wide eyes, as if wondering how anyone could have put a cradle in such a ridiculous place. In this strange world, *nobody speaks.* The artist who can suggest the universe-quaking[5] quality of rage and violence can also suggest a strange twilight world of silence. There is in these nursery-rhyme illustrations a magical combination of humour and hush. Kitamura's nursery-rhyme illustrations represent a child's bedtime dream-world, a world of ancient nonsense narratives, baffling, astonishingly vivid, and associated with quietness and falling asleep.

Kitamura's artwork is more than technique. Before or alongside execution there is reflection. Decisions have to be made about how to approach the subject. In the case of the nursery-rhyme illustrations, he seems to have thought deeply about the very nature of the rhymes themselves, and how very young children are likely to experience them. He has created his own imagined nursery-rhyme landscape for them; perhaps all Mother Goose illustrators have to do this. With Kitamura's nursery rhymes, the approach has produced a visionary quality which precisely expresses that curious mixture of quietness and alarm. Perhaps this imaginative thinking — this grasping of a vision of how the picture ought to be — is what he meant when he said that he sought some kind of 'integrity based on an understanding of one's own ideas and intention'.

Similar moments of pictorial calm also occur in the picture books. Plate 3 is taken from *Captain Toby*.[6] After the eponymous young hero has survived a violent storm at sea and the attack of a giant octopus, we are shown here his 'house-boat' and Captain Grandpa's 'house-submarine' sailing to safety. This is an important point in the narrative, immediately after the defeat of the octopus, when the climax is over and the mood is one of peace, not triumph. There are many pictorial indications of what is going on. Gunner Grandma's periscope can be seen protruding from one of the chimneys as she and Grandpa lead the small convoy to safety. The slight tilt of the houses, the hint of a following wake, and the direction of the gently rising smoke, suggest the houses' leftward movement towards the distant shore, where there are signs of habitation — and that most reassuring symbol of safety in trouble, the lighthouse. Its light is out, however, because dawn is rising above the distant horizon. For this, Kitamura has used bands of colour — the orange paling into yellow, then the whiteness, and the blue of the sky darkening gradually as the eye rises into the lingering shadows of the night. The character of the dawn clouds lit by the still invisible sun is achieved by Kitamura's judicious use of colour pencils on the textured paper. Above it, the blue water-colour 'drifts' slightly, suggesting that there is a gentle wind, or perhaps some lingering rain in the distance. The illustration is firmly contained within its frame, and the composition is mostly of horizontal lines, indicating a period of quiet and contrasting with the violently disruptive zig-zags and verticals of earlier illustrations. However, the swell of the sea is not entirely still — the undulating lines and the variations in the darkness of the blue indicate a gradually subsiding movement.

Kitamura is always attentive to words and their relationship with image and mood. Here, the simple caption gives no more information than the illustration provides. But its tone provides reassurance: there is still a good deal of darkness and possible menace in the picture, and so it is important that the simple words, with their biblical resonance ('The seas grew calm ...') should promise us that all will be well. And all is, in fact, well — it is typical of Kitamura's gentle humour that this picture book ends with Toby and his cat fishing at sea from a bathtub with a rudder, while the giant octopus has contentedly taken up knitting.

Jane Doonan has many helpful things to say about Kitamura's art. In connection with the illustrations in *When Sheep Cannot Sleep*,[7] for example, she rightly points out that each frame is drawn free-hand and 'has an organic quality, as if it is expanding and contracting very very gently against the life of the pictured world'.[8] We can see that in Plate 4. *When Sheep Cannot Sleep* is a complex text. It is simultaneously an adventure story about the insomniac Woolly, a joke about counting sheep at night, a counting book (but only if the reader wants it to be and discovers how to do it), and, implicitly, a quiet celebration of creative art.[9] The illustration is from quite early in the narrative, showing Woolly walking confidently in from the preceding picture. The place of this illustration within a developing narrative is indicated by the apple he is about to eat plucked from a tree in earlier illustrations (symbolic of an appetite for arithmetical knowledge, perhaps), and by the way the lines representing the grasses are leaning towards the right in the same direction as Woolly is walking. The result is to suggest that there is no conflict here (unlike a later picture, in which Kitamura wants to indicate fear, and where Woolly is running *against* the grain of the grass). Here all is well, as the expression on his face tells us — content but not sheepish. Woolly himself is a solid and almost circular shape of white; this is appropriate, for he has his delighted eye on the dancing fireflies, which are also white, and which intensify the darkness in the background. The darkness is very important in this story, for it is partly about what to do in the middle of the night when you cannot sleep. Here, there is a gradation from light to dark as the eye moves up the illustration, indicating that, despite Woolly's cheerful confidence, night is slowly falling. In most of the preceding illustrations the darkness has been descending steadily lower on each successive page, and here the effect is intensified by the shadowy river in the middle distance. The undergrowth beyond the river is done with a variety of light greens, but the more distant trees and bushes are darker, suggesting no more than a hint of distant menace in the landscape. All is well, this picture seems to say — but not for much longer.

Satoshi Kitamura's admission that he knows little about children and does not read many children's picture books by other artists amounts to a bracing rejection of many of our cherished assumptions about children. He was asked if he was ever worried that his books might confuse some children. 'No,' he replied, 'it's not my responsibility to worry about children. I was often confused by films when I was a child.' This concern for the integrity of his work rather than with his popularity with child readers indicates a different professionalism — one that does not regard children's books as invested with a special aura of preciousness *simply because they are for children*. They may be both special and precious — but it will be because of their quality, their 'integrity' perhaps, and not because of their intended readers. Although he prefers working with picture books, he accepts that they are part of the commercial world along with advertising, poster design and the greetings-cards industry.

His picture books have helped thousands of children to become successful readers, and yet Satoshi Kitamura is not concerned with education. He does not consciously address children, and yet children feel that they have been spoken to. Is it possible that his books are particularly liberating for the minds of young readers precisely because he pays them the compliment of *not* making special allowances?

Illustrations © Satoshi Kitamura.

Publications by Satoshi Kitamura

Angry Arthur, text by Hiawyn Oram, Andersen Press, London, 1982.

Ned and the Joybaloo, text by Hiawyn Oram, Andersen Press, London, 1983.

Sky in the Pie, text by Roger McGough, Kestrel, London, 1983.

In the Attic, text by Hiawyn Oram, Andersen Press, London, 1984.

What's Inside? A. & C. Black, London, 1985.

Paper Jungle, Andersen Press, London, 1985.

When Sheep Cannot Sleep, A. & C. Black, London, 1986.

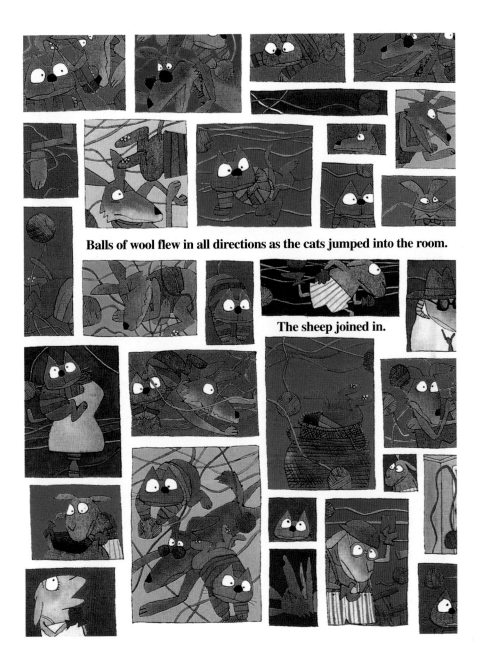

Balls of wool flew in all directions as the cats jumped into the room.

The sheep joined in.

Plate 1 Illustration from *Sheep in Wolves' Clothing,* © 1995 Satoshi Kitamura. Reproduced with the permission of the publisher, Andersen Press, London.

Plate 2 Greetings card, published by Merlin Cards, Bridgwater, Somerset. © Satoshi Kitamura. Reproduced with permission of the artist.

The seas grew calm and, as the sun rose,
both captains made for harbour.

Plate 3   A moment of pictorial calm in *Captain Toby*, first published by Blackie, Glasgow, 1987.

It was a lovely calm evening
and Woolly was not a bit sleepy.
Fireflies were dancing in the air . . .

Plate 4 Illustration from *When Sheep Cannot Sleep: The Counting Book*, published by A. & C. Black, London, 1986. © Satoshi Kitamura. Reproduced with permission of the publisher.

Lily Takes a Walk, Blackie, Glasgow, 1987.

Captain Toby, Blackie, Glasgow, 1987.

My Friend Mr Morris, text by Pat Thompson, Victor Gollancz, London, 1987.

UFO Diary, Andersen Press, London, 1989.

A Boy Wants a Dinosaur, text by Hiawyn Oram, Andersen Press, London, 1990.

From Acorn to Zoo, Andersen Press, London, 1991.

A Creepy Crawlie Song Book, story by Hiawyn Oram, music by Carl Davis, Andersen Press, London, 1993.

Paper Dinosaurs, Andersen Press, London, 1994.

Fly with the Birds — The Oxford Book of Words and Rhymes, text by Richard Edwards, Oxford University Press, Oxford, 1995.

Sheep in Wolves' Clothing, Andersen Press, London, 1995.

Notes

1. On reading this reference to a clue, Kitamura wrote: 'Almost like a detective story, Watson, but you made the culprit sound more intriguing than he really is.'
2. Jane Doonan, *Looking at Pictures in Picturebooks*, Thimble Press, Stroud, 1993.
3. Jane Doonan, *op. cit.*, pp. 23–24.
4. Satoshi Kitamura, *Sheep in Wolves' Clothing*, Andersen Press, London, 1995.
5. 'Arthur's anger became a universequake.' Satoshi Kitamura, *Angry Arthur*, Andersen Press, London, 1982.
6. Satoshi Kitamura, *Captain Toby*, Blackie, Glasgow, 1987.
7. Satoshi Kitamura, *When Sheep Cannot Sleep: The Counting Book*, A. & C. Black, London, 1986.
8. Jane Doonan, *op. cit.*, p. 32.
9. '[Woolly] is an example of this particular artist's oeuvre, taking his place with all the other independent, creative, resourceful Kitamura protagonists.' Jane Doonan, *op. cit.*, p. 33.

CHAPTER 16

Voices on Stage

Helen Nicholson

In this chapter, Helen Nicholson combines a scholarly knowledge of contemporary critical theory and dramatic texts with excellent practical ideas for using picture books with older pupils to extend their dramatic repertoires. Helen Nicholson notes how teachers make the reading of picture books a communal activity in the early years and how this encourages children to 'speculate, improvise, interpret and exercise critical judgement', setting up right from the start a dynamic relationship between text and reader. She suggests that activities such as memorizing lines, imitating voices and rehearsing written language as speech have many parallels with the actor's craft which, after all, seeks to re-create the narrative in a different mode of representation. Helen Nicholson stresses the importance of giving pupils the critical tools and vocabulary to explore the effects of their own work on their audience and value themselves as makers of art. In a delightful conclusion, she shows how 4-year-old Kate reading Angry Arthur *(but not yet able to decode print) is already able to read between the lines, interpret the pictures and 'knows that it is a narrative voice, and not Arthur, who has given anger a language'.*

Each one of us stretches out language to reconstruct, remake, extend and understand our experience in social contact with each other. When we want to make new meanings we need metaphor.[1]

Everything which is presented to the spectator within a theatrical frame is a sign. Reading signs is the way in which we set about making sense of the world.[2]

[T]he artist is not necessarily the best interpreter of his work ... the spectator too has a legitimate role to play in the organisation of what he sees.[3]

From an early age, children are adept at reading visual and oral narratives. As Margaret Meek has explained, picture books play a large part in encouraging children to decode complex narratives, and the meanings they create are vocalized, heard and shared with others. This is also true of drama, which is a communal activity and live art form, both in the making and performing. If children are already proficient makers of meaning before they can read written words, how then do we encourage their development as readers, makers and interpreters of dramatic narratives?

It is this question which has motivated this chapter. It seems surprising that most writers in drama education have shown more interest in reading still images rather than interpreting movement, and with the content of speech rather than the aural qualities of vocalized language. To focus on explicit understanding of how the visual and aural qualities of theatrical and dramatic texts are composed and make meaning has not been a widespread educational objective. Children do, however, receive and interpret a wide range of drama, in what Raymond Williams has called our contemporary 'dramatised society',[4] and this has a powerful influence on the lives and attitudes of young people. If, as Margaret Meek has argued,[5] texts teach what readers learn, children's interest in television drama frequently leads them, understandably enough, to draw on the dramatic conventions most familiar to them, those of television naturalism. Whilst electronic texts hold a valued place in education, there are live dramatic forms which might be part of a drama curriculum. In common with those interested in developing children's experiences in reading and writing, as a drama educationalist I, too, am interested in extending children's repertoires. Through introducing them to new or unfamiliar styles of dramatic art, I hope to give children a wider range of dramatic genre, style and convention to use in composing their own creative work. In this way, the dramatic texts made and interpreted by children might be informed by rich traditions of aural and visual narratives.

Children are already familiar with relating written, aural and visual text through their cultural understanding of picture books. Because of the important place these texts have in the lives of many young children, I have chosen to evoke the memory of early literacy as a starting point and touchstone for creating drama. The text I have chosen to use as a basis for this drama is Hiawyn Oram and Satoshi Kitamura's picture book *Angry Arthur*.[6] The book offers wonderful opportunities for the dramatist, which I shall explore in greater detail later. For me, one of the fascinations of the book lies in its combination of the naturalistic with the symbolic, and the imaginative way in which abstract emotions are made concrete. If dramatic narratives are representative of both personal and collective experience, this combination gives potential for use of a variety of dramatic styles and the necessity to graft everyday language with the poetic and metaphorical.

I have drawn on three distinct theoretical disciplines: the pedagogy of readership, drama semiotics and interpretation of visual art. Through their juxtaposition I hope to link the allied arts of literary studies, dance, music and visual art, and thus to encourage children to make drama which is complex both intellectually and artistically. As John Agard has pointed out, these arts have become 'sadly compartmentalized'.[7] Although the work I describe has been practised with older children in secondary school, I am grateful to experienced teachers who have been able to show me the potential for this theoretical link to inform the teaching and learning of much younger children.

Picture books as theatre

The practice of reading picture books to children has much in common with drama. Unlike the later emphasis on reading as a private, individual enterprise, when young children read picture books it is a shared and communal activity: good readers for children encourage discussion of visual narratives, and do the voices or actions. The activity of reading with children often has a dramatic setting, a *mise-en-scène*, in which the reader becomes a performer and the audience an active participant. Frequently there are rituals associated with reading picture books, in schools there are carpets to sit on for sharing stories, and children may habitually climb on to the adult's knee at home to share books. There is a recognizable pattern and the atmosphere surrounding reading assumes an importance beyond the text; it is a time for intimacy and entertainment in which the readers share an enjoyment of a fictional other world.[8]

The cultural setting for reading has much in common with the social significance of going to the theatre or sharing the viewing of favourite television dramas. As Margaret Meek has explained, successful reading partnerships between adults and children rely on trust, entertainment and mutual enjoyment.[9] Like theatre-going, sharing a story is sociable and friendly. Physical arrangements between adult and child dictate the degree of contact between readers, and, as with an audience in a theatre, this may influence the involvement with the reading. In such an environment, the book becomes a script waiting to be animated by the readers, and a text beyond the page is opened, where the picture book is a powerful focus for conversation and discussion of shared experience. Such a dialogic relationship with a text is part of the learning, and, as Myra Barrs suggests, 'Reading aloud becomes a bridge between orality and literacy, the way of demonstrating the tunes on the page.'[10] In this way, talking about the formal qualities of a picture book is a central part of children's experiences as readers, where the chance to speculate, improvise, interpret and exercise critical judgement is intrinsic to children's development as readers. Significantly, it gives considerable authority to children as active makers of meaning.

The overturning of the power relationship between text and reader is not exclusive to pedagogic practice. 'Reader-response theory' is equally central to those involved in reading dramatic texts in performance. What the shared reading of picture books has in common with decoding dramatic texts in performance is that the focus is on how the texts are heard and seen, rather than read privately and silently as a 'writerly' text. This makes for a different dynamic between text and reader; where the experience is shared, there is already a community established in the initial act of reading. Stanley Fish has argued that this makes for an 'interpretive community' which gives the work its meaning:

> Interpretive communities are made up of those who share interpretive strategies not for reading (in the conventional sense) but for writing texts, for constituting their properties and assigning their intentions. In other words, these strategies exist prior to the act of reading and therefore determine the shape of what is read rather than, as is usually assumed, the other way round.[11]

Not only do we read and interpret within a cultural frame, but, in Fish's discourse, there is an active break from text-centred objectivity towards an understanding that responses to texts will reflect the shared cultural assumptions of the readers. Just as drama depends on the reception of the audience for critical discourse, so too does the picture book. Reading is a political practice, and interpretation is informed by the context in which meanings are construed. The authority of the reader to interpret is therefore not based on an individualized act of self-expression; where children read in partnership, their interpretations indicate recognition and acceptance of their social roles as participants in the community of critical and speculative readers.

So far I have only hinted at the aspect of shared reading which most closely resembles a dramaturgy. I have concentrated on the environment for reading (the *mise-en-scène*), and the way in which interpretation is mediated and shaped by this context for reading (as a responsive audience). But those involved in reading with children will be aware that there are further elements of performance involved. The mediating voice of reader subverts the authority of the written word of the author. In a very real sense, the text of a picture book is produced and translated by its readers and audiences, physically and aurally. In the sharing of picture books the text jumps off the page as a series of non-written signs — the story assumes a physical presence, heard and seen, with the reader as actor. On one level, children become not only apprentice readers but fellow performers, memorizing the lines and imitating the voices (and sometimes facial expressions and gestures) of the initial reader. Margaret Meek has identified this aural aspect of reading:

> Children meet it [the language of writing] as the special tone which

accompanies reading and stories. For some time they may wonder where it comes from. Then they discover that whoever is reading the book makes it talk.[12]

The patterns and rhythms of language in many picture books, including *Angry Arthur*, have a particularly musical resonance: the words invite repetition. The sounds of the words are often as important to young children as their meanings, and an enjoyment of the texture of language is a part of the pleasure. It is in this act of rehearsing written language as speech that children gain access to the rich physicality of oral language which is the basis of the actor's craft.

Reading picture books with children is active and interactive. The rhythms, sounds and pictures are enacted and interpreted, and as such both experienced and apprentice readers are involved with creating a dramatic text. I have likened this physical presence of the text to drama, which equally communicates aurally and visually beyond the page. Thus the picture book shifts into the realm of lived experience, where the boundaries between book-as-artefact and text-as-script are unclear and unstable. Shared readings of picture books rely on intertextuality: a multi-layered process of linking the visual, aural and oral qualities of the text.

The dramatic potential of reading with children has been left without much explicit explanation. After all, the main focus is usually on encouraging children to become readers rather than dramatists. But there is a residue of experience here which may be brought to children's artistic education. In using the expressive tools of voice and body, the craft of the actor begins at a young age. As Barrs points out, stories prompt children to imitate the intonation of the adult reader, and to improvise the stories in performance.[13] As experienced audiences, children's first contact with live performance comes from listening to stories. As critics, they learn to make meanings from what they see and hear. It is a rich dramatic inheritance.

Semiotics of drama

At this point I should like to turn attention to the theory of performance in a specifically dramatic context. My primary educational concern is not with reading picture books with young children, but with using such texts in the creation of drama with students of secondary school age. The suitability of picture books for drama lies, as I have explained, in their intertextuality; they are often intended for shared reading, with all the dramatic potential that this involves. But in order for children to become conscious makers of dramatic narratives, the spontaneity of improvisation might be developed into the more formal skills of composition which are particular to dramatic art. For this, there is much to be gained from an understanding of semiotics.

A semiotics of performance simply suggests that drama has its own language and sign-systems. It is concerned with how drama operates in performance, how it leaves the written page and becomes a theatrical process. In this context, the study of drama leaves traditional critical practices of dramatic literature, and looks at the way in which meaning is created in performance. In short, drama semiotics is about how drama is 'done', collectively and collaboratively, by those who make drama live. It acknowledges, therefore, that the notion of individual authorship is a fallacy; playwrights, directors, actors, designers and audience all have a part to play in making drama.

A classification of dramatic signs has been developed by theatre semioticians.[14] This takes into account the auditory and visual signs of drama, integral to dramatic performance. In this way the dramatic 'text' is seen as more than the written script; a semiotic study acknowledges that the words are transformed through the act of production into a synthesis of the aural and visual languages of drama. Semiotics can serve a purpose in the creation of new dramatic texts or where there is no published script: much work in schools involves the devising of drama, and an awareness of how theatrical meaning is created and read gives a powerful focus to the act of dramatic composition.

Kowzan's system of classification indicates a web of dramatic signs which are identified with cultural conventions of signified meaning.[15] For the purpose of codifying drama, Kowzan established an analysis which distinguishes the signs which exist outside the actor, such as properties, set, lighting, music and sound, from those which relate specifically to the actor — dialogue, mime, movement, costume, gesture and so on. In this context, extra-dialogic features of the performance text assume critical importance as well as the printed play text. Semiotics thus enables description of the play as a present, living art form. In practice, this leads to reading several 'texts' simultaneously — those which are generated by the actor, and those which come from music, sound effects or design.

In Kowzan's classification, reading the structures of drama depends on knowing something about theatrical conventions. Implicit is a relationship of meaning between the sign and the signified, which has been challenged by post-structuralist semioticians.[16] But the radical departure here is in discussing the 'bones' of dramatic art, the view that dramatic effectiveness relies on an integration between the act of creation and the way in which the art is read, interpreted and understood. In other words, there needs to be both a consistency in the interpretation of a dramatic text by those involved in bringing it to life, and an awareness of how performance text is read. This has practical application for teachers; semiotics is instrumental in exposing the element of craft to those who are learning to make, perform and respond to drama. Above all it lays bare the workings of drama as an art form, and is a method whereby the art, artifice and illusion of theatre may be opened for scrutiny.

Extending the dramatic repertoire

As Carol Fox has observed, children at play reveal their awareness of the rhythmic pattern of speech, and of the conventions of different oral discourses. They know by experience the differences between ordinary conversation and the formal conventions of particular genres of narrative (those of weather forecasters, for example). Fox has identified this implicit understanding in children as young as 3 or 4 years old.[17] This is an invaluable prerequisite for drama, and one which is much employed by children in dramatic role-play. For the teacher of drama, then, there is already a repertoire of speech patterns and oral lexical structures which children may be invited to draw upon in making drama. It is a case of making such knowledge and understanding explicit, of recognizing its dramatic potential in the creation of character and situation, and consciously selecting its appropriate use. In this way, children might become active makers of dramatic meaning, rather than unconsciously echoing adult discourse. The development from the 'natural' repetition of lived experience, into the realm of illusion and artifice, distinguishes the art-maker from the imitator.

   In the past, some drama educationalists have given a privileged position to the exploration of content, rather than drawing attention to dramatic form. This division is regarded as misleading by contemporary semioticians, and has been put into an educational context by some practitioners.[18] How material is manipulated into dramatic form is of paramount importance, and there is a fundamental awareness that form and content are inseparable. Keir Elam affirms that dramatic storytelling is directly affected by the mode of representation. As such, how the plot is ordered, the use of time, narrative perspectives and so on, changes the meaning.[19] If, for example, the story of Antigone is told as a series of newspaper broadcasts, with flashbacks to her childhood, the basic content of her story may be unaltered, but the form gives it a significant new meaning. In this way, fictional drama adheres to recognizable conventions, located in a cultural or historical context, and its interpretation is seen to change over time. This is not a case of cobbling together diverse components of dramatic structure, but of recognizing the metaphorical in drama, and of the place this holds in making new meanings. Margaret Meek has identified the place of metaphor in literacy; I should like to extend the analogy to the metalanguage of drama.

   If form and content are indivisible, to extend the dramatic repertoire of children is to encourage them to use a wide variety of dramatic conventions from a range of historical periods, cultural traditions, contemporary styles and genres. Each has its own set of conventions and crafts which might be brought into play, and combined with children's own lived experience. As Susan Melrose points out, the question for production theory is 'just how it manages to be simultaneously "social" *and* highly varyingly personal.'[20] To borrow from children's individual and social experiences, *and* to teach them unfamiliar conventions, is to extend the dramatic repertoire. It is in this way that there will be a context and need for new metaphor.

Angry Arthur

The appeal of this picture book for the dramatist is in the tension between, and convergence of, the exterior world of lived experience and the interior world of the emotions. The plot is simple: a boy who is not allowed to stay up late to watch a Western on television becomes increasingly angry until his mood subsides and he has forgotten the reason for his rage. But the story is a complex web of the real figures in his life — his parents and grandparents — with his imaginary and increasingly fantastic world of the emotions. As Arthur's anger grows, it is enacted, destroying his house, street, town, world and universe. This is, of course, an extended metaphor — the text represents abstract emotions as if they were concrete and visible. Thus the focus of the drama lies in exploring the relationship between the implied narrative of Arthur's 'real' life at home, and the imaginative representation of the senses. This binary opposition lends to the drama a potential combination of the conventions of naturalism with those of non-naturalistic or physical theatre. Such a blend requires a conscious awareness of how the aural, visual and physical elements of drama make meaning.

The work I describe is not an attempt to 'act out' the story. It is intended to re-create the narrative in a different artistic mode of representation. Indeed, the participants do not see Oram and Kitamura's picture book until the end of the workshop. The idea is to encourage the exploration of the text in a variety of ways, and to transform it into a dramatic composition. This process is outlined at the end of this chapter, and suggests a framework which might easily be enlarged or adapted. In line with the National Curriculum Council *Arts in Schools* project, I have seen the process of art-making in four distinct phases: investigating, experimenting, presenting and responding. Although the final 'product' might be described as drama, in this workshop I have encouraged the use of a variety of artistic modes — aural, visual, enactive, verbal and kinaesthetic.[21]

The children I have worked with at Key Stage 3 on this project have detected two narratives in the written text. One stems from the familiar language of the home: the dialogue, 'No, that's enough,' is easily recognized as that of figures of authority — disciplinary phrases that young children imitate to perfect their 'adult' tone. The other story derives from the poetic language, indicating the protagonist's emotions, where anger is metaphorically described as a mounting storm. The narrative is linear; while the anger grows and subsides, the protagonist goes on a symbolic journey in space. We are invited to identify with this sense of frustration through metaphor. Hiawyn Oram's poetic language, particularly the alliterative 'hurricane hurling rooftops and chimneys and church spires' and 'typhoon tipping whole towns', the simile 'an earth tremor cracking the surface of the earth like a giant cracking eggs' and the invented 'universequake', gives the written text a musical and rhythmic dynamic. The poetic devices — simile, alliteration, onomatopoeia — tempt the reader to vocalize the words, and are rich in the dramatic potential of crescendo and diminuendo. As the anger subsides, so does the storm, with the becalming evocation of the addresses one writes as a child — 'Arthur's country and Arthur's town, his street, his house, his garden and bedroom' — suggesting a linguistic move from the metaphorical to the everyday.

In using the written text as dramatic script, there is a sense of the imaginary set against the real, the poetic in contrast to the naturalistic. It is through representing the inner world of the protagonist as external phenomena that the drama takes its shape. The challenge to the dramatist lies in how these contrasts and opposites might be portrayed in dramatic form. This extends beyond naturalism, and relies on finding a dramatic style which captures the abstract world of the emotions in physical, visual and oral media. For children habituated to the conventions of television, this text presents a context for extending the dramatic repertoire.

The process of making drama in this context is carefully structured. The stages of working allow for children to experiment with sound, movement and pictures within a prescribed context and framework. By limiting the canvas, children are asked to find ways of saying words in a way which evokes an atmosphere, of linking vocal collage to movement, and of considering the pictorial and visual in drama. The rhythms, the patterns, the dynamics and the motifs developed in the process of investigating and experimenting with the text draw knowledge and understanding from musical composition, choreography and abstract art, as well as developing their skills as makers of drama. In structuring the drama into a performance, there is potential for the theatre as illusion, where the symbolic world of the emotions is juxtaposed with that of everyday life.

Reading pictures

Richard Wollheim has argued that the activity and process of art-making does not make something a work of art. The status of 'art' is conferred by those who describe it as such: 'Painters make paintings, but it takes a representative of the art world to make it art.'[22] In this way, the act of interpretation becomes central to arts education, where children are invited to describe and interpret what they see. For the educationalist, there are two important lessons here. The first is concerned with giving children the critical tools and vocabulary with which to evaluate their work and that of others, and the second recognizes that in order to value children's art, it should be subject not only to the educationally evaluative practice of 'assessment' but also to critical interpretation. If Wollheim's thesis that the artist is not necessarily the best critic of his or her work is treated seriously, then as teachers we can enable children to explore the effects of their own work on their audience.

In the work on *Angry Arthur*, there are two pictorial texts available. One is Hiawyn Oram and Satoshi Kitamura's picture book, with Kitamura's wonderfully graphic interpretations of anger. The other comprises the children's own kinaesthetic dramatic images. By setting these side by side, there is scope for relating one to another, of questioning how the mood has been depicted, and of exploring how the formal qualities of the text make meaning. It is for this reason that I do not show the book until the words of the text have been used to create a drama. I am interested in how children look, and encouraging them to see 'into' a picture. Working from the same starting point, but in a different artistic medium, when introduced to Kitamura's pictures children begin to identify the effect of colour, line, repetition and perspective on the narrative thread and the creation of character. As a result of working in this way, children have compared their own use of an off-stage voice for the mother figure with the shadow of the mother that appears in the second picture in *Angry Arthur*.

The picture of the 'universequake' has all the density and intensity of a dramatic climax reached in response to the final 'That's enough,' in my experience often shouted in chorus in children's drama. As Arthur's anger ebbs away, he tumbles through space, pictorially suggested by repetition of Arthur's image from the left of the page to the right. Interestingly, this movement has been unknowingly mirrored in children's drama by a choreographed travelling from one side of the stage to another with decreasing speed. When these children looked at the book, they observed the dynamic relationship between mood, movement and patterns in the pictures, and the increasingly calm tone of the language. Transforming the genre is one way in which young artists and interpreters might learn to respond with a sense of ownership of the artistic process, and to value themselves as makers of art.

Voices on

Katie White, who is 4, tells me that you know that Arthur is cross, because his mouth is all wiggly. She also takes much pleasure in finding his cat in every picture. The cat, Katie volunteers, is sad but he has to stay with Arthur until he feels better. You can tell he is sad because his eyes are going pop a lot. In this way, Katie has interpreted the pictures and added to the story. She has speculated on the feelings of the cat and understands that a silent character has emotions. In this, she has hit on the nub of the story — the implication in the text is that Arthur does not express his anger in words, but in facial expression, gesture and actions. To transfer this attribute to the cat indicates a reader who has read between the lines, interpreted the pictures and knows that it is a narrative voice, and not Arthur, who has given anger a language.[23]

To use a picture book to create drama is to focus on the aural and visual qualities already available in the text. In so doing, we invoke the cultural experiences as readers and read-to, as performers and as audience. When young children share picture books they are entering a community of readers; when older children make drama, they are learning to participate in another form of cultural iconography. Drawing both on personal experience and social convention, making drama becomes a process in which linguistic metaphor becomes artistic symbol. The act of dramatic composition employs techniques and styles of presentation which can be read as signs, and the signified text awaits critical response and interpretation. In this way drama becomes a living metaphor, with new meanings present in the dramatic discourses of sound, movement and images.

Artistic process	Teaching strategies	Areas of learning
Investigating sound	*Bathing in sound* Group in a circle, one person blindfold in centre. Group bathe him or her in sound with words associated with: i. a storm ii. a hurricane iii. an earthquake Repeat process, but using non-verbal sounds.	Heightens auditory awareness Encourages vocal colour Creates atmosphere in sound

Artistic process	Teaching strategies	Areas of learning
Investigating words	*Speaking dialogue* Still in a circle, every other member of the group is given a line of dialogue from the text to memorize. They then repeat them, simultaneously, in the style of: i. a racing commentator ii. a weather forecaster iii. a slowing-down tape recorder etc.	Enhances awareness of tone in language Gives a sense of the 'tune' of the words in creating meaning
Investigating sounds and movement	*Exaggerating the moment* In pairs, one with and one without a line of dialogue, put a movement with the line to show the mood which it conveys. Show to the group.	Enables movement and sound to combine in creating meaning
Investigating the character	*Describing the feelings* One member of the group lies on a large roll of paper and is drawn round. It is explained that this is the character who is angry. Inside the figure, words are written which express how he feels; on the paper outside the figure, they write what they think he may be doing.	See contrast between interior and exterior life of character Speculation about action

Artistic process	Teaching strategies	Areas of learning
Experimenting with sound, movement and poetry	*Making a dramatic sequence* The class divides into five groups. Each group is given a different extract from the text which represents Arthur's anger: 1. 'a stormcloud exploding thunder and lightning and hailstones' 2. 'a hurricane hurling rooftops and chimneys and church spires' 3. 'a typhoon tipping whole towns into the seas' 4. 'an earth tremor cracking the surface of the earth like a giant cracking eggs' 5. 'a universequake' They are asked to combine these words with their representation in movement.	Consideration of the texture and tone of poetic language Use poetry to create dramatic atmosphere in sound and movement Development of the aural and visual aspects of drama: rhythm dynamic, pattern, pace, tone, space
Experimenting with visual images	*Making abstract pictures* Each group is given a large sheet of paper and chalks. They are asked to draw the shape and mood that they have created in their group drama. As a whole class, they are then asked to sequence the work in order of 'noise' and intensity. They use the quotations as titles for the pictures.	Changing theatrical images into abstract art: enhances sense of mood and atmosphere created through colour, line, shape, texture

Artistic process	Teaching strategies	Areas of learning
Experimenting with dramatic composition	*Structuring the drama* The groups use their work with the dialogue and with the poetic language as a basis for the structure of a whole-class play. They need to decide: 1. the order of the storm (the sequence of the pictures may help here) 2. how to portray the naturalistic scenes between Arthur and others 3. how these two interrelated elements of the drama might be woven together	Selecting, ordering and rehearsing material Comparing the language of everyday registers with the poetic Juxtaposing two contrasting dramatic styles
Experimenting with narrative	*Telling the story* The groups have told the story only as far as the climax of Arthur's anger. The ending now needs to be considered. It is read to the whole group. They are asked in their small groups to choreograph a way of showing a travel motif appropriate to one of Arthur's places to another (e.g. his country to his town). This is developed into a piece of movement with the words spoken by the group as they choose to reflect the atmosphere.	Awareness of dramatic form Dance motifs to show travel and changing mood Vocal interpretation of changing mood of character

Artistic process	Teaching strategies	Areas of learning
Presenting to the group	*Rehearsal* Time to practise both small- and whole-group drama. Groups work in pairs, acting as directors for each other. Attention should be drawn to: 1. the way in which dramatic tension is created aurally and visually 2. pace and delivery 3. audience awareness	Rehearsing and responding Consideration of theatrical style and dramatic effectiveness Focus on the craft of actor and director
Presenting to an audience	*Final performance*	Communicating with an audience Use of dramatic technique
Responding	*Read* Angry Arthur Focus on the discussion of the qualities of the pictures. Discuss the relationship between visual narrative and dramatic narrative.	Use of critical vocabulary Relationship between form, content and artistic medium

Notes

1 Margaret Meek, *How Texts Teach What Readers Learn*, The Thimble Press, Stroud, 1988, p. 16.
2 Elaine Aston and George Savona, *Theatre as Sign System*, Routledge, London and New York, 1991, p. 99.
3 Richard Wollheim, *Painting as an Art*, Princeton University Press, Princeton, NJ, 1987; reprinted in Charles Harrison and Paul Wood (eds), *Art in Theory 1990*, Blackwell, Oxford and Cambridge, 1992, p. 787.
4 See Raymond Williams, *Communications*, Penguin, Harmondsworth, 1962.
5 Meek, *How Texts Teach What Readers Learn*.
6 Hiawyn Oram and Satoshi Kitamura, *Angry Arthur*, Andersen Press, London, 1993.

7 John Agard, introducing 'Celebration Song', a tribute to James Berry, 9 December 1994, The Royal Horticultural Society Hall, London.
8 Margaret Meek, *Learning to Read*, Bodley Head, London, 1982, pp. 29–30.
9 *Ibid.*, p. 62.
10 Myra Barrs, in K. Kimberley, M. Meek and J. Miller (eds), *New Readings; Contributions to Understanding*, A. & C. Black Ltd, London, 1992, p. 19.
11 Stanley Fish, *Is There a Text in This Class?* Harvard University Press, Cambridge, MA, 1980, p. 171.
12 Meek, *Learning to Read*, p. 32.
13 Barrs, *op. cit.*, p. 20.
14 See Patrice Pavis, *Theatre at the Crossroads of Culture*, Routledge, London, 1992; and Susan Melrose, *A Semiotics of the Dramatic Text*, Macmillan, London, 1994.
15 Tadeusz Kowzan, *Littérature et Spectacle* (Thomas Sebeok, ed.), Mouton Press, Warsaw, 1975.
16 See Melrose, *op. cit.*
17 Carol Fox, in Kimberley, Meek and Miller, *op. cit*, p. 12.
18 See Patrice Pavis, *Languages of the Stage*, Performing Arts Journal Publications, New York, 1982; Gavin Bolton, *New Perspectives on Classroom Drama*, Simon & Schuster, Hemel Hempstead, 1992; and Andy Kempe, *The GCSE Drama Coursebook*, Simon & Schuster Education, Hemel Hempstead, 1993.
19 Keir Elam, *The Semiotics of Theatre and Drama*, Methuen, London, 1980.
20 Melrose, *op. cit.*
21 NCC, *The Arts 5–16: Curriculum Framework*, Oliver and Boyd, Edinburgh, 1990.
22 Richard Wollheim, *Painting as an Art*, Princeton University Press, Princeton, NJ, 1987.
23 Katie White, daughter of my former pupil, Emma Humphris, who was on the receiving end of my teaching practice, and survived. With thanks.

CHAPTER 17

Encountering the Different

Gabrielle Cliff Hodges

'It sounds boring because there are no secret alien bases ... no UFOs zapping people's brains.' This is what one of Gabrielle Cliff Hodges's Year 7 pupils wrote in his reading journal about beginning Gaffer Samson's Luck. *He changes his tune, and a couple of days later describes the novel as 'brilliant' after Jill Paton Walsh had drawn him into her rewarding narrative. In this chapter Gabrielle Cliff Hodges seeks to understand the need for familiarity and comfort that young people look for in their reading and how it is often based on warm family and peer group social practices. By giving pupils insights into the constructedness of texts (including their own writing), by helping to extend individual pupils in their own reading journeys to tolerate the 'different', and by encouraging oppositional reading in the classroom, Gabrielle Cliff Hodges demonstrates how it is possible (in Robert Scholes's words) to 'alienate the domestic' and tempt pupils to become more critical readers of a wider range of texts.*

I don't feel like reading much today because I am tired and have ridden to school in the wind and rain and I've got a headache.

Despite his initial reservations, Matthew did manage to concentrate on what was being read that morning: the section of Jill Paton Walsh's *Gaffer Samson's Luck*[1] in which James goes out for a long cycle ride across the flat Cambridgeshire countryside on Gaffer Samson's old black bicycle. Later Matthew added in his journal:

This part of the story was good and I liked the biking part. In the bit about biking I imagined that I was riding on my bike round all the country roads near St Neots and Eaton Socon because I go on ten mile rides sometimes when the weather is nice.

Further on in the novel, James finds himself being pursued by hostile members of the village gang, also on bikes, riding along parallel fen roads, threateningly keeping pace with him. Janine (in the same class) wrote in her journal afterwards:

Today when we read the book I really could imagine myself being there like when they were on their bikes I could imagine myself being a camera man going along with them watching them ride.

Janine didn't want to read *Gaffer Samson's Luck* at first either:

It looks a bit boring from the pictures inside. I don't think it's my sort of book. I am in a sort of reading mood but I would rather read my own book.

Jill Paton Walsh's richly poetic prose and the powerful narrative momentum of *Gaffer Samson's Luck* seldom fail to engage the attention of young readers, however uninterested they seem when first handed a copy:

We have to read a book called *Gaffer Samson's Luck*. It sounds boring because there are no secret alien bases, no tripods striding across the skyline and no UFOs zapping people's brains. The blurb tells us that there is a hunt for an ancient luck charm.
(Brian, Year 7)

Brian, too, changed his opinion. His various journal entries chart his shifting positions:

Quite good. Differs from what I expected ... I moved myself into the book ... and out of the classroom.

And a day or so later:

Brilliant. Miles better than what I expected. I am really into the book now and I love it. I hate the school and the village and estate playground. I envy and love James's room.

These pupils' comments capture something of the complexity and pleasure which the business of becoming engaged in 'class reading' may involve. All sorts of things are being experienced: coercion ('we *have* to read a book'); expectations of tedium ('it looks a bit boring'/'sounds boring'); feelings of fatigue ('I am tired ... and I've got a headache'). And, if they have got to read at all, what they would rather be doing is reading their own books. Brian, in particular, is vociferous in his preference for stories of aliens and UFOs, stories about which he is knowledgeable and enthusiastic. His attention is, however, arrested by the mention in the blurb for *Gaffer Samson's Luck* of the ancient luck charm, enough for him to tack it on to the end of his diatribe. As we later see, the novel turns out not to be what he expected and he finds himself enjoying it after all. Perhaps, although it is not science fiction, the novel shares one of Robert Scholes' defining features of good science fiction: 'When science fiction really works it does not domesticate the alien but alienates the domestic. It takes us on journeys where we meet the alien and find that he is us.'[2] Whilst there are no science fiction aliens in *Gaffer Samson's Luck*, there is much to do with alienation in all-too-familiar settings — classroom, playground, village. Jill Paton Walsh's prose style, furthermore, alienates (in Margaret Meek's[3] sense of 'making strange') this domestic familiarity. But the reading process allows the reader to 'meet the alien and find ...'.

Reconsidering the familiar

The word 'familiarity', used in connection with reading, summons up for most people associations which are both warm and positive. This may have something to do with the fact that when examined closely these associations can often be seen to be concerned with reading practices which are also social practices, for example the reading aloud of letters, newspapers, or holy books.

For many people the practices of reading (though not necessarily the ability to read itself) are first learnt within the family from parents or siblings. They involve physical closeness, joint attention to the book being read and, usually, discussion of possible meanings, interpretations and responses. The latter may not always be harmonious; indeed, arguments which arise over conflicting readings themselves sometimes become the focus of stories. The four offspring of Mr and Mrs Large, the elephants in Jill Murphy's *A Quiet Night In*,[4] nearly lose the opportunity to stay up and read together with their tired father when Laura protests that the story they have selected is a 'boy's story'. Mr Large's threats of bed-with-no-story if they argue, however, ensure temporary peace. Jill Murphy's pictures of the elephant family comfortably squashed together on a bulging sofa capture and mirror for the reader the physical warmth which marks for many children their earliest experiences of reading.

Within 'family' reading the part of the more experienced reader is sometimes taken by older siblings who may themselves have only recently learned to read. Daniel, whose father is a farmer, is a typical example. Although his reading material is, perhaps, slightly out of the ordinary, his family reading experiences are not. Daniel describes how when he was very young his father used to read *Farming News* with him. Now he himself reads to his 3-year-old sister. He says:

> I went to the East of England show, farming show and I brought back this book, farming book and it's got all the MF tractors, they're sort of ones with faces on and I read that to her ... she thinks the faces are funny.

Another aspect of reading and 'familiarity' which is learnt by many in early childhood and carried through the rest of life is the pleasure of re-reading familiar texts or the complete works of favourite authors. As readers move into more demanding territory, taking on texts which offer fewer visual and more verbal challenges, the inclination is to travel in the company of reliable friends — Enid Blyton, Roald Dahl, Judy Blume — or to take clearly signposted routes through series books — Point Horror or Sweet Valley High. Although the *act* of reading itself may have become more solitary for the young reader, there are important ways in which the processes remain fundamentally social practices.

Choosing to read books by favourite authors implies some kind of relationship with the writer. It might take the form of actual communication: all three writers mentioned above are known to have received hundreds of letters from their readers, and indeed Dahl and Blume, through television programmes about books and writers-in-schools schemes, will also have provided many of their readers with the opportunity to 'meet' them on television or in person.

Reading and social relationships

But there are yet other elements of 'familiarization' involved in reading. Firstly, there is the world of created friends and imaginary other families, that 'fabulously populated solitude which is a reader's', described by the parent in Daniel Pennac's *Reads Like a Novel*. Referring to his son's early experiences of having stories read to him, he says:

> The stories ... were swarming with brothers, sisters, parents, ideal doubles, flights of guardian angels, cohorts of watchful friends to sort out his woes, but who, for their part, were struggling with their own ogres, and so found refuge in the worried beatings of his heart.[5]

Then there is the sense in which readers are often led to feel as if they are in what D. W. Harding has described as 'social communication of a special sort with the author'.[6] Researchers working for *The Effective Use of Reading* project describe experienced readers' engagement with texts in a different way again. For these readers:

> reading is often a kind of conversation with the text ... their reading suggests a flow of questions and preliminary assumptions to which they can find answers and confirmation (or contradiction) in the course of further reading.[7]

These kinds of relationships, for all that they are described in explicitly social terms, should not lead us to assume that young readers necessarily confuse the characters about whom they read with real people. That is *not* the level of communication which D. W. Harding has in mind, although it may be a stage in its development. The more sophisticated reader, he suggests,

> knows that the characters of the novel are not real people but only *personae* created by the author for the purpose of communication ... and

he bears in mind that the represented participants are only part of a convention by which the author discusses, and proposes an evaluation of, possible human experience.[8]

Harding's comment not only serves as a useful reminder of the relationships that are involved in reading between writer, text and reader, but can also provide a framework for thinking about reading development, as I shall show later.

As readers grow more sophisticated, the dynamics involved are not only text-focused. They are also firmly related to important social relationships in the reader's life. A few examples should serve to remind us of some of the many ways in which reading habits and textual preferences are developed and to show how deeply embedded they are in the web of our social lives. Here is Daniel again, talking about his favourite book from the school library read during his first year at secondary school. It is, once more, a book about farming.

> I really like to read it [because it] tells me things that I don't already know about farming because my dad's a farmer and he tells me a lot and it's good to read for me because I really enjoy reading and looking at the old and new ways of doing things.

Other reading relationships develop around series books which, like magazines, are often passed around in reading networks which also demarcate certain social or family groupings. The transcript of a conversation about the Point Horror series between a researcher, Charles Sarland, and a group of 12-year-olds from a class in a middle school illustrates this phenomenon:[9]

CS: How did you get to hear about Point Horror, how did you start ...?
Alison: Mary brought them.
Liz: Her [indicating Mary].
Alison: Well, my stepbrother gave my sister *The Lifeguard* for Christmas, and then Mary lent me a book and I thought 'Oh that's really good' ....
Mary: ... I decided to get *The Boyfriend* 'cause it sounded quite good and, um, Laura, this girl that I know, she read it before me and she said that was really good, so I read it.

Elaine Millard, in *Developing Readers in the Middle Years*,[10] is another researcher who provides evidence of girls and boys using fiction and non-fiction respectively for the same social purposes, namely the maintenance of friendships. Millard cites one girl who describes the sharing and swapping of favourite books, especially in the Sweet Valley High series, and the friendly conversations involved in the process of making recommendations and reflecting on them afterwards. A boy in the same class describes how, for him and his friends, it is non-fiction books which are the source of their conversations. In his opinion, talking about a *story* does not constitute having something to say, whereas swapping information and data with his friend is a significant, social act.

Television viewing shares a great many social features with reading, as David Buckingham[11] has shown. Viewing is often done in the presence of parents and siblings, squabbles over programmes are likely to arise and children compromise their tastes and opinions (like the Large elephant children in *A Quiet Night In*) if there is a chance of being able to put off the moment of going to bed. Buckingham, however, also describes how programmes can be used both to include and exclude members of a social group. Some girls discussing *Ghostbusters* with the interviewer initially suggest that they think it is very good. When, however, another girl who is not too popular with the rest admits that she has a *Ghostbusters* book, related school bag and toys, the group are scornful and use this information to marginalize her.

> A preference for *Ghostbusters* is used here almost as an accusation, when not two minutes previously the same girls had been expressing their own preference for the programme. In this instance, it is very clear that the existing interpersonal relationships among the group supersede the judgments they appear to make about television.[12]

While remaining firmly in the realm of the social, we are beginning to see how familiarity can also breed contempt.

It is common to find comments about television programmes and books being used to establish, maintain or destabilize people's standing within a particular social group. Young readers who feel the need to select something safe from the school library, something they read first perhaps several years earlier, or maybe a picture book, run the risk of being ridiculed by peers who perceive themselves as more sophisticated readers; teachers and parents may likewise be disparaging in the attitudes they express towards, for example, Enid Blyton or some of the series books; government quangos can certainly be so when they attempt to prescribe fixed canons of literary texts for study in schools. However, this dismissiveness is a result of perhaps too little attention being paid to the purposes for which people often choose to read what is familiar, and to the fact that almost everyone does it from time to time. People's preferred 'safe' reading may be Jane Austen or Joanna Trollope, Terry Pratchett or Isaac Asimov — but if safe reading is what is desired, then readers choose comfortable texts. Part of feeling comfortable, furthermore, may well be that the enjoyment of Terry Pratchett or Jane Austen brings you into a fellowship of readers with whom you can share your pleasure and enjoyment. Such groups are rarely self-conscious or deliberately set up. Alastair West[13] has noted that in schools they may frequently be almost invisible, particularly to teachers. They are, however, extremely important to know about if pupils are to be helped across any divide there might be between the familiar and the different. It seems to me that the ideal place to start from is where readers feel comfortable and in good company. Brian Street[14] has said of the acquisition of literacy that it is 'a socialisation process rather than a technical process' and the development of readers seems to be so, too. Of course there are technicalities, new forms and structures to be made sense of and understood, but there are also social reading patterns and behaviours to be learned.

Encouraging reading for pleasure

I would like to look more closely at how teachers might build on some of these understandings about the social practices of reading in order to encourage pupils to continue reading for pleasure, at home and at school, the sorts of texts they already like. I would then like to consider how we might teach reading practices which encourage pupils to explore texts which are new to them and different, and support them as they move into a range of other, perhaps more sophisticated, reading relationships.

Given adequate curriculum time and sufficient flexibility it is possible, though not by any means inevitable, that teachers will help pupils develop successfully as readers who enjoy both reading for pleasure independently and reading together as a class right up until they leave school. The two activities are not, however, identical because, as West's research into pupils' perceptions of 'home' and 'school' books shows,

> the essential nature of the home/school distinction drawn by students does not primarily concern the source of the text, or, indeed any inherent properties of the text, but the social practices with which it is associated. It is a distinction relating to the uses to which a piece of writing is put, rather than between kinds of writing. It is a distinction between kinds of reading rather than kinds of writing. Insofar as it is a distinction between texts it is based upon criteria of ownership and control.[15]

Nevertheless, the two activities should not be seen as mutually exclusive. The reason why becomes clearer when we look at the rather startling findings of *The Effective Use of Reading* project in the late 1970s. From the researchers' extensive observations of pupils reading in schools they found the following: 'Approximately half of all classroom reading occurs in bursts of less than fifteen seconds in any one minute.'[16] The researchers add that it is unlikely that 'short burst' reading provides pupils with an adequate means for developing a critical or evaluative approach. (An American National Assessment of Educational Progress survey undertaken during 1979–80 found that 17-year-olds' responses to texts were 'generally superficial, abstract, undeveloped and lacking in specifics', a situation which by some is attributed to 'multiple choice testing and the kind of classroom discussion and text books that aim at quick, easy answers'.[17])

However, in *The Effective Use of Reading* it is also noted that:

> By far the greatest incidence of continuous reading took place when children were reading privately to suit their own purposes rather than to complete an assigned learning task .... Certainly this type of reading resulted in continuous attention to print which was observed only rarely on other occasions. The pupils were finding both pleasure and absorption in their chosen task.[18]

The lesson for us here appears to be that reflective, critical reading can only be successfully encouraged if sufficient time for reading is created. But that is not all.

Reading development: the role of the teacher and the text

What I wish to consider now is how these kinds of important observations about the differences between self-motivated reading and school-organized reading (dealt with here necessarily very briefly) might provide some useful starting points for thinking about the whole issue of reading development in more fluent readers. Let us consider a few practical points first.

Good resources and easy access to them are essential, but not sufficient. There must also be class time; opportunities for pupils to exercise some choice over their reading; encouragement for pupils to set up and pursue their own tasks in relation to their own reading. (It will not, of course, go unnoticed that these are all features of both Key Stage 3 and Key Stage 4 work that were marginalized recently as a result of the new assessment and testing rearrangements in secondary English in the early 1990s.)[19]

It is also important for teachers to know their pupils as individual readers, something not always easy to achieve unless specific practices are established and recognized, for example the use of reading and response journals in which pupils can engage in a dialogue with the teacher about their individual reading. There also needs to be plenty of time for discussion, with individuals and whole groups, in classroom or library, about what is currently being read, enjoyed and passed around, as well as what might be recommended.

However, these practices are likely to be less than fully effective in the development of 'sophisticated readers' unless they are related to some theory of reading development which provides a context and rationale for our teaching. I would like to devote the last part of this chapter to making some suggestions about a rationale for reading development.

I believe it is helpful to have a clear understanding of the relationship between familiarity and difference. The familiar — properly recognized for its value and importance, including the obvious pleasure it provides — makes a good starting point for reading journeys. But it needs to be a starting point, not an end in itself, as otherwise our pupils simply go round in circles and may not discover anything new. Discovering the new is important for, as Jonathan Culler has said, 'one who is continually encountering the unexpected can make momentous, unsettling findings'.[20] Most teachers would, I think, like to feel that they have the potential to introduce their pupils to texts which lead to exciting discoveries about reading. The fact that these discoveries might also be unsettling gives us an important role to play if our pupils are not to be disillusioned and discouraged. We can enact this role in a variety of ways. I would like to consider four here.

Firstly, an important job for the teacher is to recommend to pupils new and different texts, to be studied in class or to be read by individuals. For this to begin to work successfully the teacher must know the pupils' individual reading preferences as well as those of the whole class. What he or she recommends should be in some way different. 'We make sense of our lives,' says Robert Scholes, 'as we make sense of any text, by accommodating new instances to old structures of meaning and experience.'[21] The teacher must be widely read in all kinds of literature so that he or she can be a networker of kinds, one who suggests connections for pupils between a wide range of texts.

Class teaching and class reading, furthermore, provide ideal opportunities for pupils to encounter new and different kinds of texts, not by simplifying them but by making them accessible. Recent developments in approaches to reading in schools have taught us ways to work with pupils on what Clifford Geertz describes (in an anthropological context)[22] as the 'deeply different' so that it can be 'deeply known without becoming any less different'. What we learn, for example, from the best work of the Shakespeare in Schools project or Theatre in Education groups is not how to make Shakespeare's work easy for pupils but how to enable them to know it better; different understandings in our knowledge about language and its relationship to society, culture and power help us to teach the reading of literature from different cultures in ways which do not domesticate it but rather enrich pupils' understanding of difference and otherness; new attitudes to literature of other historical periods and new ways of reading it allow us to introduce our pupils to texts and writers whom they can get to know without having to be in awe of them. To quote Clifford Geertz again, we can attempt to show pupils the possibility of bringing 'the enormously distant enormously close without becoming any less far away'.[23]

Secondly, as teachers we can engage in the process described by Appleyard (echoing Harding) in *Becoming a Reader* of the move to see the text as something someone has made, 'as something problematic and therefore demanding interpretation'.[24] This is, of course, an understanding that many young readers will already have; but some may not; and few will tear themselves voluntarily from the seductive pleasures of reading a good story in order to focus on its constructedness. Indeed, it is debatable whether both can be done simultaneously anyway. Like looking at a *Magic Eye* design, it requires a different focus of attention to see the three-dimensional graphic from that which you use to look at the two-dimensional patterning. However, awareness and evaluation of a text's constructedness can in itself be both pleasurable and informative, leading the reader towards making new or different sense of it.

The Directed Activities Related to Texts (DARTs) — Cloze procedure, sequencing, and so on — pioneered by *The Effective Use of Reading* research team arose from their determination to redefine the term 'reading comprehension', about which they have this to say:

> individual differences in reading comprehension should not be thought of in terms of a multiplicity of specialized aptitudes. To all intents and purposes such differences reflect only one general aptitude: this being the pupil's ability and willingness to reflect on whatever he is reading.[25]

DARTs activities, therefore, are one way to make texts (familiar or unfamiliar) appear 'problematic', thus requiring interpretation — usually more than one interpretation — and reflection. If pupils are secure in their knowledge of some of the purposes and pleasures of reading, they are more likely to be willing, interested and confident enough to spend time in schools exploring texts in this way.

A third role for teachers is to develop these same pupils as writers who make connections between what they read and what they write. There are implications here for reading development as well. Much progress has recently been made in the development of writing in schools, not least because of the influential National Writing Project. But how often do we provide opportunities for pupils' *own* writing to be treated as 'something problematic and demanding interpretation' in the same way as we treat published adult writers' work? What happens when we subject pupils' writing to some of the reading activities we apply to class readers, for example trying out different ways of reading it aloud, transforming it into other genres, interpreting its symbolism?[26] In these cases, writers and readers may be one and the same person but they are positioned differently when engaged in the two processes, as this Year 7 writer knows when she says of a central character in one of her stories:

> When I write the story I don't think of myself as Mark but when I read it I do. [Sarah]

Does the process of subjecting their own work to the same scrutinies as those to which we ask them to subject other writers' work help them to recognize that they, too, have a part to play in the process of textual production, rather than always being on the receiving end of it? Does it make it easier for them to see that textual production and reception can have complementary parts to play? Can making visible the constructedness of their own texts lead to greater awareness of the constructedness of others?

The final idea about reading development which I want to focus on here is one which Robert Scholes sets out in *Textual Power*. He suggests that an important aspect of teachers' work is to develop in pupils a 'textual competence' which he divides, for the purposes of clarity and teaching practice, into three otherwise integrated parts: reading, interpretation and criticism. Teachers who read and discuss books with very young children know that at an early stage many readers will be engaging in all these three processes — many, but not all. They are, however, processes which, I believe, all teachers of reading might valuably encourage. With more fluent readers in particular, teachers will also want to be developing pupils' explicit awareness of them as processes.

Scholes writes about *reading* that 'The ideal reader shares the author's codes and is able to process the text without confusion or delay.'[27] As I have suggested earlier, this achievement is a foundation which must be firmly laid if (although not necessarily before) *interpretation* and *criticism* are also to be practised. Scholes then continues: 'Any hitches in this scheme will cause a shift from reading to interpretation, and certain texts are constructed to force exactly this shift.'[28] Explaining what he means by the 'shift' to interpretation, Scholes explains:

> This activity depends upon the failures of reading. It is the feeling of incompleteness on the reader's part that activates the interpretive process. This incompleteness can be based upon such simple items as a word the reader cannot understand, or such subtleties as the reader's sense that a text has a concealed or non-obvious level of meaning that can only be found by an active, conscious process of interpretation.[29]

What are some of those 'certain texts' which we might select to facilitate this shift? Janni Howker's 'The Topiary Garden'[30] is, perhaps, a good example. I am thinking of a comment made by the old woman, Sally Beck, whom the young Liz Jackson has just met in a twilit lane. Liz has complained to Sally that sometimes she wishes she were a boy. Sally replies:

> Now there's a funny thing. I was a boy once upon a time — oh yes, yes I was.

Initially the reader has to try to make some sense of Sally Beck's strange words, or live for a while with uncertainty. Whilst Janni Howker does eventually explain this mysterious comment, it has served to shift the reader into other modes of reading, of speculation about ideas, into realization that the words used can frequently be read in a variety of ways.

To return to Scholes' comments, 'failure' is an interesting but tricky word to use in connection with teaching and reading. In that context it can resonate too readily with ideas of inadequacy and inferiority. But there are other ways of reading the word which are supported by the notion of a 'feeling of incompleteness' which 'activates the reading process'. Since the publication of Wolfgang Iser's *The Act of Reading*,[31] the concept of filling textual gaps has become more familiar and many illuminating classroom practices have been constructed around it. Can they — do they — help to provide pupils with the increasing confidence necessary for recognizing 'failures of reading' as challenges to be faced or problems solved rather than insurmountable obstacles? If they do, we can continue to recommend to our pupils a wider and wider range of different texts for them to explore.

But reading, as Scholes sees it, requires both interpretation *and* criticism for its completion: 'Criticism involves a critique of the themes developed in a given fictional text, or a critique of the codes themselves out of which a given text has been constructed.'[32] Furthermore, the move towards this completion is one which involves gradually increasing the exercise of 'textual power': 'We move from a submission to textual authority in reading, through a sharing of textual power in interpretation, toward an assertion of power through opposition in criticism.'[33] In the case of 'The Topiary Garden' this opposition might derive from discussion of different-gendered readings of the story, and analysis of the male and female characters in it in that light. Or, via a consideration of the writer's use of register and dialect, oppositional readings might explore representation of social class and how it affects and is affected by the structure of the story.

Here, then, we end up where we started, describing the reading process again in social terms — exploring representations of social power through the exercise of criticism which itself forms part of the 'complex web of textual power'. If, as teachers, we succeed in developing enthusiastic habitual readers as part of our work in schools and classrooms we do much — but not enough. If, however, we attempt both to make visible and to teach the processes of interpretation and criticism, we at least begin to show our pupils the various ways in which it is possible to position themselves in relation to reading and texts of all kinds.

To return to the Year 7 readers with whom this chapter began and their reading of *Gaffer Samson's Luck*: later on they would come to an episode in which James goes to Ely with his parents. From the car he sees Ely

Cathedral a long way off across the flatness of the fens, first a distant speck on the horizon and later as something 'standing up complicated from the simple flatness of the land'. He realizes that:

> Someone had seen what to do. Someone crawling, or drowning, in this vastness had answered flatness with height, and distance with huge size ... someone had built something that would not shrink out of sight while in your line of vision.

Gaffer Samson's Luck can be seen as a similarly complex structure providing for its readers not only a contrast with more familiar narrative landscapes, but also a vantage point from which to view them. It is for precisely this kind of 'encounter with the different' that teachers of reading must aim, if their pupils are not just to enjoy reading for pleasure but to develop as critical, reflective readers as well.

Notes

I would like to thank pupils from Ernulf Community School for comments in their reading journals and discussions which have helped with this chapter.

1 Jill Paton Walsh, *Gaffer Samson's Luck*, Farrar, Strauss and Giroux, 1984; Puffin Books, Harmondsworth, 1987.
2 Robert Scholes, *Textual Power*, Yale University Press, New Haven, 1985, p. 128.
3 Margaret Meek, *How Texts Teach What Readers Learn*, Thimble Press, Stroud, 1988.
4 Jill Murphy, *A Quiet Night In*, Walker Books, London, 1993.
5 Daniel Pennac, *Reads Like a Novel*, Quartet, London, 1994.
6 D. W. Harding, 'Psychological processes in the reading of fiction', in M. Meek (ed.), *The Cool Web*, Bodley Head, London, 1977.
7 Eric Lunzer and Keith Gardner (eds), *The Effective Use of Reading*, Heinemann Educational Books for the Schools Council, London, 1979, p. 31.
8 Harding, *op. cit.*, p. 72.
9 Charles Sarland, 'Revenge of the teenage horrors: pleasure, quality and canonicity in (and out of) popular series fiction', *Signal* 74 (1994), 125–6. Reprinted as Chapter 4 of this volume.
10 Elaine Millard, *Developing Readers in the Middle Years*, Chapter 2, Open University Press, Buckingham, 1994.
11 David Buckingham, *Children Talking Television*, Falmer Press, London, 1993.
12 *Ibid.*, p. 56.
13 Alastair West, 'A reading community and the individual response to literature', unpublished D. Phil. thesis, Department of Educational Studies, University of Oxford, 1986.
14 Brian Street, *Literacy in Theory and Practice*, Cambridge University Press,

1984.
15 West, *op. cit.*
16 Lunzer and Gardner, *op. cit.*, p. 124.
17 Referred to in J. A. Appleyard, *Becoming a Reader*, Cambridge University Press, Cambridge, 1990, p. 114.
18 Lunzer and Gardner, *op. cit.*, p. 130.
19 Evidence is provided in two recent surveys carried out by the National Association for the Teaching of English: *Nothing but Facts* (English Teachers and the SATs) 1993; *The Enterprise Is Sick* (GCSE/KS4 English and English Literature Survey) 1994.
20 Jonathan Culler, *On Deconstruction*, Routledge and Kegan Paul, London, 1983, p. 72.
21 Robert Scholes, *Protocols of Reading*, Yale University Press, New Haven, 1989, p. 10.
22 Clifford Geertz, *Local Knowledge*, Fontana Press, London, 1993, p. 48.
22 *Ibid.*
23 Appleyard, *op. cit.*
24 Lunzer and Gardner, *op. cit.*, p. 64.
25 Bernard Clare describes these sorts of activities in more detail in *A Rest from Shakespeare*, a booklet produced by the NATE 12–16 Committee in 1994.
26 Scholes, *op. cit.*, pp. 21–2.
27 *Ibid.*, p. 22.
28 *Ibid.*
29 Janni Howker, 'The Topiary Garden', in *Badger on the Barge*, Julia MacRae Books, London, 1984.
30 Wolfgang Iser, *The Act of Reading*, Routledge and Kegan Paul, 1978.
31 Scholes, *op. cit.*, p. 23.
32 *Ibid.*, p. 39.

PART V

Voices of Authority

In the final section of the book we turn our attention to the complex ways in which power operates in the relationship between children and their reading. Hopeful and responsible voices are examined, as well as those which could be accused of bullying and exploiting young readers. We begin on an upbeat note with Jill Paton Walsh, who considers the authorial voice in fiction and decides that authors necessarily wear 'the mask of the narrator' when they write. She argues that none of the voices audible in a work of fiction is simply that of the author. In that triangular relationship of text, reader and author, the latter wears the narrator's mask and gets out of the way to allow the reader, unpestered, to experience the subject. And if this 'potent transaction' is to work, readers also wear masks as they enter for a while the secondary world of the book. Jill Paton Walsh argues passionately for the good that fiction can do, particularly when there is equality of respect between writers and readers for the duration of the 'transaction'. She believes that although novels can't fill moral vacuums, they can aspire to a 'state of grace' between reader and writer when the masks of the narrator find 'better, wiser, finer voices than their own'.

Mary Hilton is less sanguine about the good effects of literature on its readers. Taking a historical viewpoint, she explores the connections between the boys' adventure story and the ideological acceptance by most young men of the adventure, honour, death-and-glory values with which they entered World War I. She also uses David Vincent's work to consider how the low-level literacy offered to working-class children in schools during the late nineteenth century and up to 1914 made them fair game for imperialist, escapist, highly gendered popular fiction. Mary Hilton goes on to voice her concerns about the current 'popular culture industry', which she describes as an updated version of the imperialist adventure story, producing violent, sexist, male-fantasy products, skilfully manu-factured to appeal to the worst 'desires' of little boys and promoted in media texts, comics and popular fiction. She believes that classrooms where children are free to express their own voices, orally and in writing, and which offer alternative models of maleness, can counteract this worrying trend.

Eve Bearne believes that the voices of children, parents and teachers working together resist these negative forces through the natural subversiveness of the young and in classrooms where a critical theory of literacy is understood and practised. While recognizing the crucial relationship between literacy and power, she has faith that with the help of their teachers, children can withstand the worst attacks of ideologically driven directives in education, on the one hand, and the seduction of the worst excesses of the 'popular culture industry' on the other. Her chapter resonates with the uplifting, yet down to earth, voices of the young and their teachers who strive to understand and operate a sophisticated and sympathetic all-inclusive kind of critical literacy.

CHAPTER 18

The Masks of the Narrator

Jill Paton Walsh

In a stirring chapter, Jill Paton Walsh reflects on technical aspects of the writer's voice in fiction, and queries the effects on readers of the moral content of the fiction they read .... She argues that authors do not enter works of fiction as themselves, but with the storyteller's voice or 'mask of the narrator'. Although this mask is only partial and authors give themselves away by idiosyncrasies and distinctive styles of writing, Jill Paton Walsh affirms that this professional stance allows them to write about the world as it is, not the world as they would like it to be. While claiming that the best fiction confers grace on the reader, she does not avoid the difficult area of censorship.

My title is 'The Masks of the Narrator' and a good deal of my script is a writer's eye view of some technical aspects of what is usually called 'voice' in fiction. My reason for wishing to explore it is that it has a strong bearing on a controversy that is never very far from our working lives as friends of children's books, and often right in the forefront. The controversy is about the effects on the beliefs and, more remotely, on the conduct of readers, of the moral content of the books they read. People who become steamed up about this are nearly always advocates of censorship, although the authors subjected to the inquisitions that ensue get pretty steamed up about it too.

The defenders of literature find themselves in a tight corner. All too often those who defend freedom of speech, and find nothing wrong with a book which is under attack, sound as though they are defending racism or sexism or violence themselves, rather than saying that such things may have a place in a book that is not sexist or racist, or glorifying violence. Many people do not understand us when we object to a request that books should show an idealized world, or when we say that showing the world as it is, and teaching that the way it is is the way it should be, are not the same.

The anxiety to control the content of children's books is fundamentally, of course, a desire to control children, and make sure that they do not think for themselves; or rather, that when they think for themselves they come to the conclusions we wish them to come to. Too often, we see the desire of a section of society to limit the influence of the opinions of another section of society on future generations. The objections raised against particular books often have an air of wild implausibility about them, as though nursery copies of *Little Black Sambo* could create racism in an otherwise innocent society, or one reading of *Charlie and the Chocolate Factory* could make children cruel.

It is not only those who attack children's books who ascribe this powerful moral influence to them. Zena Sutherland's book, *The Best in Children's Books*,[1] published in 1973, and rightly still in widespread use, because it is an excellent source of information, actually has an index described as a 'Developmental Values Index'. Some of the headings in this index are as follows: Adaptability — Aesthetic discrimination — Age-mate relations — Animals, kindness to — Appreciation of beauty — Baby, adjustment to — Boy–girl relations — Bravery — Brothers — Community life — Consideration for others — Co-operation — Courage — Cousins — Creativity — Cultural awareness — Death, adjustment to — Democratic understanding — Devotion to a cause — Divorce, adjustment to — Economic differences, understanding — Education, valuing and seeking. It is not clear to me why, if children's books are stuffed with wholesome moral nutrition like this, adult fiction also should not be full of moral goodness. With the aid of this bibliotherapists' pharmacopoeia, let us try it.

> Adaptability? — *Dr Jekyll and Mr Hyde*
> Animals, kindness to? — *Moby Dick*
> Brothers — well, Karamazov, obviously
> Community life — *The Rule of St Benedict*
> Death, adjustment to — *Hamlet*
> Divorce, adjustment to — *Anna Karenina*
> Economic differences, understanding — Adam Smith, *The Wealth of Nations*
> Education, valuing and seeking — *Jude the Obscure*

We may well laugh; and yet we do not want to assert that children do not learn from reading fiction. Far from it — we would rather wish to assert that they can learn supremely important and morally valuable things from reading fiction, things which cannot easily be learnt at all in other ways.

The unavoidable conclusion is that many people do not understand how fiction works. And the element in fiction that seems to be confusing is the nature of the storytelling voice.

From a writer's point of view, what is commonly called 'voice' has two elements, a voluntary and an involuntary one. A narrative voice might mean the strategy deliberately adopted by the writer, fully self-aware, for telling a story, and it might mean that indefinable quality which makes it possible to recognize small fragments of a writer's work, and which distinguishes it, even in dialogue, where it mimics the voices of characters, from the work of other writers. Just as with one's real voice, one can control what one says, and many aspects of utterance — how loud, how fast, whether angry, loving, authoritative — but yet one cannot control what one sounds like, or easily sound like someone else, and voices, once known, are intensely recognizable and identifiable, even if they are those of actors speaking in dialects or accents different from those in use the last time one heard them.

It is obviously easiest to discuss the consciously controllable aspects of narrative voices. And the first thing to realize is that none of the voices audible in a work of fiction is simply that of the author. When we open a book and start to read, it is natural to think that it must be the author whose words we read, the author who is telling us the story. This natural assumption, which is wholly untrue, is a booby-trap for writers as much as for readers, and is made much worse by that lethal phrase 'self-expression' so often applied to literary art. But it is not as themselves that authors enter their works, and those who wish to express themselves require the services of a lover, or a psychiatrist; the services of a reader have to be otherwise earned.

To illustrate my meaning I would like to refer to Thackeray's *Vanity Fair*,[2] in which the author introduces himself to us on the first page as a puppeteer, and keeps jumping up and down apostrophizing the reader and making comments on the 'puppets' as the story progresses. Is the puppeteer Thackeray himself? Is it his voice which tells us in the opening paragraphs that 'the famous little Becky puppet has been pronounced to be uncommonly flexible in the joints' and if so, whose is the voice which opens Chapter 1, 'While the present century was in its teens, and on one sunshiny morning in June, there drove up to the great iron gate of Miss Pinkerton's academy for young ladies, on Chiswick Mall, a large family coach'? Is this second voice, which tells us the vast majority of the story, also Thackeray's? When the puppeteer pops up, and makes a comment — 'in a word, everybody went to wait upon this great man — everybody who was asked, as you, the reader (do not say nay), or I the writer, would go if we had an invitation' — is Thackeray interrupting himself?

I think it is rather obvious that the puppeteer, though presented to us as the author, is simply another character in the book. Detached, cynical, Olympian, and often making comments to guide the reader's reaction, and to produce a particular 'shrinking' effect, constantly nudging us into remembering how insignificant human lives are, he is part of the apparatus for telling the story. Perhaps in some ways he does resemble the real-life Thackeray. But there is no need for him to do so. Even if one of the characters in the book is actually called the author, the author is not on oath to be sincere, or to speak in his own voice. If the real-life Thackeray was not a cynic at all, but a sentimental old duffer (and we might feel free to think that he was, in the light of his portrayal of Amelia, his heroine), it is very obvious that he presents himself within the book as just what the book requires him to be. Within the book the author is a 'persona', not a person.

It is only one step less obvious that the other voice, the anonymous disembodied one which tells the bulk of the tale, is also a character in the book, however nebulous, and not the author. The narrative voice is not the voice of the author in private life, it is a professional 'stance'. And much the clearest way to think about this is to think in terms of masks. The mask of the narrator is worn while the utterance which forms the words on the page is not being spoken through the mask of any of the characters, though we must not forget that characters too are narrators. The author's self must be set aside, or be concealed by the masks. It is a *story* which is being expressed through the speaking masks, not a *self*.

Very many otherwise promising books have been wrecked by the intrusion of the author — the real-life one whom you can invite to dinner, or ask to speak at your conference — because the anonymous nature of the narrative voice has not been understood. It is simply that if you are wearing a mask your own face is covered and unseen. To understand this is to grasp a fundamental truth about literary technique.

Of course, people often think that whereas writing for adults may require a sophisticated understanding of technique, writing for children requires only a simple kit of tools. They think this because they are focusing on the children, not on the task of writing fiction. And children are usually thought of as needing simple books. I don't think this idea can have originated among people who know a lot about children, but even if children were simple, it would not follow that simple literary technique would be all that you needed to please them. An understanding of narrative voice is in fact very complicated, but there is nothing we would call a story which does not involve this voice, so that thinking about it is lesson one, whoever you are writing for.

Before we go any further I need to make another point. A good deal of talk about literary works contrives to consider author and reader, while forgetting about the subject. Now books tend to be about something. And all literary devices stand or fall by their usefulness in getting the reader to think and feel about that something. Because the subjects of fiction tend to be rather grand and shapeless — 'the human predicament', 'time and change', 'love', 'growth' and so on — the subject and the setting can get confused and the subject overlooked. This produces a rather unpractical and eerie feel to discussions, as though one were taking a course on how to be a museum guide, without ever learning, or asking, what is *in* the museum around which one will conduct people.

It is important to remember the central position of the subject in our minds while the book is being written, and, if the strategies are working well, in the reader's mind while the book is being read, because once you see that we are involved in a triangle, you see why mask-dropping is so disastrous. Quite simply, if the real author pops out from behind the mask, and starts showing his or her own feelings, then the reader's attention is distracted from the subject.

Three different temptations make authors want to drop the mask for a few sentences, or pages, and get into the act as themselves.

One is a little touch of megalomania; the author is deeply interested in his or her own feelings or opinions, and in writing fiction is chiefly motivated by a desire for self-expression. If it's getting rather difficult to manœuvre the story into voicing the great *me*, then perhaps the author thinks 'If I get on stage myself, and just say a few words ....' Even more frequent than mask-dropping of the mask of the narrator is mask-dropping from the face of one of the characters in the story, to allow the character to express the author's views and feelings. We have probably all had a wince and a giggle at modern liberal opinions suddenly voiced by characters in historical novels — by ancient Romans expressing detestation of slavery, by Vikings who are opposed to violence, by feudal lords in favour of equality for women — but this mistake comes in many shades of obviousness, and less obviousness. The opinion gets expressed at the cost of revealing the character as a cardboard cut-out; and although I risk being thought whimsical in saying that there is a morality which governs, or should govern, the way an author treats his or her characters, I know that I can make that claim and be understood by the readership of this book. It is brutally inconsiderate to the created characters to reveal them as cardboard placeholders for one's own views.

The second temptation, and it particularly afflicts writers for children, is a lack of trust in the audience, a terrible anxiety that they won't understand art. If you show them something cruel happening, you are afraid that they will think you are in favour of cruelty. Just in case you are misunderstood, you had better get just a word in here, speaking in your own voice ... but the problem is that masks are magic, and if you drop them you break the spell. The problem is that the aim of fiction is to arouse emotion and understanding *in the reader*, and you do that by showing them the subject. Once you make yourself into the subject of the book, you are guaranteed to bore everyone!

Writing is actually a very self-abnegating activity, in which you subordinate yourself to the job in hand. If an ugly, cruel mask is the best one for the story you are telling, then you must wear it, and not be vaingloriously concerned in case someone thinks you are cruel in your real, personal opinions.

I will try to illustrate what I mean with an example. In *A Chance*

Child,[3] a book of mine published some years ago, I wrote about cruelty to children in the English Industrial Revolution. I found myself reading, while researching for this book, personal testimonies from little children of the early nineteenth century which were harrowing and heart-breaking in the extreme. In fact I found the reading so upsetting that I could do it only for quite short periods at a time, and then I had to rest from the emotional battering I was getting. For the purposes of fiction, how I felt was useless. Can I move the reader to tears by explaining that I, J.P.W., upwards of 140 years later, am bitterly opposed to the practice of sending little girls of five down coal mines for 12-hour shifts, with only a tallow candle for comfort in the dark? So what? Who doesn't disapprove of that? Who cares what I disapprove of? The disapproval must be kept well out of sight, behind the mask, and I must simply tell the reader about the subject — what it was like then, how people lived. The subject will move many to sorrow and anger, as it has done me. That's what the narrative mask is for — to get the author out of the way, and allow the reader, unpestered and unobstructed, to experience the subject.

The third of my three temptations to mask-dropping is what one might call instrumentality. While you have the audience mesmerized, you might as well take the opportunity to put in a plug for some right attitude or other — people sometimes simply cannot see why the children's author is unwilling to be a teacher in disguise. If you say that it spoils the story, you find that they can see no value in stories for their own sake, but only as instruments for inculcating values. I am seldom opposed to the inculcation of the values which pressure groups want inculcated; but the only value I personally wish to instil is a love of literature, and I can best do that when safely behind a narrative mask.

But once one has learned that one's book is not going to be a platform for one's personal opinions and feelings, that one must go masked, there is then a choice of masks. There are many to choose from. There are a number of different first-person masks, for example; any of the characters in a story can serve as a mask for the narrative voice. An older or wiser version of one of the characters is a much-used mask — both interesting and easy, that one, but hard to make sympathetic to very young readers. Then there is the mask marked 'author' which Thackeray was wearing in the passages from *Vanity Fair* referred to above. There are a number of invisible-man masks, allowing the storytelling character to follow along, closely observing the characters, but not be among them so as to be observed by them, and playing no part in the action. And then there are the masks of gods, who know and see everything, unlimited by time and space. The advantages and disadvantages of these masks are very well known, and, in the higher reaches of literature, form the subject of a good deal of critical analysis. My own strong preference is for simply choosing a mask and wearing it to tell a story — a fictional use — rather than messing about with the very fact that masks are being worn — a metafictional use.

I will return now to the more shadowy meaning of 'voice' and consider the meaning which 'narrative voice' has when we recognize a passage as being by a certain author, or feel that the whole effect of a work is recognizably that of a personality we know from other books. For in one sense an author's voice is not designed or chosen, and cannot be altered any more than a speaking voice can, or a fingerprint, or a time in which to be born or die. You might think, after what I have been saying about masks, that the mask would entirely eliminate this personal aura. But an intention to go masked is only partly achievable. Nobody need be afraid that a mask will reduce them to a nonentity. We worry too much about lacking originality, about getting confused with another writer who uses the same masks. That part of one's personality which is still present when one goes masked, may, rather, like it or not, be more distinctive than the full-face version.

For mask-wearing has some wonderful effects. The masks put the author in touch with things which the flesh-and-blood author did not know he or she knew; sometimes they give extra stature, extra understanding, in a way which astonishes everyone.

Somewhere here is the source of that mysterious sense of the spiritual benefit that fiction confers on its participants. Readers too must go masked. For the duration of the reading of a book they must agree to be the reader that the book requires; they too must stand themselves, their prejudices, their private point of view, their specialized knowledge and ignorance aside. A wonderful party is in progress, music is audible through the open windows of the house; everyone is invited, but at the door stands a servant who hands you a mask and will not let you in unless you put it on. I am sure we have all heard someone say that they refused to wear the mask for some author's party. 'I can't read D.H. Lawrence,' they say, or 'I don't find P.G. Wodehouse funny,' or 'I never read romances, I hate all science fiction, I'm afraid I haven't read your books, my children are grown-up.' There are even some people who can't read fiction at all, either because they are so insecure that any mask threatens them intolerably, or because they are so snooty that they think any party involving mask-wearing is too frivolous for them.

But when the reader accepts the invitation, puts on the mask designed for the reader of a book, and leaves for the moment his or her own personality, and when the writer stands aside from personal utterance, and masks every aspect of self that the story does not require, they each act unselfishly. And each receives a sense of grace, almost like the glow which follows an unselfish deed in ordinary life, a glow which seems so like virtue that some people have thought that literature could fill the moral vacuum left by the decay of religion.

I wouldn't go that far myself; and yet I do say that the beneficent effects of fiction, writing it or reading it, are connected with the fact that the need to go masked while we write, while we read, paroles us briefly from what is otherwise an absolute prison, the prison of the self.

I need an example here, and I shall take a children's book — *The Nature of the Beast*, by Janni Howker.[4] The whole trajectory of this book brings us round to total sympathy with an outcast, with a character who is going to wage war on society with all his force. We are almost caught approving of extreme antisocial and criminal conduct. Whatever the boy does now, we have been made to feel, he is justified. He is not the kind of character with whom the predominantly middle-class readers of books habitually sympathize — sympathizing with him enlarges our range of understanding. And that enlargement is a grace conferred by the process of fiction — the process of reading, but also, and earlier, the process of writing, which is also a learning process.

For the process of writing, when you stand yourself out of the way, sometimes allows the mask to speak with a better, wiser, finer voice than your own. But alas! There are limits. For one thing, not everyone can wear every mask. Some are too heavy, too difficult, too light, too small, somehow outside one's range. Even masked, a brilliant elderly male actor would have trouble playing Miranda; the most wonderful schoolgirl actress, however masked, would have trouble with Prospero.

And however professionally you have laid aside your personal, conscious feelings and opinions, the things you don't know you think, the feelings you wish you did not feel, somehow get into the utterance through the mask. These uncontrollable things are part of the impression you give as a mask-wearer; they are nearly impossible to pin down, yet hallmark every paragraph you write. This penumbra is what we love, like and hate in the writers that we read, as it is in the people that we know. If you dislike someone, it may be for something they cannot help; if you don't like a writer's work, it may be just the same thing, and you may not be able to help this either!

And here we have reached a matter which is at the heart of writing for children. Some adults don't like children much. Many more think they like children but they cannot bring themselves to take them very seriously. The only mask they think appropriate for telling stories to children is a cheap and vulgar one. Children like fooling, and will watch a clown for an hour or two. The pretend friend, who wears a vulgar mask because they assume you would be baffled by a finer one, is not much liked. And most tiresome of all is the person who is only pretending to be a storyteller, who dodges round the mask all the time, telling you what to do and what to think and spoiling the show.

The masked narrator and the masked reader are engaged in a potent transaction, an ancient dance of feeling and meaning with very unpredictable effects. Children love dressing up, trying on roles and pretending, and once they get the hang of it they love wearing one after another the masks for readers implicit in the books they read. The mask-wearers are disguised, and disguises liberate people. Being in their unmasked lives remarkably powerless, and at the disposal of other people, children are more in need of this escapism, this empowerment, than many, perhaps most, adult readers. Those who prefer their children meek, obedient and pliable would do well to fear literature. The proponents of fixed and authoritarian systems of belief have always feared literature; that is why the Catholic church has an index of prohibited books, why there was a Gulag in Russia, and why Salman Rushdie is in imminent danger.

Are we then caught out in an indefensible position, saying that literature can do immense good, but can never do any harm? That you can learn adaptability, age–mate relations, animals, kindness to, appreciation of beauty, etc., all the way to truthfulness, uncle–nephew relations, value building and visual perception, from books which never teach animosity, bigotry, cruelty, deception, envy, greed, hatred, licentiousness or narrow-mindedness, all the way to woolly-mindedness and xenophobia? Are we claiming that fiction is the only one-way pendulum in the wide world?

Yes, I am saying that; and my defence would be to repeat that I believe that the very process of writing and reading fiction confers a grace; paroles us from the prison of self. And this self-expanding, self-multiplying, self-dethroning process can only be good for us; it is unambiguously good in the way that sight is better than blindness when you have to make your way in the world.

I will make one final point. The narrative masks we have available to choose from are almost all very ancient, and were first made in societies which did not divide the audience into young and old, educated and ignorant. They do not adapt very well to talking down to people. They sit most comfortably, and work best, when they are used to enable the author to claim — just for a while, while the story is told — equality with the audience. There are masks for enacting superiority to an audience — the masks of preachers, and teachers, and visionaries. But the narrative masks are all apt to fall off if you look down with them, leaving you bare-faced. You must find an audience you can look level at, or leave the masks on the wall.

Notes

1 Zena Sutherland, *The Best in Children's Books*, University of Chicago Press, Chicago, 1973.
2 William Makepeace Thackeray, *Vanity Fair* (first published 1847–48).

3   Jill Paton Walsh, *A Chance Child*, Macmillan, London, 1978.
4   Janni Howker, *The Nature of the Beast*, Julia MacRae, London, 1985.

CHAPTER 19

Lost Boys?

Violence and Imperialism in Popular Constructions of Masculinity

Mary Hilton

In a provocative and fiercely argued chapter, Mary Hilton examines continuities between texts currently popular with boys, which display what she describes as violence, militarism and assaultive images of masculinity, with what she argues are their precursors, the widely read racist and imperialist boys' adventure stories of the late nineteenth and early twentieth century. Drawing on the work of Diana Loxley, she goes on to argue that the island myth in nineteenth-century Britain, which became a site for a discourse of nationalistic, masculine adventure, is mirrored in the space fiction of twentieth-century America. She argues that in both these fictional universes militarist imperialism is promoted through heroes of the mother country, who are set against a savage and barbaric enemy, thus naturalizing a language of masculine conquest and colonization. In addition, she argues that the literacy practices of late-nineteenth-century schooling failed to promote the critical and creative resistance necessary to interrogate these militarist fictions, resulting in a generalized, heightened optimism about World War I. Ending on a cautious but more positive note, Mary Hilton believes that many teachers help boys to 'negotiate multiple, often contradictory subject positions within a range of discourses and social practices'. In classrooms that welcome children's own voices through allowing both popular fictions and male vernacular speech, teachers can encourage boys to understand how cultural representations of masculinity challenge and constrain their growing subjective identities.

Brian and literacy

Brian and I have reached an *impasse*. His rich, ironic and very funny stories of the neighbourhood, the urban landscape where he roams freely, simply cannot be written down. He cannot capture his own voice in writing; I find it impossible to help because his stories are full of adult prejudices and obscenities which only his innocence and his gifted form of oral expression rescue from the banal. Only his male peer group can really appreciate his ability to manipulate the tropes and slogans, to parody the songs and snatches, to mimic and co-opt the language of the adults and characters around him. As in any branch of learned culture they can 'read' his references.

And it's not just Brian. They can all do it: I've heard them shaping and sharpening their stories, feeding each other the lies and laughter necessary to polish the discourse. Although the talk is mysteriously male-gendered, the girls sometimes help them, throwing in a comment to get a laugh. Yet with all their verbal facility these boys are often struggling writers. Setting aside Brian's lack of steady application, his infantile hand, the blots and crossings out, the misspellings, the endless time it takes him to write anything, and not including the many pleasurable times we have spent on developing other forms of self-expression, I feel there is a deep and recognizable cultural cleft between him and what we are told is the 'standard' literate discourse of school. The oral vernacular of which he is such a brilliant exponent is created by popular culture: the tabloids and sporting magazines his dad reads (he has no mother), the sci-fi comics and soccer papers he swaps with his friends. He has few models to show him how to cut and shape his stories in writing, how to develop plot and character, or how to consider feelings, and falls back, like many boys, on recycled, extremely violent stories of aliens and mechanical heroes.

However, around Brian and his friends there now clusters a set of concerns which are becoming acknowledged as wider and deeper than can be solely expressed as the daily responsibilities of their class teacher. A plurality of literacies, of texts and messages, is implicated in new anxieties about childhood innocence itself. I have known for some time that very little they read or watch is concerned with relationships or feelings other than anger or frustration, or action other than brutality and violence. I know that in spite of a constant effort on my part to engage him with books, Brian's most serious reading material is Marshall and Cavendish's *Images of War*.[1] With these true-life stories of recent wars, complete with photographs of modern battles, weapons and destruction, Brian becomes completely absorbed. His male friends are allowed to borrow them in exchange for a violent computer game or video. But now wider public evidence, such as the recent OFSTED report *Boys and English*,[2] is beginning to show that *many* boys of Brian's age have completely given up reading literature and this is affecting their performance in English. And deeper than this runs the fear that because the common discourses of male-gendered popular culture are predominantly violent, and often xenophobic, militarist, consumer-oriented, American-imperialist and without the ballast of serious thought, this is deeply affecting the moral outlook of British youth. As Marina Warner has expressed in her Reith Lectures of 1994:

> in the arenas of contemporary culture — the tv channel, the computer game, the toy shop, the street — traditional mythic figures of masculinity like the warrior and the rapist — circulate and recirculate everyday, setting up models, not counter examples, and the forms which contain them do not contain argument or counter argument, as in a Greek tragedy, but reiterate the message, as in an advertisement .... They don't cry, 'Beware', but rather 'Aspire!'[3]

In short, what is happening to our boys?

Culture and masculinity

In the early 1980s, when Mrs Thatcher called those on the left of the Conservative Party 'wets', she was publicly articulating a discourse of masculinity which was identified with individual enterprise, efficiency, competition and the pursuit of profit.[4] Anyone who had a more tenderminded and collective sense of the delicacy of the social fabric was thus implicitly 'feminized'. The 'nanny' state began to be attacked and dismantled. Women such as Thatcher and Edwina Curry could overtake men in public life by proving themselves more ruthless and devoted capitalists, more 'masculine' than moderate, thoughtful or cautious males. Supported by the main organs of working-class male chauvinism, the tabloids, this right-wing masculinity blossomed and flourished, in spite of its obvious inconsistencies and anxieties.[5]

What has been termed the 'popular culture industry' — which is a common term for the highly profitable modern amalgam of the media, pulp fiction and associated parts of the music and toy industry, much of which is in cross-ownership, which was previously sanctioned by such organizations as the Press Council and rather precariously glued together with a series of 'gentlemen's' agreements about decency and truth — became unbridled. Nearly anything which would sell could be sold, as cultural codes about what was fair and suitable for different audiences and consumers were ignored, allowing 'the market' and the individual to apply sanctions. Violent videos and pornographic computer games became easily accessible to young children through casual or even cynical procurement by older brothers and sisters and through the not very well protected 'private' channels of cable television. In addition, the loosened potential of electronic media and enterprise profit meant larger and larger markets for cultural goods.[6]

But wider audiences often result in the production of different cultural formations. The American and Japanese domination of the popular culture industry has meant the rapid growth of universalistic discourses with less personal, particular and regional representation. To older people in Britain it has seemed that many of the cultural products and features that had been recognizably local — newspapers, magazines, comics and toys — have disappeared and been replaced by massive and more distant American bourgeois monoculture. Differentiation in plot, character and pace is achieved, not by developing nuances of local colour and character, but by highly gendered constructions, with sex and violence as central and repetitive themes. The dominant discourses in popular culture are about sexuality and gender and repeatedly construct men and women as different sorts of persons. The male roles are portrayed as active, aggressive, thrusting and powerful, and female ones as essentially passive, powerless, submissive and receptive. And between these two opposing, idealized gender positions is a relationship of *hierarchy*, so that, as with Thatcher's articulation, people who are deemed inferior are represented as feminized, controlled and subordinate. Much of the violence (and humour) in the products is generated through contradictions and conflicts in the hierarchy of these idealized discursive gender positions and their tenuous relationship to the lives of 'real' men and women. New women often appear as a resisting discourse — strong, slim and powerful — while the male enemy (such as the Joker in *Batman*) is 'feminized': often overdressed, and dishonourable. As Robert Cornell has pointed out, the advertising industry constantly plays with these idealized dominant gender discourses, representing 'new women' and 'even tougher men' without fundamentally challenging their veracity or dominance.[7]

Teachers working with children know that they, like the adults around them, do not simply take up these idealized gender positions. Rather, they, like all people, need time and imaginative space to negotiate multiple, often contradictory subject positions within a range of discourses and social practices. Through play, drama, discussion, writing and reading, girls can learn to transform these dominant gender constructions presented to them in popular culture, and women teachers have an exciting relationship to this resistance, often using literature to explore and mediate the deceptions and stereotypes of the culture industry. But with many pre-adolescent boys, with their apparent relish of violence, their disinclination to discuss relationships and their lack of interest in serious literature, the problems seem more entrenched.

Recent scholars, turning their attention to masculinity, have, strangely, emphasized its psychic fragility. According to the feminist psychoanalyst Nancy Chodorow, masculinity is always at risk. Chodorow claims that, whilst a girl becomes a woman by identifying with and becoming her mother, there is a break and a separation for boys in becoming men, one where they must free themselves from infant identification with their mother: 'Compared to a girl's love for her father, a boy's oedipal love for his mother, because it is an extension of the intense mother–infant unity, is more overwhelming and threatening for his ego and sense of (masculine) independence.'[8] Through these object relations in infancy, and their development at adolescence, she offers a psychodynamic explanation for what she perceives as men's anxiety about their gender. Whether she is correct and infant experience is its source or not, cross-cultural work seems to point to the idea that in many cultures the passage from boyhood to manhood is often difficult for the individual to achieve.[9] In tribal societies it is often marked out by initiation rites and ceremonies. In Western cultures it is probably never fully possessed, but must constantly be asserted and renegotiated. Here, because manhood has traditionally been bound up with expectations of power, and as each boy has to achieve it for himself, and because power is in the continual process of being contested and transformed, so achievement of masculinity is likewise tenuous. Indeed, the very act of acquiring the necessary temporary social power which asserts masculinity may be subjectively experienced as loss:[10] turning away from old toys and friends to join 'the gang', for example. So at this very critical age the voices of the media and the stereotypical behaviours of gendered roles in popular culture offer male children a devastating relevance. A starting point for teachers is that boys' behaviour is not simply explained by considering the rationale and constraints of the externally derived social roles they are expected to live, but also by examining and exploring sympathetically how cultural representations of masculinity challenge and constrain their individual subjective identities.

The masculine cultural product: stories for boys

My argument is that masculinity in Britain, far from being natural and monolithic, is a historical and cultural construct made up of varying and competing forms. Many of the contexts in which men's power operated over the last one hundred years, in the structure of ideas, relations and institutions, have been challenged by feminism and a new economic order. But in the idealized construction of masculinity in such superheroes as Superman, Action Man, and, lately, Power Rangers, we can see that the adventurous and assertive male of the typical boys' cultural product of the 1890s, of the original classic boy adventure story, is still extant in popular culture. Indeed, it is possible to argue that most of the current books and comics for boys in the 1990s are inherited in structural form from that period of high imperialism in Britain, the decades leading up to World War I.

When children were nearly all accounted for in schools by the 1890s there was in place the system of standards, where classes of up to 80 children were grouped according to their ability to read and memorize some set texts (only the highest standard, seven, included some Shakespeare and other classic texts). The corresponding payment to the schools based on the number of children at each standard led to unprecedented levels of boredom and docility of working-class children with regard to school literacy, as teachers battled to instil, usually by rote, the necessary rudiments of literate behaviour at each standard. Robert Roberts remembers: 'All day long the roar of a work-a-day world invaded the school hall, where each instructor, shouting in competition, taught up to sixty children massed together.'[11]

David Vincent has pointed out that although the rubric of the separate standards was often revised, the picture presented by the results of the frequent examinations remains fairly stable and sobering. By 1882 less than half of the three and a half million children crowded into elementary schools could pass Standard IV, which required the most minimal rudiments of reading, spelling and forming letters; at the top end fewer than 2 per cent could read a passage of one of Shakespeare's plays or had taken the first steps towards using a pen to make up their own sentences. Again and again in this period, the inspectorate complained that the children they examined lacked 'intelligence' in comprehending what they had read. 'The task was,' as Vincent puts it, 'to convince the pupils that written language was not an enclosed body of signs, an artificial game played to amuse the teacher ... rather ... they should know that these words stand for things with which they are familiar.'[12] The level of intellectual control necessary *to create written communications for an audience was simply not taught.* Up to World War I thousands of children left their elementary schools without development of critical consciousness expressed through the empowering mode of writing.

But out of school, however, this rudimentary but essentially passive literacy, which rested on reading with an absence of composing, that is, no other writing skills than those required for copying letters and sentences, eventually led many of the newly literate to great pleasure in reading cheap books and papers written specifically for them by shrewd members of the upper middle classes. Voracious escapist readings of highly gendered and imperialist stories, comics, magazines and novels turned out by enterprising publishers soon began to fill the imaginative gap left by the mechanical skills-based approach to reading in school.[13] The school system articulated the class system with regard to literacy practices: at one end passive and mechanical for the lower classes and, with its public schools, at the other end active and prolific for the upper classes.[14] This, combined with the mass-production possibilities of the new steam presses, meant that in Britain male adolescence became the basis for a new popular cultural product. In many thousand stories for boys, written by the well-educated about public school and Empire for the considerably less-educated, technology and social power were brought together in the late nineteenth century to form a widespread and apparently infinitely desirable cultural artefact. The public school story was to last until World War II. The imperialist adventure story was to be inherited, substantially updated and reproduced by American capitalism in the late twentieth century.

The Forster Education Act of 1870 which ushered in compulsory schooling convinced publishers that with the expansion of schools and rudimentary literacy for all children, there would emerge a large, new and untapped source of readers. Mainstream publishers like Blackie and Macmillan launched a wide range of juvenile fiction to tap the new market. School and Sunday school prizes were a particular area of growth, their content carefully supervised to appeal to church and parental authority. At the same time the effects on boys of the steadily increasing market of 'penny dreadfuls', widely distributed story papers which were supposed to glamorize crime and violence, were being debated. It is now possible to see that the penny dreadfuls were in fact linked to, and mirrored in content and plot, the more serious fiction for boys:

> In fact many of the dreadfuls were suffused with racism, patriotism and crude imperialism which will have played their own part in cementing Empire into the youthful consciousness. It was elements like these, toned down and cleaned up, which found their way into the approved boys' books.[15]

In response to the perceived threat from the dreadfuls in 1879 the Religious Tract Society produced the famous, long-running *Boys Own Paper* in which the Empire was promoted as the ideal vehicle for Christian civilization. Later its sales were rivalled at the turn of the century by *Chums* and *The Captain*, and in the Edwardian period by *The Magnet* and *The Gem*. These two were to be overtaken in the 1920s by *The Wizard* and *The Hotspur*, which remained influential until the 1950s. What all these journals shared was 'a commitment to gentlemanly ideals and imperial values'.[16]

In his essay 'Healthy papers for manly boys: imperialism and race in the Harmsworths' halfpenny boys' papers of the 1890s and 1900s', John Springhall shows how widely read and consistently racist and imperialist were the halfpenny boys' papers of this period. He argues that such cheap and desirable popular fiction also worked in helping to construct the political themes and racial stereotypes which were then transmitted back into social consciousness in the 1890s, linking together 'elements of commercial distribution, mass persuasion and conservative ideology, in forms which only the cinema was able to rival successfully in succeeding decades'.[17] Harmsworth's halfpenny boys' paper *Pluck*, for example, ran endless adventure tales of daring deeds in an empire setting, particularly Afghanistan, South Africa, Egypt and India. 'Titles like "Fighting for the Flag" were common, soldier heroes being drawn from fictionalised re-runs of such recent colonial conflicts as the Zulu, Matabele, Boer and Ashanti wars.'[18]

According to Jeffrey Richards, boys' fiction reflected the changing nature of imperialism over this period. The evangelicalism and commercial imperialism in the work of Ballantyne and Kingston of the mid-nineteenth century gave way at the end of the century to the aggressive militarism of the works of G. A. Henty and Gordon Stables. Imperialism became almost a new religion, formed by blending the Protestant work ethic with the public school code. This was a concept of chivalry which lay at the heart of public school fiction, the other chief genre of boys' reading in this period. Based on a concept of clean-limbed, clean-living, manly superiority, it was a reaction against the older concept of hard-living, hard-drinking and brutal masculinity. This older alternative masculinity lay submerged until the 1960s, when it re-emerged with the acceptance of the loss of empire.

So boys' adventure and school stories were spread across all classes in Britain, as popular among working boys as among the wealthy. A survey of 790 boys in different kinds of school in 1888 revealed three of the four favourite titles as *Robinson Crusoe*, *Swiss Family Robinson* and *Ivanhoe*, and a survey in 1908 in the boys' paper *The Captain* yielded the twelve most popular titles as *Treasure Island*, *Tom Brown's Schooldays*, *Robinson Crusoe*, *Westward Ho!*, *The Adventures of Sherlock Holmes*, *Ivanhoe*, *King Solomon's Mines*, *Coral Island*, *Fifth Form at St Dominics*, *Last of the Mohicans*, *Mr Midshipman Easy* and *J.O. Jones*.

Here I want to explore two major themes in the boys' adventure story, which contributed to the construction of masculinity in the period and which I believe are still extant, indeed rampant, in gendered reading for boys.

Imperialism and masculinity: constructing and conquering the other

In her brilliant examination of the centrality of the topos of the island to nineteenth-century imperial ideology, *Problematic Shores: The Literature of Islands*, Diana Loxley takes five texts — Verne's *The Mysterious*

Island, Marryat's *Masterman Ready* and three which we have seen feature in the list of twelve most popular books for boys, *The Swiss Family Robinson*, *Coral Island* and *Treasure Island* — and shows how the island motif provides an ideal discourse, a model formula for the assimilation of the language of conquest, masculinity, supremacy and authority and also for the supposedly inherent, eternal values of that language.[19] She traces how popular literature and imperialist ideology both advanced an imperial dream, which by managing to eliminate a problematic past and an exploitative and acquisitive present, and offering a new and wonderful destiny for all men of the imperial nation if they should choose it, carefully and drastically excluded and deformed the historical realities of colonial exploitation and experience. Through the constant reproduction of the island myth in literature (and then in countless stories for boys), the British imperialist urge toward the acquisition of territory and the consolidation of power was visible in its cultural artefacts as in its political strategy:

> The multiple complexities — historic, economic, geographic, political, racial — which in fact characterise Britain's overseas acquisitions are here dissolved at a stroke by the creation of a single image, that of fertility and abundance which serves to protect the fullness of this colonial 'beginning'. 'Fertile continents' and 'wide spaces', 'spice-lands', 'cornlands', 'timberlands', existent colonies and prospective, become merged into one undifferentiated, mythic site, an island of potential civility amidst those 'many sounding seas' of savagery.[20]

So, in this imperialist discourse, history is made hygienic and cultural 'otherness' is defined in terms of savagery, barbarity, bestiality and inhumanity.

> Soon after we arrived, the attack was made with great fury. There was no science displayed. The two bodies of savages rushed headlong upon each other and engaged in a general melee, and a more dreadful set of men I have never seen. They wore grotesque war-caps made of various substances and decorated with feathers .... 'You do not know' he said to Jack 'the danger you are running in venturing amongst these ferocious savages ... you may die in the attempt.' ... 'Well' said Jack, quietly, 'I am not afraid to die in a good cause.'[21]

Central to the dream is the question of authority, of the establishment of colonial law and order. Nature itself, together with these racist constructions of 'the other', must be made to conform to European authority. The island is finally made safe from the tamed or removed original inhabitants; made to resemble 'home' with all the comforting effects of European luxury: 'We were never tired of admiring our warm and well-arranged apartments, lighted with windows and well secured with doors .... We had formed a convenient portion of our dwelling into a small chapel.'[22]

So the construction of a masculine imperialist discourse was completed, embellished and made deeply desirable, and simultaneously worked in process with the configurations of the British social world: its school system, its class system and its machinery of cultural production in the later nineteenth century. In *The Boy's Own Paper* this discourse is constantly offered as one where boys can cross over, become men. 'Greatness' becomes a state to which all new boys, through courage, hard work and striving, can aspire: 'the outside world is opened out before the young, male Briton as a universe of possibility'.[23]

Culturally shaped and perfected for an imperialist nation, the American market soon took cognizance of this product. The world of 'outer space' began, between the wars, to provide just the same kind of discursive schema for an idealized discourse of imperialism. The harsh realities, historical, geographical, cultural and eventually military, of US imperialism began to be smoothed out in popular culture. After World War II US power and its responsibilities required a cultural authority, an ideological production accessible to all classes which could locate and develop a natural discourse of colonialism. Outer space required sophisticated technology, and 'masculine' trappings of leadership: the inherited hard, lean bodies of the decision-makers of British imperial discourse, and the 'rightness' of the American 'democratic' way of life, provided similar possibilities. The 'other' could now be again characterized as savage, scarcely human, their regimes ones of bestiality, waiting to be tamed and governed by thinly disguised US authority:

> 'I understand' Kirk persisted, 'but does it explain how it started? Why it started? There have to be reasons, and if we're to be of any help, we have to find them.'
>
> Kaulidren frowned, then shrugged. 'If you speak with the rebels perhaps they will be able to explain .... After [Delkondros] became president of the council he began beating the drums for instant independence and making outrageous accusations about our colonial administrators. But then he turned to violence although several of the more rational members of the Council repudiated him. There was no reasoning with him, and in the end, we had no choice but to declare him and the council members who remained with him outlaws. They went into hiding and have conducted a terrorist campaign against us ever since.'[24]

The colonialist discourse of *Star Trek* must be one of the most familiar and popular male-gendered literary artefacts of its genre,[25] but there is far more: such titles as *Star Wars* and *Return of the Jedi* are household names, and the industry spawns dozens of computer games, comics, figures of aliens, interactive space games and projects. Science fiction of outer space is recognized as a bestselling male-gendered construction in all its forms. Again, the male preoccupation with invasion, control, authority and power is located within the discourse of acquisitive enterprise, manliness, rationality and civilization, with the fiction of a contactable but savage universe waiting to be discovered and tamed.

Men and war: militarism, violence and the body

In her essay 'Towards a feminist peace politics' Sara Ruddick points out:

> Nearly everyone agrees that war is in some sense 'masculine'. Throughout history and across the globe, whatever the 'race' or history of particular cultures, men have greatly predominated among the generals, chiefs of staff, and heads of cadre, tribe, nation, or state who direct wars. In technologically developed states men predominate among the business entrepreneurs who fund wars and among the defense intellectuals and philosophers who justify them. Still today men predominate among the soldiers who execute war's strategies.[26]

This overwhelming conjunction between manliness and war confronts us in Western culture at every turn. Gendered war toys, talk, games, stories and behaviour are seeped into male children's consciousness from every corner: from television, peer groups, shopping trips, comics, films and books. Assaultive masculinity is presented by the culture industry in many forms and images: such as the close brotherhood of soldiers — *comrades in arms* — in action suffering from physical vulnerability together, or the *just warrior*, restrained and self-sacrificing, or yet again the *conquering hero* who enacts the national glory. And yet it often requires quite specific intention and action on the part of adults to deny and conceal war's vileness, to make 'soldiers' of boys. There are competing discourses of tender masculinity, of incipient peace politics, of justice administered through talk and feeling rather than violence against the body. There are 'many men who struggle with and against a gender identity that would immerse them by "nature" in violence.'[27]

In his innovative and compelling book *Soldier Heroes*, Graham Dawson points out:

> The soldier hero has proved to be one of the most durable and powerful forms of idealised masculinity within Western cultural traditions since the time of the Ancient Greeks. Military virtues such as aggression, strength, courage and endurance have repeatedly been defined as the natural and inherent qualities of manhood, whose apogee is attainable

only in battle. Celebrated as a hero in adventure stories telling of his dangerous and daring exploits, the soldier has become the quintessential figure of masculinity.[28]

He traces how in the growth of popular imperialism in the mid-to-late nineteenth century, heroic masculinity became fused with notions of British imperial identity. His study of adventure narratives straddles imperialist adventure fictions and life history work, and sensitively suggests, in the light of the Falklands/Malvinas War – to him a 'shocking recapitulation of the imperial past' – how elements of that past can persist in the psychic lives of post-imperial generations.

So within an imperial nation such as Britain in the nineteenth century and the USA in the later twentieth century, the popular culture industry works hard at keeping the dominant discourse of masculinity one of swaggering, assaultive militarism. The virtues of manhood, with war as the ultimate test, are the virtues of patriotism. The world of the boy is constructed through narratives of action and violence, many of them military, 'combat' clothes and accoutrements and a variety of 'masculine' consumer goods, usually directed at aggressive play fantasies. To return to Chodorow, the psychodynamic theory that masculinity is constantly threatened by the female body, its ability to give birth, and its smothering affection from which the male child has had to 'escape', is one explanation of male attraction to the industry's repetitive discourse of violence against the body.

Competing discourses and male subjectivity

So our classrooms are full of boys who are perpetually confronted with a dominant discourse of masculinity which 'naturalizes' male power and violence. Marina Warner states:

> Boys will be boys is what people say when they mean aggression, violence, noise, guns .... The biological and genetic revolution already upon us can alter and save bodies, but stories which feature such bodies assume that their natures are static, determined, doomed — rare is the character in a video game or comic strip who develops or learns to be different. Yet anthropology has shown that, in the territory of sexuality as well as other human areas, social expectation affects character. Masculinity varies from group to group, place to place, and its varieties are inculcated, not naturally so.[29]

This dominant 'natural' masculinity, which is so often associated with global capitalism, is extremely powerful and there is no doubt that our male children seem sometimes to accept without question or resistance its ordering of gendered identity. Here history has important lessons for us. The recent literature on the experience of British soldiers during World War I provides the last part of my argument. A generation of unquestioning and unreflective masculinity propagated through popular texts to a newly literate generation up to the war was put to impossible test by the realities of the horror of trench warfare. In *The Great War and Modern Memory*, Paul Fussell writes of the innocence and the prevailing certainties which two generations of imperialist boys' stories had delivered and made secure. He sets out the raised, essentially feudal language of the male romance: such words as *comrade*, a horse is *a steed*, danger is *peril*, the enemy is the *foe*. 'One read Hardy and Kipling and Conrad and frequented worlds of traditional moral action delineated in traditional moral language.'[30]

But for this unreflectiveness there was a terrible price: not only the death of the flower of British male youth, a decimation still difficult to comprehend, but a psychic wound which simply refused to heal. Between those who had witnessed the realities of war and those who had not, there was an unbridged silence. For thousands, words could not be found to describe its horror and meaninglessness: 'shell-shock' is now described as a resulting form of male hysteria. Poetic diction changed overnight. Before seeing action at the Somme in January 1917 Wilfred Owen wrote to his mother: 'There is a fine heroic feeling about being in France, and I am in perfect spirits.' But soon things changed:

> I can see no excuse for deceiving you about these 4 days. I have suffered seventh hell.
> I have not been at the front.
> I have been in front of it.

As Fussell writes: 'There is no dialect capable of synthesising those two moments in Owen's experience.'[31] After being shipped home with neurasthenia and trench fever, Owen was to meet Siegfried Sassoon, who was at the same hospital. It was Sassoon who first broke through the bitter silence between civilian and serving soldier. In *The Old Huntsman* and *Counter Attack*, first published in 1917, Sassoon shattered the high diction, rhetoric and sentiment which had surrounded the war. Sassoon's soldiers slid and lurched blindly through slimy sludge-filled trenches. They belonged in 'death's gray land' and dwelled in a place 'rotten with death'.[32] Sassoon told Owen to simplify his verse, to introduce colloquialisms into it, and to purge the high diction and sickly sentimentalism that were a legacy of his education. Out of the trauma produced by the shattering of the imperial dream of victory and honour and the breaking up of the chivalric language of romance, of elevated sentiment and diction, there arose among the ranks of the elite a new poetry and ultimately a new literature.[33]

Where were the cultures of resistance among ordinary people in the decades leading up to World War I? In *The Classic Slum*, Robert Roberts writes of the new literates:

> For nearly half a century before 1914 the newly literate millions were provided with an increasing flow of fiction based on war and the idea of its imminence .... Popular fiction and mass journalism now combined to condition the minds of the nation's new readers to a degree never possible before the advent of general literacy. In France and Germany, too, writings in the same genre were equally successful in stimulating romantic conceptions about the carnage to come. When the final cataclysm did arrive, response to such ideas set the masses cheering wildly through the capitals of Europe. *Der Tag!* — The Day — was here at last! They could hardly wait![34]

Is it too strong to claim that, even when all texts are filtered and mediated through the social world itself, they can be responsible for producing a mindless and unquestioning drift to war? Certainly, historians have looked at all corners of Edwardian society and have come to the conclusion that militarism and imperialism, the sense of 'rightness of the British way of life', was incredibly widespread in social consciousness and closely associated with popular constructions of masculinity.[35] This unreflectiveness was linked with the failure of literacy to help develop a newly critical generation. The original working-class radical papers of the 1830s and 1840s had, by 1900, disappeared and been replaced by a press which, according to Ramsay MacDonald, soon to be secretary of the Labour representation committee, 'has been gradually passing out of the control of the reader, and has been becoming the organ of the advertisers and the convenience of the capitalist'.[36] Press economics had, by 1900, become self-restricting in the same way as other industries, an economic logic of larger and fewer. The discourses of mass newspaper readership were therefore likely to be less radical, less sensitive to local power and opinion.

The assumption by Fabians and early members of the Labour Party that access to a common literary heritage would *in itself* help the newly literate to subvert the distinctions between polite and popular culture and *naturally* empower the generations of new readers was misguided. The structural rigidities of the class system were not so easily broken down. But clearly also *the model of literacy learning*, with its lack of critical consciousness, was implicated and I feel it is important that this early twentieth-century nightmare remains with us today — as a terrible warning. If children are presented with a mechanical approach to deciphering text without empowerment in considering its meanings, if they are taught to read without having their own language reproduced in school texts, even more if they are not encouraged to create in writing their own meanings for themselves, then clearly the discourses and narratives of the mass culture industries will rush in to fill the imaginative void. Here for boys the imperialist, militarist and violent constructions of the dominant masculinity will again prevail, and at the same time the written language of 'school literacy' will become elevated beyond the use of the common people: a generation potentially 'silenced' without the cultural resources to resist. Is it possible that the twin forces of a widespread arid and mechanical English curriculum and an unbridled popular culture industry could yet again produce this nightmare of mindless imperialist militarism?

Challenge and resistance: teachers understanding emergent masculinity

Anyone who has worked with children and teenagers in Britain cannot but be aware that there are many alternative, often tender and caring, masculinities expressed in schools and playgroups. Watching my class of 10-year-olds reading individually to a class of 5-year-olds was a heartwarming experience, as the younger children expected and accepted a patient kindness from some of the toughest of characters. British boys are, presumably, no more likely to grow into violent and militarist adults than boys of other nations. But there is a recognizable growing problem with their relationship to literate text and the often increasingly formal literacy practices of school, overtly concerned with surface features of writing which are apparently favoured by new assessment-orientated short-term thinking. Literacy, like masculinity, is not monolithic but made up of a variety of practices, events, genres and readings. Empowerment in practice takes cognizance of the development of critical thinking developed through active creation of text. When this is allowed it becomes apparent that boys often seem to have gender anxieties which are expressed in a variety of literate behaviours, many of which foreground the assaultive masculinity of popular culture. Their group stories are often one long collaborative effort in recalling and extending scenes from violent films, with obvious relish of horrific violence against the body. Teaching, then, involves an understanding of both the cultural and psychodynamic forces at work, and a sympathetic engagement with their anxieties.

In her examination of the behaviours and writings of young teenagers with regard to popular culture, Gemma Moss argues that because certain genres pre-exist the growth of young writers, genres which are embedded and constantly used in the literature culture around them, they use them naturally in their stories and creative compositions to explore the conditions of their lives and to express their gender anxieties. She argues that the action-based violence of the boys' stories and discourse is used by them to question and mediate masculinity in a parallel way that romance is used by teenage girls to discuss relationships and position themselves *vis-à-vis* male power. She states that for English teachers and examiners to be perpetually asking for an original autobiographical voice ignores the discursive practices that are residing in the children's culture:

> Teachers too often imagine that in reproducing popular fictions children reproduce one solitary closed meaning. The genres of popular fiction are seen as bearing a single message .... Instead meaning is produced by the way in which particular elements are recombined in each case.[37]

So sympathetic classrooms can encompass, mediate and transform these popular constructions. Gemma Moss argues:

> Once we start to take writing based on popular fiction seriously, there would be other consequences for our practice. We could encourage children to articulate what they already know about how such fictions work and help to refine that knowledge.[38]

As women are slowly developing a separate, powerful and feminine voice in the public domain, they are pointing to the inadequacies of the ways in which masculinity is constructed and how many boys feel constrained by the traditional ways in which they were expected to become men. A consistent feminist critique of masculine power and the way it can damage men as well as women is emerging which hopes to be liberating to both sexes. Men should be able to mother, to express emotion, to talk about relationships, to look inwards. But this doesn't threaten their masculinity; rather, it accepts that around the male body clusters a separate set of discourses which are rich with possibilities. So I am arguing that whether or not gender is a product of cultural and linguistic practice, sexual difference has its own physiological and psychological reality, and that recognition of this must affect the way we teach.[39] In the effort of crossing over to manhood, boys are often suffering; there are silences, gaps, over-shrill violences, cruelties, and above all inconsistencies, in their fumbling construction of adult subjectivity. These are reflected in their jokes, their stories and their retellings of popular fictions. Subordinated forms of masculinity can be revealed and valued, gendered narratives deconstructed and recon- structed, and children encouraged to play with different subject positions.

There are other masculinities in literature which are now highly valued. The two latest winners of Britain's top prize for literature (the Booker) are celebrations of the 'male' vernacular. Boys have a distinct wit and irony, a restlessness of body and mind, and many of them are tuned to a robust discourse which has grown up around the young male and his relationship to his neighbourhood which Roddy Doyle captures so brilliantly in *Paddy Clarke Ha Ha Ha*. Here is his sketch of the man who mothers his two children, since his wife has died. Its young male voice is touchingly unmistakable as it looks inwards to the heartlands of masculinity, deft but 'different':

> Mister O'Connell made brilliant dinners. Chips and burgers; he didn't make them, he brought them home. All the way from town in the train, cos there was no chipper in Barrytown then.
>
> — God love them, said my ma when my da told her about the smell of chips and vinegar that Mr O'Connell had brought with him onto the train.
>
> He made them mash. He shovelled out the middle of the mountain till it was like a volcano and then he dropped in a big lump of butter, and covered it up. He did that to every plate. He made them rasher sandwiches. He gave them a can of Ambrosia Creamed Rice each and let them eat it out of the can. They never got salad.[40]

How do we give our male children the confidence to write in this way in their own vernacular voices? Here, at the highest literary level are, I believe, the seeds of a critical masculine discourse, which Brian and his friends can produce *verbally* with ease. Certainly not through strictures of correctness, or worksheet and sentence construction, not through fear of incipient misbehaviour, not through silence, passivity and high-toned literary models, but rather through celebration of the young writer's growing masculine self, his voice, his fears, his wit, his craft. Perhaps in classrooms, where popular constructions are allowed, where stories from life, coarseness, mistakes and gender differences are valued, not ignored, we can collaborate with our boys in dissolving and transforming the violent and militarist masculinity of the popular culture industry.

Notes

1 Marshall Cavendish, London. *Images of War*, serialized magazine which is ordered through newsagents.
2 OFSTED *Boys and English*, Report on Standards of English Teaching in Schools, London, 1994.
3 Marina Warner, *Managing Monsters: Six Myths of Our Time*, The Reith Lectures 1994, Vintage Press, London, 1994, p. 27.
4 Hugo Young, *One of Us*, Macmillan, London, 1989.
5 The *Sun* has a recognizable ambivalence concerning many issues — royalty for example — and its relationship to 'yobbo' culture, hallowing and disapproving at the same time. Its anxiety about gender runs through its constant reiteration of male–female difference.
6 William Shawcross, *Biography of Rupert Murdoch*, Chatto and Windus,

London, 1992.

7   Robert Cornell, *Gender and Power*, Polity Press, Cambridge, 1987.

8   Nancy Chodorow, *The Reproduction of Mothering: Psychoanalysis and the Sociology of Gender*, Berkeley, University of California Press, 1978, p. 131.

9   Penelope Harvey and Peter Gow (eds), *Sex and Violence: Issues in Representation and Experience*, Routledge, London, 1994.

10 Michael Roper and John Tosh (eds), *Manful Assertions: Masculinities in Britain since 1800*, Routledge, London, 1991.

11 Robert Roberts, *The Classic Slum: Salford Life in the First Quarter of the Century*, University of Manchester Press, Manchester, 1971, p. 134.

12 David Vincent, *Literacy and Popular Culture: England 1750–1914*, Cambridge University Press, Cambridge, 1989, p. 91.

13 For the elite it was the great age of writing: many of the upper classes wrote poems, letters, essays, diaries, articles, pamphlets, hymns and stories.

14 Jeffrey Richards (ed.), *Imperialism and Juvenile Literature*, Manchester University Press, Manchester, 1989, p. 4.

15 *Ibid.*

16 John Springhall, 'Healthy papers for manly boys: imperialism and race in the Harmsworths' halfpenny boys' papers of the 1890s and 1900s', in Jeffrey Richards (ed.), *Imperialism and Juvenile Literature*, Manchester University Press, Manchester, 1989.

17 *Ibid.*

18 *Ibid.*

19 Diana Loxley, *Problematic Shores: The Literature of Islands*, Macmillan, London, 1990.

20 *Ibid.*, p. 2.

21 R. M. Ballantyne, *Coral Island*, first published 1858.

22 Johann David Wyss, *The Swiss Family Robinson*, first published 1812–13.

23 Loxley, *op. cit.*

24 Gene Deweese, *Star Trek Renegade*, first broadcast 19 .

25 In fact *Star Trek* represents Liberal America and incorporates a certain degree of cultural relativism, but the essential imperialist vision remains.

26 Sara Ruddick, 'Towards a feminist peace politics', in Miriam Cooke and Angela Woollacott (eds), *Gendering War Talk*, Princeton University Press, Princeton, NJ, 1993, p. 110.

27 *Ibid.*, p. 112.

28 Graham Dawson, *Soldier Heroes: British Adventure, Empire and the Imagining of Masculinity*, Routledge, London, 1994, p. 1.

29 Warner, *op. cit.*, pp. 27–8.

30 Paul Fussell, *The Great War and Modern Memory*, Oxford University Press, Oxford, 1975, p. 81.

31 *Ibid.*

32 Siegfried Sassoon, *The Old Huntsman* (1917) and *Counter-Attack* (1918).

33 Robert Wohl, *The Generation of 1914*, Weidenfeld and Nicholson, London, 1980, p. 95

34 Roberts, *op. cit.*, pp. 179–80.

35 John MacKenzie (ed.), *Imperialism and Popular Culture*, Manchester

University Press, Manchester, 1986.
36 Quoted in Alan J. Lee, *The Origins of the Labour Press 1855–1914*, Croom Helm, London, 1976, p. 217.
37 Gemma Moss, *Un/Popular Fictions*, Virago Press, London, 1989, p. 119.
38 Ibid., p. 117
39 This idea comes from Lyndal Roper, *Oedipus and the Devil? Witchcraft, Sexuality and Religion in Early Modern Europe*, Routledge, London, 1994.
40 Roddy Doyle, *Paddy Clarke Ha Ha Ha*, Minerva Press, London, 1993.

CHAPTER 20

Mind the Gap

Critical Literacy as a Dangerous Underground Movement

Eve Bearne

In the final chapter of this book, Eve Bearne argues that literacy encompasses a set of culturally developed practices occupying political space. She reminds us that literacy is not ideologically neutral and that the links between literacy and power are too important to neglect. Eve Bearne shows how scare-mongering and assertion without evidence has dominated the public debate about literacy and how the real voices of parents, teachers and children need to challenge those 'ignorant armies'. Critical literacy, she asserts, is actually reflected in the everyday practice of the classroom and exhibited in 'what children say about the texts they encounter and produce'. She believes that children can enjoy, use and subvert the fantasies of popular culture without being seduced by its often limiting, stereotyped and violent manifestations. In an exhilarating and uplifting demonstration of what writing and reading by teachers and pupils can do, Voices Off *ends on a positive note: as we near the millennium, our priorities must be in putting 'children in a position where they can feel some courage about the dangerous business of getting to be literate in the political setting'.*

Reading is a dangerous activity — look what happened to Emma Bovary. Writing is equally dangerous. Anyone who has ever tried to capture thoughts on a page knows the immediately hazardous sense which accompanies the act. But it isn't just that literacy is personally risky — it is also politically dangerous. There are enough public examples of the ways in which literacy and literature have become politically significant that I do not need to go into detail here. But even more than that, if literacy is a political act, then it also occupies political space; recent experience bears this out where literacy in education is so frequently described publicly in the language of crisis. The politically high profile of literacy means that it needs to be viewed critically as a social and cultural reality, to be carefully and thoughtfully examined and theorized, yet children daily tread this dangerous path. In this chapter I want to look at some of the dangers — real and imagined — and to suggest how young readers and writers might be encouraged to face literacy with confidence.

It is clear now that literacy and literature aren't definable in terms of texts alone — as books, or even films, television, comics, and so on — but that any discussion of literature and literacy has to be seen in terms of the contexts in which those texts are written, produced, presented and, most importantly, read. Literacy encompasses a set of culturally developed practices. Raymond Williams ended his important (and still relevant) book *Culture* with this careful formulation: 'A fully responsible sociology of culture, itself significantly developing just at this point of general change, has then to be analytically constructive as well as constructively analytic.'[1] By this he was suggesting that instead of simply analysing the social relations of cultural production, we should use that analysis to take a hand in shaping and reconstructing definitions of cultural production. And this is just as true for the mid-to-late 1990s as it was for the 1980s. Of course, Williams was working in the more general area of social and cultural analysis and not specifically in education. However, this is where I think those of us who are involved in education have the edge; we don't just have to review and analyse the cultural formations of literacy (or literacies) in a 'constructively analytical' way, but we have the opportunity to develop an educational theory of cultural production which is embedded in practice. We can theorize practice and be 'analytically constructive'.

It sounds wonderful, but I have a sense that it will be pretty tough. The recent approaches to the curriculum, which diminish and impoverish, have so occupied all of us involved in education that some important gaps and silences have gone unnoticed. (I shall go on to describe some of these later.) There has been a lot of noise, much of it, I think, coming from ignorant armies that clash at night. There has been some regrettable groping in the dark, where assertion and scare-mongering have replaced sensible investigation illuminated by those who genuinely want to find out what is really going on. But underneath the clamour are some quiet voices offering to lead the way out of the dark, if only we take the time to pause from expressing our own views in order to listen. I think we have some powerful voices with us; I mean the voices of children and their parents — as well as their teachers' voices as they theorize practice. For me, the analytically constructive approach lies in building a critical theory of literacy in education which can take into account the cultures of home and school. Such a theory would be able to draw on the ways in which children read texts, produce them — and talk about them. To do any of these things involves a view of teaching and learning which carries with it certain assumptions about how teachers create opportunities for children 'growing in interpretation'.[2] Not only can teachers make it possible for children to become more developed as interpreters of text, but also listen out for already existing evidence of children's perceptive interpretations of the texts they meet, drawn from the cultural settings of their homes and communities. Part of an analytically constructive approach lies in finding out what children think and know.

Critical literacy in its wider theoretical sense, then, is reflected in the everyday practice of the classroom, and the evidence for its existence and extension will be found in what children have to say about the texts they encounter and produce. By this I am not suggesting that teachers should simply sit back and hear what children have to say without any further intervention. Emphatically I do not mean that. It is all too easy to assume that children have been 'empowered' by teachers 'handing over' responsibility. There are greater threats to children's independent thinking through their unreflective parroting of the prejudices of adult opinion. What I am arguing for is a theory of literacy which can offer even the very youngest children in schools a critical framework with which to test out their interpretations as they grow. This requires some attentive and careful work by teachers. It may involve taking some risks, too. I want to suggest that such a planned and developmental approach can not only allow children to adopt a critical view of the texts they come across, but also give them the means to analyse the cultural conditions in which these texts are produced. This means acknowledging that literacy has an ideological component; it is not innocent, nor can it ever be neutral. It also means acknowledging the diversity of cultural contexts in which texts are read and produced.

Literacy and power

There is no doubt that being able to read matters — between the lines, behind the images, in the gaps. So does not being able to read matter, if you haven't got the hang of the literacy which counts most in your society. Enough has been said and written about entitlement and literacy rights that the links between literacy and power do not need restating here. But if getting to grips with literacy is critically important, it follows that developing a critical approach to literacy is equally important. This means re-examining the idea that literacy is to do with power; it means a complex analysis of a whole set of factors which goes beyond considering the power of the individual in relation to some view of literacy held 'out there', important though this is. In other words, it isn't just a view which equates literacy with human rights or which asserts that those who are more literate have power over those who aren't. It is a more complex matter than a crude view that one more powerful group of people is controlling the access to literacy of another less powerful group. What is critical is that those who have power to define what *counts* as valuable or valid literacy hold the greatest power. Literacy can be exclusive as well as inclusive. Frank Smith points out the importance of 'joining the literacy club', and this is important, of course, for any child, but questions remain about who writes the rules for the club and what if they change?[3] Margaret Meek, who constantly helps to shift educational perspectives on literacy, challenges any possible complacency about stating the simple platitude that literacy 'is a matter of human rights': 'have we also asked ourselves about the ways in which reading and writing can be used against people? Differences in literacy are not only the result of social differences. Literacy also helps to perpetuate them.'[4] Taking a critical view of literacy, then, means taking on the idea that lack of power over the written word isn't just the result of an individual's failure to get the hang of the literacy offered in school. It also means that the ways in which literacy opportunities are presented in schools (and elsewhere) can themselves create divisions and exclude some children from ever having the chance to exercise power over their own literacy, or over the social rights which literacy confers. The texts children read and write are often linked with the values held by society about what counts as valued literacy. Jenny Cook Gumpertz describes literacy as 'a socially constructed phenomenon':

> In early modern times literacy was regarded as a virtue, and some elements of moral virtue still seem to attach to it in that judgements about literacy skills tend to have prescriptive or normative overtones. A literate person was not only seen as a good person, but as someone capable of exercising good and reasonable judgement, for a literate person's taste and judgement depended upon access to a written tradition — a body of texts — reflecting centuries of collective experience.[5]

Judgements about what counts as valid or valuable literacy seem to be tied up with judgements about an individual's worth or value. The issue of what literacy is all about becomes more and more complex. It isn't just about how we help children to become successful readers and writers, but also about the kinds of texts they read and write and the value placed upon those texts. Further than that, it's also about how professionals involved in 'the literacy business' actually do their jobs. The way literacy is described by teachers, parents and others involved in education, and the kinds of texts which are given value or status, are part of a society's theory of literacy. This theory will, in turn, underpin the ways in which literacy is introduced by governments and in schools. It makes even more sense, then, to attempt to develop a critical educational theory of literacy and, importantly, one which can develop a critique of the cultural values attached to traditional and popular texts.

In her extraordinary book *Always Coming Home*, the continually intriguing Ursula Le Guin challenges all our existing notions of what a traditional work of fiction might be like. This 'novel' is a collection of fragments drawn, as it were, from an anthropologist's notebook; in it Ursula Le Guin creates a future people called the Kesh. In a conversation about the community's archives, the archivist explains that they find it 'safer' to give information than to keep it:

> Giving involves a good deal of discrimination; as a business it requires a more disciplined intelligence than keeping, perhaps. Disciplined people come here ... historians, learned people, scribes and reciters and writers, they're always here ... going through the books, copying out what they want, annotating. Books no-one reads go; books people read go after a while. But they all go. Books are mortal. They die. A book is an act; it takes place in time, not just in space. It is not information, but relation.[6]

This is tough to digest and, as might be expected from Le Guin, shakes established ideas. But in pointing to the idea of literacy and literature as processes to be experienced, to be placed in relation to other literacy events and practices, rather than seen as unchanging objects of study or unquestioning reverence, she certainly offers a new and complicated perspective on the values attached to literacy in any society. She also draws attention to the powerful forces needed if access to 'valuable' texts is to be restricted — keeping is more dangerous and difficult than giving, she says, although even giving isn't unproblematic. Anyone who has an interest in presenting texts of any kind to children will be aware that 'giving involves a good deal of discrimination'. This is where one of the significant gaps opens up; it is in children's homes, before they even reach schools, that 'giving' literacy begins, yet there is still very little evidence to suggest any attempt by government to fill in this gap in the English curriculum — to discover what children know about literacy before they come to school. Allied to this is another resounding silence; where are the sounds of laughter, pleasure and satisfaction? There is little mention of this in the documentation, yet in the home, the very place where awareness of texts begins, there is far more emphasis laid on shared pleasure than on the solemn business of interpreting words on the page or images on the screen. In homes, these interpretations are heard in conversations — about what we think about the actions of characters in soaps, in picture books or on the news. It is in homes that children begin their interpretations of actions and events which build towards the view of what the world ought to be like according to the culture of home and community.

Home and school literacies

One of the most fruitful recent areas of theorized practice by teachers, despite (or perhaps because of?) the shortcomings of the National Curriculum, has been to recognize the resources represented by the linguistic and cultural diversity of the children and the communities feeding schools. Attention to those links and partnerships for literacy and the acceptance of a view of 'difference' become more critical when faced with some of the generalized fears expressed by commentators. These tend to suggest either that certain kinds of homes do not offer children 'acceptable' kinds of textual experience or that they allow too much experience of texts which the commentators themselves find disturbing. There is no substitute for authentic information, however, as Sally Wilkinson explains in her study of home and school experiences of literacy:

> The knowledge I gained about the individual children and their families was more helpful to me as a classroom teacher than generalisations based on large samples ... which if accepted blindly by teachers can cause them to form stereotypes of the families and the children they teach.[7]

One of the striking silences in the National Curriculum for English has been, and remains, an acknowledgement of the importance of the social and cultural contexts for literacy. To balance the lists of written texts which 'ought' to be taught, there needs to be a view of the contexts within which those texts are constructed and read. To make the picture even more complex, it is becoming increasingly clear that the kinds of texts which are included in literacy are becoming more varied and diverse. We are now educating children not just for one kind of literacy, but for a range of literacies or 'notations' as Margaret Meek puts it:

> We *must* extend our notions of literacy, the uses and functions by which it is described, to include the images and *notations* which are common, current and important in our world beyond language in print. Representations of the world can be read in other places than books.[8]

In that case, she argues, although the children themselves might outstrip adults in their speedy use of new technologies, teachers need ways to help children describe and frame what they already know. It is becoming daily more and more evident that children have recourse to, and sometimes sophisticated knowledge of, a wide range of texts besides printed books: forms of popular literacy — newspapers, advertisements, computer games, comics, films, pop videos, television news coverage with graphs, maps, inserts and computer graphics, magazines, letters, computer printouts, street literacy. We can add to these the increasing attention given in school to children's own writing, picture books, visual texts, maps, charts, diagrams etc. Children know about the range of literacies they are exposed to; Kirsty Edwards is just one of the Year 4 pupils in a Cambridgeshire primary school who recorded her home reading in a pictorial form, thus emphasizing the visual awareness which young readers have. Not only does she reflect a wide range of forms of reading, but her representations show that she knows a lot about how they are put together as texts.

Spencer Gilbert, a 10-year-old from a Southwark primary school, is also aware of the effects of environmental print when he comments, among other things, that he reads 'when I don't even know I'm reading'. Also, unlike many adults, he does not confuse pictorial text with 'easy reading'. In response to the simple request for Spencer and his classmates to give me advice on how to help teachers teach reading, he has covered almost the full range of what might be included in a reading curriculum. Encouraging children to be reflective and to give us their opinions seems such a minor (and informative) move, but is all too rare, even in the most enlightened classrooms. Mike Millroy admitted to being surprised when his accomplished readers expressed concerns about reading. He had asked them if they liked reading to the teacher. Some of their replies were:

Dear Eve,

I like to do things like reading books. Every morning my class do reading. We fill in a little book called our Reading Record. I have not always liked reading. I do not like reading books without pictures, and books that are sometimes easy. I like to read books that are challenging. I read a lot of the time when I don't even know I'm reading. I like a lot of adventure and funny storys. In our class we have group reading. I like this, and I like following storys when other people are reading them. I like all Judy Blume storys. My teacher reads us first chapters of books where we write down notes and then what we think of the story. In assembly my teacher reads books After she reads them she asks us questions about the story she has read to us. I like it when our teacher asks the qeustions. I like reading through my rough drafts of work.

Yours sincerly

Spencer Gilbert

When I read to the teacher I read slower and make more mistakes ...

When you read to the teacher the teacher says words for you; I can take my own time on mistakes when I read to myself.

When I read to myself I feel like I'm there. When I read to the teacher, it feels like they're there instead of me.[9]

Having listened to what the children had to say about the cultural experience of reading in the classroom, Mike Millroy then did something about it — he introduced reading journals to provide his pupils with the chance to continue important, but silent, dialogues with him about the texts they read and the contexts that supported them. Young readers will need to learn how to put all of these elements of literacy, as well as more traditional forms, into a critical frame. The sudden and proliferated range of texts and 'representations of the world' mean that it is even more critical for children to be able to exert discrimination and choice over the literacies and literacy practices which they encounter daily. When technologies are advancing rapidly, being able to read behind the images, through the notations, or between the lines, takes on greater urgency; it becomes imperative to be able to read and write texts with the eyes of a critic.

Not only must children be able to read their own and others' representations of the world sharply and analytically, but so must teachers. Not only must children's implicit knowledge of a range of texts and contexts be brought into the open, but, crucially, teachers' own understandings need to be made explicit in order to help forge clear views of how best to tackle the classroom demands involved in helping children to energize their experience of an increasingly complex range of texts. Listening to teachers recounting conversations with children — and parents — is an important part of an 'analytically constructive' educational theory of literate practice. A clear analytical frame is perhaps most vitally needed when considering those forms of popular literacy which have attracted so much emotional and emotive comment.

Some examples might help to show just how enlightening this can be. Sally Wilkinson looked in detail at the classroom and home literacy of three of her Key Stage 1 learners: Darryl, Rashida and Sarah, all aged 6. Darryl draws considerable satisfaction and pleasure as a reader from comics. He has not just one collection of comics in his home, but two; he has never thrown a comic away since he started to buy them at 5 years old, and stores them on racks in his bedroom and in the family sitting room. His mother was a little concerned about his keenness to read comics. Sally writes of one occasion in school when he was writing the story of *Peter and the Wolf* after listening to Prokoviev's musical tale. As he wrote he said 'I'm going to use those curved things like in my comics' and went on to use brackets to separate an aside from his main narrative: 'But the boy (whose name was Peter) threw his rope around my neck and some hunters took me to the circus.' In discussion with his mother it became clear that far from needing to be concerned about his comic reading, his chosen form of pleasurable reading was feeding his considerable awareness of the notations of language.

Sally's observations of the children's literacy at home and school revealed more complexities in their diverse ways of gaining — and giving — pleasure through texts:

> Whereas much of Darryl's and Sarah's writing drew on themes and characters from books and the media, most of Rashida's writing was based on reality. Her stories would draw almost exclusively on remembered experiences, for example, a piece about someone in hospital

reflected her knowledge of injections gained when the family took Mamun (her brother) for his regular check-ups ... Her parents told me that there was not a tradition of oral storytelling in the family and that when Rashida wrote at home it was mostly letters to the neighbour's daughter, her siblings or her mother. This reflected what Rashida liked to do at school. When she was in the writing corner she would write letter after letter and post them in the class post-box. She wrote to confirm friendships and also to anyone whom she felt was sad or hadn't had a letter lately — in order to cheer them up.

Rashida, obviously a capably literate child, was having lessons in Bengali at the mosque, and Sally Wilkinson came to understand that in the classroom she was 'showing expectations of her which are different from those of her family or the community teacher at the mosque'. She goes on to explain how she used this knowledge to 'provide methods of writing at school which would have some resemblance to those she was encountering outside it'. The importance of such information is not only relevant for those children whose home culture is identifiably different in terms of bilingualism, for example. Sally Wilkinson also found that Sarah — from a local family of some long-standing — 'made a clear distinction between home and school books', preferring to read those from home which she was familiar with. At home, Sally Wilkinson discovered, Sarah liked telling stories and found reading aloud in school rather threatening, but after conversations with her mother and an agreement that they would both use the same kind of support for Sarah's reading, by the end of term her confidence was increasing and she was able to tackle unfamiliar print in the classroom with more assurance of getting meaning from it.

What might have been the consequences if the voices of these children — and their parents — had gone unheard?

Nostalgia *is* just what it used to be

Sally Wilkinson learned a lot about literacy by not making assumptions about homes and literacy, but connections between them. One of the most dangerous assumptions about homes and literacy comes, I think, from a kind of displaced nostalgia which takes the form of 'things ain't what they used to be'. While the ignorant clamour asserts that standards of literacy are falling, far from suggesting a decline, booksellers' statistics indicate that reading is on the increase, and the government's own figures indicate rising trends in secondary examination results.[10] A much more insidious form of nostalgia, however, is expressed through the view that television and film, and the images presented, are now so powerfully ubiquitous that their influences threaten whole generations of children. This is not a new formulation of a fear about popular cultural forms, of course. In the middle of the last century, Matthew Arnold was concerned that the forms of culture presented to ordinary people would be enervating: 'Plenty of people will try to give the masses, as they call them, an intellectual food prepared and adapted in the way they think proper.'[11] And Richard Hoggart, in his important book *The Uses of Literacy*, first published in 1957, described 'a temptation among some social critics to see in all this popular literature, especially in its more advanced contemporary forms, some sort of plot by "the authorities", a clever way of keeping the working-classes quietly doped'.[12] In going on to counter some of the fears expressed about images of violence, Hoggart reminds us about the sensationalism and violence of the broadsheets on executions or even *The Police News*. This is not to minimize the importance of a thoughtful examination of popular forms of culture, especially in respect of their violent and often gender-distorted images. Far from wanting to trivialize the debate about the content of popular literacies, I want to bring the issues more into the centre of educational thinking; I want, also, to suggest a more radical way of analysing — and subverting — any negative effects which popular forms of literacy might present. In order to do that, I want to oppose some of the knee-jerk reactions to the visual literacies which surround children now. I would agree with Hoggart that what is needed is an examination of what he describes as 'sensation without commitment' as expressed in popular cultural forms. In his book *Understanding Popular Culture*, John Fiske suggests that such reactions are over-deterministic and fail to recognize the other side of the equation; people do not simply consume the texts and messages.[13] He argues that the alarmist views of the literate middle class do not take into account how people use the texts, what meanings they assign to them, or what resistances they might put up to them. This echoes much of what both Raymond Williams and Richard Hoggart see as the strength of the assumed 'passive consumer' of popular texts; such readers may not offer clearly articulated analyses of the forms presented to them, but they don't just swallow them wholesale either. Fiske gives some convincing examples of how 'consumers' become 'producers' — the *Star Trek* television phenomenon, for one. 'Trekkies' or 'Trekkers' have an important part to play in shaping the series itself. John Fiske does not see viewers as passive, and is impatient with those who see popular culture as an overwhelmingly manipulative force in contemporary life; they have 'failed to produce a positive theory of popular pleasure ... the society they envision is not one in which fun plays much part, if it exists at all'.[14]

Fiske's views are not specifically focused on children and popular culture, but Kathleen McDonnell in her book *Kid Culture* agrees that 'Like adults, children make their own meanings out of the raw material of popular culture.'[15] I think that Fiske's identification of pleasure, or desire, is an important addition to any educational theory of literacy — especially one which is seeking a way of subverting traditionally held views of what count as valid or valuable literacy practices and forms. Humour — from the very earliest times — has been an effective way of dealing with oppression, and children are very powerful parodists and subverters of those things which adults regard with gravity. This is not to suggest that children don't take things seriously, but that for them the serious and the funny are not as separated as they often are for adults. Children know the value of being seriously funny. Cathy Pompe provides a reminder that:

> Children are natural critics: they mimic and make fun of everything around, mercilessly: adults, each other and themselves. Children's parody reflects the need both to get the measure of something, and to distance themselves from it. Children resist that which has power over them: adults, institutions, and even TV programmes.[16]

Helen Bromley provides a detailed observation of children's power to subvert and mimic what they have seen on screen and make it their own:[17]

> My daughter arrived home from school one evening full of anticipation for the next day. It transpired that this was not because of some inspirational delivery of the curriculum at Key Stage 2 but was due to the fact that 'We're playing this really good game in the playground.' The game was entitled 'The Land before Time' and was based on the video of the same name. The promotional material describes this as 'a tale of hope, survival and love' which will teach 'unforgettable lessons about life and sticking together'. Discussing this game with Rebecca showed that lessons had been learned, perhaps even more valuable than those suggested by its makers. Importantly, it was necessary to have seen the film before you could take part in the game ... The children had created an imaginary world in the playground, using places from the film. They were not, however, re-enacting the film but re-writing it with many original ideas. A great deal of planning was required to prepare for the next day's play and it was apparent that they found it very easy to slip in and out of the game.

Helen asked her daughter if she felt there was any way in which playing the game could help her with her work in class. Rebecca's reply was, 'I think it helps you with the past, the present and the future of thought.' This rich and fascinating study of what videos offer to a theory of literacy highlights some of the points which Margaret Meek makes about 'notations' and the value of recognizing cultural literacy practices. Helen Bromley points out that even the covers of videos provide print models for children's emergent understanding of and efforts at writing:

> Videos provide an opportunity for reading a variety of texts and symbols. Young children are able to identify the voice behind, and the audience for, the text on the box in which the video is contained ... The cover for

the video of *Beauty and the Beast*, for example, contains a mass of information in the form of words, pictures, numerals and symbols. The children I worked with were able to identify the author, audience and motives of the text.

She adds:

The print contained not only on the cover but also within the film itself helps to teach that all print conveys meaning. This is done in ways designed to attract interest. (Anyone who doubts this is the case should view the sequence of Walt Disney's *Aladdin* where the genie introduces himself.)

Stressing the social nature of video watching, where people are likely to talk about the text as they view it, she comments:

If children are aware that a video has been written by somebody, then they learn valuable lessons about the pleasures that authorship can bring. One of the main consequences of video watching seems to be a widening of the definitions of literate activities. There is no reason why children should only be aware of authors as producers of books, for example.

In recognizing the moral, social and cultural messages being presented in videos, Helen Bromley concludes 'there is work to be done here'. Indeed there is. Part of the work might well lie in finding out just what children do gain in terms of literacy from their considerable knowledge of television, films and video. It's my guess that their opinions will surprise many teachers who fear the power of televisual literacy.

Barbie as a closet feminist?

Gender is one of the areas which arouses strong concerns when considering the possible effects of the media and advertising specifically directed at children. Myra Barrs describes one such example:

In 1986 a media course at CLPE was thrown into disarray when the teachers were invited to view two episodes of *He-Man* in order to study them as an example of a popular media fiction watched by many boys (and girls). Several of the teachers present (all women) were angry at being asked to take seriously something that they regarded as sexist trash.[18]

The content of popular texts remains a persistent worry for teachers who do not want to bring into the classroom some of the aspects of culture which they find unacceptable. Yet as Myra Barrs points out, discussions of gender stereotyping tend to assume that readers are moulded by their reading in a relatively direct and unproblematic way. It isn't as straightforward as that, as Valerie Walkerdine explains: 'This approach assumes a passive learner, or rather a rationalist one, who will change as a result of receiving the correct information about how things really are.'[19] Angela Ridley discovered that when investigating gender-related influences of reading and television viewing on the writing of a group of 7- and 8-year-olds, 'It would seem that children do not always write what they believe, only what they believe to be socially acceptable'[20] to teachers. After a six-week examination of gender, reading and writing, where she found the children capable of sophisticated deconstruction of gender images in their television viewing and reading, she gave them an open writing task, designed to offer no specific gendered possibilities. She writes:

> Imagine my disbelief and dismay when the work was handed to me. I was confronted by 'boisterous', 'adventurous', 'handsome', 'tough', 'strong' boys, who were having adventures in castles and rescuing damsels in distress, and by 'pretty', 'friendly', 'weepy', 'nice', 'dopey', 'sulky', 'giggly' girls who were being rescued and falling in love!
>
> There was some attempt at resistance by a couple of the children: Andrea's heroine actually defends a boy who is caught in a fight, and Martin's rescues a boy from a swamp, even though she is totally confused about what is going on.[20]

In general, Angela explains, the children had chosen to adhere to accepted forms and content of writing despite their enlightened discussions. When challenged about this, the reply was simple:

Jill: Well, cos that's what happens in stories.
Martin: It's not the same as the real world.

In further discussions, the children made it very clear that they weren't taken in by advertising hype but that they felt that in schools teachers expected them to write in particular (gendered) ways — another example of the gap between school and 'real' experience. In reflecting on what she had found, Angela Ridley comments that two distinct systems seem to be in operation for these children and she concludes 'The relationship between children's reading, writing and the real world is perplexing.'[21] And it is much more complicated than a cause-and-effect view of popular media would suppose. Much attention has been given to 'what the reader brings to the text' as a way of describing active and engaged readership of books; the idea of multilayered readings is very clear to any of us who have observed a group of people talking about the same book, or returned in our own reading to a text we read some time ago. It is a familiar way of thinking about the complexities of written texts and the diverse satisfactions they can offer readers. It seems strange, then, to assume that media texts are going to operate in a much less complicated way, or that readers of written texts are active in constructing meaning from what they read, while those who read pictorial or television texts are not.

Through her analysis of the impact of one of the most vilified products for girls — the Barbie doll — Kathleen McDonnell suggests that in the uses which girls make of their Barbie dolls, Barbie herself takes on a kind of 'closet feminist' role. Picking up the refrain of nostalgia, she suggests that there is much misunderstanding which arises from the fact that 'most adults have long forgotten their own childhood play experiences' and don't fully recall the complexity of fantasy play assuming that 'toys like Barbie have a single clear message that is swallowed whole'. While acknowledging the weight of advertising which is aimed at consumerist images of what is 'beautiful', Kathleen McDonnell argues that children 'have a much better intuitive grasp of the multi-faceted relationship between reality and fantasy'.[22] Far from Barbie being taken as the model of desirable female appearance or a direct route to marriage with a man modelled on Ken, young girls do, in fact, set up a strongly female world which opposes the feared intended messages of this particular element of gendered popular advertising culture. Kathleen McDonnell argues not that Barbie is an 'innocent' product, but that she is, in fact, much more adaptable to the play and pleasures of children than adults might suppose. In conversations with young girls about Barbie, it emerged that she is used as part of an important all-female universe which resists the kinds of 'brainwashing' effects suggested by those who fear the weight of media marketing. If teachers are genuinely to bridge the gap between different kinds of cultural knowledge and the school literacy curriculum, then it is important to keep talking with children about what they know and understand about the texts — of whatever kind — that they come into contact with both at home and at school.[23]

Children as literary critics

It is not just in the area of popular culture that children's voices are worth listening to. Certainly, the whole area of visual literacy has alerted commentators to the need for a critical theory of literacy, and this brings me back to the beginnings of this chapter, where I argued for a critical theory of literacy in education which would build an analytically constructive approach from the very earliest years of schooling. Janet Towlson demonstrates one way in which even the very youngest readers in school can be given a chance to become literary critics. Her study contains a wealth of written and transcript material, but a couple of examples give the flavour of what she found when she challenged her 6-year-olds to write critically.[24] They had read Anthony Browne's *Changes* and were asked to write what they thought about it. (In the following extracts, the spelling and punctuation only have been edited.) Angie writes:

> I liked the bit where in the picture there was a baby pig instead of the little boy. I liked the bit where the crocodile's tail was changing into a banana. What I thought was funny was the slipper. The pictures say the changes. The writing tells you a story about a little boy gets a new sister. I thought it was going to end with Mummy and Daddy coming home with visitors, with lots of shopping and they would have a big feast. I think the title was good for Anthony to call the book *Changes*.

Another reader, Victoria, had made similar observations about the pictures and the text telling different stories, but perhaps most impressive is her concluding comment, 'I think all the little changes make up into one big change; that was the baby', displaying her ability to read beyond the literal.

This gave Janet Towlson impetus to push her class even further in seeking their critical response to what they read. In looking at Jan Ormerod's version of *The Frog Prince*, the children spent a lot of time looking at the borders to each page. Maria commented that 'The border is lizards — looks like music signs' and Janet Towlson goes on to describe a conversation with Maria and her friend Caroline:

> When I asked them 'Do you think if you look at *The Frog Prince* again you would see things there that you didn't see first, second or even third time around?' Caroline replied, 'It's a bit like when I got on my climbing frame I got to know more and more things — how to do it the more I had goes on it.'

There is no doubt that these children can be capable critical readers and writers, but Maria's opening line from her writing about *The Frog Prince* acts as a kind of metaphor. This 6-year-old writes: 'I think the text is telling you to keep a promise.'

The promise of these young reader–writers makes it clear just why it is important to have high expectations of children and their literacy. A theory of children and literacy needs to take into account the energetic expression of opinion as shown by all the children quoted in this chapter. They know that teachers should listen to them; Errol, from the same Southwark classroom as Spencer Gilbert, who was quoted earlier, points out, 'I think teachers should do a survey of what kinds of books the children like,' Ashraf argues for 'a larger variety of books' for group reading, and that 'racist books shouldn't be in school because they are very offending', and Vincent, who likes reading old books as well as comics and 'play books with my friends', wrote to me 'I think that reading is a part of learning.' It is indeed.

These London readers aren't by any means 'cute kids' from privileged backgrounds. They have, however, emerged as thoughtfully and reflectively literate because their teacher Carole Kirwan listened to what they had to say about their previous reading experience; she asked the children to write their reading autobiographies and built on the information they offered.[25]

One of the messages which comes through loud and clear when teachers do listen to the voices of children is just how robust and unsentimental they often are. Those who hurry to protect them from what are considered unacceptable experiences might perhaps reflect on their toughness. In their hot pursuit of justice they can be tireless, and they show by their preferences a highly moral view of the world. In expressing concerns about Teenage Mutant Ninja Turtles, or, currently, Power Rangers, it is often easy to forget that these are attractive and satisfying to children because they depict worlds where good is rewarded and evil punished. Adults can so easily confuse imitative behaviour with expressions of violence, forgetting the role of play in children's development in interpretation of the texts they meet. Of course, expressions of violence of any kind require thoughtful treatment and discussion if they are to be put within a context of human morality. I want to be as clear as I possibly can about this: I am not suggesting a free-for-all with no care taken about what children (or adults) watch or read — very much the opposite. I want adults to talk with children about what they watch, to find out from children themselves about the kinds of television they identify as disturbing or upsetting, to debate and reassure. In other words, I want more — but more informed — adult interest in what children know and think about popular forms of culture. Kathleen McDonnell points out that adults spend 'so much time and energy talking about violence on TV and comparatively little time talking about the fact that striking children for disciplinary purposes is still legal in most of the world'. In her view 'the violent imagery that pervades popular culture nowadays' is as much a reflection of the reality of public violence as it is a cause.[26] Returning to the theme of nostalgia, she suggests that if modern childhood 'no longer looks so carefree and innocent to us' it is because 'there has always been an underside to childhood, a darker country of pain, powerlessness and humiliation' that few adults would choose to revisit. If children are to be supported in their explorations of that country in order to emerge with greater confidence, then listening to children's views and putting our own point of view has to be part of a balanced and constructive approach to the kinds of uncomfortable realities both children and adults sometimes have to face.

Certainly children can face the painful and politically uncompromising — and often they do it through humour. Natalie Eaton, in Sarah Theaker's class of 7- to 9-year-olds drew on her knowledge of a range of sources when she wrote a poem in response to environment week in school:[27]

> Freddie is a whale, Freddie is my friend,
> The last time I saw Freddie he was this big!
> I said, 'Freddie what have you been doing?'
> 'I've eaten all the krill in the sea.'

Freddie eats all the krill in the ocean, in the world and in the universe, until the final verse:

> Freddie is a whale, Freddie is my friend,
> The last time I saw Freddie
> He was being towed away for oil.

This kind of sturdy poignancy is a reminder that children see the news on television, hear about political issues and *think about them*. They are the natural subversives to any 'received wisdom' about the effects of media influences, but their views can so readily go underground if they are not given a hearing. An analytically constructive educational theory of literacy ought to pay attention to the gaps between school and home experiences of literacy; between the earnest intent to get children to read what is on the page and the genuine pleasure which readers can get from the effortful success of reading a text which carries meaning for them. It ought to be founded on evidence of what children know and say about literacy — much of it robustly unsentimental. Such a theory would take into account the view that it is more dangerous to prohibit than to discuss.[28] It may well require teachers to take a few risks, to listen and to trust more. I do not mean to suggest licence and an 'anything goes' approach, but a theory of teaching and learning which is founded on building bridges and making connections; one which, from the very earliest years of schooling:

- recognizes the learners' existing experience and builds on it;
- creates an environment where learners can take an active part in negotiating and organizing their own learning;
- provides opportunities for collaboration, reflection and evaluation;
- makes links and forges partnerships between all those who are involved in education;
- offers challenges which can be tackled in a supportive context;
- allows for a little 'danger' and risk-taking;
- sees the development of literacy and the growth in interpretation as dynamic, recursive and cumulative rather than a linear progress through clearly defined stages.

Such an analytically constructive theory can engage in dialogues — can hear and reply. In this way it can involve teachers, children and parents. Most importantly, it is a theory which will put children in a position where they can feel some courage about the dangerous business of getting to be literate in the political setting of the late 1990s. It can assert that while getting involved in the fantasies of popular culture can be pleasurable, getting entangled in violent acts is not — and the adults who espouse the theory will lead by example. It will enable children to interrogate not only the texts they encounter but also the conditions in which those texts are produced. It is ambitious (and potentially subversive), but from the evidence of teachers' current theorizing of their practice, it is by no means impossible.

If a new critical literacy can be built to mind all these gaps, then it will really keep a promise with the future.

Acknowledgements

My thanks go to Jenny Maguire of Coton Primary School, Cambridgeshire, for allowing me to see the work of children in her class; particular thanks go to Kirsty Edwards.

Notes

1 Raymond Williams, *Culture*, Fontana, Glasgow, 1981, p. 233.
2 Margaret Meek, in her lecture *Challenging Texts* at the conference on critical literacy held at Homerton College, Cambridge, 12 March 1995.
3 Frank Smith, *Essays into Literacy*, Heinemann, London, 1984.
4 Margaret Meek, 'Literacy: redescribing reading', in Keith Kimberley, Margaret Meek and Jane Miller (eds), *New Readings: Contributions to an Understanding of Literacy*, A. & C. Black, London, 1992, p. 226.
5 Jenny Cook Gumpertz (ed.), *The Social Construction of Literacy*, Cambridge University Press, Cambridge, 1986, p. 1.
6 Ursula Le Guin, *Always Coming Home*, HarperCollins, Glasgow, 1993, p. 334.
7 Sally Wilkinson, ' "What did you do at home today?" An examination of the literacy links between home and school', unpublished thesis for the Advanced Diploma in Language and Literature, Homerton College, Cambridge, 1994.
8 Margaret Meek, 'Literacy: redescribing reading', *op. cit.*, p. 233.
9 Mike Millroy, 'I also read to Jinxy my kitten: children writing reading journals', in Eve Bearne (ed.), *Greater Expectations: Children Reading Writing*, Cassell, London, 1995.
10 OFSTED, *Boys and English 1988–1990*, DFE Publications, London, 1993.
11 Matthew Arnold, *Culture and Anarchy*, quoted in Richard Hoggart, *The Uses of Literacy*, Penguin, Harmondsworth, 1957.
12 Hoggart, *op. cit.*, p. 210.
13 John Fiske, *Understanding Popular Culture*, Routledge, London, 1989.
14 *Ibid.*, p. 162.

15 Kathleen McDonnell, *Kid Culture: Children, Adults and Popular Culture*, Second Story Press, Toronto, 1994, p. 128.

16 Cathy Pompe, 'When the aliens wanted water; media education — children's critical frontiers', in M. Styles, E. Bearne and V. Watson (eds), *After Alice — Exploring Children's Literature*, Cassell, London, 1992, p. 57.

17 Helen Bromley, 'A new way of seeing: what can young children learn from watching videos?', unpublished Advanced Diploma thesis, Homerton College, Cambridge, 1994.

18 Myra Barrs and Sue Pidgeon (eds), *Reading the Difference: Gender and Reading in the Primary School*, Centre for Language in Primary Education, London Borough of Southwark, 1993, p. 182.

19 Valerie Walkerdine, *Schoolgirl Fictions*, Verso, London, 1990.

20 Angela Ridley, 'It's not like the real world', in Bearne (ed.), *Greater Expectations: Children Reading Writing, op. cit.*, p. 183.

21 *Ibid.*

22 Kathleen McDonnell, *op. cit.*, p. 59.

23 See, for example, Jenny Daniels' chapter in this book, which examines some of the ways in which popular series books are analysed by their young readers.

24 Janet Towlson, 'Up and up: young critical readers', in Bearne (ed.), *Greater Expectations: Children Reading Writing, op. cit.*, pp. 97–8.

25 Eve Bearne, *Raising Reading Standards Course Evaluation*, for the Centre for Language in Primary Education, London Borough of Southwark, 1994.

26 Kathleen McDonnell, *op. cit.*, p. 158.

27 Sarah Theaker, 'Rhyme time — the naming of experience', in Bearne (ed.), *Greater Expectations: Children Reading Writing, op. cit.*

28 In a slightly different context from classroom literacy, David Buckingham, responding to the Alton Report through his article 'Child's play', argues that media education needs 'a positive *educational* strategy, rather than a negative one that is based on censorship'. *The English and Media Magazine*, NATE, Summer 1994.

Index of Authors and Titles

Young readers and writers

Subject Index

American children's literature 81–5
Arts in School Project 255
awards, literary 37–8, 67, 237, 306

canon, of literature 10–12, 56–71, 315
  construction of 67–71
  see also Shakespeare in schools
censorship 37, 236, 281–2, 326
childhood 1–13, 236
  consecration of 7, 245–6
  idealized in literature 1–13, 21, 74
  innocence 1–13, 74, 114–15, 292–307
  and Puritanism 77–9
children reading 17–43, 264–76
  adult assumptions about 35–43, 44–5, 54,
    56–9
  between the lines 161–3
  bridge texts 177–86
  children's opinions 18, 35–43, 44–55, 56–71
  children's spending power 36–7
  dictated stories 178–82
  dual language texts 179
  enjoyment seen as criterion 35–43, 56–71
  outside school 310–28
  parental influence 35, 266–7
  re–reading 47, 50, 58, 171–2
  reading communities 67–70, 251–2, 268–70
  series fiction 44–55
  transition between ages 6 and 9 22–32
  see also children's literature; critical literacy;
    popular fiction
children talking 187–97, 291–2
children writing 104–6, 154, 198–214, 273–4
  in role 205–14
  inexperienced writers 198–201
  letters 198–214
  see also spelling
children's literature 1–13, 19–32, 56–71,
    281–9, 291–307
  adults as judges of 39–42, 44–55, 56–71
  bias in 46, 50, 140, 281–2, 291–307

canon of 10, 11, 17, 56–71, 211
career novels 146
characterization 45, 47, 285
classics, the 59, 136, 142
didacticism in 77–82, 92–106, 108–13,
    139–51, 285–6
gendered reading of 50, 52, 71, 291–307
history of 77–90, 92–106, 107–26, 139–51,
    291–307
  boys' adventure stories 291–307
  family life in 77–90
  instructional books 77–8
  Puritan influence 77–80
  school stories 291–307
  waif novels 82
ideological values 140–2
intertextuality 7–10
moral influence of 282–9
realistic portrayal of family life 85–9
reviewing of 25–9, 39, 142–3
science fiction 265, 300–1
violence in 291–307
young adult fiction 85–90
  see also children reading; fables; popular
    fiction; publishing and marketing
comics 7, 150, 279, 297
critical literacy 18, 48–55, 56–71, 218, 248,
    264, 270–6, 279–80, 304–5, 310–28

drama 155, 187–97, 217–18, 248–62
  dramatic play 191–2
  fantasy 187
  as a means of extending language 187–97
  metalanguage of 254
  play/pretend 187–97
  role play 198–214, 254
  teacher in role 195, 206
  see also Shakespeare in schools

fables 92–106